Complementary and Alternative Medicine

SOURCEBOOK

Fifth Edition

Health Reference Series

Fifth Edition

Complementary and Alternative Medicine
SOURCEBOOK

Basic Consumer Health Information about Ayurveda, Acupuncture, Aromatherapy, Chiropractic Care, Diet-Based Therapies, Herbal and Vitamin Supplements, Homeopathy, Massage, Meditation, Naturopathy, Reflexology, Reiki, Shiatsu, Feng Shui, Tai Chi, Qi Gong, Traditional Chinese Medicine, Yoga, and Other Complementary and Alternative Medical Therapies

Along with Statistics, Tips for Selecting a Practitioner, Treatments for Specific Health Conditions, a Glossary of Related Terms, and a Directory of Resources for Additional Help and Information

OMNIGRAPHICS

155 W. Congress, Suite 200 Detroit, MI 48226

Bibliographic Note
Because this page cannot legibly accommodate all the copyright notices, the Bibliographic Note portion of the Preface constitutes an extension of the copyright notice.

* * *

Omnigraphics, Inc.
Editorial Services provided by Omnigraphics, Inc.,
a division of Relevant Information, Inc.

Keith Jones, *Managing Editor*

* * *

Library of Congress Cataloging-in-Publication Data

Complementary and alternative medicine sourcebook : basic consumer health information about ayurveda, acupuncture, aromatherapy, chiropractic care, diet-based therapies, guided imagery, herbal and vitamin supplements, homeopathy, hypnosis, massage, meditation, naturopathy, pilates, reflexology, reiki, shiatsu, tai chi, traditional chinese medicine, yoga, and other complementary and alternative medical therapies; along with statistics, tips for selecting a practitioner, treatments for specific health conditions, a glossary of related terms, and a directory of resources for additional help and information. – Fifth edition.
    pages cm
  Includes bibliographical references and index
  ISBN 978-0-7808-1378-6 (hardcover : alk. paper) – ISBN 978-0-7808-1404-2 (ebook)
  1. Alternative medicine--Popular works. I. Omnigraphics, Inc.
  R735.C66 2015
  610–dc23
                                                                    2015030054

Table of Contents

Part II: Alternative Medicine Systems

Part III: Complementary and Alternative Therapies

Part IV: Dietary Supplements

Part V: Alternative Treatments for Specific Diseases and Conditions

Part VI: Additional Help and Information

Preface

About This Book

Complementary and alternative medicine (CAM) therapies play a key role in the health care of many Americans. The National Center for Complementary and Integrative Health (NCCIH) reports that in the United States, about four in 10 adults and about one in nine children use some form of CAM, such as deep breathing, dietary supplements, massage, meditation, or yoga. CAM, alone or in conjunction with mainstream medicine, is often used to treat an increasing variety of diseases and conditions, such as arthritis, back pain, cancer, diabetes, heart disease, mental health issues and sleep problems.

Complementary and Alternative Medicine Sourcebook, Fifth Edition provides updated information for people considering these therapies for general well-being or specific health conditions. It discusses how to select a CAM practitioner, talk with a primary health care provider about using CAM, evaluate information on the internet, and pay for CAM therapies. It describes whole medical systems, such as Ayurveda, traditional Chinese medicine, Native American medicine, acupuncture, homeopathy, and naturopathy. It also talks about the safe use of dietary supplements, including vitamins, minerals, and herbs. Information on biologically based therapies, mind-body medicine, manipulative and body-based therapies, and chi-based therapies is also included. A glossary of related terms and a directory of additional resources provide additional help and information.

How to Use This Book

This book is divided into parts and chapters. Parts focus on broad areas of interest. Chapters are devoted to single topics within a part.

Part I: An Overview of Complementary and Alternative Medicine (CAM) defines CAM, identifies common therapies, and answers questions consumers often have about choosing a CAM practitioner and paying for treatments. Information and statistics on CAM use in specific populations, including children and the elderly, is also included, along with tips on avoiding health fraud and spotting internet scams.

Part II: Alternative Medicine Systems describes whole medical systems practiced in cultures throughout the world that evolved separately from conventional medicine as it is practiced in the United States. These include Ayurvedic medicine, homeopathy, naturopathy and other indigenous medical systems including Traditional Chinese medicine and Native American medicine.

Part III: Complementary and Alternative Therapies discusses a wide range of therapies that fall outside the domain of conventional medical practices. These include biologically-based therapies that strive to enhance or improve health using substances found in nature; Mind-Body medicine, which describes CAM techniques that focus on using the mind to improve health, such as yoga, meditation, music therapy, prayer and spirituality; Manipulative and Body-based therapies such as massage therapy, chiropractic care, and osteopathic manipulation; and Chi-based therapies such as Tai Chi and Qi gong, Feng Shui, Shiatsu, and Tui Na.

Part IV: Dietary Supplements identifies vitamins, minerals, herbs and botanicals, and other food and dietary substances taken to improve health or nutrition. Readers will also find tips on ensuring supplement safety and selecting specific products to support bone and joint health, immune system functioning, mood regulation, and weight loss efforts.

Part V: Alternative Treatments for Specific Diseases and Conditions highlights scientific research of CAM therapies for treating arthritis, asthma and allergies, cancer, chronic pain, dementia, diabetes, eye conditions, fibromyalgia, headache, heart disease, hepatitis, irritable bowel syndrome, low back pain and sleep disorders. The use of CAM for treating mental health problems, including stress and addiction, is also discussed.

Part VI: Additional Help and Information provides a glossary of important terms related to complementary and alternative medicine. A directory of organizations that provide information to consumers about complementary and alternative therapies is also included.

Bibliographic Note

This volume contains documents and excerpts from publications issued by the following U.S. government agencies: Centers for Disease Control and Prevention (CDC); Eunice Kennedy Shriver National Institute of Child Health and Human Development (NICHD); National Cancer Institute (NCI); National Center for Complementary and Integrative Health (NCCIH); National Heart, Blood and Lung Institute (NHLBI); National Institute on Aging (NIA); National Toxicology Program (NTP); NIHSeniorHealth; Office of Dietary Supplements (ODS); Office on Women's Health (OWH); U.S. Department of Agriculture (DA); U.S. Department of Veteran Affairs (VA); U.S. Food and Drug Administration (FDA).

It may also contain original material produced by Omnigraphics, Inc. and reviewed by medical consultants.

About the Health Reference Series

The *Health Reference Series* is designed to provide basic medical information for patients, families, caregivers, and the general public. Each volume takes a particular topic and provides comprehensive coverage. This is especially important for people who may be dealing with a newly diagnosed disease or a chronic disorder in themselves or in a family member. People looking for preventive guidance, information about disease warning signs, medical statistics, and risk factors for health problems will also find answers to their questions in the *Health Reference Series*. The *Series*, however, is not intended to serve as a tool for diagnosing illness, in prescribing treatments, or as a substitute for the physician/patient relationship. All people concerned about medical symptoms or the possibility of disease are encouraged to seek professional care from an appropriate health care provider.

A Note about Spelling and Style

Health Reference Series editors use *Stedman's Medical Dictionary* as an authority for questions related to the spelling of medical terms and the *Chicago Manual of Style* for questions related to grammatical structures, punctuation, and other editorial concerns. Consistent adherence is not always possible, however, because the individual volumes within the *Series* include many documents from a wide variety of different producers, and the editor's primary goal is to present material from each source as accurately as is possible. This sometimes means that information in different chapters or sections may follow other guidelines and alternate spelling authorities.

Medical Review

Omnigraphics contracts with a team of qualified, senior medical professionals who serve as medical consultants for the Health Reference Series. As necessary, medical consultants review reprinted and originally written material for currency and accuracy. Citations including the phrase, "Reviewed (month, year)" indicate material reviewed by this team. Medical consultation services are provided to the Health Reference Series editors by:

Dr. Vijayalakshmi, MBBS, DGO, MD
Dr. Senthil Selvan, MBBS, DCH, MD
Dr. K. Sivanandham MBBS, DCH, MS (Research), PhD

Our Advisory Board

We would like to thank the following board members for providing guidance to the development of this Series:

- Dr. Lynda Baker, Associate Professor of Library and Information Science, Wayne State University, Detroit, MI

- Nancy Bulgarelli, William Beaumont Hospital Library, Royal Oak, MI

- Karen Imarisio, Bloomfield Township Public Library, Bloomfield Township, MI

- Karen Morgan, Mardigian Library, University of Michigan-Dearborn, Dearborn, MI

- Rosemary Orlando, St. Clair Shores Public Library, St. Clair Shores, MI

Health Reference Series Update Policy

The inaugural book in the *Health Reference Series* was the first edition of Cancer Sourcebook published in 1989. Since then, the *Series* has been enthusiastically received by librarians and in the medical community. In order to maintain the standard of providing high-quality health information for the layperson the editorial staff at Omnigraphics felt it was necessary to implement a policy of updating volumes when warranted.

Medical researchers have been making tremendous strides, and it is the purpose of the *Health Reference Series* to stay current with the most recent advances. Each decision to update a volume is made on an individual basis. Some of the considerations include how much new information is available and the feedback we receive from people who use the books. If there is a topic you would like to see added to the update list, or an area of medical concern you feel has not been adequately addressed, please write to:

Managing Editor
Health Reference Series
Omnigraphics, Inc.
155 W. Congress, Ste. 200
Detroit, MI 48226

Part One

An Overview of Complementary and Alternative Medicine (CAM)

Chapter 1

What Is Complementary and Alternative Medicine (CAM)?

Complementary and alternative medicine (CAM) is the term for medical products and practices that are not part of standard medical care.

- **Standard medical care** is medicine that is practiced by health professionals who hold an M.D. (medical doctor) or D.O. (doctor of osteopathy) degree. It is also practiced by other health professionals, such as physical therapists, physician assistants, psychologists, and registered nurses. Standard medicine may also be called biomedicine or allopathic, Western, mainstream, orthodox, or regular medicine. Some standard medical care practitioners are also practitioners of CAM.

- **Complementary medicines** is treatments that are used along with standard medical treatments but are not considered to be standard treatments. One example is using acupuncture to help lessen some side effects of cancer treatment.

This chapter includes excerpts from "Complementary and Alternative Medicine," National Cancer Institute (NCI), April 10, 2015; and text from "Complementary, Alternative, or Integrative Health: What's In a Name?" National Center for Complementary and Integrative Health (NCCIH), National Institute of Health (NIH), March 2015.

- **Alternative medicines** is treatments that are used instead of standard medical treatments. One example is using a special diet to treat cancer instead of anti-cancer drugs that are prescribed by an oncologist.

- **Integrative medicine** is a total approach to medical care that combines standard medicine with the CAM practices that have shown to be safe and effective. They treat the patient's mind, body, and spirit.

Are CAM approaches safe?

Some CAM therapies have undergone careful evaluation and have found to be safe and effective. However, there are others that have been found to be ineffective or possibly harmful. Less is known about many CAM therapies, and research has been slower for a number of reasons:

- Time and funding issues

- Problems finding institutions and cancer researchers to work with on the studies

- Regulatory issues

CAM therapies need to be evaluated with the same long and careful research process used to evaluate standard treatments. Standard cancer treatments have generally been studied for safety and effectiveness through an intense scientific process that includes clinical trials with large numbers of patients.

Natural Does Not Mean Safe

CAM therapies include a wide variety of botanicals and nutritional products, such as dietary supplements, herbal supplements, and vitamins. Many of these "natural" products are considered to be safe because they are present in, or produced by, nature. However, that is not true in all cases. In addition, some may affect how well other medicines work in your body. For example, the herb St. John's wort, which some people use for depression, may cause certain anti-cancer drugs not to work as well as they should.

Herbal supplements may be harmful when taken by themselves, with other substances, or in large doses. For example, some studies have shown that *kava kava*, an herb that has been used to help with stress and anxiety, may cause liver damage.

4

Vitamins can also have unwanted effects in your body. For example, some studies show that high doses of vitamins, even vitamin C, may affect how chemotherapy and radiation work. Too much of any vitamin is not safe, even in a healthy person.

Tell your doctor if you're taking any dietary supplements, no matter how safe you think they are. This is very important. Even though there may be ads or claims that something has been used for years, they do not prove that it's safe or effective.

Supplements do not have to be approved by the federal government before being sold to the public. Also, a prescription is not needed to buy them. Therefore, it's up to consumers to decide what is best for them.

National Cancer Institute (NCI) and the National Center for Complementary and Integrative Health (NCCIH) are currently sponsoring or cosponsoring various clinical trials that test CAM treatments and therapies in people. Some study the effects of complementary approaches used in addition to conventional treatments, and some compare alternative therapies with conventional treatments.

Complementary versus Alternative

Many Americans—more than 30 percent of adults and about 12 percent of children—use health care approaches developed outside of mainstream Western, or conventional, medicine. When describing these approaches, people often use "alternative" and "complementary" interchangeably, but the two terms refer to different concepts:

- If a non-mainstream practice is used **together with** conventional medicine, it's considered "complementary."

- If a non-mainstream practice is used **in place of** conventional medicine, it's considered "alternative."

True alternative medicine is uncommon. Most people who use non-mainstream approaches use them along with conventional treatments.

Integrative Medicine

There are many definitions of "integrative" health care, but all involve bringing conventional and complementary approaches together in a coordinated way. The use of integrative approaches to health and wellness has grown within care settings across the United States. Researchers are currently exploring the potential benefits of integrative health in a variety of situations, including pain management for military personnel and veterans, relief of symptoms in cancer patients and survivors, and programs to promote healthy behaviors.

Integrative Approaches for Pain Management for Military Personnel and Veterans

Chronic pain is a common problem among active-duty military personnel and veterans. NCCIH, the U.S. Department of Veterans Affairs, and other agencies are sponsoring research to see whether integrative approaches can help. For example, NCCIH-funded studies are testing the effects of adding mindfulness meditation, self-hypnosis, or other complementary approaches to pain management programs for veterans. The goal is to help patients feel and function better and reduce their need for pain medicines that can have serious side effects.

Integrative Approaches for Symptom Management in Cancer Patients and Survivors

Cancer treatment centers with integrative health care programs may offer services such as acupuncture and meditation to help manage symptoms and side effects for patients who are receiving conventional cancer treatment. Although research on the potential value of these integrative programs is in its early stages, some studies have had promising results. For example, NCCIH-funded research has suggested that:

- Cancer patients who receive integrative therapies while in the hospital have less pain and anxiety.
- Massage therapy may lead to short-term improvements in pain and mood in patients with advanced cancer.
- Yoga may relieve the persistent fatigue that some women experience after breast cancer treatment.

Integrative Approaches and Health-Related Behaviors

Healthy behaviors, such as eating right, getting enough physical activity, and not smoking, can reduce people's risks of developing serious diseases. Can integrative approaches promote these types of behaviors? Researchers are working to answer this question. Preliminary research suggests that yoga and meditation-based therapies may help smokers quit, and NCCIH-funded studies are testing whether adding mindfulness-based approaches to weight control programs will help people lose weight more successfully.

So, What Terms Does NCCIH Use?

NCCIH generally uses the term "complementary health approaches" when we discuss practices and products of non-mainstream origin. We use "integrative health" when we talk about incorporating complementary approaches into mainstream health care.

Types of Complementary Health Approaches

Most complementary health approaches fall into one of two subgroups—natural products or mind and body practices.

Natural Products

This group includes a variety of products, such as **herbs** (also known as botanicals), **vitamins and minerals**, and **probiotics**. They are widely marketed, readily available to consumers, and often sold as dietary supplements.

According to the 2012 National Health Interview Survey (NHIS), which included a comprehensive survey on the use of complementary

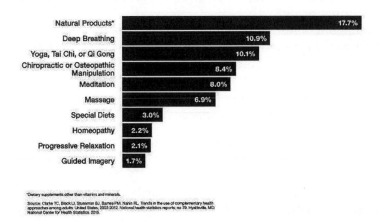

Figure 1.1. *10 most common complementary health approaches among adults*

health approaches by Americans, 17.7 percent of American adults had used a dietary supplement other than vitamins and minerals in the past year. These products were the most popular complementary health approach in the survey. The most commonly used natural product was fish oil.

Researchers have done large, rigorous studies on a few natural products, but the results often showed that the products didn't work. Research on others is in progress. While there are indications that some may be helpful, more needs to be learned about the effects of these products in the human body and about their safety and potential interactions with medicines and other natural products.

Mind and Body Practices

Mind and body practices include a large and diverse group of procedures or techniques administered or taught by a trained practitioner or teacher. The 2012 NHIS showed that **yoga, chiropractic and osteopathic manipulation, meditation**, and **massage therapy** are among the most popular mind and body practices used by adults. The popularity of yoga has grown dramatically in recent years, with almost twice as many U.S. adults practicing yoga in 2012 as in 2002.

Other mind and body practices include **relaxation techniques** (such as breathing exercises, guided imagery, and progressive muscle relaxation), **tai chi, qi qong, healing touch, hypnotherapy**, and **movement therapies** (such as Feldenkrais method, Alexander technique, Pilates, Rolfing Structural Integration, and Trager psychophysical integration).

The amount of research on mind and body approaches varies widely depending on the practice. For example, researchers have done many studies on yoga, spinal manipulation, and meditation, but there have been fewer studies on some other practices.

Other Complementary Health Approaches

The two broad areas discussed above—natural products and mind and body practices—capture most complementary health approaches. However, some approaches may not neatly fit into either of these groups—for example, the practices of **traditional healers, Ayurvedic medicine, traditional Chinese medicine, homeopathy**, and **naturopathy**.

Chapter 2

Common Questions and Answers about CAM

Are you Considering a Complementary Health Approach?

Millions of Americans use complementary health approaches. Like any decision concerning your health, decisions about whether to use complementary approaches are important. The National Center for Complementary and Integrative Health (NCCIH) has developed this content to assist you in your decision making about complementary health products and practices.

Take Charge of Your Health

- Be an informed consumer. Find out and consider what scientific studies have been done on the safety and effectiveness of any health approach that is recommended to or interests you.

- Discuss the information and your interests with your health care providers before making a decision.

This chapter includes excerpts from "Frequently Asked Questions about Cancer and CAM," Office of Cancer Complementary and Alternative Medicine (OCCAM), November 9, 2012; and text from "Are You Considering a Complementary Health Approach?" National Center for Complementary and Integrative Health (NCCIH), August 2014.

- Choose a complementary health practitioner, such as an acupuncturist, as carefully as you would choose a conventional health care provider.

- Before using any dietary supplement or herbal product, make sure you find out about potential side effects or interactions with medications you may be taking.

- Only use treatments for your condition that have been proven safe. Do not use a product or practice that has not been proven to be effective to postpone seeing your health care provider for your condition.

- Tell all your health care providers—complementary and conventional—about all the health approaches you use. Give them a full picture of what you do to manage your health. This will help ensure coordinated and safe care.

What does CAM include?

CAM may include dietary supplements, megadose vitamins, herbal preparations, special teas, acupuncture, massage therapy, magnet therapy, spiritual healing, and meditation.

Why should CAM therapies be evaluated scientifically?

It is important that CAM therapies receive the same scientific evaluation that is used to assess standard healthcare approaches. As CAM therapies are proven safe and effective, they may become part of standard health care.

What do "complementary,""alternative," and "integrative" mean?

"Complementary and alternative medicine," "complementary medicine," "alternative medicine," "integrative medicine"—we have all seen these terms on the Internet and in marketing, but what do they really mean? While the terms are often used to mean the array of health care approaches with a history of use or origins outside of mainstream medicine, they are actually hard to define and may mean different things to different people.

The terms **complementary** and **integrative** refer to the use of such non-mainstream approaches **together with** conventional medical approaches.

Alternative health approaches refer to the use of non-mainstream approaches in place of conventional medicine. NCCIH advises against using any product or practice that has not been proven safe and effective as a substitute for conventional medical treatment or as a reason to postpone seeing your health care provider about any health problem. In some instances, stopping—or not starting—conventional treatment can have serious consequences. Before making a decision not to use a proven conventional treatment, talk to your health care providers.

How can I get reliable information about a complementary health approach?

It's important to learn what scientific studies have discovered about the complementary health approach you're considering, because evidence from research studies is stronger and more reliable than something you've seen in an advertisement or on a Web site or because people have told you that it worked for them.

Understanding a product's or practice's potential benefits, risks, and scientific evidence is critical to your health and safety. Scientific research on many complementary health approaches is relatively new, so this kind of information may not be available for each one. However, many studies are under way, including those that NCCIH supports, and knowledge and understanding of complementary approaches are increasing all the time. Here are some ways to find reliable information:

- **Talk with your health care providers.** Tell them about the complementary health approach you're considering and ask any questions you may have about safety, effectiveness, or interactions with medications (prescription or nonprescription) or dietary supplements.

- **Visit the NCCIH Web site (nccih.nih.gov).** The "Health Information" page has information on what the science says about specific complementary approaches, and links to other objective sources of online information. The Web site also has contact information for the **NCCIH Clearinghouse,** where information specialists are available to assist you in searching the scientific literature and to suggest useful NCCIH publications. You can also find information from NCCIH on Facebook (www.facebook.com/nih.nccih), Twitter (twitter.com/NIH_NCCIH), YouTube (www.youtube.com/NCCIHgov), and Pinterest (www.pinterest.com/nccihgov).

- **Visit your local library or a medical library.** Ask the reference librarian to help you find scientific journals and trustworthy books with information on the product or practice that interests you.

11

Are complementary health approaches safe?

As with any medical product or treatment, there can be risks with complementary approaches. These risks depend on the specific product or practice. Each needs to be considered on its own. However, if you're considering a specific product or practice, the following general suggestions can help you think about safety and minimize risks.

- Be aware that individuals respond differently to health products and practices, whether conventional or complementary. How you might respond to one depends on many things, including your state of health, how you use it, or your belief in it.

- Keep in mind that "natural" does not necessarily mean "safe." (Think of mushrooms that grow in the wild: some are safe to eat, while others are not.)

- Learn about factors that affect safety. For a practice that is administered by a practitioner, such as chiropractic, these factors include the training, skill, and experience of the practitioner. For a product such as a dietary supplement, the specific ingredients and the quality of the manufacturing process are important factors.

- If you decide to use a practice provided by a complementary health practitioner, choose the practitioner as carefully as you would your primary health care provider.

- If you decide to use a dietary supplement, such as an herbal product, be aware that some products may interact in harmful ways with medications (prescription or over-the-counter) or other dietary supplements, and some may have side effects on their own.

- Tell all your health care providers about any complementary health approaches you use. Give them a full picture of what you do to manage your health. This will help ensure coordinated and safe care.

How can I determine whether statements made about the effectiveness of a complementary health approach are true?

- Is there scientific evidence (not just personal stories) to back up the statements?

- What is the source? Statements that manufacturers or other promoters of some complementary health approaches may make about effectiveness and benefits can sound reasonable and promising. However, the statements may be based on a biased view of the available scientific evidence.

- Does the federal government have anything to report about the product or practice?

    - Visit the NCCIH Web site or contact the NCCIH Clearinghouse to see if NCCIH has information about the product or practice.

    - Visit the U.S. Food and Drug Administration (FDA) online at www.fda.gov to see if there is any information available about the product or practice.

    - Information specifically about dietary supplements can be found on the FDA's Web site at www.fda.gov/Food/Dietary-Supplements and on the Web site of the National Institutes of Health (NIH) Office of Dietary Supplements at ods.od.nih.gov.

    - Visit the FDA's Web page on recalls and safety alerts at www.fda.gov/Safety/Recalls. The FDA has a rapid public notification system to provide information about tainted dietary supplements. See www.fda.gov/AboutFDA/ContactFDA/StayInformed/RSSFeeds/TDS/rss.xml.

    - Check with the Federal Trade Commission at www.ftc.gov to see if there are any enforcement actions for deceptive advertising regarding the therapy. Also, visit the site's Consumer Information section at www.consumer.ftc.gov.

- How does the provider or manufacturer describe the approach?

    - Beware of terms like "scientific breakthrough," "miracle cure," "secret ingredient," or "ancient remedy."

    - If you encounter claims of a "quick fix" that depart from previous research, keep in mind that science usually advances over time by small steps, slowly building an evidence base.

    - Remember: if it sounds too good to be true—for example, claims that a product or practice can cure a disease or works for a variety of ailments—it usually is.

Is That Health Web Site Trustworthy?

If you're visiting a health Web site for the first time, the following five quick questions can help you decide whether the site is a helpful resource.

13

Who? Who runs the Web site? Can you trust them?

What? What does the site say? Do its claims seem to good to be true?

When? When was the information posted or reviewed? Is it up-to-date?

Where? Where did the information come from? Is it based on scientific research?

Why? Why does the site exist? Is it selling something?

Are You Reading Real Online News or Just Advertising?

In April 2011, the Federal Trade Commission warned the public about fake online news sites promoting an acai berry weight-loss product. For example, one described an investigation in which a reporter used the product for several weeks, with "dramatic" results. The site looked real, but it was actually an advertisement. Everything was fake: there was no reporter, no news organization, and no investigation. The only real things were the links to a sales site that appeared in the story and elsewhere on the Web page. Similar fake news sites have promoted other products, including work-at-home opportunities and debt reduction plans.

You should suspect that a news site may be fake if it:

- Endorses a product. Real news organizations generally don't do this.

- Only quotes people who say good things about the product.

- Presents research findings that seem too good to be true or fail to point out any limitations in research. (If something seems too good to be true, it usually is.)

- Contains links to a sales site.

- Includes positive reader comments only, and you can't add a comment of your own.

How to Protect Yourself

If you suspect that a news site might be fake, look for a disclaimer somewhere on the page (often in small print) that indicates that the site is an advertisement. Also, don't rely on Internet news reports when making important decisions about your health. If you're considering a health product described in the news, discuss it with your health care provider.

Are complementary health approaches tested to see if they work?

While scientific evidence now exists regarding the effectiveness and safety of some complementary health approaches, there remain many yet-to-be-answered questions about whether others are safe, whether they work for the diseases or medical conditions for which they are promoted, and how those approaches with health benefits may work. As the federal government's lead agency for scientific research on health interventions, practices, products, and disciplines that originate from outside mainstream medicine, NCCIH supports scientific research to answer these questions and determine who might benefit most from the use of specific approaches.

I'm interested in an approach that involves seeing a complementary health practitioner. How do I go about selecting a practitioner?

- Your primary health care provider or local hospital may be able to recommend a complementary health practitioner.

- The professional organization for the type of practitioner you're seeking may have helpful information, such as licensing and training requirements. Many states have regulatory agencies or licensing boards for certain types of complementary health practitioners; they may be able to help you locate practitioners in your area.

- Make sure any practitioner you're considering is willing to work in collaboration with your other health care providers.

Can I receive treatment or a referral to a complementary health practitioner from NCCIH?

NCCIH does not provide treatment or referrals to complementary health practitioners. NCCIH's mission is to define, through rigorous scientific investigation, the usefulness and safety of complementary health approaches and their roles in improving health and health care.

Can I participate in a clinical trial of a complementary health approach?

NCCIH supports clinical trials on complementary health approaches. These trials are taking place in many locations, and study participants are needed. To learn more or to find trials that are recruiting participants, visit NIH Web site. The site includes questions and answers about clinical trials, guidance on how to find clinical trials through ClinicalTrials.gov, and other resources and stories about the personal experiences of clinical trial participants.

If you don't have access to the Internet, contact the NCCIH Clearinghouse for information.

Chapter 3

Use of CAM in the United States

Complementary health approaches include an array of modalities and products with a history of use or origins outside of conventional Western medicine. Previous studies have shown that individuals often use complementary health approaches to improve health and well-being or to relieve symptoms associated with chronic diseases or the side effects of conventional medicine. In the United States, most persons who use complementary health approaches do so to complement conventional care, rather than as a replacement. Using data from the 2002 National Health Interview Survey (NHIS), found that less than 5% of all U.S. adults used complementary health approaches but not conventional care. Previous research has also shown differences in the use of complementary health approaches by demographic characteristics such as sex and age. While knowledge of various types of complementary health approaches has increased among the U.S. population, the use of individual approaches has fluctuated across the years.

To better understand the patterns of use of complementary health approaches, this report describes the prevalence of adults using

Text in this chapter is excerpted from "Trends in the Use of Complementary Health Approaches Among Adults: United States, 2002–2012," Centers for Disease Control and Prevention (CDC), February 10, 2015.

selected complementary health approaches and characterizes selected sociodemographic characteristics of such users. Because nonvitamin, nonmineral dietary supplements are the most commonly used complementary health approach among U.S. adults, after vitamins and prayer, individual supplements are also examined.

Methods

Data source

Analyses in this report were based on data collected from a combined sample of 88,962 adults aged 18 and over as part of the 2002, 2007, and 2012 Adult Alternative Medicine (ALT) supplements to NHIS, with demographic and other health information from the Household, Sample Adult Core, and Family Core components. NHIS is a nationally representative, cross-sectional household interview survey that is fielded continuously by the Centers for Disease Control and Prevention's (CDC) National Center for Health Statistics (NCHS), and it produces annual estimates of the health of the U.S. civilian noninstitutionalized population. Interviews are conducted in the home using a computer-assisted personal interview questionnaire, with telephone follow-up permitted if necessary. A detailed description of the NHIS sample design and the survey questionnaires for specific years are available elsewhere.

The Household and Family Core of NHIS collect health and sociodemographic information on each member of all families residing within a sampled household. Within each family, additional information is collected from one randomly selected adult (the "sample adult") aged 18 and over with the Sample Adult Core.

In 2002, 2007, and 2012, the ALT supplement was administered to the sample adult respondent. Sponsored by the National Center for Complementary and Integrative Health [(NCCIH) formerly the National Center for Complementary and Alternative Medicine], part of the National Institutes of Health (NIH), the ALT supplement was implemented in order to provide a national data source on complementary medicine use. Since its inception in 2002, much of the content of the ALT supplement has remained constant, but modifications have been made in order to accommodate emerging scientific information, expert panel input, and societal shifts. Although the approaches included have varied slightly across survey years, the following were included in all three questionnaires: acupuncture; Ayurveda; biofeedback; chelation therapy; chiropractic care; energy healing therapy; hypnosis; massage; naturopathy; nonvitamin, non-mineral dietary supplements; homeopathic treatment; diet-based therapies; yoga; tai chi; qi gong; and meditation and other relaxation techniques.

Detailed differences between the three NHIS ALT supplement questionnaires can be found elsewhere. Briefly, use of a practitioner for chiropractic care was asked about in 2002. In 2007, participants were asked about use of a chiropractor or osteopath, however no real specificity was gained, as use of both types of manipulation were grouped together. This question was repeated in 2012, with the addition of follow-up questions asking whether a chiropractor, osteopath, or both were seen. Also, in 2007, a list of named traditional healers replaced the more general question of seeing a practitioner of folk medicine, and questions about the use of movement therapies were added. In 2012, craniosacral therapy was added to the questionnaire.

In order to provide greater detail on meditation, in 2012 the type of meditation practiced was specified as mantra, mindfulness, or spiritual. Combining the prevalence of all three types of meditation may permit the comparison of the general practice of meditation across the three time points; however, these comparisons may be affected by the change in question format on the 2012 supplement. Based on cognitive testing and recommendations from a NCCIH think tank in 2012, information about the use of deep-breathing exercises was not asked as a stand-alone question but was collected as part of other approaches, including hypnosis, biofeedback, meditation, guided imagery, progressive relaxation, yoga, tai chi, and qi gong.

While this change reduced the percentage of false-positive responses, direct comparison to previous survey years was lost. The list of nonvitamin, nonmineral dietary supplements was expanded from 35 in 2002, to 45 in 2007, and 119 in 2012. In addition, the 2002 questionnaire included a 12-month recall period for use of named nonvitamin, nonmineral dietary supplements, whereas the 2007 questionnaire included a 30-day recall period. As an improvement, the 2012 survey included both 30-day and 12-month recall periods for named nonvitamin, nonmineral dietary supplements. Comparisons of use in the past 30 days were consequently restricted to 2007 and 2012.

In order to compare overall use of complementary health approaches across all three time points, recalculation of approaches that changed across years was restricted to the narrowest definition on any one questionnaire. Individual approaches that were not directly comparable across all three time points were not included in trend analyses.

Measure of complementary health approach use

For this report, the definition of any complementary approach included the use of one or more of the following during the past 12 months: acupuncture; Ayurveda; biofeedback; chelation therapy; chiropractic care; energy healing therapy; special diets (including vegetarian and vegan, macrobiotic, Atkins, Pritikin, and Ornish); folk medicine or traditional healers; guided imagery; homeopathic treatment; hypnosis; naturopathy; nonvitamin, nonmineral dietary supplements; massage; meditation; progressive relaxation; qi gong; tai chi; or yoga. Due to the modifications in the three questionnaires as outlined above, only these approaches were asked about consistently across the three time points. Their use creates the most uniformed definition to assess trends.

Demographic variables

Demographic characteristics of U.S. adults presented in this report include sex, age group, Hispanic or Latino origin and race, educational attainment, poverty status, and health insurance coverage. All demographic characteristics were measured at the time of the interview.

Hispanic or Latino origin and race were determined from two separate questions, and individuals may have identified as Hispanic or Latino origin regardless of race. For conciseness, the text and tables in this report use shorter versions of the 1997 Office of Management and Budget terms for Hispanic origin and race. For example, the category "Non-Hispanic or non- Latino, black or African American, single race" is referred to as "non-Hispanic black." Due to insufficient sample size, "non-Hispanic Asian," "non-Hispanic Other Pacific Islander," and "non-Hispanic American Indian Alaska Native" were combined to form the category "non-Hispanic other races."

Educational attainment was collected from all adults aged 18 and over and was categorized in reference to the highest degree completed at the date of the interview. Household income was also collected, and percentage of poverty level was based on a comparison of each respondent's household income with the poverty thresholds for the family size, as defined by the U.S. Census Bureau. Imputations for income were not used.

Health insurance was categorized into three mutually exclusive categories: private, public, and uninsured. Persons with more than one type of health insurance were assigned to their primary insurance category in the following hierarchy: private, public, and uninsured. A more detailed description of these demographic variables can be found in Technical Notes.

Statistical analyses

Estimates in this report were calculated using the sample adult sampling weights and are representative of the noninstitutionalized population of U.S. adults aged 18 and over. Data weighting procedures are described in more detail elsewhere. Point estimates, and estimates of their variances, were calculated using SAS-callable SUDAAN version 11.0.0, a software package that accounts for the complex sample design of NHIS. Estimates were age-adjusted using the projected 2000 U.S. population as the standard population in order to compare various demographic subgroups that have different age distributions. Unless otherwise specified, the denominator used was all adults aged 18 and over. Calculations excluded persons with unknown information.

Estimates were compared using two-sided t tests at the 0.05 level and assuming independence. Terms such as "greater than" and "less than" indicate a statistically significant difference. Terms such as "not significantly different" or "no difference" indicate that there were no statistically detectable differences between the estimates being compared. Reliability of estimates was evaluated using the relative standard error (RSE), which is the standard error divided by the point estimate. Estimates with RSEs greater than 30% and less than or equal to 50% are considered unreliable and are preceded by a dagger symbol (†) in Table 3.1.

The SAS procedure PROC SURVEYLOGISTIC with orthogonal polynomial trend contrasts was used to perform weighted linear or quadratic regressions of the annual design-adjusted rates for each variable of interest. This procedure incorporates the complex survey sample design of NHIS, including stratification, clustering, and unequal weighting. This model tests the parallel-lines assumption by simultaneously testing the equality of separate slope parameters for each variable. The variances of the regression parameters were computed using the Taylor series (linearization) method to estimate the sampling errors of estimators based on the complex sample design. This method will be used for all trend analyses in this report series.

Strengths and limitations of data

A major strength of these analyses is that the data are from a nationally representative sample of U.S. adults, allowing for population estimates. The large sample size allows for estimation of the use of complementary health approaches by a wide variety of population subgroups and other self-reported health characteristics collected in NHIS.

21

The data in this report also have some limitations. NHIS is a cross-sectional survey, and causal associations cannot be made. Responses are dependent on participants' recall of complementary health approaches that they used in the past 12 months, as well as their willingness to report their use accurately. Additionally, in an effort to improve the validity of the questions asked and to meet NCCIH's research priorities, revisions to the content and structure of some questions preclude direct comparison across years, limiting analysis of trends to approaches that were asked about consistently on each questionnaire.

Results

Adult use of selected complementary health approaches

Complementary health approaches encompass a wide range of modalities. Table 3.1. presents the prevalence of and trends in the use of commonly used complementary health approaches in 2002, 2007, and 2012. Although there was consistency in the types of approaches that were most popular, there was variation in the trends across time points.

- Nonvitamin, nonmineral dietary supplements were the most commonly used complementary health approach at each of the three time points: 18.9% in 2002 and unchanged from 2007 to 2012 (17.7%).

- Whether used independently or as a part of other approaches, deep- breathing exercises were the second most commonly used complementary health approach in 2002 (11.6%), 2007 (12.7%), and 2012 (10.9%).

- The use of yoga, tai chi, and qi gong increased linearly over the three time points, beginning at 5.8% in 2002, 6.7% in 2007, and 10.1% in 2012. Yoga was the most commonly used of these three approaches at all three time points (Figure 3.1.)

- There was a small but significant linear increase in the use of homeopathic treatment, acupuncture, and naturopathy.

- The use of chiropractic care or chiropractic and osteopathic manipulation was the fourth most commonly used approach in 2002 (7.5%), 2007 (8.6%), and 2012 (8.4%).

- Meditation was used by 7.6% of adults in 2002, 9.4% in 2007, and 8.0% in 2012, keeping it among the top five most commonly used approaches for each time point.

- Ayurveda, biofeedback, guided imagery hypnosis, and energy healing therapy had a consistently low prevalence and had no significant changes across the three time points.

Overall use of complementary health approaches, by selected characteristics

Among U.S. adults aged 18 and over in 2002, 2007, and 2012, the percentage who used any complementary health approach in the past 12 months ranged from 32.3% in 2002 to 35.5% in 2007 and was most recently 33.2% in 2012. Table 3.2. highlights trends in the use of complementary health approaches by sex, age group, Hispanic or Latino origin and race, education, poverty status, and health insurance coverage.

- There was a quadratic change in the overall use of any complementary health approach across the three time points with a peak of 35.5% in 2007.

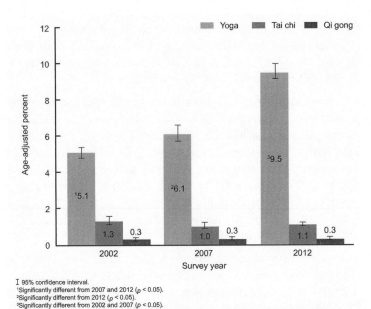

I 95% confidence interval.
[1]Significantly different from 2007 and 2012 ($p < 0.05$).
[2]Significantly different from 2012 ($p < 0.05$).
[3]Significantly different from 2002 and 2007 ($p < 0.05$).
NOTES: Estimates are age-adjusted using the projected 2000 U.S. population as the standard population and four age groups: 18–24, 25–44, 45–64, and 65 and over. Estimates are based on household interviews of a sample of the civilian noninstitutionalized population.
SOURCE: CDC/NCHS, National Health Interview Survey, 2002, 2007 and 2012.

Figure 3.1. *Use of yoga, tai chi, and qi gong among adults in the past 12 months: United States, 2002, 2007, and 2012*

- There was a significant quadratic trend in the use of complementary health approaches among both men and women across the three time points. The use of any complementary health approach increased by 3.5 percentage points among men from 2002 to 2007 but decreased by 2.5 percentage points from 2007 to 2012. There was a 3.0 percentage point increase in use among women from 2002 to 2007; however, there were no further significant differences between other time points.

- There were no significant changes in the prevalence of any complementary health approach between each time point for adults aged 18–44 (33.0% in 2002, 34.2% in 2007, and 32.2% in 2012). There was an increase from 36.5% in 2002 to 40.1% in 2007, and then a decrease to 36.8% in 2012 among adults aged 45–64. The use of any complementary health approach also increased among adults aged 65 and over from 2002 to 2007, from 22.7% to 31.1%; but no significant change was observed between 2007 and 2012 (31.1% to 29.4%).

- From 2002 to 2012, there was a significant quadratic trend for Hispanic adults (26.4% in 2002, 21.6% in 2007, and 22.0% in 2012) and non-Hispanic white adults (34.4% in 2002, 40.2% in 2007, and 37.9% in 2012). However, a significant linear trend was observed for non-Hispanic black adults (22.9% in 2002 and 2007 and 19.3% in 2012) and non-Hispanic other adults (41.5% in 2002, 39.6% in 2007, and 37.3% in 2012).

- There were significant quadratic trends in the use of complementary approaches among adults with less than a high school diploma (18.6% in 2002, 18.9% in 2007, and 15.6% in 2012); adults with a high school diploma or GED (General Educational Development high school equivalency diploma) (26.6% in 2002, 28.1% in 2007, and 24.4% in 2012); adults with some college education (35.6% in 2002, 41.3% in 2007, and 36.5% in 2012); and those with a college degree or higher (42.1% in 2002, 46.7% in 2007, and 42.6% in 2012).

- There was a significant quadratic trend in the use of complementary approaches among poor adults (25.1% in 2002, 26.6% in 2007, and 20.6% in 2012) and not-poor adults (36.8% in 2002, 40.3% in 2007, and 38.4% in 2012); and a linear trend among near-poor adults (27.7% in 2002, 27.9% in 2007, and 25.5% in 2012).

- There was a significant quadratic trend in the use of any complementary health approach among all insured groups: those with private insurance (34.6% in 2002, 39.0% in 2007, and 38.0%

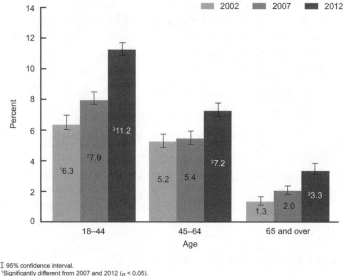

I 95% confidence interval.
[1]Significantly different from 2007 and 2012 ($p < 0.05$).
[2]Significantly different from 2012 ($p < 0.05$).
[3]Significantly different from 2002 and 2007 ($p < 0.05$).
NOTE: Estimates are based on household interviews of a sample of the civilian noninstitutionalized population.
SOURCE: CDC/NCHS, National Health Interview Survey, 2002, 2007 and 2012.

Figure 3.2. *Use of yoga among adults in the past 12 months, by age group: United States, 2002, 2007, and 2012*

in 2012) and public coverage (25.8% in 2002, 27.0% in 2007, and 24.8% in 2012) as well as the uninsured (28.4% in 2002, 27.8% in 2007, and 22.9% in 2012).

Use of selected nonvitamin, nonmineral dietary supplements in 2007 and 2012

Although there was no change in the percentage of overall use of nonvitamin, nonmineral dietary supplements among adults from 2007 to 2012, there was variability in the use of specific types of supplements. Table 3.3. presents the prevalence of selected nonvitamin, nonmineral dietary supplements used in the past 30 days. Estimates are limited to 2007 and 2012 because a 30-day supplement recall was not included in the 2002 questionnaire.

- Fish oil supplements and glucosamine, chondroitin, or a combination supplement were consistently the two most common nonvitamin, nonmineral dietary supplements used in the past 30 days in 2007 and 2012.

25

- Fish oil use among adults increased from 4.8% in 2007 to 7.8% in 2012. Probiotic or prebiotic use was four times as high in 2012 as it was in 2007 (1.6% and 0.4%, respectively), rising to the third most commonly used nonvitamin, nonmineral dietary supplement in 2012.

- The use of melatonin more than doubled in use from 0.6% in 2007 to 1.3% in 2012.

- There was a decrease in use of glucosamine, chondroitin, or a combination pill from 2007 to 2012, from 3.2% to 2.6%.

- From 2007 to 2012, there was also a significant decline in the use of echinacea (1.3 percentage points), garlic (0.6), ginseng (0.8), ginkgo biloba (0.6), methylsulfonylmethane (MSM) (0.2), and saw palmetto (0.3).

Use of yoga by age group and year

The most notable differences in the use of any complementary health approach were seen by age group. To further understand age differences, Figure 3.2. presents one of the most commonly used approaches, yoga, by age group for 2002, 2007, and 2012.

- While all age groups showed an increased use of yoga over the 10-year period, the use of yoga decreased with age (from 6.3% in 2002 to 11.2% in 2012 among those aged 18–44; 5.2% in 2002 to 7.2% in 2012 among those 45–64; and 1.3% in 2002 to 3.3% in 2012 among those 65 and over) (Figure 3.2.)

- Adults aged 18–44 had the highest prevalence of use across all three time points. The increase in use of yoga among this group from 2007 to 2012 (3.3 percentage points) was more than twice the increase in use between 2002 and 2007 (1.6 percentage points).

- There were no significant differences observed in the use of yoga between 2002 and 2007 among adults aged 45–64 and those aged 65 and over; however, there was an increase in the use of yoga between 2007 and 2012 for both age groups (1.8 and 1.3 percentage points, respectively).

Use of yoga by Hispanic or Latino origin and race and year

The use of yoga varied by Hispanic or Latino origin and race over the three time points; Figure 3.3. presents these changes.

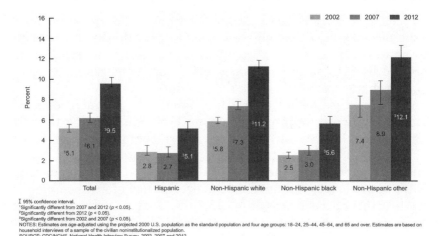

Figure 3.3. *Use of yoga among adults in the past 12 months, by Hispanic origin and race: United States, 2002, 2007, and 2012*

- There was no significant change in the use of yoga among Hispanic adults between 2002 (2.8%) and 2007 (2.7%); however, the use of yoga among this group almost doubled between 2007 and 2012 (5.1%). Non-Hispanic black adults demonstrated a similar pattern of use across time (2.5% in 2002, 3.0% in 2007, and 5.6% in 2012) (Figure 3.3.)

- Non-Hispanic white adults demonstrated a consistent increase in the use of yoga across the three time points, from 5.8% in 2002 to 11.2% in 2012.

- While there was no significant difference in the use of yoga among non-Hispanic other adults from 2002 (7.4%) to 2007 (8.9%), their use increased by almost 30% from 2002 to 2012 (12.1%).

Discussion

In response to queries from researchers, practitioners, and users of complementary health approaches, this report presents data from the 2002, 2007, and 2012 NHIS on the use of complementary health approaches among civilian noninstitutionalized U.S. adults aged 18 and over. It focuses on the prevalence and trends of selected complementary health approaches used in the past 12 months, selected characteristics of adults who used any complementary health approach, and the use of selected nonvitamin, nonmineral dietary supplements in the past 30 days. The objective was to provide the most current estimates of a wide range of complementary health approaches that are used by U.S. adults, to characterize user demographics, and to monitor changes over the three time points.

This report is one of the first to estimate the prevalence of complementary health approaches among U.S. adults using the 2012 NHIS. Overall, 34% of adults used any complementary health approach in 2012. Despite the lack of a consistent definition as to which approaches are included in the measure of complementary health approaches, estimates of the overall use of any complementary health approach presented in this study are consistent with previous research. Estimates for the use of individual approaches and demographic characteristics are also consistent with previous reports. Because a narrower definition was used in this report, it is not surprising that the revised prevalence estimates for 2002 and 2007 were lower than those published previously: 32.3% compared with 35.0% for 2002 and 35.5% compared with 38.0% for 2007. Without taking into consideration which complementary health approaches are included in the definition of any complementary health approach, comparison of the prevalence may be misleading across studies. This confusion with definitions has led to an effort to establish an internationally accepted standard for what approaches should be included in prevalence surveys of complementary health approaches.

Previous research using NHIS and other surveys found that the use of any complementary health approach has been increasing, and some reports speculated that this increasing trend would continue. However, results from this report show that while the overall use of complementary health approaches displayed a slight increase between 2002 and 2007, in 2012 use among U.S. adults was not significantly different from 2002. Distinct from the trend in use of any complementary health approaches, there have been variations in the magnitude and direction of the trends of individual approaches. Nonvitamin, nonmineral dietary supplements; deep-breathing exercises; yoga, tai chi, and qi gong; and chiropractic or osteopathic manipulation were consistently popular approaches over the three time points, regardless of changes to some questions across survey time points. Among these approaches, yoga, tai chi, and qi gong showed an increase, and deep-breathing exercises and chiropractic or osteopathic manipulation had no significant change between 2002 and

2012. Although some questions have been changed every survey year, the estimates do not reflect overly abundant increases or decreases in any one approach.

In addition to comparing the prevalence in use between time points, further examination of selected approaches revealed significant differences among age and Hispanic or Latino origin and race groups. The only group of approaches to significantly increase each year was the use of yoga, tai chi, or qi gong. Given that all three often incorporate low-intensity forms of exercise that can be scaled to an individual's abilities, the increased popularity across all ages and Hispanic origin and race groups was expected. Offered in a variety of settings ranging from self-practice to specialized studios, the yoga industry has experienced growth in recent years, making it more accessible to adults of all ages.

Previous research has noted variations in use of complementary health approaches by race and Hispanic origin. This report found that Hispanic and non-Hispanic black adults had a decreasing pattern of use of any complementary health approach while non-Hispanic white adults had an increasing pattern of use. Other studies have examined how length of stay in the United States and race and ethnicity may help explain differences in the use of complementary health approaches.

The health benefits of nonvitamin, nonmineral dietary supplements are unclear. Despite this, such supplements were consistently the most used complementary health approach across the three time points. Overall trends in the prevalence of use of any nonvitamin, nonmineral supplements need to be qualified by the observations of a significant increase in the use of certain individual supplements: fish oil; probiotics or prebiotics; and melatonin; and decreases in the use of glucosamine, chondroitin, or both; echinacea; garlic; ginseng; ginkgo biloba; MSM; and saw palmetto (Table 3.3.)

Health advocates and physicians have been recommending fish oil supplementation, although its benefits are not well understood. Research has suggested that fish oil can reduce blood pressure and inflammation, increase brain blood flow, and provide structural strength for neurons. The data for this report showed a 60% increase in the 30-day prevalence of using fish oils between 2007 and 2012. The use of other supplements such as melatonin and probiotics or prebiotics also increased. Consistent with the report's findings, market research indicates a significant increase in sales of these products over the past 5 years.

Although beyond the scope of this report, the reasons for using complementary health approaches may help explain the differences in the trends among demographic groups. The NHIS ALT supplements were designed to help guide the NIH research agenda, and they have evolved to adapt to NCCIH's evolution in priorities from disease treatment to a focus on symptom management and the promotion of optimal health. These supplements provide the most comprehensive source of information on complementary health approaches used by U.S. adults. Building upon previous reports, this report is helpful for monitoring changing patterns in complementary health approach use. Additionally, this report shows that looking exclusively at the overall use of complementary health approaches can miss meaningful differences in the use of individual approaches.

While substantial revisions to the content and structure of the ALT supplements since 2002 preclude direct comparisons of some approaches across all three time points, it is still possible to compare the prevalence of some of these approaches between two consecutive supplements. The prevalence rates of complementary health approaches will differ by survey year and by publication without using uniformed definitions. As such, data users are advised to carefully define the broad term of complementary health approaches and recalculate specific therapies, where possible, to facilitate direct comparisons.

Table 3.1. Trends in the use of selected complementary health approaches during the past 12 months, by type of approach: United States, 2002, 2007, and 2012

Complementary health approach	2002		2007		2012		Test for trend			
							Percentage point change			
	Number (in thousands)	Age-adjusted percent[1] (standard error)	Number (in thousands)	Age-adjusted percent[1] (standard error)	Number (in thousands)	Age-adjusted percent[1] (standard error)	2002–2007	2007–2012	2002–2012	Trend
Nonvitamin, nonmineral dietary supplements	38,183	18.9 (0.28)	38,797	17.7 (0.37)	40,579	17.7 (0.37)	††	0	††	††
Deep-breathing exercises[2]	23,457	11.6 (0.24)	27,794	12.7 (0.30)	24,218	10.9 (0.26)	§1.1	††	††	††
Yoga, tai chi, and qi gong	11,766	5.8 (0.17)	14,436	6.7 (0.22)	22,281	10.1 (0.25)	0.9	§2.5	§3.4	*Linear
Chiropractic or osteopathic manipulation[3]	15,226	7.5 (0.19)	18,740	8.6 (0.27)	19,369	8.4 (0.22)	††	–0.2	††	††
Meditation[4]	15,336	7.6 (0.20)	20,541	9.4 (0.27)	17,948	8.0 (0.21)	§1.8	††	††	††
Massage therapy	10,052	5.0 (0.16)	18,068	8.3 (0.23)	15,411	6.9 (0.15)	§3.3	§–1.6	§1.9	*Quadratic
Special diets[5]	6,765	3.3 (0.12)	6,040	2.8 (0.14)	6,853	3.0 (0.13)	0.1	§–0.6	–0.5	**Quadratic
Homeopathic treatment[6]	3,433	1.7 (0.09)	3,909	1.8 (0.11)	5,046	2.2 (0.11)	0.1	0.4	0.5	***Linear
Progressive relaxation	6,185	3.0 (0.12)	6,454	2.9 (0.15)	4,766	2.1 (0.10)	–0.1	§–0.8	§–0.9	*Linear
Guided imagery	4,194	2.1 (0.10)	4,866	2.2 (0.16)	3,846	1.7 (0.10)	0.1	–0.5	–0.4	None
Acupuncture	2,136	1.1 (0.07)	3,141	1.4 (0.10)	3,484	1.5 (0.08)	0.3	0.1	0.4	***Linear
Energy healing therapy	1,080	0.5 (0.05)	1,216	0.5 (0.06)	1,077	0.5 (0.05)	0	0	0	None
Naturopathy	498	0.2 (0.03)	729	0.3 (0.04)	957	0.4 (0.04)	0.1	0.1	0.2	**Linear

Table 3.1. *Continued*

Complementary health approach	2002		2007		2012		Test for trend			
							Percentage point change			
	Number (in thousands)	Age-adjusted percent[1] (standard error)	Number (in thousands)	Age-adjusted percent[1] (standard error)	Number (in thousands)	Age-adjusted percent[1] (standard error)	2002–2007	2007–2012	2002–2012	Trend
Hypnosis	505	0.2 (0.03)	561	0.2 (0.04)	347	0.1 (0.03)	0	–0.1	–0.1	None
Biofeedback	278	0.1 (0.02)	362	0.2 (0.04)	281	0.1 (0.02)	0.1	–0.1	0	None
Ayurveda	154	†0.1 (0.02)	214	†0.1 (0.03)	241	0.1 (0.02)	0	0	0	None

† Estimates are considered unreliable. Data have a relative standard error greater than 30% and less than or equal to 50% and should be used with caution.

†† Direct comparisons are not available.

§ Difference between both years is statistically significant at p < 0.05.

0.0 Quantity more than zero but less than 0.05.

*Significance of the chi-squared statistics is < 0.001.

**Significance of the chi-squared statistics is < 0.01.

***Significance of the chi-squared statistics is < 0.05.

[1] The denominator used in the calculation of percentages was all sample adults.

[2] In 2012, deep-breathing exercises included deep-breathing exercises as part of hypnosis; biofeedback; Mantra meditation (including Transcendental Meditation, Relaxation Response, and Clinically Standardized Meditation); mindfulness meditation (including Vipassana, Zen Buddhist meditation, mindfulness-based stress reduction, and mindfulness-based cognitive therapy); spiritual meditation (including centering prayer and contemplative meditation); guided imagery; progressive relaxation; yoga; tai chi; or qi gong. In 2002 and 2007, the use of deep-breathing exercises was asked broadly and not if used as part of other complementary health approaches. No trend analyses were conducted on the use of deep-breathing exercises.

[3] In 2002, the use of chiropractic care was asked broadly, and osteopathic approach was not specified on the survey. No trend analyses were conducted on the use of chiropractic or osteopathic manipulation.

[4] In 2012, meditation included Mantra meditation (including Transcendental Meditation, Relaxation Response, and Clinically Standardized Meditation); mindfulness meditation (including Vipassana, Zen Buddhist meditation, mindfulness-based stress reduction, and mindfulness-based cognitive therapy); spiritual meditation (including centering prayer and contemplative meditation); and meditation used as a part of other practices (including yoga, tai chi, and qi gong). In 2002 and 2007, the use of meditation was asked broadly and not if practiced as part of other complementary health approaches.

[5] Respondents used one or more named special diets for 2 weeks or more in the past 12 months. Special diets included vegetarian (including vegan), macrobiotic, Atkins, Pritikin, and Ornish diets.

[6] No distinction was made between persons who sought treatment from a homeopathic practitioner and those who self-medicated.

NOTES: Estimates were age-adjusted using the projected 2000 U.S. population as the standard population and using four age groups: 18–24, 25–44, 45–64, and 65 and over. The denominators for statistics shown exclude persons with unknown complementary and alternative medicine information. Estimates are based on household interviews of a sample of the civilian noninstitutionalized population.

SOURCE: CDC/NCHS, National Health Interview Survey, 2002, 2007, and 2012.

Table 3.2. Trends in the use of complementary health approaches among adults aged 18 and over, by selected characteristics: United States, 2002, 2007, and 2012

Selected characteristic	2002		2007		2012		Percentage point change			Trend
	Number (in thousands)	Age-adjusted percent[1] (standard error)	Number (in thousands)	Age-adjusted percent[1] (standard error)	Number (in thousands)	Age-adjusted percent[1] (standard error)	2002–2007	2007–2012	2002–2012	
Total[2]	65,169	32.3 (0.37)	77,032	35.5 (0.37)	76,222	33.2 (0.37)	†3.2	†-2.3	0.9	*Quadratic
Sex										
Men	27,115	27.9 (0.49)	32,884	31.4 (0.61)	31,818	28.9 (0.54)	†3.5	†-2.5	1	**Quadratic
Women	38,053	36.4 (0.48)	44,148	39.4 (0.61)	44,404	37.4 (0.54)	†3.0	-2.0	1	*Quadratic
Age group (years)										
18–44	34,842	33.0 (0.48)	36,705	34.2 (0.63)	34,600	32.2 (0.57)	1.2	-2.0	-0.8	*Linear
45–64	23,041	36.5 (0.64)	29,507	40.1 (0.80)	29,048	36.8 (0.63)	†3.6	†-3.3	0.3	*Quadratic
65 and over	7,286	22.7 (0.64)	10,820	31.1 (0.92)	11,789	29.4 (0.73)	†8.4	-1.5	†6.9	*Quadratic
Hispanic or Latino origin and race										
Hispanic	5,626	26.4 (0.80)	6,162	21.6 (0.91)	7,525	22.0 (0.76)	†-4.8	0.4	†-4.4	*Quadratic
Non-Hispanic white	50,219	34.4 (0.44)	59,814	40.2 (0.60)	57,008	37.9 (0.53)	†5.8	†-2.3	†3.5	***Quadratic
Non-Hispanic black	5,181	22.9 (0.66)	5,688	22.9 (0.90)	4,957	19.3 (0.75)	0	†-3.6	†-3.6	*Linear
Non-Hispanic other[3]	4,142	41.5 (1.59)	5,368	39.6 (1.66)	5,946	37.3 (1.21)	-1.9	-2.3	-4.2	***Linear
Education										
Less than high school diploma	5,918	18.6 (0.68)	6,440	18.9 (0.85)	4,980	15.6 (0.72)	-0.3	-2.0	†-3.0	***Quadratic
High school diploma or GED[4]	15,777	26.6 (0.53)	17,457	28.1 (0.85)	14,744	24.4 (0.64)	-1.5	†-3.7	†-2.2	***Quadratic
Some college education	14,244	35.6 (0.75)	23,189	41.3 (0.80)	16,762	36.5 (0.82)	†5.7	†-4.8	0.9	*Quadratic
College degree or higher	28,953	42.1 (0.67)	29,743	46.7 (0.82)	39,586	42.6 (0.64)	†4.6	†-4.1	0.5	*Quadratic

33

Table 3.2. Continued

Selected characteristic	2002		2007		2012		Percentage point change			Trend
	Number (in thousands)	Age-adjusted percent[1] (standard error)	Number (in thousands)	Age-adjusted percent[1] (standard error)	Number (in thousands)	Age-adjusted percent[1] (standard error)	2002–2007	2007–2012	2002–2012	
Poverty status[5]										
Poor	4,127	25.1 (0.99)	6,107	26.6 (1.02)	6,315	20.6 (0.76)	1.5	†-6.0	†-4.5	***Quadratic
Near-poor	6,961	27.7 (0.79)	8,380	27.9 (0.98)	9,283	25.5 (0.79)	0.2	-2.4	-2.2	***Linear
Not-poor	41,962	36.8 (0.48)	55,953	40.3 (0.64)	55,490	38.4 (0.53)	†3.5	-1.9	1.6	***Quadratic
Health insurance[6]										
Private	49,839	34.6 (0.42)	56,900	39.0 (0.59)	54,389	38.0 (0.50)	†4.4	-1.0	†3.4	*Quadratic
Public	6,402	25.8 (0.92)	9,401	27.0 (1.00)	11,387	24.8 (0.84)	1.2	-2.2	-1.0	**Quadratic
Uninsured	8,730	28.4 (1.21)	10,382	27.8 (1.66)	9,505	22.9 (1.09)	-0.6	†-4.9	†-5.5	***Quadratic

† Difference between both years is statistically significant at p < 0.05. 0.0 Quantity more than zero but less than 0.05.

*Significance of the chi-squared statistics is < 0.001.

**Significance of the chi-squared statistics is < 0.01.

***Significance of the chi-squared statistics is < 0.05.

[1] The denominator used in the calculation of percentages was all sample adults.

[2] Total was defined by a "yes" response to use of one or more of the following in the past 12 months: acupuncture; Ayurveda; biofeedback; chelation therapy; chiropractic care; energy healing therapy or Reiki; vegetarian and vegan, macrobiotic, Atkins, Pritikin, and Ornish diets; folk medicine; guided imagery; homeopathic treatment; hypnosis; naturopathy; nonvitamin, nonmineral, dietary supplements; massage; meditation; progressive relaxation; qi gong; tai chi; or yoga. The use of prayer for health reasons, mega-vitamin supplements, and special diets not listed, was not included. Respondents may have reported using more than one type of approach.

[3] Non-Hispanic other and persons of multiple races is a very broad and varied category of persons from a variety of races and ethnicities. This group may be more diverse than the other racial and ethnic groups.

[4] GED is General Educational Development high school equivalency diploma.

[5] Based on family income and family size using the U.S. Census Bureau's poverty thresholds for the previous calendar year. Poor persons had a total annual income below the poverty threshold; near-poor persons had incomes of 100% to less than 200% of the poverty threshold; not-poor persons had incomes that were 200% of the poverty threshold or greater.

[6] Based on a hierarchy of mutually exclusive categories. Persons with more than one type of health insurance were assigned to the first appropriate category in the hierarchy. "Uninsured" includes persons who had no coverage and those who had only Indian Health Service coverage or had only a private plan that paid for one type of service such as accidents or dental care.

NOTES: All estimates except age groups were age-adjusted using the projected 2000 U.S. population as the standard population and using four age groups: 18–24, 25–44, 45–64, and 65 and over. Estimates are based on household interviews of a sample of the civilian noninstitutionalized population.

SOURCE: CDC/NCHS, National Health Interview Survey, 2002, 2007, and 2012.

Table 3.3. *Adults aged 18 and over who used selected types of non-vitamin, nonmineral dietary supplements during the past 30 days: United States, 2007 and 2012*

Dietary supplements[1]	2007		2012		p value
	Number (in thousands)	Age-adjusted percent[2] (standard error)	Number (in thousands)	Age-adjusted percent[2] (standard error)	
Fish oil[3]	10,923	4.8 (0.17)	18,848	7.8 (0.22)	†
Glucosamine or chondroitin	7,236	3.2 (0.14)	6,450	2.6 (0.11)	†
Probiotics or prebiotics	865	0.4 (0.05)	3,857	1.6 (0.09)	†
Melatonin	1,296	0.6 (0.06)	3,065	1.3 (0.08)	†
Coenzyme Q–10 (CoQ10)	2,691	1.2 (0.08)	3,265	1.3 (0.08)	††
Echinacea	4,848	2.2 (0.12)	2,261	0.9 (0.06)	†
Cranberry (pills or capsules)	1,560	0.7 (0.06)	1,934	0.8 (0.06)	††
Garlic supplements	3,278	1.4 (0.09)	1,927	0.8 (0.06)	†
Ginseng	3,345	1.5 (0.10)	1,752	0.7 (0.06)	†
Ginkgo biloba	2,977	1.3 (0.10)	1,619	0.7 (0.06)	†
Green tea pills (not brewed tea) or EGCG (pills)[4]	1,528	0.7 (0.06)	1,503	0.6 (0.05)	††
Combination herb pill	3,446	1.5 (0.10)	1,463	0.6 (0.05)	†
MSM (methylsulfonylme-thane)	1,312	0.6 (0.05)	1,051	0.4 (0.04)	†
Milk thistle (silymarin)	1,001	0.4 (0.05)	988	0.4 (0.04)	††
Saw palmetto	1,682	0.7 (0.07)	988	0.4 (0.04)	†
Valerian	877	0.4 (0.05)	801	0.3 (0.04)	††

† $p < 0.05$.
††Difference is not statistically significant.
[1]Respondents may have used more than one nonvitamin, nonmineral dietary supplement.
[2]The denominator used in the calculation of percentages was all sample adults.
[3]In 2007, fish oil was described as fish oil or omega 3 or DHA fatty acid. In 2012, fish oil was described as fish oil or omega 3 or DHA or EPA fatty acid.
[4]EGCG is epigallocatechin gallate.
NOTES: Estimates were age-adjusted using the projected 2000 U.S. population as the standard population and using four age groups: 18–24, 25–44, 45–64, and 65 and over. Estimates are based on household interviews of a sample of the civilian noninstitutionalized population.
SOURCE: CDC/NCHS, National Health Interview Survey, 2007 and 2012.

Chapter 4

CAM Use and Children

According to a national survey, a wide range of complementary health approaches, including dietary supplements, spinal manipulation, and yoga, are used by or given to children. This content offers information for parents who may be thinking about or are already using a complementary health approach for their child.

Key Points

- Nearly 12 percent of American children (aged 4 to 17) have used or been given a complementary health product or practice.

- Few studies have examined the effects of complementary health approaches on children.

- Tell all your child's health care providers about any complementary health approaches your child uses or is given. Give them a full picture of what you do to manage your child's health. This will help ensure coordinated and safe care.

This chapter includes excerpts from "Children and Complementary Health Approaches," National Center for Complementary and Integrative Health (NCCIH), February 2015; and text from "Report Advances Knowledge About Children's Use of Complementary Approaches," National Center for Complementary and Integrative Health (NCCIH), February 10, 2015.

Patterns in the Use of Complementary Health Approaches in Children

According to the 2012 National Health Interview Survey (NHIS), which included a comprehensive survey on the use of complementary health approaches by Americans, 11.6 percent of the more than 10,000 children aged 4 to 17 included in the survey had used or been given some form of complementary health product or practice during the past year.

The most frequently used complementary approaches for children were natural products such as fish oil, melatonin, or probiotics and chiropractic or osteopathic manipulation.

For children, complementary approaches were most often used for back or neck pain, other musculoskeletal conditions, head or chest colds, anxiety or stress, attention-deficit hyperactivity disorder (ADHD), and insomnia or trouble sleeping.

Children who use or are given complementary health products or practices vary in age and health status. For example, other studies on use show that:

• Up to 10 percent of infants are given teas or botanical supplements, usually for fussiness or stomach problems.

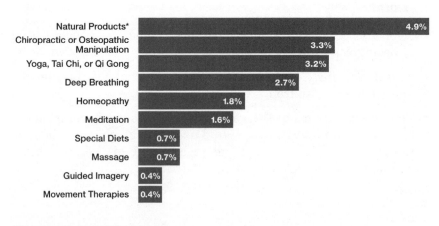

*Dietary supplements other than vitamins and minerals.

Citation: Black LI, Clarke TC, Barnes PM, Stussman BJ, Nahin RL. Use of complementary health approaches among children aged 4-17 years in the United States: National Health Interview Survey, 2007-2012. National health statistics reports; no 78. Hyattsville, MD: National Center for Health Statistics. 2015.

Figure 4.1. *10 most common complementary health approaches among children—2012*

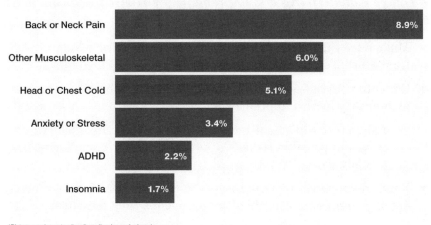

*Dietary supplements other than vitamins and minerals.

Citation: Black LI, Clarke TC, Barnes PM, Stussman BJ, Nahin RL. Use of complementary health approaches among children aged 4-17 years in the United States: National Health Interview Survey, 2007-2012. National health statistics reports; no 78. Hyattsville, MD: National Center for Health Statistics. 2015.

Figure 4.2. *Diseases/conditions for which complementary health approaches are most frequently used among children—2012*

- Between 21 and 42 percent of children take multivitamins, according to a 2012 study. Children aged 2 to 8 were the most likely to take vitamins. However, they were also the only age group who had nutritionally adequate diets whether they took multivitamins or not.

- Teens are particularly likely to use products that claim to enhance sports performance, energy levels, or weight loss.

- More than half of children with chronic medical conditions use some form of complementary health approach, usually along with conventional care.

Safety of Complementary Health Approaches for Children

Many complementary health products and practices aren't tested for safety or effectiveness in children. It's important to note that children may react differently than adults. Also, Federal regulations for dietary supplements are less strict than those for prescription and over-the-counter drugs. Some dietary supplements may be of poor quality or contain contaminants, including drugs, chemicals, or metals.

If You're Considering a Complementary Health Approach for Your Child

- Make sure that your child has received an accurate diagnosis from a licensed health care provider.

- Educate yourself about the potential risks and benefits of complementary health approaches.

  - Ask your child's health care provider about the effectiveness and possible risks of approaches you're considering or already using for your child.

- Remind your teenagers to discuss with their health care providers any complementary health approaches they may use.

- Don't use any health product or practice that hasn't been proven safe and effective to replace or delay conventional care or prescribed medications.

- If a health care provider suggests a complementary health approach, don't increase the dose or duration of the treatment beyond what is recommended (more isn't necessarily better).

- If you have any concerns about the effects of a complementary approach, contact your child's health care provider.

- As with all medications, store herbal and other dietary supplements out of the sight and reach of children.

- Tell all your child's health care providers about any complementary health approaches your child uses. Give them a full picture of what you do to manage your child's health. This will help ensure coordinated and safe care. For tips about talking with your child's health care provider about complementary health approaches, see NCCIH's Time to Talk campaign.

Selecting a Complementary Health Practitioner

- If you're looking for a complementary health practitioner for your child, be as careful and thorough in your search as you are when looking for conventional care. Be sure to ask about the practitioner's:

  - Experience in coordinating care with conventional health care providers

- Experience in delivering care to children

- Education, training, and license. Some states have licensing requirements for certain complementary health practitioners, such as chiropractors, naturopathic doctors, massage therapists, and acupuncturists.

Report Advances Knowledge about Children's Use of Complementary Approaches

A new report based on data from the 2012 National Health Interview Survey (NHIS) found that the overall use of complementary health approaches among children aged 4 to 17 years did not change significantly since the 2007 survey; however, there were significant increases in children's use of yoga, fish oil, and melatonin. The report, by the National Center for Complementary and Integrative Health (NCCIH; formerly NCCAM) and the National Center for Health Statistics (NCHS) of the U.S. Centers for Disease Control and Prevention, appears in *National Health Statistics Reports.*

The complementary health questionnaire was developed by NCCIH and the NCHS. The questionnaire is administered every 5 years as part of the NHIS, an annual study in which tens of thousands of Americans are interviewed about their health- and illness-related experiences. To identify trends in Americans' use of certain practices, 2012 survey data were compared with a version of the survey fielded in 2007. The 2007 and 2012 survey results are based on combined data from 17,321 interviews with a knowledgeable adult about children aged 4 to 17 years.

Survey Highlights on Natural Products

- The complementary health approach most commonly used by children was natural products (nonvitamin, nonmineral dietary supplements) at almost one-quarter the adult rate (4.9 percent vs. 17.7 percent). Echinacea was the most commonly used supplement in 2007, while fish oil was the most commonly used supplement in 2012.

- Melatonin ranked as the second most commonly used natural product among children. The use of melatonin among children increased significantly—from 0.1 percent in 2007 to 0.7 percent in 2012.

Survey Highlights on Mind and Body Practices

- There was a statistically significant increase in the use of movement therapies—which included yoga, tai chi, and qi gong—between 2007 (2.5 percent) and 2012 (3.2 percent). Most of this increase can be attributed to the increased use of yoga (approximately 400,000 more children used yoga since 2007).

- Only one approach, the use of traditional healers, significantly decreased among children between 2007 (1.1 percent) and 2012 (0.1 percent).

Other Survey Highlights

- Among children who used any complementary health approach, 44.2 percent used it to treat a specific health problem or condition in 2007 compared with 45.6 percent in 2012. In 2012, acupuncture had the highest percentage reporting use for treating a condition (70.1 percent).

- In 2012, as in 2007, complementary health approaches were most often used among children for back or neck pain, head or chest cold, other musculoskeletal conditions, anxiety/stress, and attention-deficit hyperactivity disorder.

The researchers noted that although the use of complementary health approaches in children, both overall and for individual modalities, is low compared to that seen in adults, these findings provide the most comprehensive snapshot of the use of these approaches and are the foundation for future studies in this area.

Chapter 5

CAM Use in Older Adults

Many older adults are turning to complementary and integrative health approaches, often as a reflection of a healthy self-empowered approach to well-being. Natural products often sold as dietary supplements are frequently used by many older people for various reasons despite safety concerns or a lack of evidence to support their use. Although there is a widespread public perception that the botanical and traditional agents included in dietary supplements can be viewed as safe, these products can contain pharmacologically active compounds and have the associated dangers.

Mind and body practices, including relaxation techniques and meditative exercise forms such as yoga, tai chi, and qi gong are being widely used by older Americans, both for fitness and relaxation, and because of perceived health benefits. A number of systematic reviews point to the potential benefit of mind and body approaches for symptom management, particularly for pain. However, research on these mind and body approaches is still hampered by methodological issues, including a lack of consensus on appropriate controls and lack of intervention standardization. While much of the clinical data is inconclusive, these approaches may help older adults maintain motivation to incorporate physical exercise into their regular activities.

This chapter includes excerpts from "Complementary and Integrative Health for Older Adults," National Center for Complementary and Integrative Health (NCCIH), April 2015; and text from "Tips for Older Dietary Supplement Users," U.S. Food and Drug Administration (FDA), May 11, 2014.

This chapter provides information on complementary and integrative health approaches for conditions clinically relevant to older adults.

Osteoarthritis (OA)

Mind and Body Practices for OA

In 2012, the American College of Rheumatology issued recommendations for using pharmacologic and nonpharmacologic approaches for OA of the hand, hip, and knee:

- The guidelines conditionally recommend tai chi, along with other non-drug approaches such as manual and thermal therapies, self-management programs, and walking aids, for managing knee OA.

- Acupuncture is also conditionally recommended for those who have chronic moderate-to-severe knee pain and are candidates for total knee replacement but are unwilling or unable to undergo surgical repair.

Acupuncture for OA

Studies of acupuncture for OA have focused primarily on OA of the knee. There is also evidence that acupuncture may help to improve pain and function in other joints such as the hip.

The Evidence Base

- The best evidence on the efficacy of acupuncture for OA consists of a few systematic reviews and one meta-analysis, as well as the 2012 American College of Rheumatology guidelines for pharmacologic and nonpharmacologic approaches for OA of the hand, hip, and knee, which conditionally recommend acupuncture for people with chronic moderate-to-severe knee pain and are candidates for total knee replacement but can't or won't undergo the procedure.

Safety

- There are few complications associated with acupuncture, but adverse effects such as minor bruising or bleeding can occur; infections can result from the use of nonsterile needles or poor technique from an inexperienced practitioner.

Massage for OA

Although there has been much research on massage therapy for pain, there are very few studies that specifically examine the effects of massage therapy on OA symptoms.

The Evidence Base

- The best evidence on the efficacy of massage therapy for OA comes from small randomized controlled trials. Very few studies have examined massage therapy for OA specifically.

Safety

- Massage therapy appears to have few risks if it is used appropriately and provided by a trained massage professional.

Tai Chi for OA

A few studies of tai chi for OA have been promising for managing symptoms of OA of the knee.

The Evidence Base

- The best evidence on the efficacy of tai chi consists of a few small randomized controlled trials, as well as the 2012 American College of Rheumatology guidelines for pharmacologic and nonpharmacologic approaches for OA of the hand, hip, and knee, which conditionally recommend tai chi, along with other non-drug approaches such as self-management programs and walking aids, for managing knee OA.

Safety

- Tai chi is considered to be a safe practice.

Natural Products for OA

Glucosamine, Chondroitin Sulfate, or the Combination

Glucosamine and chondroitin sulfate—taken separately or together—are marketed for supporting joint health. They have also been widely used for treating OA. The preponderance of evidence indicates little or no meaningful effect on pain or function. Independent clinical practice guidelines published in 2012 by the American College of Rheumatology (ACR) and in 2010 by the American Academy of Orthopaedic Surgeons (AAOS) recommend not using glucosamine or chondroitin for OA. Recommendations from Osteoarthritis Research Society International (OARSI) published in 2014 conclude that current evidence does not support use of glucosamine or chondroitin in knee OA for disease-modifying effects, but leave unsettled the question of whether either may provide symptomatic relief.

The Evidence Base

- The evidence base on the effects of glucosamine and chondroitin sulfate for osteoarthritis is of sufficient size and quality to permit independent systematic reviews and meta-analyses, and inclusion of specific recommendations in independent clinical practice guidelines.

Safety

Glucosamine and chondroitin appear to be relatively safe and well tolerated when used in suggested doses over a 2-year period. In a few specific situations, however, possible side effects or drug interactions should be considered:

- No serious side effects have been reported in large, well-conducted studies of people taking glucosamine, chondroitin, or both for up to 3 years. However, glucosamine or chondroitin may interact with warfarin.

- Although recent studies conducted by the U.S. Food and Drug Administration show that high doses of glucosamine hydrochloride taken by mouth in rats may promote cartilage regeneration and repair, this dose was also found to cause severe kidney problems in the rats—a serious side effect of the treatment.

Cognitive Decline and Alzheimer's Disease

Natural Products for Cognitive Decline and Alzheimer's Disease

Although a few trials of natural products for the prevention of cognitive decline or dementia have shown some modest effects, direct evidence is lacking.

The Evidence Base

- The evidence base on efficacy of natural products for cognitive function and dementia, including Alzheimer's disease, consists of many randomized controlled trials, particularly on omega-3 fatty acids and *ginkgo biloba* supplementation.

Safety

- Omega-3 fatty acid supplements usually do not have negative side effects. When side effects do occur, they typically consist of minor gastrointestinal symptoms. Omega-3 supplements may extend bleeding time. People who take anticoagulants or nonsteroidal anti-inflammatory drugs, should use caution.

- Side effects of ginkgo supplements may include headache, nausea, gastrointestinal upset, diarrhea, dizziness, or allergic skin reactions. More severe allergic reactions have occasionally been reported. There are some data to suggest that ginkgo can increase bleeding risk.

Sleep Disorders

Mind and Body Practices for Sleep Disorders

Relaxation Techniques

Relaxation techniques include progressive relaxation, guided imagery, biofeedback, self-hypnosis, and deep breathing exercises. The goal is similar in all: to consciously produce the body's natural relaxation response, characterized by slower breathing, lower blood pressure, and a feeling of calm and well-being. Relaxation techniques are also used to induce sleep, reduce pain, and calm emotions.

Evidence suggests that using relaxation techniques before bedtime can be helpful components of a successful strategy to improve sleep habits. Other components include maintaining a consistent sleep schedule; avoiding caffeine, alcohol, heavy meals, and strenuous exercise too close to bedtime; and sleeping in a quiet, cool, dark room.

The Evidence Base

- The best evidence on the efficacy of relaxation techniques for insomnia consists of independent systematic reviews and meta-analyses, and inclusion of specific recommendations in independent clinical practice guidelines of the American Academy of Sleep Medicine (AASM).

Safety

- Relaxation techniques are generally considered safe. There have been rare case reports of worsening of symptoms in people with epilepsy or certain psychiatric conditions, or with a history of abuse or trauma.

47

- Relaxation techniques are generally used as components of a treatment plan, and not as the only approach for potentially serious health conditions.

Other Mind and Body Practices for Sleep Disorders

Other mind and body practices which have been studied for their effects on insomnia and other sleep disorders include mindfulness-based stress reduction, yoga, massage therapy, and acupuncture. Current evidence of these therapies is either too preliminary or inconsistent to draw conclusions about whether they are helpful for sleep disorders.

The Evidence Base

- The best evidence on the efficacy of mindfulness-based stress reduction, yoga, and massage therapy consists of clinical trials reports, mostly from small preliminary studies.

- While there have been many studies of acupuncture for insomnia, the evidence base suffers from trials of poor methodological quality, and high levels of publication bias and heterogeneity in study design.

Safety

- Meditation is considered to be safe for healthy people. There have been rare reports that meditation could cause or worsen symptoms in people who have certain psychiatric problems, but this question has not been fully researched. People with physical limitations may not be able to participate in certain meditative practices involving physical movement. Individuals with existing mental or physical health conditions should speak with their health care providers prior to starting a meditative practice and make their meditation instructor aware of their condition.

- Overall, clinical trial data suggest yoga as taught and practiced in these research studies under the guidance of skilled teacher has a low rate of minor side effects. However, injuries from yoga, some of them serious, have been reported in the popular press. People with health conditions should work with an experienced teacher who can help modify or avoid some yoga poses to prevent side effects.

- Massage therapy appears to have few risks when performed by a trained practitioner. However, massage therapists should take some precautions with certain health conditions. In some cases, pregnant women should avoid massage therapy. Forceful and deep tissue massage should be avoided by people with conditions such as bleeding disorders or low blood platelet counts, and by people taking anticoagulants. Massage should not be done in any potentially weak area of the skin, such as wounds. Deep or intense pressure should not be used over an area where the patient has a tumor or cancer, unless approved by the patient's health care provider.

- Acupuncture is generally considered safe when performed by an experienced practitioner using sterile needles. Reports of serious adverse events related to acupuncture are rare, but include infections and punctured organs.

Natural Products for Sleep Disorders

Melatonin

Melatonin is a hormone known to shift circadian rhythms. Current evidence suggests that melatonin may be useful in treating several sleep disorders, such as jet lag, delayed sleep phase disorder, and sleep problems related to shift work.

The Evidence Base

- The best evidence on efficacy of melatonin for sleep disorders consists of several systematic reviews and meta-analyses, and inclusion of recommendations in independent clinical practice guidelines of the American Academy of Sleep Medicine (AASM).

Safety

- Melatonin supplements appear to be relatively safe for short-term use, although modest adverse effects on mood were seen with melatonin use in elderly people (most of whom had dementia) in one study. The long-term safety of melatonin supplements has not been established.

- Melatonin can have additive effects with alcohol and other sedating medications, and older people should be cautioned about its use.

Menopausal Symptoms

Mind and Body Practices for Menopausal Symptoms

Overall, evidence suggests that some mind and body approaches, such as yoga, tai chi, and meditation-based programs may provide some benefit in reducing common menopausal symptoms.

The Evidence Base

- The evidence base on the efficacy of mind and body practices for the symptoms of menopause consists of a few reviews of randomized controlled trials.

Safety

- Meditation is considered to be safe for healthy people. There have been rare reports that meditation could cause or worsen symptoms in people who have certain psychiatric problems, but this question has not been fully researched. People with physical limitations may not be able to participate in certain meditative practices involving physical movement. Individuals with existing mental or physical health conditions should speak with their health care providers prior to starting a meditative practice and make their meditation instructor aware of their condition.

- Overall, clinical trial data suggest yoga as taught and practiced in these research studies under the guidance of skilled teacher has a low rate of minor side effects. However, injuries from yoga, some of them serious, have been reported in the popular press. People with health conditions should work with an experienced teacher who can help modify or avoid some yoga poses to prevent side effects.

- Tai chi is considered to be a safe practice.

- There are few complications associated with acupuncture, but adverse effects such as minor bruising or bleeding can occur; infections can result from the use of nonsterile needles or poor technique from an inexperienced practitioner.

Natural Products for Menopausal Symptoms

Many natural products have been studied for their effects on menopausal symptoms, but there is little evidence that they are useful. While some herbs and botanicals are often found in over-the-counter formulas and combinations, many of these combination products have

50

not been studied. Further, because natural products used for menopausal symptoms can have side effects and can interact with other botanicals or supplements or with medications, research in this area is addressing safety as well as efficacy.

Black Cohosh (Actaea racemosa, Cimicifuga racemosa)

The Evidence Base

- The evidence base on efficacy of black cohosh for menopausal symptoms consists of many randomized controlled trials and a 2012 Cochrane review.

Safety

- United States Pharmacopeia experts suggest that **women should discontinue use of black cohosh and consult a health care practitioner if they have a liver disorder or develop symptoms of liver trouble**, such as abdominal pain, dark urine, or jaundice.

- There have been several case reports of hepatitis, as well as liver failure, in women who were taking black cohosh. It is not known if black cohosh was responsible for these problems. Although these cases are very rare and the evidence is not definitive, there is concern about the possible effects of black cohosh on the liver.

Benign Prostatic Hyperplasia (BPH)

Natural Products for BPH

Although several small studies have suggested modest benefit of saw palmetto for treating symptoms of BPH, a large study evaluating high doses of saw palmetto and a Cochrane review found that saw palmetto was not more effective than placebo for treatment of urinary symptoms related to BPH.

The Evidence Base

The evidence base on efficacy of saw palmetto *(Serenoa repens)* for benign prostatic hyperplasia consists of several randomized controlled trials and systematic reviews.

Safety

- Saw palmetto appears to be well tolerated by most users. It may cause mild side effects, including stomach discomfort.

Age-Related Macular Degeneration (AMD)

Natural Products for AMD

There is some evidence that natural products such as antioxidant vitamins and minerals may delay the development of AMD in people who are at high risk for the disease. However, other studies of vitamin E and beta carotene supplementation did not show benefit in preventing the onset of AMD.

The Evidence Base

- The evidence base on the efficacy of dietary supplements on preventing or slowing the progression of AMD consists of a few randomized controlled trials and a few systematic reviews.

Safety

- Although generally regarded as safe, vitamin supplements may have harmful effects, and clear evidence of benefit is needed before they can be recommended.

- Omega-3s appear to be safe for most adults at low-to-moderate doses. The FDA has concluded that omega-3 dietary supplements from fish are "generally recognized as safe." Fish oil supplements may cause minor gastrointestinal upsets, including diarrhea, heartburn, indigestion, and abdominal bloating.

- Side effects of ginkgo supplements may include headache, nausea, gastrointestinal upset, diarrhea, dizziness, or allergic skin reactions. More severe allergic reactions have occasionally been reported. There are some data to suggest that ginkgo can increase bleeding risk.

Herpes zoster (Shingles)

Mind and Body Practices for Herpes zoster

There have only been a few studies on the effects of tai chi on cell-mediated immunity to varicella zoster virus following vaccination, but the results of these studies have shown some benefit. Other interventions such as acupuncture, cupping, neural therapy, and intravenous vitamin C (ascorbic acid) have been studied for their effects on duration of neuropathic pain and post-herpetic neuralgia due to herpes zoster, but these studies have been small.

Tai Chi

The Evidence Base

* The evidence base on efficacy of tai chi for shingles immunity and health functioning consists of only a few small randomized controlled trials.

Safety

* Tai chi is considered to be a safe practice.

Tips for Older Dietary Supplement Users

Can Dietary Supplements Help Older Consumers?

Even if you eat a wide variety of foods, how can you be sure that you are getting all the vitamins, minerals, and other nutrients you need as you get older? If you are over 50, your nutritional needs may change. Informed food choices are the first place to start, making sure you get a variety of foods while watching your calorie intake. Supplements and fortified foods may also help you get appropriate amounts of nutrients. To help you make informed decisions, talk to your doctor and/or registered dietitian. They can work together with you to determine if your intake of a specific nutrient might be too low or too high and then decide how you can achieve a balance between the foods and nutrients you personally need.

What Are Dietary Supplements?

Today's dietary supplements are not only vitamins and minerals. They also include other less-familiar substances, such as herbals, botanicals, amino acids, enzymes, and animal extracts. Some dietary supplements are well understood and established, but others need further study. Whatever your choice, supplements should not replace the variety of foods important to a healthful diet.

Unlike drugs, dietary supplements are not pre-approved by the government for safety or effectiveness before marketing. Also, unlike drugs, supplements are not intended to treat, diagnose, prevent, or cure diseases. But some supplements can help assure that you get an adequate dietary intake of essential nutrients; others may help you reduce your risk of disease. Some older people, for example, are tired due to low iron levels. In that case, their doctor may recommend an iron supplement.

Supplement Facts

Serving Size 1 Capsule

Amount Per Capsule	% Daily Value
Calories 20	
Calories from Fat 20	
Total Fat 2 g	3%*
Saturated Fat 0.5 g	3%*
Polyunsaturated Fat 1 g	†
Monounsaturated Fat 0.5 g	†
Vitamin A 4250 IU	85%
Vitamin D 425 IU	106%
Omega-3 fatty acids 0.5 g	†

* Percent Daily Values are based on a 2,000 calorie diet.
† Daily Value not established.

Ingredients: Cod liver oil, gelatin, water, and glycerin.

Figure 5.1. *Supplement Facts*

At times, it can be confusing to tell the difference between a dietary supplement, a food, or over-the-counter (OTC) medicines. This is because supplements, by law, come in a variety of forms that resemble these products, such as tablets, capsules, powders, energy bars, or drinks. One way to know if a product is a dietary supplement is to look for the Supplement Facts label on the product.

Are There Any Risks, Especially to Older Consumers?

While certain products may be helpful to some older individuals, there may be circumstances when these products may not benefit your health or when they may create unexpected risks. Many supplements contain active ingredients that have strong biological effects in the body. This could make them unsafe in some situations and hurt or complicate your health. For example:

- Are you taking both medicines and supplements? Are you substituting one for the other? Taking a combination of supplements, using these products together with medications (whether prescription or over-the-counter), or substituting them in place of medicines your doctor prescribes could lead to harmful, even life-threatening results. Be alert to any advisories about these products. Coumadin (a prescription medicine), ginkgo biloba (an herbal supplement), aspirin (an over-the-counter drug), and vitamin E (a vitamin supplement) can each thin the blood. Taking any of these products alone or together can increase the potential for internal bleeding or stroke. Another example is St. John's wort that may reduce the effectiveness of prescription drugs for heart disease, depression, seizures, certain cancers, or HIV.

- Are you planning surgery? Some supplements can have unwanted effects before, during, and after surgery. It is important to fully inform your healthcare professional, including your pharmacist, about the vitamins, minerals, herbals, and any other supplements you are taking, especially before surgery. You may be asked to stop taking these products at least 2–3 weeks ahead of the procedure to avoid potentially dangerous supplement/drug interactions - such as changes in heart rate, blood pressure, or bleeding risk that could adversely affect the outcome of your surgery.

- Is taking more of a good thing better? Some people might think that if a little is good, taking a lot is even better. But taking too much of some nutrients, even vitamins and minerals, can also cause problems. Depending on the supplement, your age, and the status of your health, taking more than 100% of the Daily Value (DV) (see the Supplements Facts panel) of certain vitamins and minerals, e.g. Vitamin A, vitamin D, and iron (from supplements and food sources like vitamin-fortified cereals and drinks) may actually harm your health. Large amounts can also interfere with how your medicines work.

Remember: Your combined intake from all supplements (including multivitamins, single supplements, and combination products) plus fortified foods, like some cereals and drinks, could cause health problems.

Why Speak to My Healthcare Provider about Dietary Supplements?

You and your health professionals (doctors, nurses, registered dietitians, pharmacists, and other caregivers) are a team working toward a common goal—to develop a personalized health plan for you. Your doctor and other members of the health team can help monitor your medical condition and overall health, especially if any problems develop. Although they may not immediately have answers to your questions, these health professionals have access to the most current research on dietary supplements.

There are numerous resources that provide information about dietary supplements. These include TV, radio, newspapers, magazines, store clerks, friends, family, or the Internet. It is important to question recommendations from people who have no formal training in nutrition, botanicals, or medicine. While some of these sources, like the Web, may seem to offer a wealth of accurate information, these same sources may contain misinformation that may not be obvious. Given the abundance and conflicting nature of information now available about supplements, it is more important than ever to partner with your healthcare team to sort the reliable information from the questionable.

Chapter 6

Health Care Providers and CAM

How To Find a Complementary Health Practitioner

National Center for Complementary and Integrative Health (NCCIH) is the federal government's lead agency for scientific research on complementary and integrative health. As a research institution, NCCIH does not provide referrals or care for the general public.

Does NCCIH provide complementary health care or treatments?

No, NCCIH does not provide care or financial assistance for care. We are a research institution.

How can I get a referral to a complementary health practitioner?

NCCIH does not provide referrals to private practitioners. For a list of practitioners in your area, contact your doctor or a local hospital.

This chapter includes excerpts from "How To Find a Complementary Health Practitioner," National Center for Complementary and Integrative Health (NCCIH), January 29, 2015; text from "6 Things To Know When Selecting a Complementary Health Practitioner," National Center for Complementary and Integrative Health (NCCIH), June 25, 2015; and text from "4 Tips: Start Talking With Your Health Care Providers About Complementary Health Approaches," National Center for Complementary and Integrative Health (NCCIH), June 4, 2015.

Professional organizations also may be useful places to find complementary health practitioners. TheMedlinePlus Directories page from the National Library of Medicine lists organizations for some professions and provides links to directories of libraries and various types of health professionals, services, and facilities.

Talk to your health care provider

Tell all your health care providers about any complementary health approaches you use. Give them a full picture of what you do to manage your health. This will help ensure coordinated and safe care.

Things To Know When Selecting a Complementary Health Practitioner

If you're looking for a complementary health practitioner to help treat a medical problem, it is important to be as careful and thorough in your search as you are when looking for conventional care.

Here are some tips to help you in your search:

1. **If you need names of practitioners in your area, first check with your doctor or other health care provider.** A nearby hospital or medical school, professional organizations, state regulatory agencies or licensing boards, or even your health insurance provider may be helpful. Unfortunately, the National Center for Complementary and Integrative Health (NCCIH) cannot refer you to practitioners.

2. **Find out as much as you can about any potential practitioner, including education, training, licensing, and certifications.** The credentials required for complementary health practitioners vary tremendously from state to state and from discipline to discipline.

Once you have found a possible practitioner, here are some tips about deciding whether he or she is right for you:

1. **Find out whether the practitioner is willing to work together with your conventional health care providers.** For safe, coordinated care, it's important for all of the professionals involved in your health to communicate and cooperate.

2. **Explain all of your health conditions to the practitioner, and find out about the practitioner's training and experience in working with people who have your**

conditions. Choose a practitioner who understands how to work with people with your specific needs, even if general well-being is your goal. And, remember that health conditions can affect the safety of complementary approaches; for example, if you have glaucoma, some yoga poses may not be safe for you.

3. **Don't assume that your health insurance will cover the practitioner's services.** Contact your health insurance provider and ask. Insurance plans differ greatly in what complementary health approaches they cover, and even if they cover a particular approach, restrictions may apply.

4. **Tell all your health care providers about all complementary approaches you use and about all practitioners who are treating you.** Keeping your health care providers fully informed helps you to stay in control and effectively manage your health.

4 Tips: Start Talking With Your Health Care Providers about Complementary Health Approaches

When patients tell their providers about their use of complementary health practices, they can better stay in control and more effectively manage their health. When providers ask their patients, they can ensure that they are fully informed and can help patients make wise health care decisions.

Here are 4 tips to help you and your health care providers start talking:

1. **List the complementary health practices you use on your patient history form.** When completing the patient history form, be sure to include everything you use—from acupuncture to zinc. It's important to give health care providers a full picture of what you do to manage your health.

2. **At each visit, be sure to tell your providers about what complementary health approaches you are using.** Don't forget to include over-the-counter and prescription medicines, as well as dietary and herbal supplements. Make a list in advance, or download and print this wallet card and take it with you. Some complementary health approaches can have an effect on conventional medicine, so your provider needs to know.

3. **If you are considering a new complementary health practice, ask questions.** Ask your health care providers about its safety, effectiveness, and possible interactions with medications (both prescription and nonprescription).

4. **Don't wait for your providers to ask about any complementary health practice you are using.** Be proactive. Start the conversation.

Chapter 7

Insurance Issues and Paying for CAM Treatments

Introduction

Many Americans using, or thinking about using, complementary health products or practices may have questions about paying for them. This chapter provides a general overview of related topics and suggests sources for additional information.

Spending on Complementary Health Approaches in the United States

According to the 2007 National Health Interview Survey (NHIS), U.S. adults spent an estimated $33.9 billion out-of-pocket on complementary health approaches in the previous 12 months. They spent about two-thirds ($22.0 billion) on self-care costs (i.e., products, classes, and materials), and the remaining one-third ($11.9 billion) on visits to complementary health practitioners. The $33.9 billion represented approximately 1.5 percent of total health care spending but 11.2 percent of total out-of-pocket health care spending in the United States.

Text in this chapter is excerpted from "Paying for Complementary Health Approaches," National Center for Complementary and Integrative Health (NCCIH), August 2013.

Paying for Complementary Health Approaches Out-of-Pocket

People often pay for complementary health services and products themselves—that is, "out-of-pocket." For example, the 2007 NHIS found that about one-third of uninsured respondents younger than age 65 used complementary health approaches. Also, even if you have health insurance, your plan may not cover some or all complementary products or practices.

Insurance Coverage of Complementary Health Approaches

Insurance coverage of complementary health approaches is complex and confusing—so much so that it's almost impossible to make any general statements about it. Coverage may vary greatly depending on state laws, regulations, and differences among specific insurance plans. If you would like to use a complementary approach and you're wondering whether your health insurance will cover it, it's a good idea

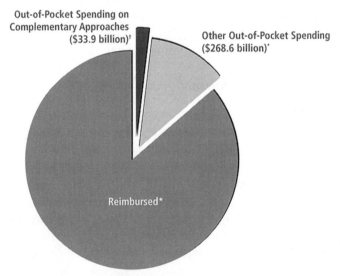

Out-of-Pocket Spending on Complementary Approaches ($33.9 billion)†

Other Out-of-Pocket Spending ($268.6 billion)*

Reimbursed*

*National Health Expenditure Data for 2007. Centers for Medicare & Medicaid Services Web site. Accessed at www.cms.hhs.gov/NationalHealthExpendData/02_NationalHealthAccountsHistorical.asp#TopOfPage on June 25, 2009.

†Nahin RL, Barnes PM, Stussman BJ, Bloom B. Costs of Complementary and Alternative Medicine (CAM) and Frequency of Visits to CAM Practitioners: United States, 2007. *CDC National Health Statistics Report #18. 2009.*

Figure 7.1. *Total Annual Health Care Spending $2.2 Trillion*

to do some investigating. Contacting your health insurance provider is a good way to start.

Questions you may want to ask your insurance provider include the following:

- Is this complementary approach covered for my health condition?

- Does it need to be

  - Preauthorized or preapproved?

  - Ordered by a prescription?

- Do I need a referral?

- Do I have to see a practitioner in your network to be covered?

- Do I have any coverage if I go out-of-network?

- Are there any limits and requirements—for example, on the number of visits or the amount you will pay?

- How much do I have to pay out-of-pocket?

It's always a good idea to keep records about all contacts you have with your insurance company, including notes on calls and copies of bills, claims, and letters. This will help if a dispute arises about a claim.

If you're choosing a new health insurance plan, you may want to ask the insurance provider about coverage of complementary health approaches. Some insurance plans cover selected complementary approaches by allowing participants to purchase special "riders"—or supplements—to their standard health insurance plans. Some offer discount programs, in which plan members pay for complementary approaches out-of-pocket but at a discounted rate.

Sources of Information on Insurers

Your state insurance department may be able to help you determine which insurance companies cover specific complementary health approaches.

Professional associations for complementary health specialties may monitor insurance coverage and reimbursement in their field. You can ask a reference librarian for help or search for them on the Internet. The National Library of Medicine's Directory of Health Organizations is a database that contains information about a variety of health organizations and associations.

Asking Complementary Health Practitioners about Payment

If you are planning to use a complementary approach provided by a practitioner, it is important to understand about payment. Here are some questions to ask the practitioner:

- **Costs:** What does the first appointment cost? What do followup appointments cost? How many appointments am I likely to need? Are there any additional costs (e.g., tests, equipment, supplements)?

- **Insurance:** Do you accept my insurance plan? What has been your experience with my plan's coverage for people with my condition? Do I file the claims, or do you take care of that?

Tax-Related Matters

Two kinds of **tax-exempt accounts** help people save money for health expenses and may help you cover the costs of some complementary health approaches. The **flexible spending arrangement** is a benefit offered by some employers; it allows you to set aside pretax dollars (generally, each pay period) for health-related expenses. The **health savings account** is for people who participate in high-deductible health plans; you, not an employer, establish this kind of account.

Some expenses related to complementary health approaches may be tax deductible.

Federal Health Benefit Programs

The federal government helps with at least some health expenses of people who are eligible for federal health benefit programs, such as programs for veterans, people aged 65 and older (Medicare), and people who cannot afford health care (Medicaid, funded jointly with the states).

Information on health benefits for veterans is available from the U.S. Department of Veterans Affairs. Information on Medicare and Medicaid is available from the Centers for Medicare & Medicaid Services. Two other Internet resources—(Benefits.gov and USA.gov)—explain federal health benefit programs. Benefits.gov has a test you can take about qualifying for programs. The Medicare program has a handbook that explains what services Medicare covers.

NCCIH's Role

The National Center for Complementary and Integrative Health (NCCIH) funds research that helps to build the evidence base used to make decisions about whether complementary health approaches are safe and effective.

NCCIH, like other components of the National Institutes of Health (NIH), is a medical research agency. NCCIH does not provide financial assistance to individuals who are seeking health care.

Chapter 8

Health Fraud Awareness

Chapter Contents

Section 8.1

Health Fraud Scams

Text in this section is excerpted from "6 Tip-offs to Rip-offs: Don't
Fall for Health Fraud Scams," United States Food and Drug
Administration (FDA), March 4, 2013.

Bogus product! Danger! Health fraud alert!

You'll never see these warnings on health products, but that's what
you ought to be thinking when you see claims like "miracle cure,"
"revolutionary scientific breakthrough," or "alternative to drugs or
surgery."

Health fraud scams have been around for hundreds of years. The
snake oil salesmen of old have morphed into the deceptive, high-tech
marketers of today. They prey on people's desires for easy solutions
to difficult health problems—from losing weight to curing serious diseases like cancer.

According to the Food and Drug Administration (FDA), a health
product is fraudulent if it is deceptively promoted as being effective
against a disease or health condition but has not been scientifically
proven safe and effective for that purpose.

Scammers promote their products through newspapers, magazines,
TV infomercials and cyberspace. You can find health fraud scams in
retail stores and on countless websites, in popup ads and spam, and
on social media sites like Facebook and Twitter.

Not Worth the Risk

Health fraud scams can do more than waste your money. They can
cause serious injury or even death, says Gary Coody, R.Ph., FDA's
national health fraud coordinator. "Using unproven treatments can
delay getting a potentially life-saving diagnosis and medication that
actually works. Also, fraudulent products sometimes contain hidden
drug ingredients that can be harmful when unknowingly taken by
consumers."

Mr. Coody says fraudulent products often make claims related to:

- weight loss
- sexual performance
- memory loss
- serious diseases such as cancer, diabetes, heart disease, arthritis and Alzheimer's.

A Pervasive Problem

Fraudulent products not only won't work—they could cause serious injury. In the past few years, FDA laboratories have found more than 100 weight-loss products, illegally marketed as dietary supplements, that contained sibutramine, the active ingredient in the prescription weight-loss drug Meridia. In 2010, Meridia was withdrawn from the U.S. market after studies showed that it was associated with an increased risk of heart attack and stroke.

Fraudulent products marketed as drugs or dietary supplements are not the only health scams on the market. FDA found a fraudulent and expensive light therapy device with cure-all claims to treat fungal meningitis, Alzheimer's, skin cancer, concussions and many other unrelated diseases. Generally, making health claims about a medical device without FDA clearance or approval of the device is illegal.

"Health fraud is a pervasive problem," says Mr. Coody, "especially when scammers sell online. It's difficult to track down the responsible parties. When we do find them and tell them their products are illegal, some will shut down their website. Unfortunately, however, these same products may reappear later on a different website, and sometimes may reappear with a different name."

Tip-Offs

FDA offers some tip-offs to help you identify rip-offs.

- **One product does it all.** Be suspicious of products that claim to cure a wide range of diseases. A New York firm claimed its products marketed as dietary supplements could treat or cure senile dementia, brain atrophy, atherosclerosis, kidney dysfunction, gangrene, depression, osteoarthritis, dysuria, and lung, cervical and prostate cancer. In October 2012, at FDA's request, U.S. marshals seized these products.

- **Personal testimonials.** Success stories, such as, "It cured my diabetes" or "My tumors are gone," are easy to make up and are not a substitute for scientific evidence.

- **Quick fixes.** Few diseases or conditions can be treated quickly, even with legitimate products. Beware of language such as, "Lose 30 pounds in 30 days" or "eliminates skin cancer in days."

- **"All natural."** Some plants found in nature (such as poisonous mushrooms) can kill when consumed. Moreover, FDA has found numerous products promoted as "all natural" but that contain hidden and dangerously high doses of prescription drug ingredients or even untested active artificial ingredients.

- **"Miracle cure."** Alarms should go off when you see this claim or others like it such as, "new discovery," "scientific breakthrough" or "secret ingredient." If a real cure for a serious disease were discovered, it would be widely reported through the media and prescribed by health professionals—not buried in print ads, TV infomercials or on Internet sites.

- **Conspiracy theories.** Claims like "The pharmaceutical industry and the government are working together to hide information about a miracle cure" are always untrue and unfounded. These statements are used to distract consumers from the obvious, common-sense questions about the so-called miracle cure.

Even with these tips, fraudulent health products are not always easy to spot. If you're tempted to buy an unproven product or one with questionable claims, check with your doctor or other health care professional first.

Section 8.2

Fraudulent Dietary Supplements

Text in this section is excerpted from "Beware of Products Promising
Miracle Weight Loss," United States Food and Drug Administration
(FDA), January 5, 2015.

"This year, I'm going to lose some weight."
If you find yourself making this common New Year's resolution,
know this: many so-called "miracle" weight loss supplements and foods
(including teas and coffees) don't live up to their claims. Worse, they
can cause serious harm, say FDA regulators. The agency has found
hundreds of products that are marketed as dietary supplements but
actually contain hidden active ingredients (components that make a
medicine effective against a specific illness) contained in prescription
drugs, unsafe ingredients that were in drugs that have been removed
from the market, or compounds that have not been adequately studied
in humans.

"When the product contains a drug or other ingredient which is
not listed as an ingredient we become especially concerned about the
safety of the product," says James P. Smith, M.D., an acting deputy
director in FDA's Office of Drug Evaluation.

Tainted Products

For example, FDA has found weight-loss products tainted with
the prescription drug ingredient sibutramine. This ingredient was
in an FDA-approved drug called Meridia, which was removed from
the market in October 2010 because it caused heart problems and
strokes.

"We've also found weight-loss products marketed as supplements
that contain dangerous concoctions of hidden ingredients including
active ingredients contained in approved seizure medications, blood
pressure medications, and antidepressants," says Jason Humbert,
a senior regulatory manager at FDA. Most recently, FDA has found
a number of products marketed as dietary supplements containing

71

fluoxetine, the active ingredient found in Prozac, a prescription drug marketed for the treatment of depression and other conditions. Another product contained triamterene, a powerful diuretic (sometimes known as "water pills") that can have serious side-effects and should only be used under the supervision of a health care professional.

Many of these tainted products are imported, sold online, and heavily promoted on social media sites. Some can also be found on store shelves.

And if you're about to take what you think of as "natural" dietary supplements, such as bee pollen or Garcinia cambogia, you should be aware that FDA has found some of these products also contain hidden active ingredients contained in prescription drugs.

"The only natural way to lose weight is to burn more calories than you take in," says James P. Smith, M.D. That means a combination of healthful eating and physical activity.

Dietary Supplements are not FDA-Approved

Under the Federal Food, Drug and Cosmetics Act (as amended by the Dietary Supplement Health and Education Act of 1994), dietary supplement firms do not need FDA approval prior to marketing their products. It is the company's responsibility to make sure its products are safe and that any claims made about such products are true.

But just because you see a supplement product on a store shelf does not mean it is safe, Humbert says. FDA has received numerous reports of harm associated with the use of weight loss products, including increased blood pressure, heart palpitations (a pounding or racing heart), stroke, seizure and death. When safety issues are suspected, FDA must investigate and, when warranted, take steps to have these products removed from the market.

FDA has issued over 30 public notifications and recalled 7 tainted weight loss products in 2014. The agency also has issued warning letters, seized products, and criminally prosecuted people responsible for marketing these illegal diet products.

To help people with long-term weight management, FDA has approved prescription drugs such as Belviq, Qysmia, and Contrave, but these products are intended for people at least 18 years of age who:

- have a body mass index (BMI, a standard measure of body fat) of 30 or greater (considered obese); or

- have a BMI of 27 or greater (considered overweight) and have at least one other weight-related health condition.

Moreover, if you are going to embark on any type of weight control campaign, you should talk to your health care professional about it first, Smith says.

Know the Warning Signs

Look for potential warning signs of tainted products, such as:

- promises of a quick fix, for example, "lose 10 pounds in one week."
- use of the words "guaranteed" or "scientific breakthrough."
- products marketed in a foreign language.
- products marketed through mass e-mails.
- products marketed as herbal alternatives to an FDA-approved drug or as having effects similar to prescription drugs.

Advice for Consumers

Generally, if you are using or considering using any product marketed as a dietary supplement, FDA suggests that you:

- check with your health care professional or a registered dietitian about any nutrients you may need in addition to your regular diet.
- ask yourself if it sounds too good to be true.
- be cautious if the claims for the product seem exaggerated or unrealistic.
- watch out for extreme claims such as "quick and effective" or "totally safe."
- be skeptical about anecdotal information from personal "testimonials" about incredible benefits or results from using a product.

If you suspect a product marketed as a dietary supplement sold online may be tainted, FDA urges you to report that information online. You or your health care professional can also report an illness or injury you believe to be related to the use of a dietary supplement by calling 1-800-FDA-1088 or visiting FDA online.

Chapter 9

Finding and Evaluating Online Resources for Complementary Health Approaches

The number of Web sites offering health-related resources—including information about complementary health approaches (often called complementary and alternative medicine)—grows every day. Social media sites have also become an important source of online health information for some people. Many online health resources are useful, but others may present information that is inaccurate or misleading, so it's important to find sources you can trust and to know how to evaluate their content. This chapter provides help for finding reliable Web sites and outlines things to consider in evaluating health information from Web sites and social media sources.

Key Facts

Not all online health information is accurate. Be cautious when you evaluate health information on the Internet, especially if the site

Text in this chapter is excerpted from "Finding and Evaluating Online Resources on Complementary Health Approaches," National Center for Complementary and Integrative Health (NCCIH), September 2014.

- Is selling something

- Includes outdated information

- Makes excessive claims for what a product can do

- Is sponsored by an organization whose goals differ from yours.

Checking Out a Health Web Site: Five Quick Questions

If you're visiting a health Web site for the first time, these five quick questions can help you decide whether the site is a helpful resource.

Who? Who runs the Web site? Can you trust them?

What? What does the site say? Do its claims seem too good to be true?

When? When was the information posted or reviewed? Is it up-to-date?

Where? Where did the information come from? Is it based on scientific research?

Why? Why does the site exist? Is it selling something?

Keep in Mind

Don't rely exclusively on online resources when making decisions about your health. If you're considering a complementary health approach, discuss it with your health care provider.

Talk to Your Health Care Provider about Complementary Health Approaches

If you are considering a complementary health approach and find information on the Web site, it's a good idea to share the information with all your health care providers and get their opinions.

Finding Health Information on the Internet: How to Start

You can find accurate health information quickly and easily if you start with one of these organized collections of high-quality, up-to-date resources:

- MedlinePlus, sponsored by the National Library of Medicine, which is part of the National Institutes of Health (NIH)

- healthfinder.gov, sponsored by the Office of Disease Prevention and Health Promotion in the U.S. Department of Health and Human Services.

If you're specifically looking for information about complementary health approaches:

- You can use the National Center for Complementary and Integrative Health (NCCIH) Web site as a starting point. NCCIH is the federal government's lead agency for scientific research on the diverse medical and health care systems, practices, and products that aren't generally considered part of conventional medicine.

- Follow along with NCCIH via its official Facebook, Twitter, and Pinterest accounts. These accounts are updated and managed by NCCIH and provide the latest resources on a variety of complementary health approaches.
  - Facebook—www.facebook.com/nih.nccih
  - Twitter—twitter.com/NIH_nccih
  - Pinterest—www.pinterest.com/nccihgov

- For information on dietary supplements, visit both the NCCIH Web site and the Web site of NIH's Office of Dietary Supplements (ODS).

- For additional resources on complementary health approaches, visit NCCIH's Links to Other Organizations page. All of the resources listed there come from federal agencies or the World Health Organization; they all provide reliable information.

Questions to Ask When Evaluating a Health-Related Web Site

Your search for online health information may start on a known, trusted site, but after following several links, you may find yourself on an unfamiliar site. Can you trust this site? Here are some key questions you need to ask.

Health Information in Social Media

About one-third of American adults use social networking sites, such as Facebook or Twitter, as a source of health information.

Here are two ideas that may help you evaluate health information in social media:

- **Evaluate the sponsor's Web site.** Health information presented on social networking sites is often very brief, and details about the sponsoring organization may be very limited. Fortunately, organizations with social media accounts usually have Web sites as well, where they discuss the same health topics at greater length and provide additional details about themselves and their policies. You can usually find a link to the Web site in the organization's profile on the social networking site. On Twitter, it's usually in the header above the tweets; on Facebook, it's usually in the *About* section. Once you find the link, you can visit the Web site and evaluate it just as you would any other Web site, using the ideas in this guide.
- **Make sure the social media account is authentic.** Special tools can help you verify that social media accounts are what they claim to be. Some social networking sites have symbols that indicate that an account has been verified. For example, Twitter uses a blue badge. The federal government has a tool to verify social media accounts that claim to belong to federal agencies:www.usa.gov/Contact/verify-social-media.shtml. Another way to find out whether an account is real is to go to the organization's Web site and look for a link to the social networking site. That link should take you to the organization's legitimate account. Additionally, many organizations will include the fact that the platform is "official" in their information. Either in the Twitter biography or Facebook About section, many organizations state "the official Facebook/Twitter page of [name of organization]."

Who runs and pays for the Web site?

Any reliable health-related Web site should make it easy for you to learn who's responsible for the site. For example, on the NCCIH Web site, each major page clearly identifies NCCIH and, because NCCIH is part of NIH, provides a link to the NIH homepage. If it isn't obvious who runs the Web site, look for a link on the homepage to an *About This Site* page.

You can also learn about who runs a Web site by looking at the letters at the end of its Web address. For example, Web addresses (such as NCCIH's) that end in ".gov" mean it's a government-sponsored site; ".edu" indicates an educational institution, ".org" a noncommercial organization, and ".com" a commercial organization.

You can trust sites with ".gov" addresses. You can also trust sites with ".edu" addresses if they're produced by the educational institution. Personal pages of individuals at an educational institution may not be trustworthy, even though they have ".edu" addresses. The presence of ".org" in an address doesn't guarantee that a site is reputable; there have been instances where phony ".org" sites were set up to mislead consumers. Also, some legitimate ".org" sites belong to organizations that promote a specific agenda; their content may be biased.

You should know how the site supports itself. Is it funded by the organization that sponsors it? Does it sell advertising? Is it sponsored by a company that sells dietary supplements, drugs, or other products or services? The source of funding can affect what content is presented, how it's presented, and what the site owners want to accomplish.

What is the purpose of the site?

The site's purpose is related to who runs and pays for it. The *About This Site* page should include a clear statement of purpose. To be sure you're getting reliable information, you should confirm information that you find on sales sites by consulting other, independent sites where no products are sold.

What is the source of the information?

Many health/medical sites post information collected from other Web sites or sources. If the person or organization in charge of the site didn't create the material, the original source should be clearly identified. For example, the *Health Topics A–Z* page on the NCCIH site provides links to some documents that NCCIH didn't create; in those instances, the source of the documents is always identified.

What is the basis of the information?

In addition to identifying the source of the material you're reading, the site should describe the evidence (such as articles in medical journals) that the material is based on. Also, opinions or advice should be clearly set apart from information that's "evidence-based" (that is, based on research results). For example, if a site discusses health benefits people can expect from a treatment, look for references to scientific research that clearly support what's said. Keep in mind that testimonials, anecdotes, unsupported claims, and opinions aren't the same as objective, evidence-based information.

Is the information reviewed?

You can be more confident in the quality of medical information on a Web site if people with credible professional and scientific qualifications review the material before it's posted. Some Web sites have an editorial board that reviews content. Others put the names and credentials of the individuals who reviewed a Web page in the *Acknowledgments* section near the end of the page.

How current is the information?

Some types of outdated medical information can be misleading or even dangerous. Responsible health Web sites review and update much of their content on a regular basis, especially informational content such as fact sheets and lists of frequently asked questions (FAQs). Other types of site content, however, such as news reports or summaries of scientific meetings, may never be updated; their purpose is to describe an event, rather than to provide the most up-to-date information on a topic.

To find out whether information on a Web page is old or new, look for a date on the page (it's often near the bottom).

What is the site's policy about linking to other sites?

Web sites usually have a policy about establishing links to other sites. Some sites take a conservative approach and don't link to any other sites. Some link to any site that asks or pays for a link. Others only link to sites that have met certain criteria. You may be able to find information on the site about its linking policy. (For example, you can find information about NCCIH's linking policy on the NCCIH Web Site Information and Policies page at nccih.nih.gov/tools/privacy.htm.) Unless the site's linking policy is strict, don't assume that the sites that it links to are reliable. You should evaluate the linked sites just as you would any other site that you're visiting for the first time.

How does the site handle personal information?

Many Web sites track visitors' paths to determine what pages are being viewed. A health Web site may ask you to "subscribe" or "become a member." In some cases, this may be so that it can collect a user fee or select information for you that's relevant to your concerns. In all cases, this will give the site personal information about you.

Any credible site asking for this kind of information should tell you exactly what it will and will not do with it. Many commercial sites sell "aggregate" (collected) data about their users to other companies—information such as what percentage of their users are women older than 40. In some cases, they may collect and reuse information that's "personally identifiable," such as your ZIP Code, gender, and birth date. Be sure to read any privacy policy or similar language on the site, and don't sign up for anything you don't fully understand. You can find NCCIH's privacy policy at nccih.nih.gov/tools/privacy.htm#privacy.

How does the site manage interactions with users?

You should always be able to contact the site owner if you run across problems or have questions or feedback. If the site hosts online discussion areas (forums or message boards), it should explain the terms of using this service. If the site is affiliated with social networking sites such as Twitter, Facebook, or YouTube, it should explain the terms of using them. Look for a social media comments policy on the Web site. NCCIH's social media comments policy is here: nccih.nih.gov/tools/commentpolicy.htm. Spend some time reading what has been posted before joining in to see whether you feel comfortable with the environment. You may also be able to review past discussions. For example, NCCIH has an archive of its Twitter chats here: nccih.nih.gov/news/events/twitterchat/archive.

Are You Reading Real Online News or Just Advertising?

In April 2011, the Federal Trade Commission warned the public about fake online news sites promoting an acai berry weight-loss product. On a typical fake "news" site, a story described an investigation in which a reporter used the product for several weeks, with "dramatic" results. The site looked real, but it was actually an advertisement. Everything was fake: there was no reporter, no news organization, and no investigation. The only real things were the links to a sales site that appeared in the story and elsewhere on the Web page. Similar fake news sites have promoted other products, including work-at-home opportunities and debt reduction plans.

You should suspect that a news site may be fake if it:

- Endorses a product. Real news organizations generally don't do this.
- Only quotes people who say good things about the product.
- Presents research findings that seem too good to be true. (If something seems too good to be true, it usually is.)
- Contains links to a sales site.
- Includes positive reader comments only, and you can't add a comment of your own.

How to Protect Yourself

If you suspect that a news site is fake, look for a disclaimer somewhere on the page (often in small print) that indicates that the site is an advertisement. Also, don't rely on Internet news reports when making important decisions about your health. If you're considering a health product described in the news, discuss it with your health care provider.

Part Two

Alternative Medicine Systems

Chapter 10

Acupuncture

What's the Bottom Line?

How much do we know about acupuncture?

There have been extensive studies conducted on acupuncture, especially for back and neck pain, osteoarthritis / knee pain, and headache. However, researchers are only beginning to understand whether acupuncture can be helpful for various health conditions.

What do we know about the effectiveness of acupuncture?

Research suggests that acupuncture can help manage certain pain conditions, but evidence about its value for other health issues is uncertain.

What do we know about the safety of acupuncture?

Acupuncture is generally considered safe when performed by an experienced, well-trained practitioner using sterile needles. Improperly performed acupuncture can cause serious side effects.

Text in this chapter is excerpted from "Acupuncture: What You Need To Know," National Center for Complementary and Integrative Health (NCCIH), November 2014.

What Is Acupuncture?

Acupuncture is a technique in which practitioners stimulate specific points on the body—most often by inserting thin needles through the skin. It is one of the practices used in traditional Chinese medicine.

What the Science Says about the Effectiveness of Acupuncture

Results from a number of studies suggest that acupuncture may help ease types of pain that are often chronic such as low-back pain, neck pain, and osteoarthritis/knee pain. It also may help reduce the frequency of tension headaches and prevent migraine headaches. Therefore, acupuncture appears to be a reasonable option for people with chronic pain to consider. However, clinical practice guidelines are inconsistent in recommendations about acupuncture.

The effects of acupuncture on the brain and body and how best to measure them are only beginning to be understood. Current evidence suggests that many factors—like expectation and belief—that are unrelated to acupuncture needling may play important roles in the beneficial effects of acupuncture on pain.

For Low-Back Pain

- A 2012 analysis of data on participants in acupuncture studies looked at back and neck pain together and found that actual acupuncture was more helpful than either no acupuncture or simulated acupuncture.

- A 2010 review by the Agency for Healthcare Research and Quality found that acupuncture relieved low-back pain immediately after treatment but not over longer periods of time.

- A 2008 systematic review of studies on acupuncture for low-back pain found strong evidence that combining acupuncture with usual care helps more than usual care alone. The same review also found strong evidence that there is no difference between the effects of actual and simulated acupuncture in people with low-back pain.

- Clinical practice guidelines issued by the American Pain Society and the American College of Physicians in 2007 recommend acupuncture as one of several nondrug approaches physicians should consider when patients with chronic low-back pain do not respond to self-care (practices that people can do by themselves, such as remaining active, applying heat, and taking pain-relieving medications).

For Neck Pain

- A 2014 Australian clinical study involving 282 men and women showed that needle and laser acupuncture were modestly better at relieving knee pain from osteoarthritis than no treatment, but not better than simulated (sham) laser acupuncture. Participants received 8 to 12 actual and simulated acupuncture treatments over 12 weeks. These results are generally consistent with previous studies, which showed that acupuncture is consistently better than no treatment but not necessarily better than simulated acupuncture at relieving osteoarthritis pain.

- A 2009 analysis found that actual acupuncture was more helpful for neck pain than simulated acupuncture, but the analysis was based on a small amount of evidence (only three studies with small study populations).

- A large German study with more than 14,000 participants evaluated adding acupuncture to usual care for neck pain. The researchers found that participants reported greater pain relief than those who didn't receive it; the researchers didn't test actual acupuncture against simulated acupuncture.

For Osteoarthritis/Knee Pain

- A 2014 Australian clinical study involving 282 men and women showed that needle and laser acupuncture were modestly better at relieving knee pain from osteoarthritis than no treatment, but not better than simulated (sham) laser acupuncture. Participants received 8 to 12 actual and simulated acupuncture treatments over 12 weeks. These results are generally consistent with previous studies, which showed that acupuncture is consistently better than no treatment but not necessarily better than simulated acupuncture at relieving osteoarthritis pain.

- A major 2012 analysis of data on participants in acupuncture studies found that actual acupuncture was more helpful for osteoarthritis pain than simulated acupuncture or no acupuncture.

- A 2010 systematic review of studies of acupuncture for knee or hip osteoarthritis concluded that actual acupuncture was more helpful for osteoarthritis pain than either simulated acupuncture or no acupuncture. However, the difference between actual and simulated acupuncture was very small, while the difference between acupuncture and no acupuncture was large.

For Headache

- A 2012 analysis of data on individual participants in acupuncture studies looked at migraine and tension headaches. The analysis showed that actual acupuncture was more effective than either no acupuncture or simulated acupuncture in reducing headache frequency or severity.

- A 2009 systematic review of studies concluded that actual acupuncture, compared with simulated acupuncture or pain-relieving drugs, helped people with tension-type headaches. A 2008 systematic review of studies suggested that actual acupuncture has a very slight advantage over simulated acupuncture in reducing tension-type headache intensity and the number of headache days per month.

- A 2009 systematic review found that adding acupuncture to basic care for migraines helped to reduce migraine frequency. However, in studies that compared actual acupuncture with simulated acupuncture, researchers found that the differences between the two treatments may have been due to chance.

For Other Conditions

- Results of a systematic review that combined data from 11 clinical trials with more than 1,200 participants suggested that acupuncture (and acupuncture point stimulation) may help with certain symptoms associated with cancer treatments.

- There is not enough evidence to determine if acupuncture can help people with depression.

- Acupuncture has been promoted as a smoking cessation treatment since the 1970s, but research has not shown that it helps people quit the habit.

The Challenges of Studying Acupuncture

Studying acupuncture is challenging because:

- Clinical trials often differ in terms of technique, the number of acupuncture points, the number of sessions, and the duration of those sessions.

- Results of an acupuncture session may be associated with a person's beliefs and expectations about their treatment or from their relationship with the therapist, rather than from acupuncture treatment itself.

What Is Simulated Acupuncture?

In some clinical trials, researchers test a product or practice against an inactive product or technique (called a placebo) to see if the response is due to the test protocol or to something else. Many acupuncture trials rely on a technique called simulated acupuncture, which may use blunt-tipped retractable needles that touch the skin but do not penetrate (in real acupuncture, needles penetrate the skin). Researchers also may simulate acupuncture in other ways. However, in some instances, researchers have observed that simulated acupuncture resulted in some degree of pain relief.

What the Science Says about Safety and Side Effects of Acupuncture

- Relatively few complications from using acupuncture have been reported. Still, complications have resulted from use of nonsterile needles and improper delivery of treatments.

- When not delivered properly, acupuncture can cause serious adverse effects, including infections, punctured organs, collapsed lungs, and injury to the central nervous system.

The U.S. Food and Drug Administration (FDA) regulates acupuncture needles as medical devices for use by licensed practitioners and requires that needles be manufactured and labeled according to certain standards. For example, the FDA requires that needles be sterile, nontoxic, and labeled for single use by qualified practitioners only.

More to Consider

- Don't use acupuncture to postpone seeing a health care provider about a health problem.

- If you decide to visit an acupuncturist, check his or her credentials. Most states require a license, certification, or registration to practice acupuncture; however, education and training standards and requirements for obtaining these vary from state to state. Although a license does not ensure quality of care, it does indicate that the practitioner meets certain standards regarding the knowledge and use of acupuncture. Most states require a diploma from the National Certification Commission for Acupuncture and Oriental Medicine for licensing.

- Some conventional medical practitioners—including physicians and dentists—practice acupuncture. In addition, national acupuncture organizations (which can be found through libraries or by searching the Internet) may provide referrals to acupuncturists. When considering practitioners, ask about their training and experience.

- Ask the practitioner about the estimated number of treatments needed and how much each treatment will cost. Some insurance companies may cover the costs of acupuncture, while others may not.

Help your health care providers give you better coordinated and safe care by telling them about all the health approaches you use. Give them a full picture of what you do to manage your health.

Chapter 11

Ayurvedic Medicine

Ayurvedic medicine (also called Ayurveda) is one of the world's oldest medical systems. It originated in India more than 3,000 years ago and remains one of the country's traditional health care systems. Its concepts about health and disease promote the use of herbal compounds, special diets, and other unique health practices. India's government and other institutes throughout the world support clinical and laboratory research on Ayurvedic medicine, within the context of the Eastern belief system. However, Ayurvedic medicine isn't widely studied as part of conventional (Western) medicine. This chapter provides a general overview of Ayurvedic medicine.

Key Points

- **Is Ayurvedic medicine safe?**

  Ayurvedic medicine uses a variety of products and practices. Some of these products—which may contain herbs, minerals, or metals—may be **harmful, particularly if used improperly or without the direction of a trained practitioner.** For example, some herbs can cause side effects or interact with conventional medicines. Also, **ingesting some metals, such as lead, can be poisonous.**

Text in this chapter is excerpted from "Ayurvedic Medicine: An Introduction," National Center for Complementary and Integrative Health (NCCIH), January 2015.

- **Is Ayurvedic medicine effective?**

  Studies have examined Ayurvedic medicine, including herbal products, for specific conditions. However, there aren't enough well-controlled clinical trials and systematic research reviews—the gold standard for Western medical research—to prove that the approaches are beneficial.

Keep in Mind

Tell all your health care providers about any complementary and integrative health approaches you use. Give them a full picture of what you do to manage your health. This will help ensure coordinated and safe care.

What Is Ayurveda?

The term "Ayurveda" combines the Sanskrit words *ayur* (life) and *veda* (science or knowledge). Ayurvedic medicine, as practiced in India, is one of the oldest systems of medicine in the world. Many Ayurvedic practices predate written records and were handed down by word of mouth. Three ancient books known as the Great Trilogy were written in Sanskrit more than 2,000 years ago and are considered the main texts on Ayurvedic medicine—*Caraka Samhita, Sushruta Samhita, and Astanga Hridaya.*

Key concepts of Ayurvedic medicine include universal interconnectedness (among people, their health, and the universe), the body's constitution *(prakriti)*, and life forces *(dosha)*, which are often compared to the biologic humors of the ancient Greek system. Using these concepts, Ayurvedic physicians prescribe individualized treatments, including compounds of herbs or proprietary ingredients, and diet, exercise, and lifestyle recommendations.

The majority of India's population uses Ayurvedic medicine exclusively or combined with conventional Western medicine, and it's practiced in varying forms in Southeast Asia.

What the Science Says about the Safety and Side Effects of Ayurvedic Medicine

Ayurvedic medicine uses a variety of products and practices. Ayurvedic products are made either of herbs only or a combination of herbs, metals, minerals, or other materials in an Ayurvedic practice called *rasa shastra*. Some of these **products may be harmful if used improperly or without the direction of a trained practitioner.**

Toxicity

Ayurvedic products have the potential to be toxic. Many materials used in them haven't been studied for safety in controlled clinical trials. In the United States, Ayurvedic products are regulated as dietary supplements. As such, they aren't required to meet the same safety and effectiveness standards as conventional medicines.

In 2008, a study, funded by National Center for Complementary and Integrative Health (NCCIH), examined the content of 193 Ayurvedic products purchased over the Internet and manufactured in either the United States or India. The researchers found that 21 percent of the products contained levels of lead, mercury, and/or arsenic that exceeded the standards for acceptable daily intake.

Other approaches used in Ayurvedic medicine, such as massage, special diets, and cleansing techniques may have side effects as well. To help ensure coordinated and safe care, it's important to tell all your health care providers about any Ayurvedic products and practices or other complementary and integrative health approaches you use.

What the Science Says about the Effectiveness of Ayurvedic Medicine Research

Most clinical trials of Ayurvedic approaches have been small, had problems with research designs, or lacked appropriate control groups, potentially affecting research results.

- Researchers have studied Ayurvedic approaches for schizophrenia and for diabetes; however, scientific evidence for its effectiveness for these diseases is inconclusive.

- A preliminary clinical trial in 2011, funded in part by National Center for Complementary and Integrative Health (NCCIH), found that conventional and Ayurvedic treatments for rheumatoid arthritis had similar effectiveness. The conventional drug tested was methotrexate and the Ayurvedic treatment included 40 herbal compounds.

- Ayurvedic practitioners use turmeric for inflammatory conditions, among other disorders. Evidence from clinical trials show that turmeric may help with certain digestive disorders and arthritis, but the research is limited.

- Varieties of boswellia (*Boswellia serrata, Boswellia carterii*, also known as frankincense) produce a resin that has shown anti-inflammatory and immune system effects in laboratory studies. A 2011 preliminary clinical trial found that osteoarthritis patients receiving a compound derived from *B. serrata* gum resin had greater decreases in pain compared to patients receiving a placebo.

Licensing

No states in the United States license Ayurvedic practitioners, although a few have approved Ayurvedic schools. Many Ayurvedic practitioners are licensed in other health care fields, such as midwifery or massage.

More to Consider

- Do not use Ayurvedic medicine to replace conventional care or to postpone seeing a health care provider about a medical problem.

- Women who are pregnant or nursing, or people who are thinking of using Ayurvedic approaches to treat a child, should consult their (or their child's) health care provider.

- Tell all your health care providers about any complementary and integrative health approaches you use. Give them a full picture of what you do to manage your health. This will help to ensure coordinated and safe care.

Chapter 12

Homeopathy

Homeopathy, also known as homeopathic medicine, is an alternative medical system that was developed in Germany more than 200 years ago. This chapter provides a general overview of homeopathy.

Key Points

- There is little evidence to support homeopathy as an effective treatment for any specific condition.

- Although people sometimes assume that all homeopathic remedies are highly diluted and therefore unlikely to cause harm, some products labeled as homeopathic can contain substantial amounts of active ingredients and therefore could cause side effects and drug interactions.

- Homeopathic remedies are regulated by the U.S. Food and Drug Administration (FDA). However, FDA does not evaluate the remedies for safety or effectiveness.

- Several key concepts of homeopathy are inconsistent with fundamental concepts of chemistry and physics. There are significant challenges in carrying out rigorous clinical research on homeopathic remedies.

- Tell all your health care providers about any complementary health practices you use. Give them a full picture of all you

Text in this chapter is excerpted from "Homeopathy: An Introduction," National Center for Complementary and Integrative Health (NCCIH), April 2015.

do to manage your health. This will help ensure coordinated and safe care.

Overview

The alternative medical system of homeopathy was developed in Germany at the end of the 18th century. Supporters of homeopathy point to two unconventional theories: "like cures like"—the notion that a disease can be cured by a substance that produces similar symptoms in healthy people; and "law of minimum dose"—the notion that the *lower* the dose of the medication, the *greater* its effectiveness. Many homeopathic remedies are so diluted that no molecules of the original substance remain.

Homeopathic remedies are derived from substances that come from plants, minerals, or animals, such as red onion, arnica (mountain herb), crushed whole bees, white arsenic, poison ivy, belladonna (deadly nightshade), and stinging nettle. Homeopathic remedies are often formulated as sugar pellets to be placed under the tongue; they may also be in other forms, such as ointments, gels, drops, creams, and tablets. Treatments are "individualized" or tailored to each person—it is not uncommon for different people with the same condition to receive different treatments.

Use in the United States

According to the 2012 National Health Interview Survey (NHIS), which included a comprehensive survey on the use of complementary health approaches by Americans, an estimated 5 million adults and 1 million children used homeopathy in the previous year. The 2012 survey also reported that although about 1.8 percent of children used homeopathy, only 0.2 percent of children went to a homeopathic practitioner. According to the 2007 NHIS, out-of-pocket costs for adults were $2.9 billion for homeopathic medicines and $170 million for visits to homeopathic practitioners.

The Status of Homeopathy Research

Most rigorous clinical trials and systematic analyses of the research on homeopathy have concluded that there is little evidence to support homeopathy as an effective treatment for any specific condition.

A 2015 comprehensive assessment of evidence by the Australian government's National Health and Medical Research Council concluded that there are no health conditions for which there is reliable evidence that homeopathy is effective.

Homeopathy is a controversial topic in complementary medicine research. A number of the key concepts of homeopathy are not consistent with fundamental concepts of chemistry and physics. For example, it is not possible to explain in scientific terms how a remedy containing little or no active ingredient can have any effect. This, in turn, creates major challenges to rigorous clinical investigation of homeopathic remedies. For example, one cannot confirm that an extremely dilute remedy contains what is listed on the label, or develop objective measures that show effects of extremely dilute remedies in the human body.

Another research challenge is that homeopathic treatments are highly individualized, and there is no uniform prescribing standard for homeopathic practitioners. There are hundreds of different homeopathic remedies, which can be prescribed in a variety of different dilutions for thousands of symptoms.

Side Effects and Risks

- Certain homeopathic products (called "nosodes" or "homeopathic immunizations") have been promoted by some as substitutes for conventional immunizations, but data to support such claims is lacking. The National Center for Complementary and Integrative Health (NCCIH) supports the Centers for Disease Control and Prevention's recommendations for immunizations/vaccinations.

- While many homeopathic remedies are highly diluted, some products sold or labeled as homeopathic may not be highly diluted; they can contain substantial amounts of active ingredients. Like any drug or dietary supplement that contains chemical ingredients, these homeopathic products may cause side effects or drug interactions. Negative health effects from homeopathic products of this type have been reported.

- A 2007 systematic review found that highly diluted homeopathic remedies, taken under the supervision of trained professionals, are generally safe and unlikely to cause severe adverse reactions. However, like any drug or dietary supplement, these products could pose risks if they are improperly manufactured (for example, if they are contaminated with microorganisms or incorrectly diluted).

- A 2012 systematic review of case reports and case series concluded that using certain homeopathic treatments (such as those containing heavy metals like mercury or iron that are not highly diluted) or replacing an effective conventional treatment with an ineffective homeopathic one can cause adverse effects, some of which may be serious.

- Liquid homeopathic remedies may contain alcohol. The FDA allows higher levels of alcohol in these remedies than it allows in conventional drugs.

- Homeopathic practitioners expect some of their patients to experience "homeopathic aggravation" (a temporary worsening of existing symptoms after taking a homeopathic prescription). Researchers have not found much evidence of this reaction in clinical studies; however, research on homeopathic aggravations is scarce. Always discuss changes in your symptoms with your health care provider.

- The FDA has warned consumers about different products labeled as homeopathic. For example, in 2015, it warned consumers not to rely on asthma products labeled as homeopathic that are sold over-the-counter. These products have not been evaluated by the FDA for safety and effectiveness.

Regulation of Homeopathic Treatments

Homeopathic remedies are regulated as drugs under the Federal Food, Drug and Cosmetic Act (FDCA). However, under current Agency policy, FDA does not evaluate the remedies for safety or effectiveness. FDA enforcement policies for homeopathic drugs are described in FDA's Compliance Policy Guide entitled Conditions Under Which Homeopathic Drugs May be Marketed (CPG 7132.15).

FDA allows homeopathic remedies that meet certain conditions to be marketed without agency preapproval. For example, homeopathic remedies must contain active ingredients that are listed in the Homeopathic Pharmacopeia of the United States (HPUS). The HPUS lists active ingredients that may be legally included in homeopathic products and standards for strength, quality, and purity of that ingredient. In addition, the FDA requires that the label on the product, outer container, or accompanying leaflet include at least one major indication (i.e., medical problem to be treated), a list of ingredients, the number of times the active ingredient was diluted, and directions for use. If a homeopathic remedy claims to treat a serious disease such as cancer, it must be sold by prescription. Only products for minor health problems, like a cold or headache, which go away on their own, can be sold without a prescription.

Licensing

Laws regulating the practice of homeopathy in the United States vary from state to state. Usually, individuals who are licensed to practice medicine or another health care profession can legally practice homeopathy. In some states, non-licensed professionals may practice homeopathy.

Arizona, Connecticut, and Nevada are the only states with homeopathic licensing boards for doctors of medicine (holders of M.D. degrees) and doctors of osteopathic medicine (holders of D.O. degrees). Arizona and Nevada also license homeopathic assistants, who are allowed to perform medical services under the supervision of a homeopathic physician. Some states explicitly include homeopathy within the scope of practice of chiropractic, naturopathy, and physical therapy.

If You Are Thinking about Using Homeopathy

- Do not use homeopathy as a replacement for proven conventional care or to postpone seeing a health care provider about a medical problem.

- If you are considering using a homeopathic remedy, bring the product with you when you visit your health care provider. The provider may be able to help you determine whether the product might pose a risk of side effects or drug interactions.

- Follow the recommended conventional immunization schedules for children and adults. Do not use homeopathic products as a substitute for conventional immunizations.

- Women who are pregnant or nursing, or people who are thinking of using homeopathy to treat a child, should consult their (or their child's) health care providers.

- Tell all your health care providers about any complementary health practices you use. Give them a full picture of all you do to manage your health. This will ensure coordinated and safe care.

Chapter 13

Naturopathy

Naturopathy—also called naturopathic medicine—is a medical system that has evolved from a combination of traditional practices and health care approaches popular in Europe during the 19th century. Guided by a philosophy that emphasizes the healing power of nature, naturopathic practitioners now use a variety of traditional and modern therapies. This chapter provides a general overview of naturopathy and suggests sources for additional information.

Key Points

- Although some of the individual therapies used in naturopathy have been studied for efficacy and safety, naturopathy as a general approach to health care has not been widely researched.

- "Natural" does not necessarily mean "safe." Some therapies used in naturopathy, such as herbal supplements and restrictive or unconventional diets, have the potential to be harmful if not used under the direction of a well-trained practitioner.

- Some beliefs and approaches of naturopathic practitioners are not consistent with conventional medicine, and their safety may not be supported by scientific evidence. For example, some practitioners may not recommend childhood vaccinations. The

Text in this chapter is excerpted from "Naturopathy: An Introduction," National Center for Complementary and Integrative Health (NCCIH), March 2012.

benefits of vaccination in preventing illness and death have been repeatedly proven and greatly outweigh the risks.

- Tell all your health care providers about any complementary health practices you use. Give them a full picture of what you do to manage your health. This will help ensure coordinated and safe care.

Background

Naturopathy has its roots in Germany. It was further developed in the late 19th and early 20th centuries in the United States.

The word *naturopathy* comes from Greek and Latin and literally translates as "nature disease." A central belief in naturopathy is that nature has a healing power (a principle practitioners call *vis medicatrix naturae*). Practitioners view their role as supporting the body's ability to maintain and restore health, and prefer to use treatment approaches they consider to be the most natural and least invasive.

Recently, naturopathy is practiced in a number of countries, including the United States, Canada, Germany, Great Britain, Australia, and New Zealand.

Use in the United States

According to the 2007 National Health Interview Survey, which included a comprehensive survey of the use of complementary health practices by Americans, an estimated 729,000 adults and 237,000 children had used a naturopathic treatment in the previous year.

People visit naturopathic practitioners for various health-related purposes, including primary care, overall well-being, and complementary treatment (used in addition to conventional medical treatment) of chronic illnesses as well as acute conditions such as colds and flu. Many practitioners also provide complementary health care for patients with serious illnesses.

Underlying Principles

The practice of naturopathy is based on principles that are similar to and consistent with the principles of primary care medicine as practiced by conventional physicians. These include:

- **First do no harm.** Try to minimize harmful side effects and avoid suppression of symptoms.

- **Physician as teacher.** Educate patients and encourage them to take responsibility for their own health.

- **Treat the whole person.** Consider all factors (e.g., physical, mental, emotional, spiritual, genetic, environmental, social) when tailoring treatment to each patient.

- **Prevention.** Assess risk factors and, in partnership with patients, make appropriate interventions to prevent illness.

- **Healing power of nature.** Seek to identify and remove obstacles to the body's natural processes for maintaining and restoring health.

- **Treat the cause.** Focus on the causes of a disease or condition, rather than its symptoms.

Treatment

Naturopathic practitioners use many different treatment modalities. Examples include:

- Nutrition counseling, including dietary changes (such as eating more whole and unprocessed foods) and use of vitamins, minerals, and other supplements

- Herbal medicines

- Homeopathy

- Hydrotherapy

- Physical medicine, such as therapeutic massage and joint manipulation

- Exercise therapy

- Lifestyle counseling.

Some practitioners use other treatments as well or, if appropriate, may refer patients to conventional health care providers.

Efficacy and Safety

Some of the individual therapies used in naturopathy have been researched for their efficacy, with varying results. The complex treatment approaches that naturopathic physicians often use are challenging to study, and little scientific evidence is currently available on overall effectiveness. Related research is under way but is in the early stages.

Some studies have shown a few areas of scientific interest to pursue. For example, a study of warehouse employees with chronic low-back pain found that naturopathic care was a more cost-effective approach than standard physiotherapy advice. In another study, postal employees with chronic low-back pain had significantly greater improvement from naturopathic care than from standard physiotherapy advice. Researchers have also found evidence that naturopathic treatment may help improve quality of life in multiple sclerosis patients. A study of treatment approaches for patients with temporomandibular (jaw) disorders found that two complementary health practices—naturopathic medicine and traditional Chinese medicine—both resulted in greater pain reduction than state-of-the-art conventional care.

In assessing the safety of naturopathic care, points to consider include:

• Naturopathy is not a complete substitute for conventional care. Relying exclusively on naturopathic treatments and avoiding conventional medical care may be harmful or, in some circumstances (for example, a severe injury or an infection), have serious health consequences.

• Some beliefs and approaches of naturopathic practitioners are not consistent with conventional medicine, and their safety may not be supported by scientific evidence. For example, some practitioners may not recommend childhood vaccinations that are standard practice in conventional medicine (although a survey of naturopathic physicians in one state found that some provided childhood immunizations).

• Some therapies used in naturopathy have the potential to be harmful if not used under the direction of a well-trained practitioner. For example, herbs can cause side effects on their own and may interact with prescription or over-the-counter medicines or other herbs, and restrictive or other unconventional diets can be unsafe for some people.

Practitioners

In the United States, naturopathy has three general categories of practitioners: naturopathic physicians, traditional naturopaths, and other health care providers who also offer naturopathic services. The titles used by practitioners may vary (for example, both naturopathic physicians and traditional naturopaths sometimes refer to themselves as "naturopathic doctors" or by the abbreviation N.D. or N.M.D.). As of 2000, an estimated 1,500 naturopathic physicians were practicing in the United States; that estimate nearly doubled by 2006. As of 2001, an estimated 3,600 traditional naturopaths were practicing in the United States.

Naturopathic physicians generally complete a 4-year, graduate-level program at one of the North American naturopathic medical schools accredited by the Council on Naturopathic Medical Education, an organization recognized for accreditation purposes by the U.S. Department of Education. Admission requirements generally include a bachelor's degree and standard premedical courses. The study program includes basic sciences, naturopathic therapies and techniques, diagnostic techniques and tests, specialty courses, clinical sciences, and clinical training. Graduates receive the degree of N.D. (Naturopathic Doctor) or N.M.D. (Naturopathic Medical Doctor), depending on where the degree is issued. Although postdoctoral (residency) training is not required, some graduates pursue residency opportunities.

Some U.S. states and territories have licensing requirements for naturopathic physicians, but others do not. In those jurisdictions that have licensing requirements, naturopathic physicians must graduate from a 4-year naturopathic medical college and pass an examination to receive a license. They must also fulfill annual continuing education requirements. Their scope of practice is defined by law in the state in which they practice (for example, depending on the state, naturopathic physicians may or may not be allowed to prescribe drugs, perform minor surgery, practice acupuncture, and/or assist in childbirth).

Traditional naturopaths, also known simply as "naturopaths," emphasize naturopathic approaches to a healthy lifestyle, strengthening and cleansing the body, and noninvasive treatments. They do not use prescription drugs, injections, X-rays, or surgery. Several schools offer training for people who want to become naturopaths, often through distance learning (correspondence or Internet courses). Admission requirements for schools can range from none, to a high school diploma, to specific degrees and coursework. Programs vary in length and content and are not accredited by organizations recognized for accreditation purposes by the U.S. Department of Education. Traditional naturopaths are not subject to licensing.

Other health care providers (such as physicians, osteopathic physicians, chiropractors, dentists, and nurses) sometimes offer naturopathic treatments and other holistic therapies, having pursued additional training in these areas. Training programs vary.

In states that license naturopathic physicians, that title as well as "naturopathic doctor" or even "naturopath" may be protected by law for practitioners who have completed a 4-year naturopathic medical school program.

If You Are Thinking about Using Naturopathy

Keep in mind the following points:

- Naturopathy practitioners' qualifications may vary widely. Find out about the practitioner's education and training. Ask whether the practitioner is licensed by the state, and about any other documented qualifications.

- Tell the practitioner about any medical conditions you have. Ask whether the practitioner has any specialized training and experience in them.

- Ask about the practitioner's referral network and make sure the practitioner has experience coordinating care with other types of medical providers.

- Ask the practitioner about typical out-of-pocket costs and insurance coverage (if any).

- Tell the practitioner about all medications (prescription or over-the-counter) and dietary supplements you are taking. Naturopathic practitioners may use herbal remedies, or may be licensed to prescribe certain drugs. Avoiding potential interactions is important.

- Tell all of your health care providers about any complementary health approaches you use. Give them a full picture of what you do to manage your health. This will help ensure coordinated and safe care.

Chapter 14

Other Indigenous Medical Systems

Chapter Contents

Section 14.1

Traditional Chinese Medicine

Text in this section is excerpted from "Traditional Chinese Medicine:
An Introduction," National Center for Complementary and
Integrative Health (NCCIH), October 2013.

Traditional Chinese medicine (TCM) originated in ancient China
and has evolved over thousands of years. TCM practitioners use herbal
medicines and various mind and body practices, such as acupuncture
and tai chi, to treat or prevent health problems. In the United States,
people use TCM primarily as a complementary health approach. This
section provides a general overview of TCM and suggests sources for
additional information.

Key Points

Is It Safe?

Acupuncture is generally considered safe when performed by an
experienced practitioner using sterile needles. Improperly performed
acupuncture can cause potentially serious side effects.

- Tai chi and qi gong, two mind and body practices used in TCM,
  are generally safe.

- There have been reports of Chinese herbal products being contaminated with drugs, toxins, or heavy metals or not containing
  the listed ingredients. Some of the herbs used in Chinese medicine can interact with drugs, have serious side effects, or be
  unsafe for people with certain medical conditions.

Is It Effective?

- For most conditions, there is not enough rigorous scientific evidence to know whether TCM methods work for the conditions for
  which they are used.

Keep in Mind

- Tell all your health care providers about any complementary health approaches you use. Give them a full picture of what you do to manage your health. This will help ensure coordinated and safe care.

Background

TCM encompasses many different practices, including acupuncture, moxibustion (burning an herb above the skin to apply heat to acupuncture points), Chinese herbal medicine, tui na (Chinese therapeutic massage), dietary therapy, and tai chi and qi gong (practices that combine specific movements or postures, coordinated breathing, and mental focus). TCM is rooted in the ancient philosophy of Taoism and dates back more than 2,500 years. Traditional systems of medicine also exist in other East and South Asian countries, including Japan (where the traditional herbal medicine is called Kampo) and Korea. Some of these systems have been influenced by TCM and are similar to it in some ways, but each has developed distinctive features of its own.

Although the exact number of people who use TCM in the United States is unknown, it was estimated in 1997 that some 10,000 practitioners served more than 1 million patients each year. According to the 2007 National Health Interview Survey (NHIS), which included a comprehensive survey on the use of complementary health approaches by Americans, an estimated 3.1 million U.S. adults had used acupuncture in the previous year. The number of visits to acupuncturists tripled between 1997 and 2007. According to the 2007 NHIS, about 2.3 million Americans practiced tai chi and 600,000 practiced qi gong in the previous year.

Side Effects and Risks

- Herbal medicines used in TCM are sometimes marketed in the United States as dietary supplements. The U.S. Food and Drug Administration (FDA) regulations for dietary supplements are not the same as those for prescription or over-the-counter drugs; in general, the regulations for dietary supplements are less stringent. For example, manufacturers don't have to prove to the FDA that most claims made for dietary supplements are valid; if the product were a drug, they would have to provide proof.

- Some Chinese herbal products may be safe, but others may not be. There have been reports of products being contaminated with drugs, toxins, or heavy metals or not containing the listed ingredients. Some of the herbs used in Chinese medicine can interact with drugs, can have serious side effects, or may be unsafe for people with certain medical conditions. For example, the Chinese herb ephedra (ma huang) has been linked to serious health complications, including heart attack and stroke. In 2004, the FDA banned the sale of ephedra-containing dietary supplements, but the ban does not apply to TCM remedies.

- The FDA regulates acupuncture needles as medical devices and requires that the needles be sterile, nontoxic, and labeled for single use by qualified practitioners only. Relatively few complications from the use of acupuncture have been reported. However, adverse effects—some of them serious—have resulted from the use of nonsterile needles or improper delivery of acupuncture treatments.

- Tai chi and qi gong are considered to be generally safe practices.

- Information on the safety of other TCM methods is limited. Reported complications of moxibustion include allergic reactions, burns, and infections, but how often these events occur is not known. Both moxibustion and cupping (applying a heated cup to the skin to create a slight suction) may mark the skin, usually temporarily. The origin of these marks should be explained to health care providers so that they will not be mistaken for signs of disease or physical abuse.

TCM practitioners use a variety of techniques in an effort to promote health and treat disease. In the United States, the most commonly used approaches include Chinese herbal medicine, acupuncture, and tai chi.

- **Chinese herbal medicine.** The Chinese *Materia Medica* (a pharmacological reference book used by TCM practitioners) describes thousands of medicinal substances—primarily plants, but also some minerals and animal products. Different parts of plants, such as the leaves, roots, stems, flowers, and seeds, are used. In TCM, herbs are often combined in formulas and given as teas, capsules, liquid extracts, granules, or powders.

- **Acupuncture.** Acupuncture is a family of procedures involving the stimulation of specific points on the body using a variety of techniques. The acupuncture technique that has been most often studied scientifically involves penetrating the skin with thin,

Underlying Concepts

When thinking about ancient medical systems such as TCM, it is important to separate questions about traditional theories and concepts of health and wellness from questions about whether specific interventions might be helpful in the context of modern science-based medicine and health promotion practices.

The ancient beliefs on which TCM is based include the following:

- The human body is a miniature version of the larger, sur-rounding universe.
- Harmony between two opposing yet complementary forces, called *yin* and *yang*, supports health, and disease results from an imbalance between these forces.
- Five elements—fire, earth, wood, metal, and water—sym-bolically represent all phenomena, including the stages of human life, and explain the functioning of the body and how it changes during disease.
- Qi, a vital energy that flows through the body, performs multiple functions in maintaining health.

Concepts such as these are of interest in understanding the history of TCM. However, NCCIH-supported research on TCM does not focus on these ideas. Instead, it examines specific TCM practices from a scientific perspective, looking at their effects in the body and whether the practices are helpful in symptom management.

solid, metal needles that are manipulated by the hands or by electrical stimulation.

- **Tai chi.** Tai chi is a centuries-old mind and body practice. It involves gentle, dance-like body movements with mental focus, breathing, and relaxation.

Status of TCM Research

In spite of the widespread use of TCM in China and its use in the West, rigorous scientific evidence of its effectiveness is limited. TCM can be difficult for researchers to study because its treatments are often complex and are based on ideas very different from those of modern Western medicine.

Most research studies on TCM have focused on specific techniques, primarily acupuncture and Chinese herbal remedies, and there have been many systematic reviews of studies of TCM approaches for various conditions.

- An assessment of the research found that 41 of 70 systematic reviews of the scientific evidence (including 19 of 26 reviews on acupuncture for a variety of conditions and 22 of 42 reviews on Chinese herbal medicine) were unable to reach conclusions about whether the technique worked for the condition under investigation because there was not enough good-quality evidence. The other 29 systematic reviews (including 7 of 26 reviews on acupuncture and 20 of 42 reviews on Chinese herbal medicine) suggested possible benefits but could not reach definite conclusions because of the small quantity or poor quality of the studies.

- In a 2012 analysis that combined data on individual participants in 29 studies of acupuncture for pain, patients who received acupuncture for back or neck pain, osteoarthritis, or chronic headache had better pain relief than those who did not receive acupuncture. However, in the same analysis, when actual acupuncture was compared with simulated acupuncture (a sham procedure that resembles acupuncture but in which the needles do not penetrate the skin or penetrate it only slightly), the difference in pain relief between the two treatments was much smaller—so small that it may not have been meaningful to patients.

- Tai chi has not been investigated as extensively as acupuncture or Chinese herbal medicine, but recent studies, including some supported by National Center for Complementary and Integrative Health (NCCIH), suggest that practicing tai chi may help to improve balance and stability in people with Parkinson's disease; reduce pain from knee osteoarthritis and fibromyalgia; and promote quality of life and mood in people with heart failure.

If You Are Thinking about Using TCM

- Do not use TCM to replace effective conventional care or as a reason to postpone seeing a health care provider about a medical problem.

- Look for published research studies on TCM for the health condition that interests you.

- It is better to use TCM herbal remedies under the supervision of your health care provider or a professional trained in herbal medicine than to try to treat yourself.

- Ask about the training and experience of the TCM practitioner you are considering.

- If you are pregnant or nursing, or are thinking of using TCM to treat a child, you should be especially sure to consult your (or the child's) health care provider.

- Tell all your health care providers about any complementary health approaches you use. Give them a full picture of what you do to manage your health. This will help ensure coordinated and safe care.

Section 14.2

Native American Medicine

"Native American Medicine," © 2015 Omnigraphics, Inc. Reviewed September 2015.

Native American medicine refers to the healing practices used by the indigenous peoples of North America. Native American medicine originated thousands of years ago, and it encompasses the traditions and beliefs of more than 500 distinct nations that inhabited the continent before the arrival of Europeans. One of the distinguishing features of Native American medicine is its emphasis on spiritual harmony or balance as a key component of individual health.

Native American healers typically employ a holistic approach that not only addresses the patient's specific illness or injury, but also seeks to restore the patient's spirit to a state of harmonious balance with the larger world. They view humans as part of a complex, interrelated spiritual web that encompasses the individual, the community, the Creator, and the natural environment. They believe that diseases, trauma, and bad luck are indications that the relationship between these elements has been disrupted. To return a patient to good health, a healer must also restore the balance.

Although the general thrust of Native American medicine is clear, the specific techniques and practices are not well known. Since most Native American cultures never developed a written language, healing techniques were usually passed down verbally from one generation to the next. In the centuries following European contact, many Native American nations experienced dramatic population losses as a result of warfare and epidemics of unfamiliar diseases like smallpox and measles. As traditional healers died, they often took their knowledge of Native American medicine with them.

The main documentation of Native American medicine was done by people outside of the cultural tradition. Although these people could observe and describe the physical practices, they could not necessarily understand and capture their underlying spiritual meaning. In fact, some Native American healers claim that their medical practices cannot be reduced to an academic body of knowledge and technique. In addition, many Native American elders decline requests to share their healing secrets with non-natives, out of concern that their sacred practices will be dishonored or exploited and their spiritual power weakened. Some of the knowledge has survived, however, and Native American medicine continues to be practiced in the twenty-first century.

Healers

The traditional healers in Native American tribes were known as medicine men and medicine women. They mixed herbs and administered remedies to people who were sick or injured. In addition to practicing medicine, however, the healers were also religious leaders who helped maintain the connection between the tribe and the Creator or Great Spirit. Under the Native American belief system, an illness could have any number of different causes, including demons and evil spirits. The healers often wore grotesque masks to frighten away evil spirits and performed special ceremonies to purge the patient of demonic influences.

Most healers used tools made from natural sources, such as bones, crystals, feathers, fur, roots, shells, skin, and stones. These tools were used in ceremonies to invoke the help of the Great Spirit in healing illnesses and driving away evil. Many healers carried medicines tied in a cloth bundle or thick hide. The contents of these medicine bags were known only to the healer and were considered a sacred source of power.

Each healer was believed to have a unique perspective that grew out of their own individual skills, abilities, and life experiences. A person in need of medical treatment would seek a healer who had successfully treated other patients with similar conditions. The healer typically established a relationship with each patient in order to gain an understanding of their unique circumstances and preferences. Often the treatment was designed not only to cure a disease, but also to help the patient achieve spiritual growth and find a healthier balance with the larger world.

Healing Practices and Ceremonies

Although the healing methods used by various Native Americans nations differed, herbal remedies played a major role in medical treatment for all the tribes. Healers collected plants from surrounding areas that were known to be effective in treating certain ailments. They even traded over long distances to obtain herbs that were not available locally. Various herbs could be ground into powders to be inhaled, mashed into pastes to be applied to skin, or mixed with water or food to be consumed.

Native American healers also conducted special purification rituals, such as sweat lodges and sweat baths, to help remove toxins from a sick person's body. During these rituals, the healer usually prayed, chanted, sang, or played drums to help cleanse the body and increase clarity of thought. Sage, an herb that was believed to have powerful cleansing properties, was burned in a ceremony called "sweeping the smoke" in order to purify the body and soul.

Native American medicine also involved healing rituals and ceremonies in which the entire community participated. Rather than curing an individual patient, many of these rituals were intended to help restore harmony between the tribe and the Great Spirit in order to promote general health and prosperity. The ceremonies, which sometimes took place over several days, might involve prayers, songs and stories, chants, drumming, and various sacred healing objects. Some tribes used the medicine wheel or sacred hoop, which denotes the circle of life. It incorporates the four directions as well as Mother Earth and Father Sky.

Native American Medicine Today

In the late 1800s the U.S. government instituted bans on Native American religious practices, which white officials considered "heathen" rituals that interfered with their goal of "civilizing" the tribes. Since these practices were closely linked to Native American medicine, many traditional healing rituals were prohibited or strongly discouraged as well. After being suppressed for decades, many ancient medical practices were forgotten. Meanwhile, in the early twentieth century the federal Indian Health Service began opening hospitals and clinics on reservations to bring modern medicine to Native American communities. An increasing number of Native Americans turned to these facilities for their heath care needs, especially to treat "white man's diseases" that their healers had proven unable to cure.

The passage of the American Indian Religious Freedom Act in 1978 finally lifted the federal ban on Native American religious practices and healing rituals. Since then, mainstream medical theory has shifted toward a more holistic approach that recognizes a patient's mental and spiritual well-being as an important component of their physical health. As a result, Native American medicine has experienced a surge in popularity and interest in recent years.

Traditional herbal remedies drawn from Native American traditions, for instance, hold strong appeal for people who are concerned about the toxicity, addictive properties, and side effects of pharmaceutical drugs. Some people believe that these natural remedies, which have been developed over centuries, can be as effective as prescription medications in treating certain conditions.

Many Native American communities face serious health concerns in the twenty-first century, including high rates of alcoholism, obesity, diabetes, and heart disease. While most Native Americans rely on conventional medicine to treat these health problems, many find that traditional healing practices provide benefits as well. In addition, the holistic approach used by Native American healers has increasingly attracted non-native adherents. By treating the patient's body, mind, and spirit together, they believe that Native American medicine can improve their chances of healing and maintaining good health.

References:

1. Center for Health and Healing. "Traditional and Indigenous Healing Systems: Native American Medicine." Mt. Sinai Beth Israel, 2003.
2. Mehl-Madrona, Lewis. "Traditional (Native American) Indian Medicine Treatment of Chronic Illness." Healing Center Online, 2008.
3. Weiser, Kathy. "Native American Medicine." Legends of America, May 2015.

Part Three

Complementary and
Alternative Therapies

Chapter 15

Biologically Based Therapies

Chapter Contents

Section 15.1

Aromatherapy and Essential Oils

Text in this section begins with excerpts from "Aromatherapy
and Essential Oils (PDQ®) – Questions and Answers About
Aromatherapy," National Cancer Institute (NCI), December 17, 2014.
Text in this section beginning with "What's the "intended use"?" is
excerpted from "Aromatherapy," U.S. Food and Drug Administration
(FDA), August 22, 2014.

What is aromatherapy?

Aromatherapy is the use of essential oils from plants to support
and balance the mind, body, and spirit. Aromatherapy may be combined with other complementary treatments like massage therapy
and acupuncture, as well as with standard treatments, for symptom
management.

Essential oils (also known as volatile oils) are the basic materials of
aromatherapy. They are made from fragrant essences found in many
plants. These essences are made in special plant cells, often under the
surface of leaves, bark, or peel, using energy from the sun and elements
from the air, soil, and water. If the plant is crushed, the essence and
its unique fragrance are released.

When essences are extracted from plants in natural ways, they
become essential oils. They may be distilled with steam and/or water,
or mechanically pressed. Oils that are made with chemical processes
are not considered true essential oils.

There are many essential oils used in aromatherapy, including
those from Roman chamomile, geranium, lavender, tea tree, lemon,
cedarwood, and bergamot. Each type of essential oil has a different
chemical composition that affects how it smells, how it is absorbed,
and how it is used by the body. Even the oils from varieties of plants
within the same species may have chemical compositions different
from each other. The same applies to plants that are grown or har-
vested in different ways or locations.

Essential oils are very concentrated. For example, it takes about
220 lbs of lavender flowers to make about 1 pound of essential oil.

Essential oils are very volatile, evaporating quickly when they are exposed to open air.

What is the history of the discovery and use of aromatherapy as a complementary and alternative treatment?

Fragrant plants have been used in healing practices for thousands of years across many cultures, including ancient China, India, and Egypt. Ways to extract essential oils from plants were first discovered during the Middle Ages.

The history of modern aromatherapy began in the early 20th century, when French chemist Rene Gattefosse coined the term "aromatherapy" and studied the effects of essential oils on many kinds of diseases. In the 1980s and 1990s, aromatherapy was rediscovered in Western countries as interest in complementary and alternative medicine (CAM) began to grow.

How is aromatherapy administered?

Aromatherapy is used in various ways. Examples include:

- Indirect inhalation (patient breathes in essential oils by using a room diffuser or placing drops nearby).

- Direct inhalation (patient breathes in essential oils by using an individual inhaler with drops floated on top of hot water) to treat a sinus headache.

- Aromatherapy massage (massaging essential oils, diluted in a carrier oil, into the skin).

- Applying essential oils to the skin by combining them with bath salts, lotions, or dressings.

Aromatherapy is rarely taken by mouth.

There are some essential oils commonly chosen to treat specific conditions. However, the types of oils used and the ways they are combined may vary, depending on the experience and training of the aromatherapist. This lack of standard methods has led to some conflicting research on the effects of aromatherapy.

Have any preclinical (laboratory or animal) studies been conducted using aromatherapy?

Many studies of essential oils have found that they have antibacterial effects when applied to the skin. Some essential oils have antiviral activity against the herpes simplex virus. Others have antifungal activity against certain vaginal and oropharyngeal fungal infections. In addition, studies in rats have shown that different essential oils can be calming or energizing. When rats were exposed to certain fragrances under stressful conditions, their behavior and immune responses were improved.

One study showed that after essential oils were inhaled, markers of the fragrance compounds were found in the bloodstream, suggesting that aromatherapy affects the body directly like a drug, in addition to indirectly through the central nervous system.

Have any clinical trials (research studies with people) of aromatherapy been conducted?

Clinical trials of aromatherapy have mainly studied its use in the treatment of stress, anxiety, and other health-related conditions in seriously ill patients. Some patients receiving aromatherapy have reported improvement in symptoms such as nausea or pain, and have lower blood pressure, pulse, and respiratory rates. Studies of aromatherapy massage have had mixed results, with some studies reporting improvement in mood, anxiety, pain, and constipation and other studies reporting no effect.

A study of inhaled bergamot in children and adolescents receiving stem cell transplants reported an increase in anxiety and nausea and no effect on pain. Parents receiving the aromatherapy and parents receiving the placebo both showed less anxiety after their children's transplants. In a study of adult patients receiving stem cell transplants, tasting or sniffing sliced oranges was more effective at reducing nausea, retching, and coughing than inhaling an orange essential oil.

A small study of tea tree oil as a topical treatment to clear antibiotic -resistant Methicillin-resistant Staphylococcus aureus (MRSA) bacteria from the skin of hospital patients found that it was as effective as the standard treatment. Antibacterial essential oils have been studied to lessen odor in necrotic ulcers.

Have any side effects or risks been reported from aromatherapy?

Safety testing on essential oils shows very few bad side effects or risks when they are used as directed. Some essential oils have been approved as ingredients in food and are classified as GRAS (generally recognized as safe) by the U.S. Food and Drug Administration, within specific limits. Swallowing large amounts of essential oils is not recommended.

Allergic reactions and skin irritation may occur in aromatherapists or in patients, especially when essential oils are in contact with the skin for long periods of time. Sun sensitivity may develop when citrus or other oils are applied to the skin before sun exposure.

Lavender and tea tree oils have been found to have some hormone -like effects. They have effects similar to estrogen (female sex hormone) and also block or decrease the effect of androgens (male sex hormones). Applying lavender and tea tree oils to the skin over a long period of time has been linked in one study to breast enlargement in boys who have not yet reached puberty. It is recommended that patients with tumors that need estrogen to grow avoid using lavender and tea tree oils.

Is aromatherapy approved by the U.S. Food and Drug Administration (FDA) for use as a cancer treatment in the United States?

Aromatherapy products do not need approval by the Food and Drug Administration because no specific claims are made for the treatment of cancer or other diseases.

Aromatherapy is not regulated by state law, and there is no licensing required to practice aromatherapy in the United States. Professionals often combine aromatherapy training with another field in which they are licensed, for example, massage therapy, registered nursing, acupuncture, or naturopathy. Some aromatherapy courses for healthcare providers offer medical credit hours and include conducting research and measuring results.

The National Association for Holistic Aromatherapy (www.naha. org) and the Alliance of International Aromatherapists (www.alliance-aromatherapists.org) are two organizations that have national educational standards for aromatherapists. The National Association for Holistic Aromatherapy (NAHA) plans to have a standard aromatherapy certification in the United States. There are many schools that offer certificate programs approved by NAHA. A list of these schools can be found at www.naha.org/schools_level_one_two.htm. National exams in aromatherapy are held twice a year.

The Canadian Federation of Aromatherapists (www.cfacanada.com) certifies aromatherapists in Canada. See the International Federation of Aromatherapists Web site (www.ifaroma.org) for a list of international aromatherapy programs.

What's the "intended use"?

Under the law, how "aromatherapy" products are regulated depends mainly on how they are intended to be used.

FDA determines a product's intended use based on factors such as claims made in the labeling, on websites, and in advertising, as well as what consumers expect it to do. We also look at how a product is marketed, not just a word or phrase taken out of context. Finally, we make decisions on a case-by-case basis.

Is it a cosmetic?

If a product is intended only to cleanse the body or to make a person more attractive, it's a cosmetic. So, if a product such as a shower gel is intended only to cleanse the body, or a perfume or cologne is intended only to make a person smell good, it's a cosmetic.

The law doesn't require cosmetics to have FDA approval before they go on the market. But FDA can take action against a cosmetic on the market if we have reliable information showing that it is unsafe when consumers use it according to directions on the label, or in the customary or expected way, or if it is not labeled properly.

Is it a drug?

If a product is intended for a therapeutic use, such as treating or preventing disease, or to affect the structure or function of the body, it's a drug. For example, claims that a product will relieve colic, ease pain, relax muscles, treat depression or anxiety, or help you sleep are drug claims.

Such claims are sometimes made for products such as soaps, lotions, and massage oils containing "essential oils" and marketed as "aromatherapy." The fact that a fragrance material or other ingredient comes from a plant doesn't keep it from being regulated as a drug.

Under the law, drugs must meet requirements such as FDA approval for safety and effectiveness before they go on the market. To find out if a product marketed with drug claims is FDA-approved, contact FDA's Center for Drug Evaluation and Research (CDER) at druginfo@fda.hhs.gov.

Is it both a cosmetic and a drug?

Some products are both cosmetics and drugs. For example, a baby lotion marketed with claims that it both moisturizes the baby's skin and relieves colic would be both a cosmetic and a drug. Such products must meet the requirements for both cosmetics and drugs.

Is it something else?

Some fragrance products are regulated by the Consumer Product Safety Commission (CPSC). These include products such as air fresheners, scented candles, laundry detergents, and household cleansers.

If an "essential oil" or other fragrance is "natural" or "organic," doesn't that mean it's safe?

Sometimes people think that if an "essential oil" or other ingredient comes from a plant, it must be safe. But many plants contain materials that are toxic, irritating, or likely to cause allergic reactions when applied to the skin.

For example, cumin oil is safe in food, but can cause the skin to blister. Certain citrus oils used safely in food can also be harmful in cosmetics, particularly when applied to skin exposed to the sun.

FDA doesn't have regulations defining "natural" or "organic" for cosmetics. All cosmetic products and ingredients must meet the same safety requirement, regardless of their source.

Section 15.2

Oxygen Therapy

Text in this section is excerpted from "Oxygen Therapy," National Heart, Lung, and Blood Institute (NHLBI), February 24, 2012.

What Is Oxygen Therapy?

Oxygen therapy is a treatment that provides you with extra oxygen, a gas that your body needs to work well. Normally, your lungs absorb oxygen from the air. However, some diseases and conditions can prevent you from getting enough oxygen.

Oxygen therapy may help you function better and be more active. Oxygen is supplied in a metal cylinder or other container. It flows through a tube and is delivered to your lungs in one of the following ways:

- Through a nasal cannula, which consists of two small plastic tubes, or prongs, that are placed in both nostrils.
- Through a face mask, which fits over your nose and mouth.
- Through a small tube inserted into your windpipe through the front of your neck. Your doctor will use a needle or small incision (cut) to place the tube. Oxygen delivered this way is called transtracheal oxygen therapy.

Oxygen therapy can be done in a hospital, another medical setting, or at home. If you need oxygen therapy for a chronic (ongoing) disease or condition, you might receive home oxygen therapy.

Overview

To learn how oxygen therapy works, it helps to understand how your respiratory system works. This system is a group of organs and tissues that help you breathe. The respiratory system includes the airways and lungs.

The airways carry oxygen-rich air to your lungs. They also carry carbon dioxide (a waste gas) out of your lungs.

Air enters your body through your nose or mouth, which moistens and warms the air. The air then travels through your voice box and down your windpipe. The windpipe divides into two tubes called bronchi that enter your lungs.

Within your lungs, your bronchi branch into thousands of smaller, thinner tubes called bronchioles. These tubes end in bunches of tiny round air sacs called alveoli.

Each of the air sacs is covered in a mesh of tiny blood vessels called capillaries. The capillaries connect to a network of arteries and veins that move blood throughout your body.

When air reaches the air sacs, the oxygen in the air passes through the air sac walls into the blood in the capillaries.

The oxygen-rich blood then travels to the heart through the pulmonary vein and its branches. The heart pumps the oxygen-rich blood to your organs.

Certain acute (short-term) and chronic (ongoing) diseases and conditions can affect the transfer of oxygen from the alveoli into the blood. Examples include pneumonia and chronic obstructive pulmonary disease (COPD).

Your doctor will decide whether you need oxygen therapy based on the results of tests, such as an arterial blood gas test and a pulse oximetry test. These tests measure how much oxygen is in your blood. A low oxygen level is a sign that you need oxygen therapy.

Oxygen is considered a medicine, so your doctor must prescribe it.

Outlook

Oxygen therapy helps many people function better and be more active. It also may help:

• Decrease shortness of breath and fatigue (tiredness)

• Improve sleep in some people who have sleep-related breathing disorders

• Increase the lifespan of some people who have COPD

Although you may need oxygen therapy long term, it doesn't have to limit your daily routine. Portable oxygen units can make it easier for you to move around and do many daily activities. Talk with your doctor if you have questions about whether certain activities are safe for you.

A home equipment provider will work with you to make sure you have the supplies and equipment you need. Trained staff also will show you how to use the equipment correctly and safely.

Oxygen therapy generally is safe, but it can pose a fire hazard. To use your oxygen safely, follow the instructions you receive from your home equipment provider.

Who Needs Oxygen Therapy?

Your doctor may recommend oxygen therapy if you have a low blood oxygen level. Normally, your lungs absorb oxygen from the air and transfer it into your bloodstream.

Some acute (short-term) and chronic (ongoing) diseases and conditions can prevent you from getting enough oxygen.

Acute Diseases and Conditions

You may receive oxygen therapy if you're in the hospital for a serious condition that prevents you from getting enough oxygen. Once you've recovered from the condition, the oxygen will likely be stopped.

Some diseases and conditions that may require short-term oxygen therapy are:

- **Severe pneumonia.** Pneumonia is an infection in one or both of the lungs. If severe, the infection causes your lungs' air sacs to become very inflamed. This prevents the air sacs from moving enough oxygen into your blood.

- **Severe asthma attack.** Asthma is a lung disease that inflames and narrows the airways. Most people who have asthma, including many children, can safely manage their symptoms. But if you have a severe asthma attack, you may need hospital care that includes oxygen therapy.

- **Respiratory distress syndrome (RDS) or bronchopulmonary dysplasia (BPD) in premature babies.** Premature babies may develop one or both of these serious lung conditions. As part of their treatment, they may receive extra oxygen through a nasal continuous positive airway pressure (NCPAP) machine or a ventilator, or through a tube in the nose.

Chronic Diseases and Conditions

Long-term home oxygen therapy might be used to treat some diseases and conditions, such as:

- **COPD (chronic obstructive pulmonary disease).** This is a progressive disease in which damage to the air sacs prevents them from moving enough oxygen into the bloodstream. "Progressive" means the disease gets worse over time.

- **Late-stage heart failure.** This is a condition in which the heart can't pump enough oxygen-rich blood to meet the body's needs.

- **Cystic fibrosis (CF).** CF is an inherited disease of the secretory glands, including the glands that make mucus and sweat. People who have CF have thick, sticky mucus that collects in their airways. The mucus makes it easy for bacteria to grow. This leads to repeated, serious lung infections. Over time, these infections can severely damage the lungs.

- **Sleep-related breathing disorders** that lead to low levels of oxygen in the blood during sleep, such as sleep apnea.

How Does Oxygen Therapy Work?

Oxygen therapy provides you with extra oxygen, a gas that your body needs to work well. Oxygen comes in different forms and can be delivered to your lungs in several ways.

Oxygen Therapy Systems

Oxygen is supplied in three forms: as compressed gas, as liquid, or as a concentrated form taken from the air.

Compressed oxygen gas is stored under pressure in metal cylinders. The cylinders come in many sizes. Some of the cylinders are small enough to carry around. You can put one on a small wheeled cart or in a shoulder bag or backpack.

Liquid oxygen is very cold. When released from its container, the liquid becomes gas. Liquid oxygen is delivered to your home in a large container. From this container, smaller, portable units can be filled.

The advantage of liquid oxygen is that the storage units need less space than compressed or concentrated oxygen. However, liquid oxygen costs more than the other forms of oxygen. Also, it evaporates easily, so it doesn't last for a long time.

Oxygen concentrators filter out other gases in the air and store only oxygen. Oxygen concentrators come in several sizes, including portable units.

Oxygen concentrators cost less than the other oxygen therapy systems. One reason is because they don't require oxygen refills. However, oxygen concentrators are powered by electricity. Thus, you'll need a backup supply of oxygen in case of a power outage.

Delivery Devices

Most often, oxygen is given through a nasal cannula. A nasal cannula consists of two small plastic tubes, or prongs, that are placed in both nostrils.

To help hold the cannula in place, you can put the longer ends of it over your ears or attach them to a special kind of eyeglass frame that helps hide the tubing. The tubing then comes around the back of your ears and under your chin, where it joins together. From there, it's attached to the tube from the oxygen container.

The image shows how a nasal cannula and portable oxygen container are attached to a patient.

You might use a face mask instead of a nasal cannula. The mask fits over your mouth and nose. This method mainly is used if you need a high flow rate of oxygen or if your nose is clogged from a cold.

The face mask is held in place with a strap that goes around your head or with tubes that fit around your ears. The oxygen is delivered through a tube that attaches to the front of the mask.

129

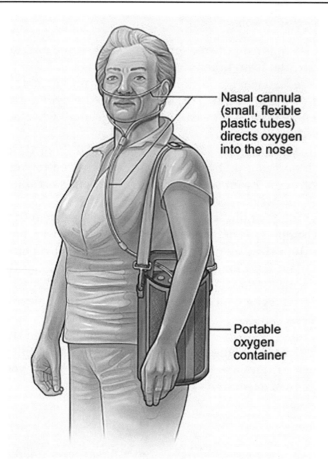

Nasal cannula
(small, flexible
plastic tubes)
directs oxygen
into the nose

Portable
oxygen
container

Figure 15.1. Oxygen Delivery Device

Oxygen also can be delivered through a small tube inserted into your windpipe through the front of your neck. Your doctor will use a needle or small incision (cut) to place the tube. Oxygen delivered this way is called transtracheal oxygen therapy.

If you're getting transtracheal oxygen therapy, you'll need to have a humidifier attached to your oxygen system. This is because the oxygen doesn't pass through your nose or mouth like it does with the other delivery systems. A humidifier adds moisture to the oxygen and prevents your airways from getting too dry.

Oxygen also can be delivered through machines that support breathing, such as CPAP (continuous positive airway pressure) devices or ventilators.

What to Expect before Oxygen Therapy?

During an emergency—such as a serious accident, possible heart attack, or other life-threatening event—you might be started on oxygen therapy right away.

Otherwise, your doctor will decide whether you need oxygen therapy based on test results. An arterial blood gas test and a pulse oximetry test can measure the amount of oxygen in your blood.

For an arterial blood gas test, a small needle is inserted into an artery, usually in your wrist. A sample of blood is taken from the artery. The sample is then sent to a laboratory, where its oxygen level is measured.

For a pulse oximetry test, a small sensor is attached to your fingertip or toe. The sensor uses light to estimate how much oxygen is in your blood.

If the tests show that your blood oxygen level is low, your doctor may prescribe oxygen therapy. In the prescription, your doctor will include the number of liters of oxygen per minute that you need (oxygen flow rate). He or she also will include how often you need to use the oxygen (frequency of use).

Frequency of use includes when and for how long you should use the oxygen. Depending on your condition and blood oxygen level, you may need oxygen only at certain times, such as during sleep or while exercising.

If your doctor prescribes home oxygen therapy, he or she can help you find a home equipment provider. The provider will give you the equipment and other supplies you need.

What to Expect during Oxygen Therapy?

During an emergency—such as a serious accident, possible heart attack, or other life-threatening event—you might be started on oxygen therapy right away.

While you're in the hospital, your doctor will check on you to make sure you're getting the right amount of oxygen. Nurses or respiratory therapists also may assist with the oxygen therapy.

If you're having oxygen therapy at home, a home equipment provider will help you set up the oxygen therapy equipment at your house.

Trained staff will show you how to use and take care of the equipment. They'll supply the oxygen and teach you how to safely handle it.

Because oxygen poses a fire risk, you'll need to take certain safety steps. Oxygen isn't explosive, but it can worsen a fire. In the presence of oxygen, a small fire can quickly get out of control. Also, the cylinder that compressed oxygen gas comes in can explode if it's exposed to heat.

Your home equipment provider will give you a complete list of safety steps that you'll need to follow at home and in public. For example, while on oxygen, you should:

- Never smoke or be around people who are smoking

- Never use paint thinners, cleaning fluids, gasoline, aerosol sprays, and other flammable materials

- Stay at least 5 feet away from gas stoves, candles, and other heat sources

When you're not using the oxygen, keep it in a large, airy room. Never store compressed oxygen gas cylinders and liquid oxygen containers in small, enclosed places, such as in closets, behind curtains, or under clothes.

Oxygen containers let off small amounts of oxygen. These small amounts can build up to harmful levels if they're allowed to escape into small spaces.

What Are the Risks of Oxygen Therapy?

Oxygen therapy can cause complications and side effects. These problems might include a dry or bloody nose, skin irritation from the nasal cannula or face mask, fatigue (tiredness), and morning headaches.

If these problems persist, tell your doctor and home equipment provider. Depending on the problem, your doctor may need to change your oxygen flow rate or the length of time you're using the oxygen.

If nose dryness is a problem, your doctor may recommend a nasal spray or have a humidifier added to your oxygen equipment.

If you have an uncomfortable nasal cannula or face mask, your home equipment provider can help you find a device that fits better. Your provider also can recommend over-the-counter gels and devices that are designed to lessen skin irritation.

Complications from transtracheal oxygen therapy can be more serious. With this type of oxygen therapy, oxygen is delivered through a tube inserted into your windpipe through the front of your neck.

With transtracheal oxygen therapy:

- Mucus balls might develop on the tube inside the windpipe. Mucus balls tend to form as a result of the oxygen drying out the airways. Mucus balls can cause coughing and clog the windpipe or tube.

- Problems with the tube slipping or breaking.

- Infection.

- Injury to the lining of the windpipe.

Proper medical care and correct handling of the tube and other supplies may reduce the risk of complications.

Other Risks

In certain people, oxygen therapy may suppress the drive to breathe, affecting how well the respiratory system works. This is managed by adjusting the oxygen flow rate.

Oxygen poses a fire risk, so you'll need to take certain safety steps. Oxygen itself isn't explosive, but it can worsen a fire. In the presence of oxygen, a small fire can quickly get out of control. Also, the cylinder that compressed oxygen gas comes in might explode if exposed to heat.

Your home equipment provider will give you a complete list of safety steps you'll need to take at home and when out in public.

For example, when you're not using the oxygen, keep it in an airy room. Never store compressed oxygen gas cylinders and liquid oxygen containers in small, enclosed places, such as in closets, behind curtains, or under clothes.

Oxygen containers let off small amounts of oxygen. These small amounts can build up to harmful levels if they're allowed to escape into small spaces.

Living with Oxygen Therapy

Oxygen therapy helps many people function better and be more active. It also may help:

- Decrease shortness of breath and fatigue (tiredness)

- Improve sleep in some people who have sleep-related breathing disorders

- Increase the lifespan of some people who have COPD

Although you may need oxygen therapy continuously, or for long periods, it doesn't have to limit your daily routine. Portable oxygen units can make it easier for you to move around and do many daily activities. Talk with your doctor if you have questions about whether certain activities are safe for you.

Portable oxygen units also can make it easier for you to travel. Often, the rules for traveling with oxygen vary depending on the transportation carrier (for example, the airline or bus company). If you need oxygen while traveling, plan in advance. Contact your transportation carrier to find out their specific rules.

Also, talk with your doctor and home equipment provider if you're planning to travel. They can help you plan for your oxygen needs and fill out any required medical forms.

Ongoing Care

To make sure you're getting the full benefits of oxygen therapy, visit your doctor regularly. Your doctor can check your progress and adjust your oxygen therapy as needed.

Never change the amount of oxygen you're taking or adjust the flow rate of your oxygen on your own. Discuss any problems or side effects with your doctor first. He or she may recommend adjusting your treatment.

Talk with your doctor about when you should contact him or her or seek emergency medical care. Your doctor can advise you about what to do if you have:

- Increased shortness of breath, wheezing, or other changes from your usual breathing.

- Fever, increased mucus production, or other symptoms of an infection.

- A blue tint to your lips or fingernails. This is a sign that your body isn't getting enough oxygen.

- Confusion, restlessness, or more anxiety than usual.

During an emergency, go to your nearest hospital emergency room or call 9–1–1. You might want to wear a medical identification (ID) bracelet or necklace to alert others to your medical needs.

Chapter 16

Diet-Based Therapies

Chapter Contents

Section 16.1

Gerson Therapy

Text in this section is excerpted from "Gerson Therapy (PDQ®) –
Questions and Answers About the Gerson Therapy," National Cancer
Institute (NCI), January 7, 2015.

What is the Gerson therapy?

The Gerson therapy has been used by some people to treat cancer
and other diseases. It is based on the role of minerals, enzymes, and
other dietary factors. There are 3 key parts to the therapy:

1. Diet: Organic fruits, vegetables, and whole grains to give the
   body plenty of vitamins, minerals, enzymes, and other nutrients. The fruits and vegetables are low in sodium (salt) and
   high in potassium.

2. Supplementation: The addition of certain substances to the
   diet to help correct cell metabolism (the chemical changes that
   take place in a cell to make energy and basic materials needed
   for the body's life processes).

3. Detoxification: Treatments, including enemas, to remove toxic
   (harmful) substances from the body.

What is the history of the discovery and use of the Gerson therapy as a complementary or alternative treatment?

The Gerson therapy was named after Dr. Max B. Gerson (1881–
1959), who first used it to treat his migraine headaches. In the 1930s,
Dr. Gerson's therapy became known to the public as a treatment for a
type of tuberculosis (TB). The Gerson therapy was later used to treat
other conditions, including cancer.

What is the theory behind the claim that the Gerson therapy is useful in treating cancer?

The Gerson therapy is based on the idea that cancer develops when
there are changes in cell metabolism because of the buildup of toxic

substances in the body. Dr. Gerson said the disease process makes more toxins and the liver becomes overworked. According to Dr. Gerson, people with cancer also have too much sodium and too little potassium in the cells in their bodies, which causes tissue damage and weakened organs.

The goal of the Gerson therapy is to restore the body to health by repairing the liver and returning the metabolism to its normal state. According to Dr. Gerson, this can be done by removing toxins from the body and building up the immune system with diet and supplements. The enemas are said to widen the bile ducts of the liver so toxins can be released. According to Dr. Gerson, the liver is further overworked as the treatment regimen breaks down cancer cells and rids the body of toxins. Pancreatic enzymes are given to decrease the demands on the weakened liver and pancreas to make enzymes for digestion. An organic diet and nutritional supplements are used to boost the immune system and support the body as the regimen cleans the body of toxins. Foods low in sodium and high in potassium are said to help correct the tissue damage caused by having too much sodium in the cells.

How is the Gerson therapy administered?

The Gerson therapy requires that the many details of its treatment plan be followed exactly. Some key parts of the regimen include the following:

- Drinking 13 glasses of juice a day. The juice must be freshly made from organic fruits and vegetables and be taken once every hour.

- Eating vegetarian meals of organically grown fruits, vegetables, and whole grains.

- Taking a number of supplements, including:

  - Potassium.

  - Lugol's solution (potassium iodide, iodine, and water).

  - Coenzyme Q10 injected with vitamin B12. (The original regimen used crude liver extract instead of coenzyme Q10.)

  - Vitamins A, C, and B3 (niacin).

  - Flaxseed oil.

  - Pancreatic enzymes.

  - Pepsin (a stomach enzyme).

- Taking coffee or chamomile enemas regularly to remove toxins from the body.

- Preparing food without salt, spices, or oils, and without using aluminum cookware or utensils.

Have any preclinical (laboratory or animal) studies been conducted using the Gerson therapy?

No results of laboratory or animal studies have been published in scientific journals.

Have any clinical trials (research studies with people) of the Gerson therapy been conducted?

Most of the published information on the use of the Gerson therapy reports on retrospective studies (reviews of past cases). Dr. Gerson published case histories (detailed reports of the diagnosis, treatment, and follow-up of individual patients) of 50 of his patients. He treated several different types of cancer in his practice. The reports include Dr. Gerson's notes, with some X-rays of the patients over time. The follow-up was contact with patients by mail or phone and included anecdotal reports (incomplete descriptions of the medical and treatment histories of one or more patients).

In 1947 and 1959, the National Cancer Institute (NCI) reviewed the cases of a total of 60 patients treated by Dr. Gerson. The NCI found that the available information did not prove the regimen had benefit. The following studies of the Gerson therapy were published:

- In 1983–1984, a retrospective study of 38 patients treated with the Gerson therapy was done. Medical records were not available to the authors of the study; information came from patient interviews. These case reviews did not provide information that supports the usefulness of the Gerson therapy for treating cancer.

- In 1990, a study of a diet regimen similar to the Gerson therapy was done in Austria. The patients received standard treatment along with the special diet. The authors of the study reported that the diet appeared to help patients live longer than usual and have fewer side effects. The authors said it needed further study.

- In 1995, the Gerson Research Organization did a retrospective study of their melanoma patients who were treated with the Gerson therapy. The study reported that patients who had stage III or stage IV melanoma lived longer than usual for patients with these stages of melanoma. There have been no clinical trials that support the findings of this retrospective study.

- A case review of 6 patients with metastatic cancer who used the Gerson therapy reported that the regimen helped patients in some ways, both physically and psychologically. Based on these results, the reviewers recommended that clinical trials of the Gerson therapy be conducted.

Have any side effects or risks been reported from use of the Gerson therapy?

Reports of three deaths that may be related to coffee enemas have been published. Taking too many enemas of any kind can cause changes in normal blood chemistry, chemicals that occur naturally in the body and keep the muscles, heart, and other organs working properly.

Is the Gerson therapy approved by the U.S. Food and Drug Administration (FDA) for use as a cancer treatment in the United States?

The Gerson therapy has not been approved by the FDA for use as a treatment for cancer or any other disease.

For most cancer patients, nutrition guidelines include eating a well-balanced diet with plenty of fruits, vegetables, and whole-grain products. However, general guidelines such as these may have to be changed to meet the specific needs of an individual patient. Patients should talk with their health care providers about an appropriate diet to follow.

Section 16.2

Vegetarianism

Text in this section begins with excerpts from "Vegetarian Eating,"
Office on Women's Health (OWH) at U.S. Department of Health and
Human Services (HHS), November 5, 2013;
Text in this section beginning with "Some tips for combining good
nutrition and physical activity," is excerpted from "Healthy eating
for an active lifestyle," United States Department of Agriculture
(USDA), March 2013.

You may wonder what it means to be vegetarian, and you may
have even considered going meatless. Well, vegetarianism can be quite
healthy if you plan carefully and make sure to eat a variety of different
foods.

Types of vegetarians

There are three main types of vegetarians. They are named for the
types of food they eat:

Lacto-ovo vegetarians eat:

- Plant-based foods

- Eggs

- Dairy products like milk

Lacto-vegetarians eat:

- Plant-based foods

- No eggs

- Dairy products

Vegans eat:

- Plant-based foods

- No eggs

- No dairy products

Some people even try just cutting out meat sometimes. They may not be official vegetarians, but they still can get the great health benefits of eating more fruits, veggies, and plant sources of protein.

Healthy eating for vegetarians

If you plan well, you can get all the nutrients you need from vegetarian foods. But dairy products are good sources of calcium, vitamin D, and the protein you need. And, eggs are a good source of vitamin B-12 and protein. So if you don't eat dairy products or eggs, you need to look elsewhere for these nutrients. Vegetarians also need to make sure that they get enough iron and zinc.

You can learn more about healthy vegetarian eating from the Web site ChooseMyPlate.gov. A dietitian can also help you come up with a vegetarian eating plan that provides you with the nutrients you need during your teen years. It's a good idea to tell your doctor if you are vegetarian, so he or she can monitor your growth. You also can ask your doctor or dietitian if you should take a vitamin and mineral supplement.

Here are some non-animal sources of nutrients that vegetarians need to make sure they get enough of:

Protein

- Tofu and other soy-based products

- Beans, peas, and lentils

- Peanuts, seeds, and nuts

- Grains

Keep in mind that no one plant food has all the amino acids your body needs. (Amino acids are the building blocks your body uses to make proteins.) So, to get all the amino acids you need, you have to eat a variety of plant foods over the course of your day. For example, eating beans and brown rice will give you complete proteins because each food contains the amino acids that the other food lacks.

Vitamin B-12

- Fortified soy and rice drinks

- Some fortified cereals

- Some meat replacement products

- Some types of nutritional yeast

Vitamin D

- Some fortified cereals
- Some fortified soy drinks, rice drinks, and orange juice
- Some fortified cereals
- Some fortified margarines

Calcium

- Tofu (if made with calcium)
- Some fortified soy drinks, rice drinks, and juices
- Some fortified cereals
- Chinese cabbage, bok choy, broccoli, kale, and collard greens

Keep in mind that vegetable products are not as good a source of calcium as milk. You will have to eat many more veggies than you would have to drink milk to get enough calcium.

Iron

- Some fortified breakfast cereals
- Green leafy vegetables, such as spinach and turnip greens
- Cooked dry beans (such as kidney beans and pinto beans) and peas (such as black-eyed peas)
- Dried fruit, like apricots, prunes, and raisins
- Tofu
- Enriched and whole grain breads

Eating foods with vitamin C, such as oranges, tomatoes, and grape-fruit, can help your body absorb iron.

Omega-3 fatty acids (n-3 fatty acids)

- Soy milks and breakfast bars with added DHA (a type of n-3 fatty acid)
- Flaxseed
- Walnuts
- Canola oil
- Soy products like tofu

Zinc

- Whole grain bread

- Cooked dry beans (such as kidney beans and pinto beans) and peas (such as black-eyed peas)

- Nuts

- Oatmeal

- Tofu

Some tips for combining good nutrition and physical activity

For youth and adults engaging in physical activity and sports, healthy eating is essential for optimizing performance. Combining good nutrition with physical activity can lead to a healthier lifestyle.

- **Maximize with nutrient-packed foods**

Give your body the nutrients it needs by eating a variety of nutrient-packed food, including whole grains, lean protein, fruits and vegetables, and low-fat or fat-free dairy. Eat less food high in solid fats, added sugars, and sodium (salt).

- **Energize with grains**

Your body's quickest energy source comes from foods such as bread, pasta, oatmeal, cereals, and tortillas. Be sure to make at least half of your grain food choices whole-grain foods like whole-wheat bread or pasta and brown rice.

- **Power up with protein**

Protein is essential for building and repairing muscle. Choose lean or low-fat cuts of beef or pork, and skinless chicken or turkey. Get your protein from seafood twice a week. Quality protein sources come from plant-based foods, too.

- **Mix it up with plant protein foods**

Variety is great! Choose beans and peas (kidney, pinto, black, or white beans; split peas; chickpeas; hummus), soy products (tofu, tempeh, veggie burgers), and unsalted nuts and seeds.

143

• **Vary your fruits and vegetables**

Get the nutrients your body needs by eating a variety of colors, in various ways. Try blue, red, or black berries; red and yellow peppers; and dark greens like spinach and kale. Choose fresh, frozen, low-sodium canned, dried, or 100 percent juice options.

• **Don't forget dairy**

Foods like fat-free and low-fat milk, cheese, yogurt, and fortified soy beverages (soymilk) help to build and maintain strong bones needed for everyday activities.

• **Drink water**

Stay hydrated by drinking water instead of sugary drinks. Keep a reusable water bottle with you to always have water on hand.

Section 16.3

Detoxification Diets

"Detoxification," © 2015 Omnigraphics, Inc.
Reviewed September 2015.

Detoxification

Detoxification is concerned with identifying and eliminating toxic substances that may accumulate in the human body. It is a common technique used in alternative medicine for the purpose of curing disease and improving general health. Detoxification has been used for centuries by practitioners of the Ayurvedic and Chinese medical systems, who have taught that eating certain types of food can help eliminate toxins from the body and restore good health. Complementary and alternative medicine (CAM) practitioners often recommend detoxification therapies for people with allergies, anxiety, asthma, cancer, depression, diabetes, headaches, heart disease, obesity, and other chronic conditions. People who are exposed to high levels of toxic substances in the environment due to industrial accidents or pollution may also benefit from detoxification therapy.

Detoxification programs have increased in popularity in recent years. The trend may have started with celebrities touting the benefits of various regimens designed to cleanse the body of chemicals and impurities, cure chronic illnesses, promote weight loss, or end addictions. Such programs have quickly gained adherents among ordinary people hoping to reverse the ill effects of fast food, sugar, caffeine, and other dietary excesses.

Detoxification has emerged as a major nutrition and health industry worldwide, with hundreds of different diets, supplements, and holiday retreats promising to help people cleanse their bodies of toxins. The options range from simple diets based on cucumber or grapefruit juice to elaborate vacation packages offering fasts, mud baths, and colonic irrigation. Many people sign up for detoxification therapies as inpatients in order to speed up the process and gain the reassurance of having a practitioner monitor their treatment.

The Idea behind Detoxification

From pollution in the air to pesticides on crops and growth hormones in meat, people are exposed to a wide variety of organic pollutants and chemical contaminants every day. While the human body naturally eliminates many harmful substances in wastes, some toxic substances can build up in fat cells and other living tissues. Heavy metals, persistent organic pollutants, and fat-soluble chemicals, for instance, tend to bioaccumulate and remain in the body's cells for a long time. The buildup of toxins can contribute to serious physiological problems, including cancer and diseases of the kidneys, liver, lungs, and heart. Detoxification programs attempt to address these problems by ridding the body of toxins that pose health risks. Detoxification thus holds an obvious appeal for many people. They like the idea that following a special diet can remove harmful substances from the body and eliminate the health risks associated with them.

The Science behind Detoxification

The mainstream medical community, however, tends to regard detoxification as a myth. Although toxins are undoubtedly present in the environment, they argue that the body is capable of eliminating those encountered by a typical person through natural mechanisms involving the skin, lungs, liver, and kidneys. If a person is exposed to such high levels of toxic substances that their bodily systems cannot process and eliminate them, then they are likely to require medical attention. Critics say that there is no scientific evidence to substantiate the lofty claims made by promoters of various detoxification programs. They argue that no special diet, supplement, or regimen can eliminate all toxins from the body, and that most of these programs are unlikely to lead to significant improvements in health.

Critics point out that the makers of detoxification products—ranging from smoothies to shampoos—do not specify exactly what toxins the products purportedly eliminate. As a result, a patient's bodily levels of these toxins cannot be measured before and after they undergo treatment in order to prove the products' efficacy. The only kind of medically validated detoxification programs are those intended to help people overcome alcohol or drug addictions.

Types of Detoxification Programs

Although there are many different detoxification diets and programs available, most are based on the same principles. They encourage people to restrict their exposure to chemicals for a specific period of time (usually five to seven days) while also consuming foods or supplements that are believed to stimulate the release of stored toxins from the body. Many detoxification diets begin with a period of fasting, which is intended to rest the organs and reset the digestive system. Ancient Chinese and Ayurvedic medical traditions claim that regular fasting cleanses the digestive tract and enhances health and longevity.

Rather than restricting food intake in general, other detoxification diets focus on eliminating certain foods that are believed to increase the toxin load in the body—such alcohol, caffeine, refined sugar, saturated fats, and processed grains. Along the same lines, some detoxification programs recommend minimizing exposure to household cleaners, personal care products, lawn treatments, and other common environmental sources of toxic chemicals, and replacing them with natural alternatives when possible.

After reducing the exposure to toxins, the next step in many detoxification programs involves stimulating the body to eliminate built-up toxins from the organs and tissues. Common strategies for achieving this goal include drinking lots of water to improve kidney function, eating foods high in fiber to improve colon function, exercising to increase blood circulation, sitting in a sauna to excrete toxins through sweating, getting a massage to release toxins in muscles and fat tissues, exfoliating to remove dead skin and chelation therapy to aid the body of heavy metals. Body therapies may also be presented including massage therapy, Shiatsu, acupressure, manual lymph drainage therapy, etc.

Finally, many detoxification programs recommend refuelling the body with healthy nutrients. Although countless detox diet plans exist, most tend to emphasize a high-fiber diet full of organic fruits and vegetables and lots of water. Some programs promote the use of dietary supplements to aid in the detoxification process. Many of these supplements are diuretics or laxatives made from herbal extracts. They should be used with care, as diuretics can cause dehydration and fatigue, while laxatives can lead to frequent bowel movements and malabsorption of nutrients.

The Pros and Cons of Detoxification

Despite the disapproval of the mainstream medical community, millions of people try detoxification programs each year, and some of them swear that they lose weight, feel better, or experience other health benefits. Some aspects of the typical detox diet can lead to healthier food choices and more mindful eating. Many people abstain from alcohol, tobacco, and caffeine during detoxification, for instance, and increase their consumption of fruits, vegetables, whole grains, and water. Completing a detoxification program can help people break bad eating habits by retraining the palate to enjoy whole foods and reject processed foods. It can also help people recover from disorders like emotional eating or binge eating.

By temporarily limiting food choices, detox diets can also help people consume fewer calories and lose weight. In many cases, though, the weight loss takes the form of water and stored glycogen, and people will typically regain the pounds once they resume a normal eating pattern. The restrictions in some detoxification plans can also create nutritional deficiencies, especially for teenagers, pregnant or lactating women, or people with health conditions like diabetes or cardiovascular disease. Doctors warn that detox diets—and especially those that involve fasting—can be harmful to the health and well-being of these groups of people. Finally, detoxification programs and supplements can be very expensive.

References:

1. Smith, Deborahann. "10 Ways to Detoxify Your Body." *Gaiam Life,* 2014.

2. Torrens, Kerry. "What Is a Detox Diet?" BBC *GoodFood,* n.d.

Chapter 17

Mind-Body Medicine

Chapter Contents

Section 17.1

Mind-Body Medicine: An Overview

This section includes excerpts from "Complementary Health
Approaches: Mind And Body Practices," National Institutes
of Health (NIH), September 2013; text from "Complementary
Health Approaches: Safety of Mind And Body Practices," National
Institutes of Health (NIH), September 2013; and text from "5 Tips
on Safety of Mind and Body Practices for Children and Teens,"
National Center for Complementary and Integrative Health
(NCCIH), June 4, 2015.

Most complementary health approaches fall into one of two categories: natural products or mind and body practices. This section
addresses mind and body practices.

Mind and body practices are a large and varied group of procedures
performed or taught by a trained practitioner or teacher.

Most meditation techniques, including transcendental meditation and mindfulness meditation, involve various approaches in which
a person learns to focus attention. Meditation has been studied for
several types of health problems, especially high blood pressure, other
cardiovascular disorders, and substance abuse disorders.

Reiki is a complementary approach in which practitioners place
their hands lightly on or just above a person, with the goal of facilitating the person's own healing response. There is a lack of high-quality
research on Reiki.

Relaxation techniques, such as breathing exercises, guided imagery, and progressive muscle relaxation, are designed to produce the
body's natural relaxation response. They have been studied for anxiety,
depression, insomnia, and other conditions.

The various styles of **yoga** used for health purposes typically combine physical postures or movement, breathing techniques, and meditation. Yoga has been studied for low-back pain, depression, arthritis,
and other conditions.

Commonly Used Practices

Several mind and body practices were among the complementary health approaches most commonly used by adults in the 2007 National Health Interview Survey. They included deep breathing, meditation, chiropractic and osteopathic manipulation, massage, yoga, progressive relaxation, and guided imagery.

Working with a Practitioner

Mind and body practices usually involve working with a practitioner or teacher. It is important to select a complementary health practitioner as carefully as you would select a conventional health care provider.

Tell all your health care providers about any complementary health practitioners you're seeing and any complementary approaches you're using to treat health problems.

Safety of Mind and Body Practices

As with any treatment, it is important to consider safety before using complementary health approaches. Safety depends on the specific approach, and each complementary product or practice should be considered on its own.

If You Have a Medical Condition

Complementary health approaches that are safe for healthy people may not be safe for people with some medical conditions. If you have any health problems, always talk with your health care provider before starting a new complementary approach. If the approach involves working with a practitioner or taking classes with an instructor, discuss your health condition with that person, too.

How Safe Are Mind and Body Practices?

Meditation is generally considered to be safe for healthy people. However, people with health conditions should talk with their health care providers before starting any type of meditation and make their meditation instructor aware of their condition.

Relaxation techniques are considered safe for healthy people. However, people with health problems should discuss the use of these techniques with their health care providers. It's particularly important for people with heart disease to consult their health care providers before using progressive muscle relaxation.

Yoga is generally safe for healthy people when practiced appropriately under the guidance of a well-trained instructor. However, people who have certain medical conditions, such as high blood pressure, glaucoma, or sciatica, need to modify or avoid some yoga poses.

5 Tips on Safety of Mind and Body Practices for Children and Teens

Nearly 12 percent of children (about 1 in 9) in the United States are using some form of complementary health product or practice, such as chiropractic care, deep breathing, and yoga. Mind and body interventions are physical techniques usually administered by a trained practitioner or teacher to help improve health and well-being, but there are things older kids can do on their own (or with the help of a parent or caregiver) such as practicing relaxation techniques and deep breathing, especially to help manage pain.

While most mind and body practices, in general, appear to be safe if used appropriately, the limited research done on the safety of mind and body practices for children has found the following:

1. Acupuncture appears to be safe for most children when performed by appropriately trained practitioners, but a 2011 research review concluded that unwanted side effects can occur when acupuncture is done by poorly trained practitioners.

2. Massage therapy is one of the most commonly reported complementary health practices for children with cancer, but direct pressure over a tumor should be avoided.

3. Relaxation techniques are generally considered safe for healthy people, including children. However, there have been rare reports that certain relaxation techniques might cause or worsen symptoms in people with epilepsy or certain psychiatric conditions, or with a history of abuse or trauma.

4. Severe complications can occur from spinal manipulation used to treat infants and children, but they appear to be rare. Spinal manipulation should never be relied on as a primary treatment for serious conditions, such as cancer.

5. There are numerous ongoing studies to determine the benefits and harms of these and other mind and body practices in children.

It's important that parents talk with their child's health care provider about any complementary health approach that is being used or considered, and parents should encourage their teenagers to do the same.

Section 17.2

Meditation

Text in this section is excerpted from "Meditation: What You Need To Know," National Center for Complementary and Integrative Health (NCCIH), November 2014.

Meditation: What You Need to Know

What's the Bottom Line?

How much do we know about meditation?

Many studies have been conducted to look at how meditation may be helpful for a variety of conditions, such as high blood pressure, certain psychological disorders, and pain. A number of studies also have helped researchers learn how meditation might work and how it affects the brain.

What do we know about the effectiveness of meditation?

Research suggests that practicing meditation may reduce blood pressure, symptoms of irritable bowel syndrome, anxiety and depression, insomnia, and the incidence, duration, and severity of acute respiratory illnesses (such as influenza). Evidence about its effectiveness for pain and as a smoking-cessation treatment is uncertain.

What do we know about the safety of meditation?

Meditation is generally considered to be safe for healthy people. However, people with physical limitations may not be able to participate in certain meditative practices involving movement.

What Is Meditation?

Meditation is a mind and body practice that has a long history of use for increasing calmness and physical relaxation, improving psychological balance, coping with illness, and enhancing overall health and well-being. Mind and body practices focus on the interactions among the brain, mind, body, and behavior.

There are many types of meditation, but most have four elements in common: a quiet location with as few distractions as possible; a specific, comfortable posture (sitting, lying down, walking, or in other positions); a focus of attention (a specially chosen word or set of words, an object, or the sensations of the breath); and an open attitude (letting distractions come and go naturally without judging them).

What the Science Says about the Effectiveness of Meditation

Many studies have investigated meditation for different conditions, and there's evidence that it may reduce blood pressure as well as symptoms of irritable bowel syndrome and flare-ups in people who have had ulcerative colitis. It may ease symptoms of anxiety and depression, and may help people with insomnia. Meditation also may lower the incidence, duration, and severity of acute respiratory illnesses (such as influenza).

For High Blood Pressure

- Results of a 2009 NCCIH-funded trial involving 298 university students suggest that practicing Transcendental Meditation may lower the blood pressure of people at increased risk of developing high blood pressure.

- The findings also suggested that practicing meditation can help with psychological distress, anxiety, depression, anger/hostility, and coping ability.

- A literature review and scientific statement from the American Heart Association suggest that evidence supports the use of Transcendental Meditation (TM) to lower blood pressure. However, the review indicates that it's uncertain whether TM is truly superior to other meditation techniques in terms of blood-pressure lowering because there are few head-to-head studies.

For Irritable Bowel Syndrome

- Results of a 2011 NCCIH-funded clinical trial that enrolled 75 women suggest that practicing mindfulness meditation for 8 weeks reduces the severity of irritable bowel syndrome (IBS) symptoms.

- A 2013 review concluded that mindfulness training improved IBS patients' pain and quality of life but not their depression or anxiety. The amount of improvement was small.

For Ulcerative Colitis

- In a 2014 pilot study, 55 adults with ulcerative colitis in remission were divided into two groups. For 8 weeks, one group learned and practiced mindfulness-based stress reduction (MBSR) while the other group practiced a placebo procedure. Six and 12 months later, there were no significant differences between the 2 groups in the course of the disease, markers of inflammation, or any psychological measure except perceived stress during flare-ups. The researchers concluded that MBSR might help people in remission from moderate to moderately severe disease—and maybe reduce rates of flare-up from stress.

For Anxiety, Depression, and Insomnia

- A 2014 literature review of 47 trials in 3,515 participants suggests that mindfulness meditation programs show moderate evidence of improving anxiety and depression. But the researchers found no evidence that meditation changed health-related behaviors affected by stress, such as substance abuse and sleep.

- A 2012 systematic review and meta-analysis of 36 randomized controlled trials found that 25 of them reported statistically superior outcomes for symptoms of anxiety in the meditation groups compared to control groups.

- In a small, NCCIH-funded study, 54 adults with chronic insomnia learned mindfulness-based stress reduction (MBSR), a form of MBSR specially adapted to deal with insomnia (mindfulness-based therapy for insomnia, or MBTI), or a self-monitoring program. Both meditation-based programs aided sleep, with MBTI providing a significantly greater reduction in insomnia severity compared with MBSR.

155

For Smoking Cessation

• Findings from a 2013 systematic review suggest that meditation-based therapies may help people quit smoking; however, the small number of available studies is insufficient to determine rigorously if meditation is effective for this.

• A 2011 randomized controlled trial comparing mindfulness training with a standard behavioral smoking cessation treatment found that individuals who received mindfulness training showed a greater rate of reduction in cigarette use immediately after treatment and at 17-week followup.

• Results of a 2013 brain imaging study suggest that mindful attention reduced the craving to smoke, and also that it reduced activity in a craving-related region of the brain.

• However, in a second 2013 brain imaging study, researchers observed that a 2-week course of meditation (5 hours total) significantly reduced smoking, compared with relaxation training, and that it increased activity in brain areas associated with craving.

Other Conditions

• Results from a 2011 NCCIH-funded study of 279 adults who participated in an 8-week Mindfulness-Based Stress Reduction (MBSR) program found that changes in spirituality were associated with better mental health and quality of life.

• Data from a 2013 literature review concluded that practicing mindfulness meditation may enhance immune function, particularly among patients with cancer or HIV/AIDS.

• Guidelines from the American College of Chest Physicians published in 2013 suggest that MBSR and meditation may help to reduce stress, anxiety, pain, and depression while enhancing mood and self-esteem in people with lung cancer.

• Clinical practice guidelines issued in 2014 by the Society for Integrative Oncology (SIC) recommend meditation as supportive care to reduce stress, anxiety, depression, and fatigue in patients treated for breast cancer. The SIC also recommends its use to improve quality of life in these people.

• Meditation-based programs may be helpful in reducing common menopausal symptoms, including the frequency and intensity of hot flashes, sleep and mood disturbances, stress, and muscle and joint pain. However, differences in study designs mean that no firm conclusions can be drawn.

- Because only a few studies have been conducted on the effects of meditation for attention deficit hyperactivity disorder (ADHD), there isn't sufficient evidence to support its use for this condition.

- A 2014 literature review and meta-analysis suggested that mind and body practices, including meditation, reduce chemical identifiers of inflammation and show promise in helping to regulate the immune system.

- Results from a 2013 NCCIH-supported study involving 49 adults suggest that 8 weeks of mindfulness training may reduce stress-induced inflammation better than a health program that includes physical activity, education about diet, and music therapy.

- There's some evidence that forms of meditation may help with chronic pain, but research has shown mixed results.

Meditation and the Brain

Some research suggests that meditation may physically change the brain and body and could potentially help to improve many health problems and promote healthy behaviors.

- In a 2012 study, researchers compared brain images from 50 adult meditators and 50 adult non-meditators. Results suggested that people who practiced meditation for many years have more folds in the outer layer of the brain. This process (called gyrification) may increase the brain's ability to process information.

- A 2013 review of three clinical studies suggests that meditation may slow, stall, or even reverse changes that take place in the brain due to normal aging.

- Results from a 2012 NCCIH-funded study suggest that meditation can affect activity in the amygdala (a part of the brain involved in processing emotions), and that different types of meditation can affect the amygdala differently even when the person is not meditating.

- Research about meditation's ability to reduce pain has produced mixed results. However, in some studies scientists suggest

157

that meditation activates certain areas of the brain in response to pain.

What the Science Says about Safety and Side Effects of Meditation

- Meditation is generally considered to be safe for healthy people.

- People with physical limitations may not be able to participate in certain meditative practices involving movement. People with physical health conditions should speak with their health care providers before starting a meditative practice, and make their meditation instructor aware of their condition.

- There have been rare reports that meditation could cause or worsen symptoms in people with certain psychiatric problems like anxiety and depression. People with existing mental health conditions should speak with their health care providers before starting a meditative practice, and make their meditation instructor aware of their condition.

More to Consider

- Don't use meditation to replace conventional care or as a reason to postpone seeing a health care provider about a medical problem.

- Ask about the training and experience of the meditation instructor you are considering.

- Help your health care providers give you better coordinated and safe care by telling them about all the health approaches you use. Give them a full picture of what you do to manage your health.

Section 17.3

Music Therapy

Text in this section is excerpted from "Other Treatments for Pain," National Cancer Institute (NCI), April 10, 2014.

Music has been used to relieve pain and anxiety caused by cancer and cancer treatments. Studies have reported that music may work on areas of the brain that increase pleasant feelings and decrease unpleasant responses. Your favorite music may help you the most. Music is more helpful if you begin listening before a procedure than it is during or after a procedure. Music may be used along with pain medicine.

There are two main types of music treatments— music therapy and music medicine:

- Music therapy is given by a trained specialist called a music therapist. The music used may be live or recorded. Therapy may include music improvisation (making up music), song writing and singing, and relaxing to music. The music therapist bases treatment on your needs, such as controlling pain, decreasing anxiety, or learning new coping skills.

- Music medicine is listening to music (usually recorded music) to take attention away from the pain. Music medicine is guided by a medical professional who does not have special training in music therapy.

The use of music for pain related to cancer is still being studied. Music is also used in relaxation exercises.

Step 1. You will need the following:

- An MP3 player, CD player, or iPod.

- Earphones or a headset. (This helps focus the attention better than a speaker does, and avoids disturbing others.)

- A recording of music you like. (Most people like fast, lively music, but some select relaxing music. Others like comedy routines, sporting events, old radio shows, or stories.)

Step 2. Mark time to the music; for example, tap out the rhythm with your finger or nod your head. This helps you think about the music instead of your discomfort.

Step 3. Keep your eyes open and focus on a fixed spot or object. If you wish to close your eyes, picture something about the music.

Step 4. Listen to the music at a comfortable volume. If the discomfort increases, try increasing the volume; decrease the volume when the discomfort decreases.

Step 5. If the music is not helping enough, try adding or changing one or more of the following:

- Massage your body in rhythm to the music.

- Try other music.

- Mark time to the music in more than one manner, such as tapping your foot and finger at the same time.

Many patients have found listening to music to be helpful. It tends to be very popular, probably because playing music is a part of daily life and easy to do. If you are very tired, you may simply listen to the music without marking time or focusing on a spot.

Section 17.4

Prayer and Spirituality

Text in this section begins with excerpts from "Spirituality in Cancer Care (PDQ®)," National Cancer Institute (NCI), May 18, 2015; and text from "Coping with Cancer – Day-to-Day Life," National Cancer Institute (NCI), December 2, 2014.

Religious and spiritual values are important to patients suffering from chronic diseases.

Studies have shown that religious and spiritual values are important to Americans. Most American adults say that they believe in God and that their religious beliefs affect how they live their lives. However, people have different ideas about life after death, belief in miracles, and other religious beliefs. Such beliefs may be based on gender, education, and ethnic background.

Many patients with chronic diseases rely on spiritual or religious beliefs and practices to help them cope with their disease. This is called spiritual coping. Many caregivers also rely on spiritual coping. Each person may have different spiritual needs, depending on cultural and religious traditions. For some seriously ill patients, spiritual well-being may affect how much anxiety they feel about death. For others, it may affect what they decide about end-of-life treatments. Some patients and their family caregivers may want doctors to talk about spiritual concerns, but may feel unsure about how to bring up the subject.

Some studies show that doctors' support of spiritual well-being in very ill patients helps improve their quality of life. Doctors may ask patients which spiritual issues are important to them during treatment as well as near the end of life.

Spirituality and religion may have different meanings.

The terms spirituality and religion are often used in place of each other, but for many people they have different meanings. Religion may be defined as a specific set of beliefs and practices, usually within

161

an organized group. Spirituality may be defined as an individual's sense of peace, purpose, and connection to others, and beliefs about the meaning of life. Spirituality may be found and expressed through an organized religion or in other ways. Patients may think of themselves as spiritual or religious or both.

Serious illness, such as cancer, may cause spiritual distress.

Serious illnesses like cancer may cause patients or family caregivers to have doubts about their beliefs or religious values and cause much spiritual distress. Some studies show that patients with cancer may feel that they are being punished by God or may have a loss of faith after being diagnosed. Other patients may have mild feelings of spiritual distress when coping with cancer. Many people with cancer look more deeply for meaning in their lives. They want to understand their purpose in life or why they got cancer. Spirituality means the way you look at the world and how you make sense of your place in it. Spirituality can include faith or religion, beliefs, values, and "reasons for being."

Having cancer may cause you to think about what you believe, whether or not you're connected to a traditional religion. It's normal to view the experience both negatively and positively at the same time. Some people find that cancer brings more meaning to their faith. Others feel that their faith has let them down and they struggle to understand why they have cancer. For example, they might question their relationship with God.

What It Means to You

Being spiritual can mean different things to everyone. It's a very personal issue. Everyone has their own beliefs about it. Some people find it through religion or faith. Others may be spiritual through meditating, teaching, volunteer work, or reading. It can mean something different for each person. Some people look for a sense of peace or bond with other people. Others seek to forgive themselves or others for past actions.

Your Values May Change

The things you own and your daily duties may seem less important. You may decide to spend more time with loved ones or do something to help others. Or you may take more time to do things in the outdoors or learn about something new. For some, faith can be an important part of both coping with and recovering from any chronic disease.

Finding Comfort and Meaning

If you want to find faith-based or spiritual support, many hospitals have chaplains who are trained to give support to people of different faiths, as well as those who aren't religious at all.

Some ideas that have helped others find comfort and meaning are:

- Praying or meditating

- Reading uplifting stories about the human spirit

- Talking with others with similar experiences

- Taking time alone to reflect on life and relationships

- Writing in a journal

- Finding a special place where you find beauty or a sense of calm

- Taking part in community or social gatherings for support and to support others

Section 17.5

Reiki

Text in this section is excerpted from "Reiki," National Center for
Complementary and Integrative Health (NCCIH), September 2014.

What's the Bottom Line?

How much do we know about Reiki?

We don't know very much because little high-quality research
has been done on Reiki.

What do we know about the effectiveness of Reiki?

Reiki hasn't been clearly shown to be useful for any
health-related purpose.

What do we know about the safety of Reiki?

Reiki hasn't been shown to have any harmful effects.
However, Reiki should not be used to replace conventional care or to postpone seeing a health care provider about
a health problem.

What is Reiki?

Reiki is a complementary health approach in which practitioners
place their hands lightly on or just above a person, with the goal of
facilitating the person's own healing response.

- Reiki is based on an Eastern belief in an energy that supports
  the body's innate or natural healing abilities. However, there
  isn't any scientific evidence that such an energy exists.

- Reiki has been studied for a variety of conditions, including pain,
  anxiety, fatigue, and depression.

What the Science Says about the Effectiveness of Reiki

Several groups of experts have evaluated the evidence on Reiki, and all of them have concluded that it's uncertain whether Reiki is helpful.

Only a small number of studies of Reiki have been completed, and most of them included only a few people. Different studies looked at different health conditions making it hard to compare their results. Many of the studies didn't compare Reiki with both sham (simulated) Reiki and with no treatment. Studies that include both of these comparisons are usually the most informative.

What the Science Says about the Safety of Reiki

Reiki appears to be generally safe. In studies of Reiki, side effects were no more common among participants who received Reiki than among those who didn't receive it.

More to Consider

- Reiki should not be used to replace conventional care or to postpone seeing a health care provider about a health problem. If you have severe or long-lasting symptoms, see your health care provider. You may have a health problem that needs prompt treatment.

- Tell all your health care providers about any complementary health approaches you use. Give them a full picture of what you do to manage your health. This will help ensure coordinated and safe care.

Section 17.6

Relaxation Training

Text in this section is excerpted from "Relaxation Techniques for Health: What You Need To Know," National Center for Complementary and Integrative Health (NCCIH), December 2014.

What's the Bottom Line?

How much do we know about relaxation techniques?

A substantial amount of research has been done on relaxation techniques. However, for many health conditions, the number or size of the studies has been small, and some studies have been of poor quality.

What do we know about the effectiveness of relaxation techniques?

Relaxation techniques may be helpful in managing a variety of health conditions, including **anxiety associated with illnesses or medical procedures, insomnia, labor pain, chemotherapy-induced nausea,** and **temporomandibular joint dysfunction**. Psychological therapies, which may include relaxation techniques, can help manage **chronic headaches and other types of chronic pain in children and adolescents**. Relaxation techniques have also been studied for other conditions, but either they haven't been shown to be useful, research results have been inconsistent, or the evidence is limited.

What do we know about the safety of relaxation techniques?

Relaxation techniques are generally considered safe for healthy people, although there have been a few reports of unpleasant experiences such as increased anxiety. People with serious physical or mental health problems should discuss relaxation techniques with their health care providers.

What Are Relaxation Techniques?

Relaxation techniques include a number of practices such as progressive relaxation, guided imagery, biofeedback, self-hypnosis, and deep breathing exercises. The goal is similar in all: to produce the body's natural relaxation response, characterized by slower breathing, lower blood pressure, and a feeling of increased well-being.

Meditation and practices that include meditation with movement, such as yoga and tai chi, can also promote relaxation.

Stress management programs commonly include relaxation techniques. Relaxation techniques have also been studied to see whether they might be of value in managing various health problems.

The Importance of Practice

Relaxation techniques are skills, and like other skills, they need practice. People who use relaxation techniques frequently are more likely to benefit from them. Regular, frequent practice is particularly important if you're using relaxation techniques to help manage a chronic health problem. Continuing use of relaxation techniques is more effective than short-term use.

Relaxation techniques include the following:

Autogenic Training

In autogenic training, you learn to concentrate on the physical sensations of warmth, heaviness, and relaxation in different parts of your body.

Biofeedback-Assisted Relaxation

Biofeedback techniques measure body functions and give you information about them so that you can learn to control them. Biofeedback-assisted relaxation uses electronic devices to teach you to produce changes in your body that are associated with relaxation, such as reduced muscle tension.

Deep Breathing or Breathing Exercises

This technique involves focusing on taking slow, deep, even breaths.

Guided Imagery

For this technique, people are taught to focus on pleasant images to replace negative or stressful feelings. Guided imagery may be self-directed or led by a practitioner or a recording.

Progressive Relaxation

This technique, also called Jacobson relaxation or progressive muscle relaxation, involves tightening, and relaxing various muscle groups. Progressive relaxation is often combined with guided imagery and breathing exercises.

Self-Hypnosis

In self-hypnosis programs, people are taught to produce the relaxation response when prompted by a phrase or nonverbal cue (called a "suggestion").

What the Science Says about the Effectiveness of Relaxation Techniques

Researchers have evaluated relaxation techniques to see whether they could play a role in managing a variety of health conditions, including the following:

Anxiety

Studies have shown relaxation techniques may reduce anxiety in people with ongoing health problems such as heart disease or inflammatory bowel disease, and in those who are having medical procedures such as breast biopsies or dental treatment. Relaxation techniques have also been shown to be useful for older adults with anxiety.

On the other hand, relaxation techniques may not be the best way to help people with generalized anxiety disorder. Generalized anxiety disorder is a mental health condition, lasting for months or longer, in which a person is often worried or anxious about many things and finds it hard to control the anxiety. Studies indicate that long-term results are better in people with generalized anxiety disorder who receive a type of psychotherapy called cognitive-behavioral therapy than in those who are taught relaxation techniques.

Asthma

There hasn't been enough research to show whether relaxation techniques can relieve asthma symptoms in either adults or children.

Childbirth

Relaxation techniques such as guided imagery, progressive muscle relaxation, and breathing techniques may be useful in managing labor pain. Studies have shown that women who were taught self-hypnosis have a decreased need for pain medicine during labor. Biofeedback has not been shown to relieve labor pain.

Depression

An evaluation of 15 studies concluded that relaxation techniques are better than no treatment in reducing symptoms of depression but are not as beneficial as psychological therapies such as cognitive-behavioral therapy.

Epilepsy

There is no reliable evidence that relaxation techniques are useful in managing epilepsy.

Fibromyalgia

Studies of guided imagery for fibromyalgia have had inconsistent results.

A 2013 evaluation of the research concluded that electromyographic (EMG) biofeedback, in which people are taught to control and reduce muscle tension, helped to reduce fibromyalgia pain, at least for short periods of time. However, EMG biofeedback did not affect sleep problems, depression, fatigue, or health-related quality of life in people with fibromyalgia, and its long-term effects have not been established.

Headache

- **Biofeedback**. Biofeedback has been studied for both tension headaches and migraines.

  - An evaluation of high-quality studies concluded that there is conflicting evidence about whether biofeedback can relieve tension headaches.

  - Studies have shown decreases in the frequency of migraines in people who were using biofeedback. However, it is unclear whether biofeedback is better than a placebo.

- **Other Relaxation Techniques**. Relaxation techniques other than biofeedback have been studied for tension headaches. An evaluation of high-quality studies found conflicting evidence on whether relaxation techniques are better than no treatment or a placebo. Some studies suggest that other relaxation techniques are less effective than biofeedback.

Heart Disease

In people with heart disease, studies have shown relaxation techniques can reduce stress and anxiety and may also have beneficial effects on physical measures such as heart rate.

High Blood Pressure

Stress can lead to a short-term increase in blood pressure, and the relaxation response has been shown to reduce blood pressure on a short-term basis, allowing people to reduce their need for blood pressure medication. However, it is uncertain whether relaxation techniques can have long-term effects on high blood pressure.

Insomnia

There is evidence that relaxation techniques can be helpful in managing chronic insomnia. Relaxation techniques can be combined with other strategies for getting a good night's sleep, such as maintaining a consistent sleep schedule; avoiding caffeine, alcohol, heavy meals, and strenuous exercise too close to bedtime; and sleeping in a quiet, cool, dark room.

Irritable Bowel Syndrome

An evaluation of research results by the American College of Gastroenterology concluded that relaxation therapy has not been shown to be beneficial for irritable bowel syndrome. However, other psychological therapies, including cognitive-behavioral therapy and hypnotherapy, are associated with overall symptom improvement in people with irritable bowel syndrome.

Menopause Symptoms

Relaxation techniques have been studied for hot flashes and other symptoms associated with menopause, but the quality of the research is not high enough to allow definite conclusions to be reached.

Menstrual Cramps

Some research suggests that relaxation techniques may be beneficial for menstrual cramps, but definite conclusions can't be reached because of the small number of participants in the studies and the poor quality of some of the research.

Nausea

An evaluation of the research evidence concluded that some relaxation techniques, including guided imagery and progressive muscle relaxation, are likely to be effective in relieving nausea when used in combination with anti-nausea drugs.

Nightmares

Some studies have indicated that relaxation exercises may be an effective approach for nightmares of unknown cause and those associated with post-traumatic stress disorder. However, an assessment of many studies concluded that relaxation is less helpful than more extensive forms of treatment (psychotherapy or medication).

Pain

Evaluations of the research evidence have found promising but not conclusive evidence that guided imagery may relieve musculoskeletal pain (pain involving the bones or muscles) and other types of pain.

Pain in Children and Adolescents

A 2014 evaluation of the scientific evidence found that psychological therapies, which may include relaxation techniques as well as other approaches such as cognitive-behavioral therapy, can reduce pain in children and adolescents with chronic headaches or other types of chronic pain. The evidence is particularly promising for headaches: the effect on pain may last for several months after treatment, and the therapies also help to reduce anxiety.

Post-Traumatic Stress Disorder

Studies of biofeedback and other relaxation techniques for post-traumatic stress disorder have had inconsistent results.

Rheumatoid Arthritis

There is limited evidence that biofeedback or other relaxation techniques might be valuable additions to treatment programs for rheumatoid arthritis.

171

Ringing in the Ears (Tinnitus)

Only a few studies have evaluated relaxation techniques for ringing in the ears. The limited evidence from these studies suggests that relaxation techniques might be useful, especially in reducing the intrusiveness of the problem.

Smoking Cessation

- Limited evidence suggests that guided imagery may be a valuable tool for people who are working to quit smoking.

- In a study that compared the two techniques, autogenic training was found to be less effective than cognitive-behavioral therapy as a quit-smoking aid. However, this study involved patients in an alcohol detoxification program, so its results may not be applicable to other people.

- Preliminary research suggests that a guided relaxation routine might help reduce cigarette cravings.

Temporomandibular Joint Dysfunction

Problems with the temporomandibular joint (the joint that connects the jaw to the side of the head) can cause pain and difficulty moving the jaw. A few studies have shown that programs that include relaxation techniques may help relieve symptoms of temporomandibular joint dysfunction.

What the Science Says about the Safety and Side Effects of Relaxation Techniques

- Relaxation techniques are generally considered safe for healthy people. However, occasionally, people report unpleasant experiences such as increased anxiety, intrusive thoughts, or fear of losing control.

- There have been rare reports that certain relaxation techniques might cause or worsen symptoms in people with epilepsy or certain psychiatric conditions, or with a history of abuse or trauma. People with heart disease should talk to their health care provider before doing progressive muscle relaxation.

More to Consider

- If you have severe or long-lasting symptoms of any kind, see your health care provider. You might have a condition that needs to be treated promptly. For example, if depression or anxiety persists, it's important to seek help from a qualified health care professional.

- Tell all your health care providers about any complementary health approaches you use. Give them a full picture of what you do to manage your health. This will help ensure coordinated and safe care.

Section 17.7

Yoga

Text in this section is excerpted from "Yoga for Health," National Center for Complementary and Integrative Health (NCCIH), June 2013.

Yoga is a mind and body practice with historical origins in ancient Indian philosophy. Like other meditative movement practices used for health purposes, various styles of yoga typically combine physical postures, breathing techniques, and meditation or relaxation. This section provides basic information about yoga and summarizes scientific research on effectiveness and safety.

Key Facts

- Recent studies in people with chronic low-back pain suggest that a carefully adapted set of yoga poses may help reduce pain and improve function (the ability to walk and move). Studies also suggest that practicing yoga (as well as other forms of regular exercise) might have other health benefits such as reducing heart rate and blood pressure, and may also help relieve anxiety and depression. Other research suggests yoga is not helpful for asthma, and studies looking at yoga and arthritis have had mixed results.

- People with high blood pressure, glaucoma, or sciatica, and women who are pregnant should modify or avoid some yoga poses.

- Ask a trusted source (such as a health care provider or local hospital) to recommend a yoga practitioner. Contact professional organizations for the names of practitioners who have completed an acceptable training program.

- Tell all your health care providers about any complementary health approaches you use. Give them a full picture of what you do to manage your health. This will help ensure coordinated and safe care.

About Yoga

Yoga in its full form combines physical postures, breathing exercises, meditation, and a distinct philosophy. There are numerous styles of yoga. *Hatha* yoga, commonly practiced in the United States and Europe, emphasizes postures, breathing exercises, and meditation. *Hatha* yoga styles include *Ananda, Anusara, Ashtanga, Bikram, Iyengar, Kripalu, Kundalini, Viniyoga*, and others.

Side Effects and Risks

- Yoga is generally low-impact and safe for healthy people when practiced appropriately under the guidance of a well-trained instructor.

- Overall, those who practice yoga have a low rate of side effects, and the risk of serious injury from yoga is quite low. However, certain types of stroke as well as pain from nerve damage are among the rare possible side effects of practicing yoga.

- Women who are pregnant and people with certain medical conditions, such as high blood pressure, glaucoma (a condition in which fluid pressure within the eye slowly increases and may damage the eye's optic nerve), and sciatica (pain, weakness, numbing, or tingling that may extend from the lower back to the calf, foot, or even the toes), should modify or avoid some yoga poses.

Use of Yoga for Health in the United States

According to the 2007 National Health Interview Survey (NHIS), which included a comprehensive survey on the use of complementary health approaches by Americans, yoga is the sixth most commonly used complementary health practice among adults. More than 13 million adults practiced yoga in the previous year, and between the 2002 and 2007 NHIS, use of yoga among adults increased by 1 percent (or approximately 3 million people). The 2007 survey also found that more than 1.5 million children practiced yoga in the previous year.

Many people who practice yoga do so to maintain their health and well-being, improve physical fitness, relieve stress, and enhance quality of life. In addition, they may be addressing specific health conditions, such as back pain, neck pain, arthritis, and anxiety.

What the Science Says about Yoga

Current research suggests that a carefully adapted set of yoga poses may reduce low-back pain and improve function. Other studies also suggest that practicing yoga (as well as other forms of regular exercise) might improve quality of life; reduce stress; lower heart rate and blood pressure; help relieve anxiety, depression, and insomnia; and improve overall physical fitness, strength, and flexibility. But some research suggests yoga may not improve asthma, and studies looking at yoga and arthritis have had mixed results.

- One NCCIH-funded study of 90 people with chronic low-back pain found that participants who practiced a *Hatha* yoga had significantly less disability, pain, and depression after 6 months.

- In a 2011 study, also funded by NCCIH, researchers compared yoga with conventional stretching exercises or a self-care book in 228 adults with chronic low-back pain. The results showed that both yoga and stretching were more effective than a self-care book for improving function and reducing symptoms due to chronic low-back pain.

- Conclusions from another 2011 study of 313 adults with chronic or recurring low-back pain suggested that 12 weekly yoga classes resulted in better function than usual medical care.

However, studies show that certain health conditions may not benefit from yoga.

- A 2011 systematic review of clinical studies suggests that there is no sound evidence that yoga improves asthma.

- A 2011 review of the literature reports that few published studies have looked at yoga and arthritis, and of those that have, results are inconclusive. The two main types of arthritis—osteoarthritis

175

and rheumatoid arthritis—are different conditions, and the effects of yoga may not be the same for each. In addition, the reviewers suggested that even if a study showed that yoga helped osteoarthritic finger joints, it may not help osteoarthritic knee joints.

If You Are Considering Practicing Yoga

- Do not use yoga to replace conventional medical care or to postpone seeing a health care provider about pain or any other medical condition.

- If you have a medical condition, talk to your health care provider before starting yoga.

- Ask a trusted source (such as your health care provider or a nearby hospital) to recommend a yoga practitioner. Find out about the training and experience of any practitioner you are considering.

- Everyone's body is different, and yoga postures should be modified based on individual abilities. Carefully selecting an instructor who is experienced with and attentive to your needs is an important step toward helping you practice yoga safely. Ask about the physical demands of the type of yoga in which you are interested and inform your yoga instructor about any medical issues you have.

- Carefully think about the type of yoga you are interested in. For example, hot yoga (such as Bikram yoga) may involve standing and moving in humid environments with temperatures as high as 105°F. Because such settings may be physically stressful, people who practice hot yoga should take certain precautions. These include drinking water before, during, and after a hot yoga practice and wearing suitable clothing. People with conditions that may be affected by excessive heat, such as heart disease, lung disease, and a prior history of heatstroke may want to avoid this form of yoga. Women who are pregnant may want to check with their health care providers before starting hot yoga.

- Tell all your health care providers about any complementary health approaches you use. Give them a full picture of what you do to manage your health. This will help ensure coordinated and safe care.

Chapter 18

Manipulative and Body-Based Therapies

Chapter Contents

Section 18.1

Chiropractic

Text in this section is excerpted from "Chiropractic: An Introduction,"
National Center for Complementary and Integrative Health
(NCCIH), February 2012.

Chiropractic is a health care profession that focuses on the relationship between the body's structure—mainly the spine—and its functioning. Although practitioners may use a variety of treatment approaches, they primarily perform adjustments (manipulations) to the spine or other parts of the body with the goal of correcting alignment problems, alleviating pain, improving function, and supporting the body's natural ability to heal itself.

Key Points

- Most research on chiropractic has focused on spinal manipulation. Spinal manipulation appears to benefit some people with low-back pain and may also be helpful for headaches, neck pain, upper- and lower-extremity joint conditions, and whiplash-associated disorders.

- Side effects from spinal manipulation can include temporary headaches, tiredness, or discomfort in the parts of the body that were treated. There have been rare reports of serious complications such as stroke, but whether spinal manipulation actually causes these complications is unclear. Safety remains an important focus of ongoing research.

- Tell all your health care providers about any complementary health approaches you use. Give them a full picture of what you do to manage your health. This will help ensure coordinated and safe care.

Overview and History

The term "chiropractic" combines the Greek words *cheir* (hand) and *praxis* (practice) to describe a treatment done by hand. Hands-on therapy—especially adjustment of the spine—is central to chiropractic care. Chiropractic is based on the notion that the relationship between the body's structure (primarily that of the spine) and its function (as coordinated by the nervous system) affects health.

Spinal adjustment/manipulation is a core treatment in chiropractic care, but it is not synonymous with chiropractic. Chiropractors commonly use other treatments in addition to spinal manipulation, and other health care providers (e.g., physical therapists or some osteopathic physicians) may use spinal manipulation.

Use in the United States

In the United States, chiropractic is often considered a complementary health approach. According to the 2007 National Health Interview Survey (NHIS), which included a comprehensive survey of the use of complementary health approaches by Americans, about 8 percent of adults (more than 18 million) and nearly 3 percent of children (more than 2 million) had received chiropractic or osteopathic manipulation in the past 12 months. Additionally, an analysis of NHIS cost data found that adults in the United States spent approximately $11.9 billion out-of-pocket on visits to complementary health practitioners—$3.9 billion of which was spent on visits to practitioners for chiropractic or osteopathic manipulation.

Many people who seek chiropractic care have low-back pain. People also commonly seek chiropractic care for other kinds of musculoskeletal pain (e.g., neck, shoulder), headaches, and extremity (e.g., hand or foot) problems.

An analysis of the use of complementary health approaches for back pain, based on data from the 2002 NHIS, found that chiropractic was by far the most commonly used therapy. Among survey respondents who had used any of these therapies for their back pain, 74 percent (approximately 4 million Americans) had used chiropractic. Among those who had used chiropractic for back pain, 66 percent perceived "great benefit" from their treatments.

Treatment

During the initial visit, chiropractors typically take a health history and perform a physical examination, with a special emphasis on the spine. Other examinations or tests such as X-rays may also be performed. If chiropractic treatment is considered appropriate, a treatment plan will be developed.

During followup visits, practitioners may perform one or more of the many different types of adjustments and other manual therapies used in chiropractic care. Given mainly to the spine, a chiropractic adjustment involves using the hands or a device to apply a controlled, rapid force to a joint. The goal is to increase the range and quality of motion in the area being treated and to aid in restoring health. Joint mobilization is another type of manual therapy that may be used.

Chiropractors may combine the use of spinal adjustments and other manual therapies with several other treatments and approaches such as:

- Heat and ice
- Electrical stimulation
- Relaxation techniques
- Rehabilitative and general exercise
- Counseling about diet, weight loss, and other lifestyle factors
- Dietary supplements.

What the Science Says

Researchers have studied spinal manipulation for a number of conditions ranging from back, neck, and shoulder pain to asthma, carpal tunnel syndrome, fibromyalgia, and headaches. Much of the research has focused on low-back pain, and has shown that spinal manipulation appears to benefit some people with this condition.

A 2010 review of scientific evidence on manual therapies for a range of conditions concluded that spinal manipulation/mobilization may be helpful for several conditions in addition to back pain, including migraine and cervicogenic (neck-related) headaches, neck pain, upper- and lower-extremity joint conditions, and whiplash-associated disorders. The review also identified a number of conditions for which spinal manipulation/mobilization appears not to be helpful (including asthma, hypertension, and menstrual pain) or the evidence is inconclusive (e.g., fibromyalgia, mid-back pain, premenstrual syndrome, sciatica, and temporomandibular joint disorders).

Safety

- Side effects from spinal manipulation can include temporary headaches, tiredness, or discomfort in the parts of the body that were treated.
- There have been rare reports of serious complications such as stroke, cauda equina syndrome (a condition involving pinched

nerves in the lower part of the spinal canal), and worsening of herniated discs, although cause and effect are unclear.

Safety remains an important focus of ongoing research:

* A 2007 study of treatment outcomes for 19,722 chiropractic patients in the United Kingdom concluded that minor side effects (such as temporary soreness) after cervical spine manipulation were relatively common, but that the risk of a serious adverse event was "low to very low" immediately or up to 7 days after treatment.

* A 2009 study that drew on 9 years of hospitalization records for the population of Ontario, Canada analyzed 818 cases of vertebrobasilar artery (VBA) stroke (involving the arteries that supply blood to the back of the brain). The study found an association between visits to a health care practitioner and subsequent VBA stroke, but there was no evidence that visiting a chiropractor put people at greater risk than visiting a primary care physician. The researchers attributed the association between health care visits and VBA stroke to the likelihood that people with VBA dissection (torn arteries) seek care for related headache and neck pain before their stroke.

If You Are Thinking about Seeking Chiropractic Care

* Ask about the chiropractor's education and licensure.

* Mention any medical conditions you have, and ask whether the chiropractor has specialized training or experience in the condition for which you are seeking care.

* Ask about typical out-of-pocket costs and insurance coverage. (Chiropractic is covered by many health maintenance organizations and private health plans, Medicare, and state workers' compensation systems.)

* Tell the chiropractor about any medications (prescription or over-the-counter) and dietary supplements you take. If the chiropractor suggests a dietary supplement, ask about potential interactions with your medications or other supplements.

* Tell all of your health care providers about any complementary health approaches you use. Give them a full picture of what you do to manage your health. This will help ensure coordinated and safe care.

Section 18.2

Massage Therapy

Text in this section is excerpted from "Massage Therapy for Health Purposes: What You Need To Know," National Center for Complementary and Integrative Health (NCCIH), May 2015.

What's the Bottom Line?

How much do we know about massage?

A lot of research on the effects of massage therapy has been carried out.

What do we know about the effectiveness of massage?

While often preliminary or conflicting, there is scientific evidence that massage may help with back pain and may improve quality of life for people with depression, cancer, and HIV/AIDS.

What do we know about the safety of massage?

Massage therapy appears to have few risks if it is used appropriately and provided by a trained massage professional.

What Is Massage Therapy?

The term "massage therapy" includes many techniques, and the type of massage given usually depends on your needs and physical condition.

- Massage therapy dates back thousands of years. References to massage appear in ancient writings from China, Japan, India, and Egypt.

- In general, massage therapists work on muscle and other soft tissue to help you feel better.

- In Swedish massage, the therapist uses long strokes, kneading, deep circular movements, vibration, and tapping.

- Sports massage combines techniques of Swedish massage and deep tissue massage to release chronic muscle tension. It is adapted to the needs of athletes.

- Myofascial trigger point therapy focuses on trigger points— areas that are painful when pressed and are associated with pain elsewhere in the body.

- Massage therapy is sometimes done using essential oils as a form of aromatherapy.

What the Science Says about the Effectiveness of Massage

A lot of the scientific research on massage therapy is preliminary or conflicting, but much of the evidence points toward beneficial effects on pain and other symptoms associated with a number of different conditions. Much of the evidence suggests that these effects are short term and that people need to keep getting massages for the benefits to continue.

Researchers have studied the effects of massage for many conditions. Some that they have studied more extensively are the following:

Pain

- A 2008 systematic review and 2011 NCCIH-funded clinical trial concluded that massage may be useful for chronic low-back pain.

- Massage may help with chronic neck pain, a 2009 NCCIH-funded clinical trial reported.

- Massage may help with pain due to osteoarthritis of the knee, according to a 2012 NCCIH-funded study.

- Studies suggest that for women in labor, massage provided some pain relief and increased their satisfaction with other forms of pain relief, but the evidence is not strong, a 2012 review concluded.

Cancer

Numerous systematic reviews and clinical studies have suggested that at least for the short term, massage therapy for cancer patients may reduce pain, promote relaxation, and boost mood. However, the National Cancer Institute urges massage therapists to take specific precautions with cancer patients and avoid massaging:

- Open wounds, bruises, or areas with skin breakdown

- Directly over the tumor site

- Areas with a blood clot in a vein

- Sensitive areas following radiation therapy

Mental health

- A 2010 meta-analysis of 17 clinical trials concluded that massage therapy may help to reduce depression.

- Brief, twice-weekly yoga and massage sessions for 12 weeks were associated with a decrease in depression, anxiety, and back and leg pain in pregnant women with depression, a 2012 NCCIH-funded randomized controlled trial showed. Also, the women's babies weighed more than babies born to women who didn't receive the therapy.

- However, a 2013 research review concluded that there is not enough evidence to determine if massage helps pregnant mothers with depression.

- A 2010 review concluded that massage may help older people relax.

- For generalized anxiety disorder, massage therapy was no better at reducing symptoms than providing a relaxing environment and deep breathing lessons, according to a small, 2010 NCCIH-supported clinical trial.

Fibromyalgia

A 2010 review concluded that massage therapy may help temporarily reduce pain, fatigue, and other symptoms associated with fibromyalgia, but the evidence is not definitive. The authors noted that it is important that the massage therapist not cause pain.

Headaches

Clinical trials on the effects of massage for headaches are preliminary and only somewhat promising.

HIV/AIDS

Massage therapy may help improve the quality of life for people with HIV or AIDS, a 2010 systematic review of four small clinical trials concluded.

Infant care

Massaging preterm infants using moderate pressure may improve weight gain, a 2010 review suggested. We don't have enough evidence to know if massage benefits healthy infants who are developing normally, a 2013 review determined.

Other Conditions

Researchers have studied massage for the following but it's still unclear if it helps:

- Behavior of children with autism or autism spectrum disorders
- Immune function in women with breast cancer
- Anxiety and pain in patients following heart surgery
- Quality of life and glucose levels in people with diabetes
- Lung function in children with asthma.

What the Science Says about the Safety and Side Effects of Massage Therapy

Massage therapy appears to have few risks when performed by a trained practitioner. However, massage therapists should take some precautions in people with certain health conditions.

- In some cases, pregnant women should avoid massage therapy. Talk with your health care provider before getting a massage if you are pregnant.

- People with some conditions such as bleeding disorders or low blood platelet counts should avoid having forceful and deep tissue massage. People who take anticoagulants (also known as blood thinners) also should avoid them. Massage should not be done in any potentially weak area of the skin, such as wounds.

- Deep or intense pressure should not be used over an area where the patient has a tumor or cancer, unless approved by the patient's health care provider.

More to Consider

Do not use massage therapy to replace conventional care or to postpone seeing a health care provider about a medical problem.

- If you have a medical condition and are unsure whether massage therapy would be appropriate for you, discuss your concerns with your health care provider, who may also be able to help you select a massage therapist.

- Ask about the training, experience, and credentials of the massage therapist you are considering. Also ask about the number of treatments that might be needed, the cost, and insurance coverage.

- For more tips on finding a complementary health practitioner, such as a massage therapist, see the National Center for Complementary and Integrative Health's (NCCIH) Web page *How To Find a Complementary Health Practitioner.*

- Tell all your health care providers about any complementary and integrative health approaches you use. Give them a full picture of what you do to manage your health. This will ensure coordinated and safe care.

Section 18.3

Lymphatic Drainage Therapy

Lymphatic drainage therapy is a manual massage technique intended to reduce fluid buildup and swelling that may occur due to problems with the lymph nodes. Lymph is a clear, watery fluid that flows through a network of tissues, organs, and vessels known as the lymphatic system. The main components of the lymphatic system include the bone marrow, spleen, and thymus, as well as lymph nodes located in the neck, armpits, chest, groin, and the lymphatic vessels.

The lymph nodes play a vital role in the functioning of the immune system. They filter out harmful substances that are carried in the lymph fluid, such as bacteria and viruses, and attack and destroy them with white blood cells called lymphocytes. If a person has an infection, injury, or a disease like cancer, the lymph nodes may become tender and swollen as they aid in the immune response.

When the lymph nodes are compromised by disease or surgically removed, the lymphatic system may lose its ability to drain fluid from a nearby region of the body, resulting in a condition called lymphedema. Problems involving the lymph nodes in the armpit, for instance, may result in painful fluid buildup and swelling in the arm. Lymphatic drainage therapy was developed to treat lymphedema and related conditions.

Causes and Symptoms of Lymphedema

Lymphedema can be related to several different factors. Primary lymphedema, which is rare, can arise at birth as a result of a malformed or dysfunctional lymphatic system. The more common condition, secondary lymphedema, can result from anything that obstructs or causes damage to the lymphatic system, including infection, injury, cancer, surgery, or radiation therapy.

Among the most common causes of secondary lymphedema are cancer and cancer treatments. When surgeons operate to remove a malignancy, they often remove lymph nodes in the area of the tumor to determine whether cancer cells are present in the lymphatic system. If the cancer has spread to the lymph nodes, the patient faces a higher risk that the disease will come back following surgery. The degree to which the cancer has affected the lymph nodes determines its stage of advancement and the type of treatment that the patient requires. Cancer in the lymph nodes, surgical removal of the lymph nodes, and radiation therapy designed to kill cancer cells can all cause lymphedema.

Regardless of the cause, the symptoms of lymphedema include swelling of the hands, arms, feet, legs, or any other part of the body; loss of mobility in the affected joints and limbs; redness, itching, and tightening of the skin; and general feelings of heaviness and discomfort.

Massage Therapy for Lymph Drainage

Chronic lymphedema has no cure, but there are a number of methods that can be used to help manage its severity and symptoms. One option is lymphatic drainage or manual massage therapy. Developed in Europe in the 1930s, it is intended to improve the natural flow of lymph and the drainage of fluids from body parts affected by lymphedema.

The manual massage technique involves gentle rubbing, tapping, and stroking of the skin using a specific speed, pressure, and pattern. The goal is to stimulate the movement of lymph out of congested areas, bypassing the damaged lymph vessels, and channel it into healthy vessels so that it can return to systemic circulation.

Manual massage treatments should begin with a certified therapist, although patients can learn to perform the technique on themselves. Generally, it does not involve risks when done correctly. However, the technique should not be used on open wounds, broken skin, or tissues that have been exposed to radiation therapy. It is also not suitable if the patient has a deep vein thrombosis (blood clot).

Proponents claim that manual massage therapy can lead to improvements in many different medical conditions, including poor circulation, injuries, burns, nervous system disorders, arthritis, pregnancy-related swelling, varicose veins, stress, and insomnia.

A few studies have indicated that women with lymphedema related to breast cancer treatment may experience a reduction in swelling following manual massage therapy. But the efficacy of the treatment must be demonstrated in larger, controlled studies for it to gain acceptance in the mainstream medical community.

References:

1. American Cancer Society. "Lymph Nodes and Cancer," 2015.

2. Dr. Vodder School International. "Manual Lymphatic Drainage," 2015.

3. National Cancer Institute. "Lymphedema for Health Professionals: Manual Lymphedema Therapy," 2015.

Section 18.4

Reflexology (Zone Therapy)

"Reflexology (Zone Therapy)," © 2015 Omnigraphics, Inc. Reviewed September 2015.

Reflexology is based on the idea that applying pressure to specific points on the feet, hands, or ears will produce beneficial effects on the corresponding body organs and a person's general health. It is utilized worldwide as a complementary and alternative treatment method for a variety of chronic painful disorders, such as anxiety, asthma, low-back pain, headaches (migraines), premenstrual syndrome (dysmenorrhea), and stress. It is particularly helpful in children and elderly people. In Europe and North America, reflexology is performed by paramedical practitioners.

Reflexology is also known as zone therapy. According to proponents of the method, the body is divided into ten longitudinal zones, with five located on each side of the body. Each zone within the body is represented by a certain point on the hands or feet. Practitioners claim to be able to detect abnormalities in the organs of each zone by feeling the corresponding areas on the hands or feet. Once the problem has been identified, the reflexologist puts pressure on the reflex points in order to stimulate a flow of energy, blood, nutrients, and nerve impulses to the zone.

Reflexology has experienced a rapid increase in popularity in Europe and Asia. In several countries, in fact, local governing bodies and private companies have begun employing reflexologists to treat their staff members. The practice has been credited with helping to increase job satisfaction and reduce absenteeism in some of these organizations.

Origin and Development of Reflexology

Reflexology has been practiced since ancient times. It is depicted in a pictograph on the Egyptian tomb of Ankhamor that dates to 2330 BCE, for instance, as well as in symbols engraved on the feet of Buddha statues in India and China. The earliest discussion of reflexology in print appears in the *Yellow Emperor's Classic of Internal Medicine,* a Chinese text written around 1,000 BCE. Marco Polo is credited with introducing reflexology methods in Europe in the 1300s by translating Chinese massage instructions into Italian.

The so-called Father of Zone Therapy in the United States was Dr. William H. Fitzgerald. In 1913, he introduced the idea that putting pressure on certain points on the feet and hands could exert an anaesthetic effect on other parts of the body. He used the zone therapy technique to relieve pain from injuries or minor medical procedures. Fitzgerald's work was expanded by Dr. Shelby Riley, who also suggested pressure points on the outer ear. Another important contribution was made by Eunice D. Ingham, a physiotherapist who mapped the body's reflex zones in the 1940s.

Reflexology Points and Areas

Although the practice of reflexology varies in different parts of the world, most practitioners agree on the major reflex points. Reflexologists use maps to represent the correspondence between these points on the feet, hands, and ears and different bodily systems. Each foot represents a vertical half of the body, for instance, with points on the left foot corresponding to organs on the left side of the body and points on the right foot corresponding to organs on the right side of the body. For instance, the liver, which is located on the right side of the abdomen, is represented by an area on the right foot.

Research on Reflexology

Medical research into the effectiveness of reflexology has yielded mixed results. Most patients find reflexology therapy relaxing, and many report that it provides such health benefits as relieving pain, reducing anxiety, improving mood, and enhancing sleep. Studies funded by the U.S. National Institutes of Health (NIH) have supported the anecdotal evidence that reflexology may help alleviate pain and reduce the psychological stress associated with injury and illness. As a result, reflexology treatments are increasingly being used as part of the palliative care of people with cancer.

The mainstream medical community generally rejects the idea that reflexology can effectively diagnose and treat potentially serious medical conditions, such as asthma, diabetes, or cancer. A 2009 systematic review of controlled studies concluded that reflexology had failed to demonstrate effectiveness in treating any medical condition. Critics argue that there is no scientific evidence to support claims that reflexology practitioners can identify problems or improve the function of bodily systems by putting pressure on reflex points. They point out that medical research has never established any nerve connection or flow of energy between reflex points and other parts of the body.

Although reflexology is not considered harmful and may aid some patients with the psychological aspects of healing, doctors warn that it should only be used in addition to, rather than in place of, appropriate medical treatment.

References:

1. Barrett, Stephen. "Reflexology: A Close Look." Quackwatch, 2015.

2. Bauer, Brent A. "What Is Reflexology? Can It Relieve Stress?" Mayo Clinic, 2015.

3. Teagarden, Karen. "Reflexology." *Taking Charge of Your Health and Well-Being,* University of Minnesota Center for Spirituality and Healing, 2013.

Chapter 19

Chi-Based Therapies

Chapter Contents

Section 19.1

Feng Shui

"Feng Shui," © 2015 Omnigraphics, Inc.
Reviewed September 2015.

Feng shui (pronounced "fung shway") is an ancient philosophical system of Chinese origin that dates back to 1700 BCE. It is based on the concept that people who live in harmony with their environment can lead healthier, happier, more productive lives. Feng shui is the art of designing the physical environment so that it balances various elements of nature. Achieving this balance is believed to enhance the flow of *qi* (pronounced "chee"), the central energy or life force that is present in all things. When qi flows gently and smoothly through a person's surroundings, it may exert a positive influence on their health, relationships, and worldly success.

History of Feng Shui

In ancient China, the principles of feng shui were widely used to select, orient, design, and decorate living spaces. Citizens relied upon the system to choose locations to build homes, grow crops, and bury departed family members. The dynasties that ruled over China applied this "art of placement" to the construction of palaces, government buildings, and even entire cities.

Over time, the principles associated with feng shui expanded to include nuances from astronomy, astrology, philosophy, cosmology, and metaphysics. During the Cultural Revolution of 1966–76, however, Chinese Communist leaders purged the country of many traditional elements of Chinese culture. Although the practice of feng shui was suppressed in mainland China, the discipline gained prominence in the United States and elsewhere in the world.

Principles of Feng Shui

Wherever it is practiced, feng shui incorporates the same basic principles:

Qi. In traditional Chinese culture, qi is the life force or energy flow that permeates all living things and connects them to the natural environment. Qi is the core principle of feng shui as well as traditional Chinese medicine and martial arts. In the practice of feng shui, people strive to arrange their surroundings to remove obstructions, create harmony, and keep qi flowing smoothly.

Yin and Yang. Feng shui also incorporates the principle of polarity or duality. Under this principle, everything in nature is comprised of two opposing, yet interconnected forces, Yin and Yang. These two forces cannot exist without each other, and they can be regarded as parts of a whole circle. Yin is considered to be a female force, and it is often characterized as soft, gentle, and nurturing. Yang, on the other hand, is considered to be a male force, characterized as hard, active, and aggressive. In feng shui, people strive to balance opposing forces—light and dark, straight and curvy, etc.—in an effort to promote harmony in their environment.

Connectedness. This principle is based on the idea that the environment can influence people, just as people can influence their environment. Due to this connectedness, organizing one's surroundings through the practice of feng shui is believed to have an impact on other aspects of one's life, such as health and success.

The Five Elements. Feng shui divides the environment into five elements: fire, earth, metal, water, and wood. The five elements are believed to relate to each other as they do in nature, in what are known as productive cycles and destructive cycles. Arranging surroundings with feng shui means striving to attain balance between the various elements. When one element is emphasized too heavily, it can obstruct the flow of qi and make the surroundings feel uncomfortable. Each element is associated with a certain shape, color, and set of characteristics or attributes:

1 Fire is represented by a triangle and the color red. Among the qualities associated with the fire element are passion, enthusiasm, expressiveness, inspiration, boldness, and leadership. In the environment, objects that incorporate the fire element include candles, fireplaces, and lamps.

2 Earth is represented by a square, and its main colors are brown and yellow. It is associated with such attributes as balance, stability, grounding, and practicality. Objects that bring the earth element into the environment might include hardwood floors, granite countertops, or clay pots.

195

3 Metal is represented by a circle, and its main colors are silver, gold, and white. Metal energy is associated with activities of the mind, such as strength, focus, and clarity of thought. This element can be featured in the environment through the use of wrought iron furniture or light fixtures, metal picture frames, or electronic devices like clocks or televisions.

4 Water is represented by wavy lines and the colors blue and black. It is regarded as a mystical element that symbolizes spirituality, reflection, movement, and flow. It can be incorporated into the environment in the form of water-filled glass vases, aquariums, fountains, or objects that have a swirling pattern.

5 Wood is represented by a rectangle and the color green. Among the attributes of wood energy are growth, vitality, and creativity. Objects that bring wood energy into the environment include anything made of wood, such as furniture or flooring, as well as live plants and flowers—especially bamboo.

The Bagua. The bagua is an important tool used in the practice of feng shui. It is an octagonal or rectangular chart containing nine equal spaces that correspond to the following critical aspects of life:

- Power and wealth
- Fame and reputation
- Love and relationships
- Children and legacy
- Compassion and travel
- Work and career
- Knowledge and wisdom
- Health and community
- Well-being and balance

The bagua is used to determine which physical part of a home, office, shop, or restaurant relates to each attribute. This information can help people decide how to decorate or place favorite personal possessions within a space in order to enhance the flow of qi.

The first step in using the bagua involves orienting it to the space, with the main entrance in the middle of the bottom row. Next, feng shui experts suggest conceptualizing the floor plan of the space as nine squares that match the ones on the bagua. Finally, they recommend decorating and accessorizing each area with objects that activate the specific energy or attributes of the corresponding square on the bagua. For example, diplomas and trophies should be placed in the area that represents fame and reputation, while family photos and children's drawings should be placed in the area that represents children and legacy. Proponents of feng shui believe that people who use these principles to organize their surroundings will achieve greater balance and experience positive changes in their lives.

References:

1. Jones, Katina Z. *The Everything Feng Shui Book.* New York: F+W Media, 2011.

2. Olmstead, Carol. "Basics." Feng Shui for Real Life, 2015.

Section 19.2

Tai Chi and Qigong

Text in this section is excerpted from "Tai Chi and Qi Gong,"
National Center for Complementary and Integrative Health
(NCCIH), August 2015.

What's the Bottom Line?

How much do we know about tai chi and qi gong?

Several clinical trials have evaluated the effects of tai chi and qi gong in people with various health conditions.

What do we know about the effectiveness of tai chi and qi gong?

Practicing tai chi may help to improve balance and stability in older people and in those with Parkinson's disease, reduce back pain and pain from **knee osteoarthritis**, and improve quality of life in people with **heart disease, cancer, and other chronic illnesses.** Tai chi and qi gong may ease fibromyalgia pain and promote general quality of life. Qi gong may reduce chronic neck pain, but study results are mixed. Tai chi also may improve reasoning ability in older people.

What do we know about the safety of tai chi and qi gong?

Tai chi and qi gong appear to be safe practices, but it's a good idea to talk with your health care providers before beginning any exercise program.

What Are Tai Chi and Qi Gong?

Tai chi and qi gong are centuries-old, related mind and body practices. They involve certain postures and gentle movements with mental focus, breathing, and relaxation. The movements can be adapted or practiced while walking, standing, or sitting. In contrast to qi gong, tai chi movements, if practiced quickly, can be a form of combat or self-defense.

What the Science Says about the Effectiveness of Tai Chi and Qi Gong

Research findings suggest that practicing tai chi may improve balance and stability in older people and those with Parkinson's, reduce pain from knee osteoarthritis, help people cope with fibromyalgia and back pain, and promote quality of life and mood in people with heart failure and cancer. There has been less research on the effects of qi gong, but some studies suggest it may reduce chronic neck pain (although results are mixed) and pain from fibromyalgia. Qi gong also may help to improve general quality of life.

Both also may offer psychological benefits, such as reducing anxiety. However, differences in how the research on anxiety was conducted make it difficult to draw firm conclusions about this.

Falling and Balance

Exercise programs, including tai chi, may reduce falling and the fear of falling in older people. Tai chi also may be more effective than other forms of exercise for improving balance and stability in people with Parkinson's disease.

- A 2012 review determined that tai chi, as well as other group- and home-based activity programs (which often include balance and strength-training exercises) effectively reduced falling in older people, and tai chi significantly reduced the risk of falling. But the reviewers also found that tai chi was less effective in older people who were at higher risk of falling.

- Fear of falling can have a serious impact on an older person's health and life. In a 2014 review, researchers suggested that various types of exercise, including tai chi, may reduce the fear of falling among older people.

- Findings from a 2012 clinical trial with 195 people showed that practicing tai chi improved balance and stability better than resistance training or stretching in people with mild-to-moderate Parkinson's disease. A 2014 followup analysis showed that people who practiced tai chi were more likely to continue exercising during the 3 months following the study compared with those who participated in resistance training or stretching.

For Pain (knee osteoarthritis, fibromyalgia, chronic neck pain, and back pain)

There's some evidence that practicing tai chi may help people manage pain associated with knee osteoarthritis (a breakdown of cartilage in the knee that allows leg bones to rub together), fibromyalgia (a disorder that causes muscle pain and fatigue), and back pain. Qi gong may offer some benefit for chronic neck pain, but results are mixed.

Knee Osteoarthritis

- Results of a small NCCIH-funded clinical trial involving 40 participants with knee osteoarthritis suggested that practicing tai chi reduced pain and improved function better than an education and stretching program.

- An analysis of seven small and moderately-sized clinical studies concluded that a 12-week course of tai chi reduced pain and improved function in people with this condition.

Fibromyalgia

- Results from a small 2010 NCCIH-supported clinical trial suggested that practicing tai chi was more effective than wellness education and stretching in helping people with fibromyalgia sleep better and cope with pain, fatigue, and depression. After 12 weeks, those who practiced tai chi also had better scores on a survey designed to measure a person's ability to carry out certain daily activities such as walking, housecleaning, shopping, and preparing a meal. The benefits of tai chi also appeared to last longer.

- A small 2012 NCCIH-supported trial suggested that combining tai chi movements with mindfulness allowed people with fibromyalgia to work through the discomfort they may feel during exercise, allowing them to take advantage of the benefits of physical activity.

- Results of a 2012 randomized clinical trial with 100 participants suggested that practicing qi gong reduced pain and improved sleep, the ability to do daily activities, and mental function. The researchers also observed that most improvements were still apparent after 6 months.

Chronic Neck Pain

Research results on the effectiveness of qi gong for chronic neck pain are mixed, but the populations that were studied and the study protocols were quite different.

- A 2009 clinical study by German researchers showed no benefit for qi gong or exercise compared with no therapy in 117 elderly adults (mostly women) with an average 20-year history of chronic neck pain. Study participants had 24 exercise or qi gong sessions over 3 months.

- In a 2011 study, some of the same researchers observed that qi gong was just as effective as exercise therapy (and both were more effective than no therapy) in relieving neck pain in the target population—123 middle-aged adults (mostly women) who had chronic neck pain for an average of 3 years. Exercise therapy included throwing and catching a ball, rowing and climbing movements, arm swinging, and stretching, among other activities. People in the study had 18 exercise or qi gong sessions over 6 months.

Back Pain

- In people who had low-back pain for at least 3 months, a program of tai chi exercises was more effective in reducing pain and improving function than whatever the individuals had been doing previously to manage their pain.

For Mental Health and Cognitive Function

While a range of research has suggested a beneficial relationship between exercise and depression and exercise and anxiety symptoms, the role of tai chi and qi gong for these and other mental health factors is less clear. However, there is evidence that tai chi may boost brain function and reasoning ability in older people.

- NCCIH-supported research suggests that practicing tai chi may help reduce stress, anxiety, and depression, and also improve mood and self-esteem. However, in their 2010 systematic review and meta-analysis, which included 40 studies and more than 3,800 participants, the researchers noted that they could not develop firm conclusions because of differences in study designs.

- In a 2010 NCCIH-supported literature review, researchers found that the results from 29 studies with more than 2,500 participants did not offer clear evidence about the effectiveness of tai chi and qi gong on such psychological factors as anxiety, depression, stress, mood, and self-esteem. But the researchers noted that most of these studies did not look at psychological distress as the primary goal and did not intentionally recruit participants with mental health issues.

- Results from another NCCIH-supported review published in 2014 suggested that practicing tai chi may enhance the ability to reason, plan, remember, and solve problems in older people without evidence significant cognitive impairment. The data also indicated that tai chi boosted cognitive ability in people who showed signs of mild cognitive impairment to dementia, but to a lesser degree than in those with no signs of cognitive impairment.

For Quality of Life

Much research suggests that physical activity enhances quality of life. Health providers who treat people with cancer often recommend exercise to reduce illness-related fatigue and improve quality of life. Some studies also suggest that physical activity helps people with heart disease and other chronic illnesses.

Cancer

Research results indicate that practicing qi gong may improve quality of life, mood, fatigue, and inflammation in adults diagnosed with different types of cancer compared with those receiving usual care. However, the researchers suggested that the attention received by the qi gong participants may have contributed to the positive study findings.

Heart Disease

- Regular practice of tai chi may improve quality of life and mood in people with chronic heart failure, according to a 2011 clinical trial funded by NCCIH.

- Results from a small study suggest that practicing tai chi improves the ability to exercise and may be an option as cardiac rehabilitation for people who have experienced a heart attack.

Other

A 2010 NCCIH-supported review of the literature examined the effects of tai chi and qi gong on quality of life in studies involving adults who were healthy, elderly, were breast cancer or stroke survivors, or had a chronic disease. The analysis suggested that practicing tai chi or qi gong may improve quality of life in healthy and chronically ill people.

What the Science Says about Safety of Tai Chi and Qi Gong

Tai chi and qi gong appear to be safe practices. One NCCIH-supported review noted that tai chi is unlikely to result in serious injury but it may be associated with minor aches and pains. Women who are pregnant should talk with their health care providers before beginning tai chi, qi gong, or any other exercise program.

More to Consider

- Learning tai chi or qi gong from a video or book does not ensure that you're doing the movements correctly or safely.

- If you have a health condition, talk with your health care provider before starting tai chi or qi gong.

- Ask a trusted source (such as your health care provider or a nearby hospital) to recommend a tai chi or qi gong instructor. Find out about the training and experience of any instructor you are considering.

- Tell all your health care providers about any complementary or integrative health approaches you use. Give them a full picture of what you do to manage your health. This will help ensure coordinated and safe care.

Section 19.3

Shiatsu

"Shiatsu," © 2015 Omnigraphics, Inc.
Reviewed September 2015.

Shiatsu (pronounced "she-AT-zoo"), which is a Japanese word meaning "finger pressure," is a form of therapeutic bodywork. Practitioners use their fingers, thumbs, and palms to knead, press, tap, and stretch various parts of the body in a rhythmic sequence. In most forms of shiatsu, the goal is to correct imbalances in the flow of energy through the body, known as *qi* (pronounced "chee") in Japanese and Chinese medical traditions. According to these traditions, obstructions or deficiencies in the qi can contribute to many chronic health issues, such as headaches, muscular pain, digestive problems, or frequent colds. Shiatsu therapists use manual techniques to access the qi, harmonize the flow of energy through the body, and thus restore the client to good health.

History of Shiatsu

The person often credited as the founder of modern shiatsu therapy is Tokujiro Namikoshi, who was born in Japan in 1905. He began using hands-on therapy techniques at the age of seven to treat his mother's rheumatoid arthritis. He eventually developed a theory of bodywork that he called shiatsu and established a school to train shiatsu therapists. Namikoshi introduced shiatsu to the United States in the 1950s, and from there it spread around the world. Although shiatsu evolved from anma, a massage system popularized in the 1600s by acupuncturist Sugiyama Waichi, it integrated this traditional Japanese form of manual therapy with modern medical knowledge. The Japanese Ministry of Health recognized shiatsu as a distinct form of therapeutic treatment in 1964.

Over the years, many shiatsu practitioners developed their own therapeutic styles. Some approaches emphasize stimulation of acupressure points, while others concentrate on influencing the flow of qi. Although the techniques may differ slightly, they all share the same basic goals. Some of the common variations include:

- Five Element Shiatsu

- Hara Shiatsu

- Macrobiotic Shiatsu

- Meridian Shiatsu

- Oha Shiatsu

- Quantum Shiatsu

- Tao Shiatsu

- Tsubo Shiatsu

- Water Shiatsu

- Zen Shiatsu

The Shiatsu Treatment Process

Regardless of the style used, a shiatsu treatment typically begins with an assessment of state of the client's qi. The practitioner performs this evaluation in order to determine what obstructions or sources of imbalance might be present. This process allows the therapist to design a treatment plan that will address the problems, restore the balance, and improve the client's health.

Following the initial assessment, the practitioner uses manual techniques—including pressing, kneading, soothing, rubbing, tapping, and stretching—to access the client's qi. The qi is believed to flow through pathways in the body called meridians. Practitioners attempt to influence the flow of energy by manipulating locations known as vital points. If the client is experiencing a great deal of stress or anxiety, the therapist may employ techniques designed to disperse energy. On the other hand, if the client is experiencing fatigue or depression, the practitioner may use techniques designed to restore energy.

Unlike some other types of massage therapy, shiatsu is performed through light, comfortable clothing and without the use of oils. The person undergoing treatment usually lies on a low massage table or on a pad on the floor. A typical session lasts between 60 and 90 minutes. Although shiatsu is considered a low-risk treatment, it may not be appropriate for people who have recently undergone surgery, have skin rashes, open wounds, or injuries, or who are in the advanced stages of pregnancy.

Research on Shiatsu

Most people find shiatsu therapy to be very soothing and relaxing. Anecdotal evidence suggests that it can offer some health benefits, such as alleviating pain from injuries or arthritis and reducing the psychological stress associated with illness. Proponents claim that it is also effective in relieving headaches, reducing anxiety, enhancing sleep, improving digestion, and treating the symptoms of premenstrual syndrome.

While shiatsu may aid in the healing process for some patients, doctors emphasize that it should complement, rather than replace, appropriate medical treatment. The mainstream medical community generally rejects the idea that shiatsu can effectively prevent, diagnose, or treat potentially serious medical conditions. Critics argue that there is no scientific evidence to support the existence of qi or the claim that shiatsu can improve the function of bodily systems.

In the U.S., the main research grants for therapeutic body work have been focused on massage and other energy therapies. While the evidence on the efficacy of Shiatsu therapy is limited at present, it may be remembered that the risk is very minimal and there are significant anecdotally-reported benefits.

References:

1. Canadian Shiatsu Society of British Columbia. "About Shiatsu," n.d.

2. Pelava, Cari Johnson. "What Is Shiatsu?" *Taking Charge of Your Health and Well-Being,* Center for Spirituality and Healing, University of Minnesota, 2013.

Section 19.4

Tui Na

"Tui Na," © 2015 Omnigraphics, Inc.
Reviewed September 2015.

Tui na (pronounced "twee naw") is a form of massage therapy that originated in China around 2,500 years ago. Its name comes from the Chinese words for two of the motions commonly used by practitioners, *tui* (meaning "push") and *na* ("squeeze"). Tui na incorporates elements from several different forms of traditional Chinese medicine and martial arts, including qi gong, shiatsu, acupuncture, fire cupping, and tai chi.

Although it employs manual manipulation techniques similar to those used in other types of body massage—such as pressing, kneading, tapping, rolling, gliding, and shaking—tui na tends to focus on identifying and addressing specific problems rather than on promoting simple relaxation. The goal for the tui na therapist is to find and correct imbalances in the flow of energy through the patient's body, known as *qi* (pronounced "chee"). According to traditional Chinese medicine, obstructions or deficiencies in the qi can contribute to many chronic health issues. Tui na therapists use manual techniques to access the qi, harmonize the flow of Yin and Yang energy through the body, and thus restore the patient to good health.

The Tui Na Treatment Process

Proponents of tui na believe that the qi must be in balance for a person to have positive energy and enjoy good health. The tui na treatment process thus focuses on enhancing the flow of qi through the body in channels called meridians. Therapists are trained to access the qi by massaging vital points along the meridians. They may employ a variety of manual techniques designed to remove obstructions in the flow of energy, such as kneading, rolling, rubbing, gliding, pulling, rocking, rotating, vibrating, and shaking. Some tui na practitioners also incorporate acupressure or spinal manipulation techniques into the treatment process.

A typical tui na therapy session lasts between 30 and 60 minutes. The client usually wears loose clothing and lies on a massage table or floor mat. The practitioner begins by examining the client to identify problem areas, whether specific pain sites or obstructions in the flow of qi. Then the therapist applies manual massage techniques to acupressure points, energy meridians, and muscles and joints to treat the problems. The client usually feels relaxed but energized at the end of the treatment. Depending on the severity of the problems, the client may need to return for additional sessions.

Benefits of Tui Na

Proponents claim that tui na massage therapy can lead to improvements in many different health conditions, including arthritis, sciatica, muscle spasms, chronic pain, insomnia, digestive problems, constipation, headaches, and stress. They believe that restoring the free flow of energy through the body relaxes muscles, relieves pain, improves circulation, and creates a feeling of vitality and emotional well-being.

While tui na may aid in the healing process for some patients, doctors warn that it should only complement, rather than replace, conventional medical treatment for potentially serious health conditions. Critics argue that there is no scientific evidence to support the existence of qi or the claim that tui na can improve the function of bodily systems. In addition, since tui na is more vigorous and intense than many other forms of massage, it may not be appropriate for everyone.

References:

1. Hafner, Christopher. "Tui Na." Center for Spirituality and Healing, University of Minnesota, 2013.

2. Henderson, Jan. "What Is Tui Na?" Balance Flow Health and Bodyworks, 2014.

3. Pacific College of Oriental Medicine. "Benefits of Tui Na Massage," 2014.

Part Four

Dietary Supplements

Chapter 20

Questions and Answers about Dietary Supplements

What is a dietary supplement?

Congress defined the term "dietary supplement" in the Dietary Supplement Health and Education Act (DSHEA) of 1994. A dietary supplement is a product taken by mouth that contains a "dietary ingredient" intended to supplement the diet. The "dietary ingredients" in these products may include: vitamins, minerals, herbs or other botanicals, amino acids, and substances such as enzymes, organ tissues, glandulars, and metabolites. Dietary supplements can also be extracts or concentrates, and may be found in many forms such as tablets, capsules, softgels, gelcaps, liquids, or powders. They can also be in other forms, such as a bar, but if they are, information on their label must not represent the product as a conventional food or a sole item of a meal or diet. Whatever their form may be, DSHEA places dietary supplements in a special category under the general umbrella of "foods," not drugs, and requires that every supplement be labeled a dietary supplement.

Text in this chapter is excerpted from "Food–Questions and Answers on Dietary Supplements," Food and Drug Administration (FDA), April 28, 2015.

What is a "new dietary ingredient" in a dietary supplement?

The Dietary Supplement Health and Education Act (DSHEA) of 1994 defined both of the terms "dietary ingredient" and "new dietary ingredient" as components of dietary supplements. In order for an ingredient of a dietary supplement to be a "dietary ingredient," it must be one or any combination of the following substances:

- a vitamin,

- a mineral,

- an herb or other botanical,

- an amino acid,

- a dietary substance for use by man to supplement the diet by increasing the total dietary intake (e.g., enzymes or tissues from organs or glands), or

- a concentrate, metabolite, constituent or extract.

A "new dietary ingredient" is one that meets the above definition for a "dietary ingredient" and was not sold in the U.S. in a dietary supplement before October 15, 1994.

What is FDA's role in regulating dietary supplements versus the manufacturer's responsibility for marketing them?

In October 1994, the Dietary Supplement Health and Education Act (DSHEA) was signed into law by President Clinton. Before this time, dietary supplements were subject to the same regulatory requirements as were other foods. This new law, which amended the Federal Food, Drug, and Cosmetic Act, created a new regulatory framework for the safety and labeling of dietary supplements. Under DSHEA, a firm is responsible for determining that the dietary supplements it manufactures or distributes are safe and that any representations or claims made about them are substantiated by adequate evidence to show that they are not false or misleading. This means that dietary supplements do not need approval from the Food and Drug Administration (FDA) before they are marketed. Except in the case of a new dietary ingredient, where pre-market review for safety data and other information is required by law, a firm does not have to provide FDA with the evidence it relies on to substantiate safety or effectiveness before or after it markets its products. Also, manufacturers need to register themselves pursuant to the Bioterrorism Act with FDA before producing or selling supplements. In June 2007, FDA published comprehensive regulations for Current Good Manufacturing Practices for those who manufacture, package or hold dietary supplement products. These regulations focus on practices that ensure the identity, purity, quality, strength and composition of dietary supplements.

When must a manufacturer or distributor notify FDA about a dietary supplement it intends to market in the U.S.?

The Dietary Supplement Health and Education Act (DSHEA) requires that a manufacturer or distributor notify FDA if it intends to market a dietary supplement in the U.S. that contains a "new dietary ingredient." The manufacturer (and distributor) must demonstrate to FDA why the ingredient is reasonably expected to be safe for use in a dietary supplement, unless it has been recognized as a food substance and is present in the food supply. There is no authoritative list of dietary ingredients that were marketed before October 15, 1994. Therefore, manufacturers and distributors are responsible for determining if a dietary ingredient is "new," and if it is not, for documenting that the dietary supplements its sells, containing the dietary ingredient, were marketed before October 15, 1994.

What information must the manufacturer disclose on the label of a dietary supplement?

FDA regulations require that certain information appear on dietary supplement labels. Information that must be on a dietary supplement label includes: a descriptive name of the product stating that it is a "supplement"; the name and place of business of the manufacturer, packer, or distributor; a complete list of ingredients; and the net contents of the product. In addition, each dietary supplement (except for some small volume products or those produced by eligible small businesses) must have nutrition labeling in the form of a "Supplement Facts" panel. This label must identify each dietary ingredient contained in the product.

Must all ingredients be declared on the label of a dietary supplement?

Yes, ingredients not listed on the "Supplement Facts" panel must be listed in the "other ingredient" statement beneath the panel. The types of ingredients listed there could include the source of dietary ingredients, if not identified in the "Supplement Facts" panel (e.g., rose hips as the source of vitamin C), other food ingredients (e.g., water

213

and sugar), and technical additives or processing aids (e.g., gelatin, starch, colors, stabilizers, preservatives, and flavors).

Are dietary supplement serving sizes standardized or are there restrictions on the amount of a nutrient that can be in one serving?

Other than the manufacturer's responsibility to ensure safety, there are no rules that limit a serving size or the amount of a nutrient in any form of dietary supplements. This decision is made by the manufacturer and does not require FDA review or approval.

Where can I get information about a specific dietary supplement?

Manufacturers and distributors do not need FDA approval to sell their dietary supplements. This means that FDA does not keep a list of manufacturers, distributors or the dietary supplement products they sell. If you want more detailed information than the label tells you about a specific product, you may contact the manufacturer of that brand directly. The name and address of the manufacturer or distributor can be found on the label of the dietary supplement.

Who has the responsibility for ensuring that a dietary supplement is safe?

By law (DSHEA), the manufacturer is responsible for ensuring that its dietary supplement products are safe before they are marketed. Unlike drug products that must be proven safe and effective for their intended use before marketing, there are no provisions in the law for FDA to "approve" dietary supplements for safety or effectiveness before they reach the consumer. Under DSHEA, once the product is marketed, FDA has the responsibility for showing that a dietary supplement is "unsafe," before it can take action to restrict the product's use or removal from the marketplace. However, manufacturers and distributors of dietary supplements must record, investigate and forward to FDA any reports they receive of serious adverse events associated with the use of their products that are reported to them directly. FDA is able to evaluate these reports and any other adverse event information reported directly to us by healthcare providers or consumers to identify early signals that a product may present safety risks to consumers.

Do manufacturers or distributors of dietary supplements have to tell FDA or consumers what evidence they have about their product's safety or what evidence they have to back up the claims they are making for them?

No, except for rules described above that govern "new dietary ingredients," there is no provision under any law or regulation that FDA enforces that requires a firm to disclose to FDA or consumers the information they have about the safety or purported benefits of their dietary supplement products. Likewise, there is no prohibition against them making this information available either to FDA or to their customers. It is up to each firm to set its own policy on disclosure of such information.

How can consumers inform themselves about safety and other issues related to dietary supplements?

It is important to be well informed about products before purchasing them. Because it is often difficult to know what information is reliable and what is questionable, consumers may first want to contact the manufacturer about the product they intend to purchase (see previous question "Where can I get information about a specific dietary supplement?").

What is FDA's oversight responsibility for dietary supplements?

Because dietary supplements are under the "umbrella" of foods, FDA's Center for Food Safety and Applied Nutrition (CFSAN) is responsible for the agency's oversight of these products. FDA's efforts to monitor the marketplace for potential illegal products (that is, products that may be unsafe or make false or misleading claims) include obtaining information from inspections of dietary supplement manufacturers and distributors, the Internet, consumer and trade complaints, occasional laboratory analyses of selected products, and adverse events associated with the use of supplements that are reported to the agency.

Does FDA routinely analyze the content of dietary supplements?

In that FDA has limited resources to analyze the composition of food products, including dietary supplements, it focuses these resources first on public health emergencies and products that may have caused injury or illness. Enforcement priorities then go to products thought to be unsafe or fraudulent or in violation of the law. The remaining funds are used for routine monitoring of products pulled from store shelves or collected during inspections of manufacturing firms. The agency does not analyze dietary supplements before they are sold to consumers. The manufacturer is responsible for ensuring that the "Supplement Facts" label and ingredient list are accurate, that the dietary ingredients are safe, and that the content matches the amount declared on the label. FDA does not have resources to analyze dietary supplements sent to the agency by consumers who want to know their content. Instead, consumers may contact the manufacturer or a commercial laboratory for an analysis of the content.

Is it legal to market a dietary supplement product as a treatment or cure for a specific disease or condition?

No, a product sold as a dietary supplement and promoted on its label or in labeling as a treatment, prevention or cure for a specific disease or condition would be considered an unapproved–and thus illegal–drug. To maintain the product's status as a dietary supplement, the label and labeling must be consistent with the provisions in the Dietary Supplement Health and Education Act (DSHEA) of 1994.

Who validates claims and what kinds of claims can be made on dietary supplement labels?

FDA receives many consumer inquiries about the validity of claims for dietary supplements, including product labels, advertisements, media, and printed materials. The responsibility for ensuring the validity of these claims rests with the manufacturer, FDA, and, in the case of advertising, with the Federal Trade Commission.By law, manufacturers may make three types of claims for their dietary supplement products: health claims, structure/function claims, and nutrient content claims. Some of these claims describe: the link between a food substance and disease or a health-related condition; the intended benefits of using the product; or the amount of a nutrient or dietary substance in a product. Different requirements generally apply to each type of claim, and are described in more detail.

Why do some supplements have wording (a disclaimer) that says: "This statement has not been evaluated by the FDA. This product is not intended to diagnose, treat, cure, or prevent any disease"?

This statement or "disclaimer" is required by law (DSHEA) when a manufacturer makes a structure/function claim on a dietary supplement label. In general, these claims describe the role of a nutrient or dietary ingredient intended to affect the structure or function of the body. The manufacturer is responsible for ensuring the accuracy and truthfulness of these claims; they are not approved by FDA. For this reason, the law says that if a dietary supplement label includes such a claim, it must state in a "disclaimer" that FDA has not evaluated this claim. The disclaimer must also state that this product is not intended to "diagnose, treat, cure or prevent any disease," because only a drug can legally make such a claim.

How are advertisements for dietary supplements regulated?

The Federal Trade Commission (FTC) regulates advertising, including infomercials, for dietary supplements and most other products sold to consumers. FDA works closely with FTC in this area, but FTC's work is directed by different laws.

How do I, my health care provider, or any informed individual report a problem or illness caused by a dietary supplement to FDA?

If you think you have suffered a serious harmful effect or illness from a dietary supplement, the first thing you should do is contact or see your healthcare provider immediately. Then, you or your health care provider can report this by submitting a report through the Safety Reporting Portal. If you do not have access to the internet, you may submit a report by calling FDA's MedWatch hotline at 1-800-FDA-1088.

FDA would like to know when a dietary supplement causes a problem even if you are unsure the product caused the problem or even if you do not visit a doctor or clinic. Anyone may report a serious adverse event or illness thought to be related to a dietary supplement directly to FDA by accessing the SRP mentioned above.

Consumers are also encouraged to report instances of product problems using the Safety Reporting Portal . Examples of product problems are foreign objects in the packaging or other apparent quality defects.

Chapter 21

Herbs at a Glance

Botanical dietary supplements are sometimes referred to as herbals or herbal dietary supplements. Botanical dietary supplements are available to consumers as plants, plant parts, or plant extracts. A dietary supplement is defined, in part, as a product intended for ingestion that may contain one or more dietary ingredients and that is intended to supplement the diet. Dietary supplements may be found in many forms such as tablets, capsules, soft gels, gel caps, liquids, or powders. Some botanical dietary supplements are used in complementary and alternative medicine, also sometimes called traditional medicine.

Acai

Common Names: acai, açaí, Amazonian palm berry
Latin Name: *Euterpe oleracea*

The acai palm tree, native to tropical Central and South America, produces a reddish-purple berry. The acai berry's name, which comes from a language of the native people of the region, means "fruit that cries." The acai berry has long been an important food source

---

This chapter includes excerpts from "NTP Botanical Dietary Supplement Program," National Toxicology Program (NTP), May 2014; and text from "Herbs at a Glance," National Center for Complementary and Integrative Health (NCCIH), March 24, 2015.

for indigenous peoples of the Amazon region, who also use acai for a variety of health-related purposes.

Acai berry products have become popular in the United States, where they have been marketed as folk or traditional remedies for weight-loss and anti-aging purposes, but there is no definitive scientific evidence to support these claims. Acai fruit pulp has been used experimentally as an oral contrast agent for magnetic resonance imaging (MRI) of the gastrointestinal tract.

Acai berry products are available as juices, powders, tablets, and capsules.

What the Science Says

- There is no definitive scientific evidence based on studies in humans to support the use of acai berry for any health-related purpose.

- No independent studies have been published in peer-reviewed journals that substantiate claims that acai supplements alone promote rapid weight loss. Researchers who investigated the safety profile of an acai-fortified juice in animals observed that there were no body weight changes in rats given the juice compared with controls.

- Laboratory studies have focused on acai berry's potential antioxidant properties (antioxidants are substances that are thought to protect cells from damaging effects of chemical reactions with oxygen). Laboratory studies also have shown that acai berries demonstrate anti-cancer and anti-inflammatory activity.

Side Effects and Cautions

- There is little reliable information about the safety of acai as a supplement. It is widely consumed as an edible fruit or as a juice.

- People who are allergic to acai or to plants in the Arecaceae (palm) family should not consume acai.

- Consuming acai might affect MRI test results. If you use acai products and are scheduled for an MRI, check with your health care provider.

Keep in Mind

Tell all your health care providers about any complementary health approaches you use. Give them a full picture of what you

do to manage your health. This will help ensure coordinated and safe care.

Aloe Vera

Common Names: aloe vera, aloe, burn plant, lily of the desert, elephant's gall
Latin Names: *Aloe vera, Aloe barbadensis*

Aloe vera's use can be traced back 6,000 years to early Egypt, where the plant was depicted on stone carvings. Known as the "plant of immortality," aloe was presented as a burial gift to deceased pharaohs.

Historically, aloe was used topically to heal wounds and for various skin conditions, and orally as a laxative. Recently, in addition to these uses, aloe is used as a folk or traditional remedy for a variety of conditions, including diabetes, asthma, epilepsy, and osteoarthritis. It is also used topically for osteoarthritis, burns, sunburns, and psoriasis. Aloe vera gel can be found in hundreds of skin products, including lotions and sunblocks. The Food and Drug Administration (FDA) has approved aloe vera as a natural food flavoring.

Aloe leaves contain a clear gel that is often used as a topical ointment. The green part of the leaf that surrounds the gel can be used to produce a juice or a dried substance (called latex) that is taken by mouth.

What the Science Says

- Aloe latex contains strong laxative compounds. Products made with various components of aloe (aloin, aloe-emodin, and barbaloin) were at one time regulated by the FDA as oral over-the-counter (OTC) laxatives. In 2002, the FDA required that all OTC aloe laxative products be removed from the U.S. market or reformulated because the companies that manufactured them did not provide the necessary safety data.

- Early studies show that topical aloe gel may help heal burns and abrasions. One study, however, showed that aloe gel inhibits healing of deep surgical wounds. Aloe gel has not been shown to prevent burns from radiation therapy.

- There is not enough scientific evidence to support aloe vera for any of its other uses.

221

Side Effects and Cautions

- Use of topical aloe vera is not associated with significant side effects.

- A 2-year National Toxicology Program (NTP) study on oral consumption of non-decolorized whole leaf extract of aloe vera found clear evidence of carcinogenic activity in male and female rats, based on tumors of the large intestine. According to the NTP, from what is known right now there is nothing that would lead them to believe that these findings are not relevant to humans. However, more information, including how individuals use different types of aloe vera products, is needed to determine the potential risks to humans.

- Abdominal cramps and diarrhea have been reported with oral use of aloe vera.

- Diarrhea, caused by the laxative effect of oral aloe vera, can decrease the absorption of many drugs.

- People with diabetes who use glucose-lowering medication should be cautious if also taking aloe by mouth because preliminary studies suggest aloe may lower blood glucose levels.

- There have been a few case reports of acute hepatitis from aloe vera taken orally. However, the evidence is not definitive.

Keep in Mind

Tell all your health care providers about any complementary health approaches you use. Give them a full picture of what you do to manage your health. This will help ensure coordinated and safe care.

Asian Ginseng

Common Names: Asian ginseng, ginseng, Chinese ginseng, Korean ginseng, Asiatic ginseng
Latin Name: *Panax ginseng*

Asian ginseng is native to China and Korea and has been used in various systems of medicine for many centuries. Asian ginseng is one of several types of true ginseng (another is American ginseng, *Panax quinquefolius*). The *herb* called Siberian ginseng or eleuthero *(Eleutherococcus senticosus)* is not a true ginseng.

Treatment claims for Asian ginseng are numerous and include the use of the herb to support overall health and boost the immune system.

Traditional and folk uses of ginseng include improving the health of people recovering from illness; increasing a sense of well-being and stamina; improving both mental and physical performance; treating erectile dysfunction, hepatitis C, and symptoms related to menopause; and lowering blood glucose and controlling blood pressure.

The root of Asian ginseng contains active chemical components called ginsenosides (or panaxosides) that are thought to be responsible for the herb's claimed medicinal properties. The root is dried and used to make tablets or capsules, extracts, and teas, as well as creams or other preparations for external use.

What the Science Says

- Some studies have shown that Asian ginseng may lower blood glucose. Other studies indicate possible beneficial effects on immune function.

- Although Asian ginseng has been widely studied for a variety of uses, research results to date do not conclusively support health claims associated with the herb. Only a few large, high-quality clinical trials have been conducted. Most evidence is preliminary—i.e., based on laboratory research or small clinical trials.

- NCCIH supports studies to better understand the use of Asian ginseng. Areas of recent NCCIH-funded research include the herb's potential role in treating insulin resistance, cancer, and Alzheimer's disease.

Side Effects and Cautions

- Short-term use of ginseng at recommended doses appears to be safe for most people. Some sources suggest that prolonged use might cause side effects.

- The most common side effects are headaches and sleep and gastrointestinal problems.

- Asian ginseng can cause allergic reactions.

- There have been reports of breast tenderness, menstrual irregularities, and high blood pressure associated with Asian ginseng products, but these products' components were not analyzed, so effects may have been due to another herb or drug in the product.

- Asian ginseng may lower levels of blood sugar; this effect may be seen more in people with diabetes. Therefore, people with diabetes should use extra caution with Asian ginseng, especially if they are using medicines to lower blood sugar or taking other herbs, such as bitter melon and fenugreek that are also thought to lower blood sugar.

Keep in Mind

Tell all your health care providers about any complementary health approaches you use. Give them a full picture of what you do to manage your health. This will help ensure coordinated and safe care.

Bilberry

Common Names: bilberry, European blueberry, whortleberry, huckleberry
Latin Name: *Vaccinium myrtillus*

Bilberry is a relative of the blueberry, and its fruit is commonly used to make pies and jams. It has been used for nearly 1,000 years in traditional European medicine. Bilberry grows in North America, Europe, and northern Asia. Historically, bilberry fruit was used to treat diarrhea, scurvy, and other conditions. Recently, the fruit is used as a folk or traditional remedy for diarrhea, menstrual cramps, eye problems, varicose veins, venous insufficiency (a condition in which the veins do not efficiently return blood from the legs to the heart), and other circulatory problems. Bilberry leaf is used for entirely different conditions, including diabetes.

The fruit of the bilberry plant can be eaten or made into extracts. Similarly, the leaves of the bilberry plant can be made into extracts or used to make teas.

What the Science Says

- Some claim that bilberry fruit improves night vision, but clinical studies have not shown this to be true.
- There is not enough scientific evidence to support the use of bilberry fruit or leaf for any health conditions.

Side Effects and Cautions

- Bilberry fruit is considered safe when consumed in amounts typically found in foods, or as an extract in recommended doses for brief periods of time. Long-term safety and side effects have not been extensively studied.

- High doses or extended use of bilberry leaf or leaf extract are considered unsafe due to possible toxic side effects.

Keep in Mind

Tell all your health care providers about any complementary health approaches you use. Give them a full picture of what you do to manage your health. This will help ensure coordinated and safe care.

Bitter Orange

Common Names: bitter orange, Seville orange, sour orange, zhi shi
Latin Name: *Citrus aurantium*

The bitter orange tree is native to eastern Africa and tropical Asia. Recently, it is grown throughout the Mediterranean region and elsewhere, including California and Florida. Bitter orange oil is used in foods, cosmetics, and *aromatherapy* products. Bitter orange oil from the tree's leaves is called petitgrain, and oil from the flowers is called neroli. Bitter orange has been used in *traditional Chinese medicine* and by indigenous people of the Amazon rainforest for nausea, indigestion, and constipation. Current folk or traditional uses of bitter orange are for heartburn, loss of appetite, nasal congestion, and weight loss. It is also applied to the skin for fungal infections such as ringworm and athlete's foot.

The dried fruit and peel (and sometimes flowers and leaves) are taken by mouth in extracts, tablets, and capsules. Bitter orange oil can be applied to the skin.

What the Science Says

- There is not enough scientific evidence to support the use of bitter orange for health purposes.
- Many herbal weight-loss products now use concentrated extracts of bitter orange peel in place of ephedra. However, bitter orange contains the chemical synephrine, which is similar to the main chemical in ephedra. The U.S. Food and Drug Administration banned ephedra because it raises blood pressure and is linked to heart attacks and strokes; it is unclear whether bitter orange has similar effects. There is currently little evidence that bitter orange is safer to use than ephedra.

225

Side Effects and Cautions

- Because bitter orange contains chemicals that may speed up the heart rate and raise blood pressure, it may not be safe to use as a *dietary supplement*. There have been reports of fainting, heart attack, and stroke in healthy people after taking bitter orange supplements alone or combined with caffeine. People should avoid taking bitter orange supplements if they have a heart condition or high blood pressure, or if they are taking medications (such as MAO inhibitors), caffeine, or other herbs/supplements that speed up the heart rate.

- Due to lack of safety evidence, pregnant women or nursing mothers should avoid products that contain bitter orange.

- Bitter orange oil used on the skin may increase the risk of sunburn, particularly in light-skinned people.

Keep in Mind

Tell all your health care providers about any complementary health approaches you use. Give them a full picture of what you do to manage your health. This will help ensure coordinated and safe care.

Black Cohosh

Common Names: black cohosh, black snakeroot, macrotys, bugbane, bugwort, rattleroot, rattleweed
Latin Names: *Actaea racemosa, Cimicifuga racemosa*

Black cohosh, a member of the buttercup family, is a plant native to North America. It was used in Native American medicine and was a home remedy in 19th-century America. Black cohosh has a history of use for rheumatism (arthritis and muscle pain) but has been used more recently as a folk or traditional remedy for hot flashes, night sweats, vaginal dryness, and other symptoms that can occur during menopause. Black cohosh has also been used for menstrual irregularities and premenstrual syndrome, and to induce labor.

The underground stems and roots of black cohosh are commonly used fresh or dried to make strong teas (infusions), capsules, solid extracts used in pills, or liquid extracts (tinctures).

What the Science Says

- Study results are mixed on whether black cohosh effectively relieves menopausal symptoms. An NCCIH-funded study found

226

that black cohosh, whether used alone or with other botanicals, failed to relieve hot flashes and night sweats in postmenopausal women or those approaching menopause.

• Most studies to date have been less than 6 months long, so the safety of long-term use is uncertain.

• NCCIH is funding studies to further understand the potential effects of black cohosh on hot flashes and other menopausal symptoms.

• There are not enough reliable data to determine whether black cohosh is effective for rheumatism or other uses.

Side Effects and Cautions

• United States Pharmacopeia experts suggest women should discontinue use of black cohosh and consult a health care practitioner if they have a liver disorder or develop symptoms of liver trouble, such as abdominal pain, dark urine, or jaundice. There have been several case reports of hepatitis (inflammation of the liver), as well as liver failure, in women who were taking black cohosh. It is not known if black cohosh was responsible for these problems. Although these cases are very rare and the evidence is not definitive, scientists are concerned about the possible effects of black cohosh on the liver.

• Some people taking black cohosh have experienced side effects such as stomach discomfort, headache, or rash. In general, clinical trials of black cohosh for menopausal symptoms have not found serious side effects.

• Although concerns have been raised about possible interactions between black cohosh and various medications, a 2008 review of studies to date concluded that the risk of such interactions appears to be small.

• It is not clear if black cohosh is safe for women who have had hormone-sensitive conditions such as breast cancer or for pregnant women or nursing mothers.

• Black cohosh should not be confused with blue cohosh (*Caulophyllum thalictroides*), which has different properties, treatment uses, and side effects than black cohosh. Black cohosh is sometimes used with blue cohosh to stimulate labor, but this therapy has caused adverse effects in newborns, which appear to be due to blue cohosh.

Keep in Mind

Tell all your health care providers about any complementary health approaches you use. Give them a full picture of what you do to manage your health. This will help ensure coordinated and safe care.

Bromelain

Common Names: bromelain, pineapple extract
Latin Name: (Pineapple Plant) *Ananas comosus L.*

Bromelain is a mixture of enzymes found in the pineapple plant. Pineapple is native to the Americas but is now grown throughout the world in tropical and subtropical regions. Historically, natives of Central and South America used pineapple for a variety of ailments, such as digestive disorders.

Currently, bromelain is used as a dietary supplement for nasal swelling and inflammation, osteoarthritis, cancer, poor digestion, and muscle soreness. Topical (applied to the skin) bromelain is used for wounds and burns.

Bromelain is obtained from the stem or fruit of the pineapple. It is sold in the form of a powder, cream, tablet, or capsule, and it may be used alone or in combination with other ingredients.

How Much Do We Know?

There have been several studies on the use of bromelain for nasal swelling and inflammation and for removing dead skin from burns. Little research has been done on other uses of bromelain.

What Have We Learned?

- A systematic review of the evidence indicates that bromelain is helpful in relieving symptoms of acute nasal and sinus inflammation when used in combination with standard medications.

- Research in human and animal studies has found that topical bromelain preparations may help remove dead skin from burns. However, not enough evidence exists to show whether topical bromelain helps to treat burns and other wounds.

- There is conflicting evidence about whether bromelain, alone or in combination with other ingredients, is helpful for osteoarthritis and for muscle soreness after exercise.

- There is not enough evidence to determine if bromelain is effective for the other conditions for which it has been used, including cancer and gastrointestinal problems.

- NCCIH-funded research is examining bromelain for inflammatory conditions and asthma.

What Do We Know about Safety?

- There have been some reports of gastrointestinal problems, increased heart rate, and menstrual problems in people who have taken bromelain orally.

- Allergic reactions may occur in individuals who are sensitive or allergic to pineapples or who may have other allergies.

Keep in Mind

Tell all your health care providers about any complementary health approaches you use. Give them a full picture of what you do to manage your health. This will help ensure coordinated and safe care.

Butterbur

Common Names: butterbur, petasites, purple butterbur. Butterbur is also known under several patented standardized extract forms, such as Petadolex.

Latin Names: *Petasites hybridus* (also known as *Petasitidis hybridus, Petasites officinalis,* or *Tussilago hybrida*).

Butterbur is a shrub that grows in Europe and parts of Asia and North America, typically in wet, marshy ground. The name, butterbur, is attributed to the traditional use of its large leaves to wrap butter in warm weather. Butterbur has historically been used for a variety of health issues such as pain, headache, anxiety, cough, fever, and gastrointestinal and urinary tract conditions. It has also been used topically to improve wound healing. Recently, traditional or folk uses include nasal allergies, allergic skin reactions, asthma, and migraine headache.

The leaves, rhizomes (underground stems), and roots of butterbur are commonly used to make solid extracts used in tablets. Some butterbur extracts are also used topically.

What the Science Says

- An NCCIH-funded literature review reports that in a clinical trial of 125 participants, butterbur was just as effective as a commonly used oral antihistamine for allergy symptoms such as itchy eyes.

- According to one systematic literature review, there is evidence to support the effectiveness of butterbur for the treatment of migraines.

- There is some evidence that butterbur extract can decrease the symptoms associated with nasal allergies.

- There is not enough evidence to show efficacy and safety of butterbur for allergic skin reactions and asthma.

Side Effects and Cautions

- The raw, unprocessed butterbur plant contains chemicals called pyrrolizidine alkaloids (PAs). PAs can cause liver damage and can result in serious illness. Only butterbur products that have been processed to remove PAs and are labeled or certified as PA-free should be used.

- Several studies, including a few studies of children and adolescents, have reported that PA-free butterbur products are safe and well tolerated when taken by mouth in recommended doses for up to 12 to 16 weeks. The safety of longer-term use has not been established.

- Butterbur can cause belching, headache, itchy eyes, gastrointestinal issues, asthma, fatigue, and drowsiness.

- Butterbur may cause allergic reactions in people who are sensitive to plants such as ragweed, chrysanthemums, marigolds, and daisies.

- Butterbur should only be given to children under the supervision of a qualified health practitioner.

Keep in Mind

Tell all your health care providers about any complementary health approaches you use. Give them a full picture of what you do to manage your health. This will help ensure coordinated and safe care.

Cat's Claw

Common Names: cat's claw, *uña de gato*
Latin Names: *Uncaria tomentosa, Uncaria guianensis*

Cat's claw grows wild in many countries of Central and South America, especially in the Amazon rainforest. The use of this woody vine dates back to the Inca civilization. Historically, cat's claw has been used for centuries in South America to prevent and treat disease. More recently, cat's claw has been used as a folk or traditional remedy for a variety of health conditions, including viral infections (such as herpes and HIV), Alzheimer's disease, cancer, and arthritis. Other folk uses include supporting the immune system and promoting kidney health, as well as preventing and aborting pregnancy.

The inner bark of cat's claw is used to make liquid extracts, capsules, and teas. Preparations of cat's claw can also be applied to the skin.

What the Science Says

- There is not enough scientific evidence to determine whether cat's claw works for any health condition.

- Small studies in humans have shown a possible benefit of cat's claw in osteoarthritis and rheumatoid arthritis, but no large trials have been done. In laboratory studies, cat's claw stimulates part of the immune system, but it has not been proven to reduce inflammation or boost the immune system in humans.

- The National Institute on Aging funded a study that looked at how cat's claw may affect the brain. Findings may point to new avenues for research in Alzheimer's disease treatment.

Side Effects and Cautions

- Few side effects have been reported for cat's claw when it is taken at recommended dosages. Though rare, side effects may include headaches, dizziness, and vomiting.

- Women who are pregnant or trying to become pregnant should avoid using cat's claw because of its past use for preventing and aborting pregnancy.

- Because cat's claw may stimulate the immune system, it is unclear whether the herb is safe for people with conditions affecting the immune system.

231

- Cat's claw may interfere with controlling blood pressure during or after surgery.

Keep in Mind

Tell all your health care providers about any complementary health approaches you use. Give them a full picture of what you do to manage your health. This will help ensure coordinated and safe care.

Chamomile

Common Names: chamomile, German chamomile
Latin Names: *Matricaria recutita, Chamomilla recutita*

Two types of chamomile have been used for health conditions: German chamomile and Roman chamomile. While the two kinds are thought to have similar effects on the body, the German variety is more commonly used in the United States.

Chamomile has been widely used in children and adults for thousands of years for a variety of health conditions. Recently, chamomile is used as a folk or traditional remedy for sleeplessness, anxiety, and gastrointestinal conditions such as upset stomach, gas, and diarrhea. It is also used topically for skin conditions and for mouth ulcers resulting from cancer treatment.

The flowering tops of the chamomile plant are used to make teas, liquid extracts, capsules, or tablets. The herb can also be applied to the skin as a cream or an ointment, or used as a mouth rinse.

What the Science Says

- Chamomile has not been well studied in people so there is little evidence to support its use for any condition.

- Some early studies point to chamomile's possible benefits for certain skin conditions and for mouth ulcers caused by chemotherapy or radiation.

- In combination with other herbs, chamomile may be of some benefit for upset stomach, for diarrhea in children, and for infants with colic.

- NCCIH-funded research includes studies of chamomile for generalized anxiety disorder and abdominal pain caused by children's bowel disorders.

232

Side Effects and Cautions

- There are reports of allergic reactions in people who have eaten or come into contact with chamomile products. Reactions can include skin rashes, throat swelling, shortness of breath, and anaphylaxis (a life-threatening allergic reaction).

- People are more likely to experience allergic reactions to chamomile if they are allergic to related plants in the daisy family, which includes ragweed, chrysanthemums, marigolds, and daisies.

Keep in Mind

Tell all your health care providers about any complementary health approaches you use. Give them a full picture of what you do to manage your health. This will help to ensure coordinated and safe care.

Chasteberry

Common Names: chasteberry, chaste-tree berry, vitex, monk's pepper
Latin Name: *Vitex agnus-castus*

Chasteberry is the fruit of the chaste tree, a small shrub-like tree native to Central Asia and the Mediterranean region. The name is thought to come from a belief that the plant promoted chastity—it is reported that monks in the Middle Ages used chasteberry to decrease sexual desire.

Chasteberry has been used for thousands of years, mostly by women to ease menstrual problems and to stimulate the production of breast milk. Currently, chasteberry is still used as a folk or traditional remedy for menstrual problems, such as premenstrual syndrome, as well as for symptoms of menopause, some types of infertility, and acne.

The dried ripe chasteberry is used to prepare liquid extracts or solid extracts that are put into capsules and tablets.

What the Science Says

- A few studies of chasteberry for premenstrual syndrome have found a benefit. However, most of these studies were not well designed, so firm conclusions cannot be drawn.

- Small studies suggest that chasteberry may help with breast pain and some types of infertility, but there is not enough

233

reliable scientific evidence to determine whether chasteberry has any effect on these conditions.

- NCCIH has funded studies on chasteberry. Projects have explored how chasteberry works in the body and how it might affect symptoms of premenstrual syndrome.

Side Effects and Cautions

- Chasteberry has not been associated with serious side effects. However, it can cause gastrointestinal problems, acne-like rashes, and dizziness.
- Chasteberry may affect certain hormone levels. Women who are pregnant or taking birth control pills or who have a hormone-sensitive condition (such as breast cancer) should not use chasteberry.
- Because chasteberry may affect the dopamine system in the brain, people taking dopamine-related medications, such as certain antipsychotic drugs and Parkinson's disease medications, should avoid using chasteberry.

Keep in Mind

Tell all your health care providers about any complementary health approaches you use. Give them a full picture of what you do to manage your health. This will help ensure coordinated and safe care.

Cinnamon

Common Names: cinnamon, cinnamon bark, Ceylon cinnamon, cassia cinnamon, Chinese cinnamon

Latin Names: *Cinnamomum zeylanicum* (also known as *Cinnamomum verum*); *Cinnamomum cassia* (also known as *Cinnamomum aromaticum*)

Cinnamon comes from the bark of trees native to China, India, and Southeast Asia. A popular cooking spice in many cultures for centuries, cinnamon also has a long history of use as a folk or traditional medicine. For example, many ancient societies used cinnamon for bronchitis. Additional folk or traditional uses include gastrointestinal problems, loss of appetite, and control of diabetes, as well as a variety of other conditions.

Cinnamon bark is used to make powders, capsules, teas, and liquid extracts. Although there are many kinds of cinnamon, Ceylon cinnamon (sometimes referred to as "true" cinnamon) and cassia cinnamon (also known as Chinese cinnamon) are the most familiar.

What the Science Says

- High-quality clinical evidence (i.e., studies in people) to support the use of cinnamon for any medical condition is generally lacking.

- An analysis of five clinical trials concluded that cinnamon does not appear to affect factors related to diabetes and heart disease.

Side Effects and Cautions

- Cinnamon appears to be safe for most people when taken by mouth in amounts up to 6 grams daily for 6 weeks or less. Some people may have allergic reactions to cinnamon or its parts.

- Cassia cinnamon contains coumarin, the parent compound of warfarin, a medication used to keep blood from clotting. Due to concerns about the possible effects of coumarin, in 2006, the German Federal Institute for Risk Assessment warned against consuming large amounts of cassia cinnamon.

- Cinnamon should not be used in place of conventional medical care or to delay seeking care if you are experiencing symptoms that are of concern; this is particularly true if you have diabetes.

Keep in Mind

Tell all your health care providers about any complementary health approaches you use. Give them a full picture of what you do to manage your health. This will help ensure coordinated and safe care.

Cranberry

Common Names: cranberry, American cranberry, bog cranberry
Latin Name: *Vaccinium macrocarpon*

Cranberries are the fruit of a native plant of North America. These red berries are used in foods and in herbal products. Historically, cranberry fruits and leaves were used for a variety of problems, such as wounds, urinary disorders, diarrhea, diabetes, stomach ailments, and liver problems. More recently, cranberry has been used as a folk or traditional remedy for urinary tract infections or *Helicobacter pylori*

(H. pylori) infections that can lead to stomach ulcers, or to prevent dental plaque. Cranberry has also been reported to have antioxidant and anticancer activity.

The berries are used to produce beverages and many other food products, as well as dietary supplements in the form of extracts, capsules, or tablets.

What the Science Says

- There is some evidence that cranberry can help to prevent urinary tract infections; however, the evidence is not definitive, and more research is needed. Cranberry has not been shown to be effective as a treatment for an existing urinary tract infection.

- Research shows that components found in cranberry may prevent bacteria, such as *E. coli*, from clinging to the cells along the walls of the urinary tract and causing infection. There is also preliminary evidence that cranberry may reduce the ability of *H. pylori* bacteria to live in the stomach and cause ulcers.

- Findings from a few laboratory studies suggest that cranberry may have antioxidant properties and may also be able to reduce dental plaque (a cause of gum disease).

- NCCIH is funding studies of cranberry, primarily to better understand its effects on urinary tract infection. The Office of Dietary Supplements and other National Institutes of Health (NIH) agencies are also supporting cranberry research; for example, the National Institute on Aging is funding a laboratory study of potential anti-aging effects.

Side Effects and Cautions

- Drinking cranberry juice products appears to be safe, although excessive amounts could cause gastrointestinal upset or diarrhea.

- People who think they have a urinary tract infection should see a health care provider for proper diagnosis and treatment. Cranberry products should not be used to treat infection.

- There are some indications that cranberry should be used cautiously by people who take blood-thinning drugs (such as warfarin), medications that affect the liver, or aspirin.

Keep in Mind

Tell all your health care providers about any complementary health approaches you use. Give them a full picture of what you do to manage your health. This will help ensure coordinated and safe care.

Dandelion

Common Names: dandelion, lion's tooth, blowball
Latin Name: *Taraxacum officinale*

Dandelion greens are edible and are a rich source of vitamin A. Dandelion has been used in many traditional medical systems, including Native American and traditional Arabic medicine. Historically, dandelion was most commonly used to treat liver diseases, kidney diseases, and spleen problems. Less commonly, dandelion was used to treat digestive problems and skin conditions. Recently, traditional or folk uses of dandelion include use as a liver or kidney "tonic," as a diuretic, and for minor digestive problems.

The leaves and roots of the dandelion, or the whole plant, are used fresh or dried in teas, capsules, or extracts. Dandelion leaves are used in salads or as a cooked green, and the flowers are used to make wine.

What the Science Says

There is no compelling scientific evidence for using dandelion as a treatment for any medical condition.

Side Effects and Cautions

- Dandelion use is generally considered safe. However, there have been rare reports of upset stomach and diarrhea, and some people are allergic to the plant.

- People with an inflamed or infected gallbladder, or blocked bile ducts, should avoid using dandelion.

Keep in Mind

Tell all your health care providers about any complementary health approaches you use. Give them a full picture of what you do to manage your health. This will help ensure coordinated and safe care.

237

Ephedra

Common Names: ephedra, Chinese ephedra, ma huang
Latin Name: *Ephedra sinica*

Ephedra is an evergreen shrub-like plant native to Central Asia and Mongolia. The principal active ingredient, ephedrine, is a compound that can powerfully stimulate the nervous system and heart. Ephedra has been used for more than 5,000 years in China and India to treat conditions such as colds, fever, flu, headaches, asthma, wheezing, and nasal congestion. More recently, ephedra was used as an ingredient in dietary supplements for weight loss, increased energy, and enhanced athletic performance.

The dried stems and leaves of the ephedra plant have been used to create capsules, tablets, tinctures, and teas.

What the Science Says

- An NCCIH-funded study that analyzed phone calls to poison control centers found a higher rate of side effects from ephedra, compared with other herbal products.

- Other studies and systematic reviews have found an increased risk of heart, psychiatric, and gastrointestinal problems, as well as high blood pressure and stroke, with ephedra use.

- According to the U.S. Food and Drug Administration (FDA), there is little evidence of ephedra's effectiveness, except for short-term weight loss. However, the increased risk of heart problems and stroke outweighs any benefits.

Side Effects and Cautions

- In 2004, the FDA banned the U.S. sale of dietary supplements containing ephedra. The FDA found that these supplements had an unreasonable risk of injury or illness—particularly cardiovascular complications—and a risk of death. The ban does not apply to traditional Chinese herbal remedies or to products like herbal teas regulated as conventional foods.

- Between 1995 and 1997, the FDA received more than 900 reports of possible ephedra toxicity. Serious adverse events such as stroke, heart attack, and sudden death were reported in 37 cases.

- Using ephedra may worsen many health conditions such as cardiovascular disease, kidney disease, and diabetes.

- Ephedra may cause seizures in otherwise healthy people as well as in people with seizure disorders.

- Taking ephedra can also result in anxiety, difficulty urinating, dry mouth, headache, heart damage, high blood pressure, irregular heart rhythms, irritation of the stomach, kidney stones, nausea, psychosis, restlessness, sleep problems, and tremors.

- Women who are pregnant or breastfeeding and children should avoid taking ephedra.

- Ephedra use may lead to serious health problems when used with other dietary supplements or medicines.

- Combining ephedra with caffeine increases the risk of potentially serious side effects.

Keep in Mind

Tell all your health care providers about any complementary health approaches you use. Give them a full picture of what you do to manage your health. This will help ensure coordinated and safe care.

European Mistletoe

Common Names: European mistletoe, mistletoe
Latin Name: *Viscum album L*

European mistletoe is a semi-parasitic plant that grows on several types of trees in temperate regions worldwide. Where the term "mistletoe" is used in this chapter, it refers to European mistletoe. (European mistletoe is different from American mistletoe, which is used as a holiday decoration.) Mistletoe has been used for centuries in traditional medicine to treat seizures, headaches, and other conditions. Recently, mistletoe is used mainly in Europe as a treatment for cancer.

The leafy shoots and berries of mistletoe are used to make extracts that can be taken by mouth. In Europe, mistletoe extracts are prescription drugs that are given by injection. In the United States, mistletoe by injection is available only in clinical trials.

What the Science Says

- Laboratory studies have found that mistletoe kills cancer cells and stimulates the immune system.

- The use of mistletoe to treat cancer has been studied in Europe in more than 30 clinical trials. Although improvements in

239

survival or quality of life have been reported, almost all of the trials had major weaknesses in their design that raise doubts about the findings. For example, many of the studies had a small number of participants or did not have a control group.

Side Effects and Cautions

- Raw, unprocessed mistletoe is poisonous. Eating raw, unprocessed European mistletoe or American mistletoe can cause vomiting, seizures, a slowing of the heart rate, and even death. American mistletoe is unsafe for medicinal use.

- In countries where commercial mistletoe is available by injection, such as Germany, those extracts are considered to be generally safe when used according to product directions and under the supervision of a health care provider.

- Injected mistletoe extract may cause itching or redness in the area of the injection. Less commonly, side effects may include more extensive skin reactions, low-grade fevers, or flu-like symptoms. There have been very rare reports of more serious allergic reactions, such as difficulty breathing.

- Because mistletoe has not yet been proven to be a safe and effective cancer treatment, it should not be used outside of clinical trials.

Keep in Mind

Tell all your health care providers about any complementary health approaches you use. Give them a full picture of what you do to manage your health. This will help ensure coordinated and safe care.

Evening Primrose Oil [EPO]

Common Names: evening primrose oil, EPO
Latin Name: *Oenothera biennis*

Evening primrose is a plant native to North America, but it grows in Europe and parts of the Southern hemisphere as well. It has yellow flowers that bloom in the evening. Evening primrose oil contains the fatty acid gamma-linolenic acid (GLA).

Evening primrose oil has been used since the 1930s as a folk or traditional remedy for eczema (a condition in which the skin becomes inflamed, itchy, or scaly because of allergies or other irritation). More recent folk uses include other conditions involving inflammation, such as rheumatoid arthritis; conditions affecting women's health, such as breast pain associated with the menstrual cycle, menopausal symptoms, and premenstrual syndrome (PMS); cancer; and diabetes.

Evening primrose oil is extracted from the seeds of the evening primrose. The oil is usually put into capsules for use.

What the Science Says

- There is not enough evidence to support the use of evening primrose oil for any health condition.

- According to a comprehensive 2013 evaluation of the evidence, evening primrose oil, taken orally (by mouth), is not helpful for relieving symptoms of eczema.

- Evening primrose oil has been studied for rheumatoid arthritis and breast pain. However, study results are mixed, and most studies have been small and not well designed.

- Evening primrose oil does not appear to affect menopausal symptoms.

- The best-designed clinical trials of evening primrose oil for PMS found no effect.

Side Effects and Cautions

- Evening primrose oil is well tolerated by most people, when taken for short periods of time. Mild side effects include gastrointestinal upset and headache.

- The safety of long-term use of evening primrose oil has not been established.

- Evening primrose oil may increase bleeding in people who are taking the anticoagulant (blood thinning) medication warfarin.

Keep in Mind

Tell all your health care providers about any complementary health approaches you use. Give them a full picture of what you do to manage your health. This will help ensure coordinated and safe care.

Fenugreek

Common Names: fenugreek, fenugreek seed
Latin Name: *Trigonella foenum-graecum*

241

The first recorded use of fenugreek is described on an ancient Egyptian papyrus dated to 1500 B.C. Fenugreek seed is commonly used in cooking. Historically, fenugreek was used for a variety of health conditions, including menopausal symptoms and digestive problems. It was also used for inducing childbirth. Recently, fenugreek is used as a folk or traditional remedy for diabetes and loss of appetite, and to stimulate milk production in breastfeeding women. It is also applied to the skin for inflammation.

The dried seeds are ground and taken by mouth or used to form a paste that is applied to the skin.

What the Science Says

- A few small studies have found that fenugreek may help lower blood sugar levels in people with diabetes.

- There is not enough scientific evidence to support the use of fenugreek for any other health condition.

Side Effects and Cautions

- Possible side effects of fenugreek when taken by mouth include gas, bloating, and diarrhea. Fenugreek can cause irritation when applied to the skin.

- Given its historical use for inducing childbirth, women should use caution when taking fenugreek during pregnancy.

Keep in Mind

Tell all your health care providers about any complementary health approaches you use. Give them a full picture of what you do to manage your health. This will help ensure coordinated and safe care.

Feverfew

Common Names: feverfew, bachelor's buttons, featherfew
Latin Names: *Tanacetum parthenium, Chrysanthemum parthenium*

Originally, a plant native to the Balkan mountains of Eastern Europe, feverfew—a short bush with daisy-like flowers—now grows throughout Europe, North America, and South America. For centuries, traditional uses of feverfew have included fevers, headaches, stomach aches, toothaches, insect bites, infertility, and problems with menstruation and with labor during childbirth. Newer folk or traditional uses for feverfew include migraine headaches, rheumatoid arthritis, psoriasis, allergies, asthma, tinnitus (ringing or roaring sounds in the ears), dizziness, nausea, and vomiting.

The dried leaves—and sometimes flowers and stems—of feverfew are used to make supplements, including capsules, tablets, and liquid extracts. The leaves are sometimes eaten fresh.

What the Science Says

- Some research suggests that feverfew may be helpful in preventing migraine headaches; however, results have been mixed and more evidence is needed from well-designed studies.

- One study found that feverfew did not reduce rheumatoid arthritis symptoms in women whose symptoms did not respond to conventional medicines. It has been suggested that feverfew could help those with milder symptoms.

- There is not enough evidence available to assess whether feverfew is beneficial for other uses.

- NCCIH-funded researchers have studied ways to standardize feverfew; that is, to prepare it in a consistent manner. Standardized preparations can be used in future studies of feverfew.

Side Effects and Cautions

- No serious side effects have been reported for feverfew. Side effects can include canker sores, swelling and irritation of the lips and tongue, and loss of taste.

- Less common side effects can include nausea, digestive problems, and bloating.

- People who take feverfew for a long time and then stop taking it may have difficulty sleeping, headaches, joint pain, nervousness, and stiff muscles.

- Women who are pregnant should not use feverfew because it may cause the uterus to contract, increasing the risk of miscarriage or premature delivery.

- People can have allergic reactions to feverfew. Those who are allergic to other members of the daisy family (which includes ragweed and chrysanthemums) are more likely to be allergic to feverfew.

243

Keep in Mind

Tell all your health care providers about any complementary health approaches you use. Give them a full picture of what you do to manage your health. This will help ensure coordinated and safe care.

Garlic

Common Name: garlic
Latin Name: *Allium sativum*

Garlic is the edible bulb from a plant in the lily family. It has been used as both a medicine and a spice for thousands of years. Garlic's most common folk or traditional uses as a dietary supplement are for high cholesterol, heart disease, and high blood pressure. Other folk or traditional uses include prevention of certain types of cancer, including stomach and colon cancers. Garlic cloves can be eaten raw or cooked. They may also be dried or powdered and used in tablets and capsules. Raw garlic cloves can be used to make oils and liquid extracts.

What the Science Says

- Some evidence indicates that taking garlic can slightly lower blood cholesterol levels; studies have shown positive effects for short-term (1 to 3 months) use. However, an NCCIH-funded study on the safety and effectiveness of three garlic preparations (fresh garlic, dried powdered garlic tablets, and aged garlic extract tablets) for lowering blood cholesterol levels found no effect.

- Preliminary research suggests that taking garlic may slow the development of atherosclerosis (hardening of the arteries), a condition that can lead to heart disease or stroke.

- Evidence suggests that taking garlic may slightly lower blood pressure, particularly in people with high blood pressure.

- Some studies suggest consuming garlic as a regular part of the diet may lower the risk of certain cancers. However, no clinical trials have examined this. A clinical trial on the long-term use of garlic supplements to prevent stomach cancer found no effect.

- Recent NCCIH-funded research includes studies on how garlic interacts with certain drugs; its effects on liver function and the dilation and constriction of blood vessels; and the bioavailability (how well a substance is absorbed by the body) of allicin, the main active compound of garlic.

Side Effects and Cautions

• Garlic appears to be safe for most adults.

• Side effects include breath and body odor, heartburn, upset stomach, and allergic reactions. These side effects are more common with raw garlic.

• Garlic can thin the blood (reduce the ability of blood to clot) in a manner similar to aspirin. This effect may be a problem during or after surgery. Use garlic with caution if you are planning to have surgery or dental work, or if you have a bleeding disorder.

• Garlic has been found to interfere with the effectiveness of saquinavir, a drug used to treat HIV infection. Its effect on other drugs has not been well studied.

Keep in Mind

Tell all your health care providers about any complementary health approaches you use. Give them a full picture of what you do to manage your health. This will help ensure coordinated and safe care.

Ginger

Common Name: ginger
Latin Name: *Zingiber officinale*

Ginger is a tropical plant that has green-purple flowers and an aromatic underground stem (called a rhizome). It is commonly used for cooking and medicinal purposes. Historically, ginger has been used in Asian medicine to treat stomach aches, nausea, and diarrhea. Recently, ginger is used as a folk or traditional remedy for postsurgery nausea; nausea caused by motion, chemotherapy, and pregnancy; rheumatoid arthritis; osteoarthritis; and joint and muscle pain.

What the Science Says

• Studies suggest that the short-term use of ginger can safely relieve pregnancy-related nausea and vomiting.

• Studies are mixed on whether ginger is effective for nausea caused by motion, chemotherapy, or surgery.

• It is unclear whether ginger is effective in treating rheumatoid arthritis, osteoarthritis, or joint and muscle pain.

- NCCIH-funded investigators have looked at whether ginger interacts with drugs, such as those used to suppress the immune system, and ginger's effects on reducing nausea and vomiting. Investigators are also studying:

  - The general safety and effectiveness of ginger's use for health purposes, as well as its active components and effects on inflammation.

  - The effects of ginger dietary supplements on joint inflammation, rheumatoid arthritis, and osteoporosis.

Side Effects and Cautions

- Few side effects are linked to ginger when it is taken in small doses.

- Side effects most often reported are gas, bloating, heartburn, and nausea. These effects are most often associated with powdered ginger.

Keep in Mind

Tell all your health care providers about any complementary health approaches you use. Give them a full picture of what you do to manage your health. This will help ensure coordinated and safe care.

Goldenseal

Common Names: goldenseal, yellow root
Latin Name: *Hydrastis canadensis*

Goldenseal is a plant that grows wild in parts of the United States but has become endangered by overharvesting. With natural supplies dwindling, goldenseal is now grown commercially across the United States, especially in the Blue Ridge Mountains. Historically, Native Americans have used goldenseal for various health conditions such as skin diseases, ulcers, and gonorrhea. Currently, folk or traditional uses of goldenseal include colds and other respiratory tract infections, infectious diarrhea, eye infections, vaginitis (inflammation or infection of the vagina), and occasionally, cancer. It is also applied to wounds and canker sores and is used as a mouthwash for sore gums, mouth, and throat.

The underground stems or roots of goldenseal are dried and used to make teas, liquid extracts, and solid extracts that may be made into tablets and capsules. Goldenseal is often combined with echinacea in preparations that are intended to be used for colds.

246

What the Science Says

- Few studies have been published on goldenseal's safety and effectiveness, and there is little scientific evidence to support using it for any health problem.

- Clinical studies on a compound found in goldenseal, berberine, suggest that the compound may be beneficial for certain infections—such as those that cause some types of diarrhea, as well as some eye infections. However, goldenseal preparations contain only a small amount of berberine, so it is difficult to extend the evidence about the effectiveness of berberine to goldenseal.

- NCCIH is funding research on goldenseal, including studies of antibacterial mechanisms and potential cholesterol-lowering effects. NCCIH is also funding development of research-grade goldenseal, to facilitate clinical studies.

Side Effects and Cautions

- Goldenseal is considered safe for short-term use in adults at recommended dosages. Rare side effects may include nausea and vomiting.

- There is little information about the safety of high dosages or the long-term use of goldenseal.

- Goldenseal may cause changes in the way the body processes drugs, and could potentially alter the effects of many drugs.

- Other herbs containing berberine, including Chinese goldthread *(Coptis trifolia)* and Oregon grape *(Mahonia aquifolium)*, are sometimes substituted for goldenseal. These herbs may have different effects, side effects, and drug interactions than goldenseal.

- Women who are pregnant or breastfeeding should avoid using goldenseal. Berberine, a chemical in goldenseal, can cause or worsen jaundice in newborns and could lead to a life-threatening problem called kernicterus.

- Goldenseal should not be given to infants and young children.

Keep in Mind

Tell all your health care providers about any complementary health approaches you use. Give them a full picture of what you do to manage your health. This will help ensure coordinated and safe care.

Grape Seed Extract

Common Name: grape seed extract
Latin Name: *Vitis vinifera*

The leaves and fruit of the grape have been used medicinally since ancient Greece. Recently, grape seed extract is used as a folk or traditional remedy for conditions related to the heart and blood vessels, such as atherosclerosis (hardening of the arteries), high blood pressure, high cholesterol, and poor circulation; complications related to diabetes, such as nerve and eye damage; vision problems, such as macular degeneration (which can cause blindness); swelling after an injury or surgery; cancer prevention; and wound healing.

The grape seeds used to produce grape seed extract are generally obtained from wine manufacturers. Grape seed extract is available in capsule and tablet forms.

What the Science Says

- Studies have found that some compounds in grape seed extract may be effective in relieving symptoms of chronic venous insufficiency (when veins have problems sending blood from the legs back to the heart) and reducing edema (swelling) after an injury or surgery.

- Small randomized trials have found beneficial effects of grape seed extract for diabetic retinopathy (an eye problem caused by diabetes) and for vascular fragility (weakness in small blood vessels). Larger trials are needed to confirm these findings.

- Grape seed extract contains antioxidants, which help prevent cell damage caused by free radicals (highly reactive molecules that can damage cell function). Preliminary studies have shown some beneficial antioxidant effects; however, more research is needed.

- A study funded by the National Cancer Institute (NCI) found that grape seed extract did not reduce the hardening of breast tissue that can occur after radiation therapy for breast cancer.

- NCI is also funding studies to evaluate whether grape seed extract is effective in preventing breast cancer in postmenopausal women and prostate cancer.

- NCCIH is studying whether the action of grape seed extract and its components may benefit the heart or help prevent cognitive decline, Alzheimer's disease, and other brain disorders. Another study is investigating the effects of grape seed extract on colon cancer.

Side Effects and Cautions

- Grape seed extract is generally well tolerated when taken by mouth. It has been used safely for up to 8 weeks in clinical trials.

- Side effects that have been reported include a dry, itchy scalp; dizziness; headache; high blood pressure; hives; indigestion; and nausea.

- Interactions between grape seed extract and medicines or other supplements have not been carefully studied.

Keep in Mind

Tell all your health care providers about any complementary health approaches you use. Give them a full picture of what you do to manage your health. This will help ensure coordinated and safe care.

Hawthorn

Common Names: hawthorn, English hawthorn, harthorne, haw, hawthorne

Latin Names: *Crataegus laevigata* (also known as *Crataegus oxyacantha*), *Crataegus monogyna*

Hawthorn is a spiny, flowering shrub or small tree of the rose family. The species of hawthorn discussed here are native to northern European regions and grow throughout the world.

Historically, hawthorn fruit has been used for heart disease since the first century. It has also been used for digestive and kidney problems. More recently, hawthorn leaf and flower have been used as folk or traditional remedies for heart failure, a weakness of the heart muscle that prevents the heart from pumping enough blood to the rest of the body, which can lead to fatigue and limit physical activities. Hawthorn is also used for other heart conditions, including symptoms of coronary artery disease (such as angina).

The hawthorn leaf and flower are used to make liquid extracts, usually with water and alcohol. Dry extracts can be put into capsules and tablets.

What the Science Says

- There is scientific evidence that hawthorn leaf and flower may be safe and effective for milder forms of heart failure, but study results are conflicting.
- There is not enough scientific evidence to determine whether hawthorn works for other heart problems.
- NCCIH-supported research to date includes a study of the mechanism by which hawthorn may affect heart failure.

Side Effects and Cautions

- Hawthorn is considered safe for most adults when used for short periods of time. Side effects are rare and can include upset stomach, headache, and dizziness.
- Although drug interactions with hawthorn have not been thoroughly studied, there is evidence to suggest that hawthorn may interact with a number of different drugs, including certain heart medications.

Keep in Mind

Tell all your health care providers about any complementary health approaches you use. Give them a full picture of what you do to manage your health. This will help ensure coordinated and safe care.

Horse Chestnut

Common Names: horse chestnut, buckeye, Spanish chestnut
Latin Name: *Aesculus hippocastanum*

Horse chestnut trees are native to the Balkan Peninsula (for example, Greece and Bulgaria), but grow throughout the Northern Hemisphere. Although horse chestnut is sometimes called buckeye, it should not be confused with the Ohio or California buckeye trees, which are related but not the same species.

For centuries, horse chestnut seeds, leaves, bark, and flowers were used for a variety of conditions and diseases. Recently, horse chestnut seed extract is used primarily as a folk or traditional remedy for chronic venous insufficiency (a condition in which the veins do not efficiently return blood from the legs to the heart). This condition is associated with varicose veins, pain, ankle swelling, feelings of heaviness, itching, and nighttime leg cramping. The seed extract has also been used as a folk or traditional remedy for hemorrhoids.

Horse chestnut seed extract standardized to contain 16 to 20 percent aescin (escin), the active ingredient, is the most commonly used form. Topical preparations have also been used.

What the Science Says

- Studies have found that horse chestnut seed extract is beneficial in treating chronic venous insufficiency. There is also preliminary evidence that horse chestnut seed extract may be as effective as wearing compression stockings.

- There is not enough scientific evidence to support the use of horse chestnut seed, leaf, or bark for any other conditions.

Side Effects and Cautions

- Do not use raw or unprocessed horse chestnut seeds, leaves, bark, or flowers. They contain esculin, which is poisonous.

- When properly processed, horse chestnut seed extract contains little or no esculin and is considered generally safe when used for short periods of time. However, the extract can cause some side effects, including itching, nausea, or gastrointestinal upset.

Keep in Mind

Tell all your health care providers about any complementary health approaches you use. Give them a full picture of what you do to manage your health. This will help ensure coordinated and safe care.

Kava

Common Names: kava, kava kava, awa, kava pepper
Latin Name: *Piper methysticum*

Kava is native to the islands of the South Pacific and is a member of the pepper family. Kava has been used as a ceremonial beverage in the South Pacific for centuries.

Historically, kava was used to help people fall asleep and fight fatigue, as well as to treat asthma and urinary tract infections. It also had a topical use as a numbing agent. More recent folk or traditional uses include anxiety, insomnia, and menopausal symptoms.

The root and rhizome (underground stem) of kava are used to prepare beverages, extracts, capsules, tablets, and topical solutions.

What the Science Says

- Although scientific studies provide some evidence that kava may be beneficial for the management of anxiety, the U.S. Food and Drug Administration (FDA) has issued a warning that using kava supplements has been linked to a risk of severe liver damage.
- Kava is not a proven therapy for other uses.
- NCCIH-funded studies on kava were suspended after the FDA issued its warning.

Side Effects and Cautions

- Kava has been reported to cause liver damage, including hepatitis and liver failure (which can cause death).
- Kava has been associated with several cases of dystonia (abnormal muscle spasm or involuntary muscle movements). Kava may interact with several drugs, including drugs used for Parkinson's disease.
- Long-term and/or heavy use of kava may result in scaly, yellowed skin.
- Avoid driving and operating heavy machinery while taking kava because the herb has been reported to cause drowsiness.

Keep in Mind

Tell all your health care providers about any complementary health approaches you use. Give them a full picture of what you do to manage your health. This will help ensure coordinated and safe care.

Lavender

Common Names: lavender, English lavender, garden lavender
Latin Name: *Lavandula angustifolia*

Lavender is native to the Mediterranean region. It was used in ancient Egypt as part of the process for mummifying bodies. Lavender's use as a bath additive originated in Persia, Greece, and Rome. The herb's name comes from the Latin lavare, which means "to wash."

Historically, lavender was used as an antiseptic and for mental health purposes. Recently, lavender is used as a folk or traditional remedy for anxiety, restlessness, insomnia, depression, headache, upset stomach, and hair loss.

Lavender is most commonly used in aromatherapy, in which the scent of the essential oil from the flowers is inhaled. The essential oil can also be diluted with another oil and applied to the skin. Dried lavender flowers can be used to make teas or liquid extracts that can be taken by mouth.

What the Science Says

- There is little scientific evidence of lavender's effectiveness for most health uses.

- Small studies on lavender for anxiety show mixed results.

- Some preliminary results indicate that lavender oil, combined with oils from other herbs, may help with hair loss from a condition called alopecia areata.

Side Effects and Cautions

- Topical use of diluted lavender oil or use of lavender as aromatherapy is generally considered safe for most adults. However, applying lavender oil to the skin can cause irritation. There have been reports that topical use can cause breast growth in young boys.

- Lavender oil may be poisonous if taken by mouth.

- When lavender teas and extracts are taken by mouth, they may cause headache, changes in appetite, and constipation.

- Using lavender with sedative medications may increase drowsiness.

Keep in Mind

Tell all your health care providers about any complementary health approaches you use. Give them a full picture of what you do to manage your health. This will help ensure coordinated and safe care.

Licorice Root

Common Names: licorice root, licorice, liquorice, sweet root, gan zao (Chinese licorice)

Latin Names: *Glycyrrhiza glabra, Glycyrrhiza uralensis* (Chinese licorice)

Most licorice is grown in Greece, Turkey, and Asia. Licorice contains a compound called glycyrrhizin (or glycyrrhizic acid). Licorice has a long history of medicinal use in both Eastern and Western systems of medicine. Recently, licorice is used as a folk or traditional remedy for stomach ulcers, bronchitis, and sore throat, as well as infections caused by viruses, such as hepatitis.

Peeled licorice root is available in dried and powdered forms. Licorice root is available as capsules, tablets, and liquid extracts. Licorice can be found with glycyrrhizin removed; the product is called DGL (for "deglycyrrhizinated licorice").

What the Science Says

- An injectable form of licorice extract—not available in the United States—has been shown to have beneficial effects against hepatitis C in clinical trials. There are no reliable data on oral forms of licorice for hepatitis C. More research is needed before reaching any conclusions.

- There are not enough reliable data to determine whether licorice is effective for any condition.

Side Effects and Cautions

- In large amounts, licorice containing glycyrrhizin can cause high blood pressure, salt and water retention, and low potassium levels, which could lead to heart problems. DGL products are thought to cause fewer side effects.

- The safety of using licorice as a dietary supplement for more than 4 to 6 weeks has not been thoroughly studied.

- Taking licorice together with diuretics (water pills), corticosteroids, or other medicines that reduce the body's potassium levels could cause dangerously low potassium levels.

- People with heart disease or high blood pressure should be cautious about using licorice.

- When taken in large amounts, licorice can affect the body's levels of a hormone called cortisol and related steroid drugs, such as prednisone.

- Pregnant women should avoid using licorice as a supplement or consuming large amounts of licorice as food, as some research suggests it could increase the risk of preterm labor.

Keep in Mind

Tell all your health care providers about any complementary health approaches you use. Give them a full picture of what you do to manage your health. This will help ensure coordinated and safe care.

Milk Thistle

Common Names: milk thistle, Mary thistle, holy thistle, silymarin.
Latin Name: *Silybum marianum*

Milk thistle is a flowering herb native to the Mediterranean region. It has been used for thousands of years as a remedy for a variety of ailments, and historically was thought to have protective effects on the liver and improve its function. Today, its primary folk uses include liver disorders such as cirrhosis and chronic hepatitis, and gallbladder disorders. Other folk uses include lowering cholesterol levels, reducing insulin resistance in people who have both type 2 diabetes and cirrhosis, and reducing the growth of breast, cervical, and prostate cancer cells.

Silymarin, which can be extracted from the seeds (fruit) of the milk thistle plant, is believed to be the biologically active part of the herb. The seeds are used to prepare capsules, extracts, powders, and tinctures.

What the Science Says

- Previous laboratory studies suggested that milk thistle may benefit the liver by protecting and promoting the growth of liver cells, fighting oxidation (a chemical process that can damage cells), and inhibiting inflammation. However, results from small clinical trials of milk thistle for liver diseases have been mixed, and two rigorously designed studies found no benefit.

- A 2012 clinical trial, cofunded by NCCIH and the National Institute of Diabetes and Digestive and Kidney Diseases, showed that two higher-than-usual doses of silymarin were no better than placebo for chronic hepatitis C in people who had not responded to standard antiviral treatment.

- The 2008 Hepatitis C Antiviral Long-Term Treatment Against Cirrhosis (HALT-C) study, sponsored by the National Institutes of Health (NIH), found that hepatitis C patients who used silymarin had fewer and milder symptoms of liver disease and somewhat better quality of life but no change in virus activity or liver inflammation.

Side Effects and Cautions

- In clinical trials, milk thistle appears to be well tolerated in recommended doses. Occasionally, people report various gastrointestinal side effects.

- Milk thistle can produce allergic reactions, which tend to be more common among people who are allergic to plants in the same family (for example, ragweed, chrysanthemum, marigold, and daisy).

- Milk thistle may lower blood sugar levels. People with diabetes or hypoglycemia, or people taking drugs or supplements that affect blood sugar levels, should use caution.

Keep in Mind

Tell all your health care providers about any complementary health approaches you use. Give them a full picture of what you do to manage your health. This will help ensure coordinated and safe care.

Noni

Common Names: noni, morinda, Indian mulberry, hog apple, canary wood
Latin Name: *Morinda citrifolia*

Noni is an evergreen shrub or small tree that grows throughout the tropical regions of the Pacific Ocean, from Southeast Asia to Australia. Noni has a history of use as a topical preparation for joint pain and skin conditions. Recently, noni fruit juice has folk uses as a general health tonic and for cancer and chronic conditions such as cardiovascular disease and diabetes.

The noni fruit is most commonly combined with other fruits (such as grape) to make juice. Preparations of the fruit and leaves are also available in capsules, tablets, and teas.

What the Science Says

- In laboratory research, noni has shown antioxidant, immune-stimulating, and tumor-fighting properties. These results suggest that noni may warrant further study for conditions such as cancer and cardiovascular disease. However, noni has not been well studied in people for any health condition.

- NCCIH-funded research includes a study on noni for cancer to determine its safety and potential effects on tumors and symptoms, as well as a laboratory study of noni's effects on prostate cancer cells. The National Cancer Institute is funding preliminary research on noni for breast cancer prevention and treatment.

Side Effects and Cautions

- Noni is high in potassium. People who are on potassium-restricted diets because of kidney problems should avoid using noni.

- Several noni juice manufacturers have received warnings from the U.S. Food and Drug Administration about making unsupported health claims.

- Few side effects from noni have been reported, but its safety has not been adequately studied.

- There have been reports of liver damage from using noni. It should be avoided if you have liver disease because it contains compounds that may make your disease worse.

Keep in Mind

Tell all your health care providers about any complementary health approaches you use. Give them a full picture of what you do to manage your health. This will help ensure coordinated and safe care.

Passionflower

Common Names: passionflower, Maypop, apricot vine, old field apricot, maracuja, water lemon
Latin Name: *Passiflora incarnata* L

Background

- Sixteenth-century Spanish explorers learned of passionflower in Peru. Native peoples of the Americas used passionflower for boils, wounds, earaches, and liver problems.

- Recently, passionflower is used as a dietary supplement for anxiety, stress, and sleep, as well as for heart ailments, asthma, attention-deficit hyperactivity disorder, burns, and hemorrhoids.

- Passionflower is available dried (which can be used to make tea), or as liquid extract, capsules, or tablets.

How Much Do We Know?

- Passionflower's effect on anxiety hasn't been studied extensively. A 2009 systematic review of two studies that included 198 people compared the ability of passionflower and two drugs to reduce anxiety. It concluded that the three substances had about the same degree of minimal effectiveness.

- There isn't enough evidence to draw conclusions about passionflower for cardiovascular conditions, asthma, hemorrhoids, burns, or sleep.

What Do We Know about Safety?

- Passionflower is generally considered to be safe but may cause dizziness and confusion.

- Taking passionflower with a sedative may increase the risk of excessive sleepiness.

- Passionflower should not be used during pregnancy as it may induce contractions.

Keep in Mind

Tell all your health care providers about any complementary health approaches you use. Give them a full picture of what you do to manage your health. This will help ensure coordinated and safe care.

Peppermint Oil

Common Name: peppermint oil
Latin Name: *Mentha x piperita*

The herb peppermint, a cross between two types of mint (water mint and spearmint), grows throughout Europe and North America. Peppermint is often used to flavor foods, and the leaves can be used fresh or dried in teas. Recently, peppermint oil is used as a folk or traditional remedy for nausea, indigestion, cold symptoms, headaches, muscle and nerve pain, stomach problems, and bowel conditions such as irritable bowel syndrome.

Essential oil of peppermint may be found in very small doses in capsule or liquid forms. The essential oil can also be diluted with another oil and applied to the skin.

What the Science Says

- Results from several studies suggest that peppermint oil may improve symptoms of irritable bowel syndrome.

- A few studies have found that peppermint oil, in combination with caraway oil, may help relieve indigestion, but this evidence is preliminary.

- Although there are some promising results, there is no clear-cut evidence to support the use of peppermint oil for other health conditions.

Side Effects and Cautions

- Peppermint oil appears to be safe for most adults when used in small doses. Possible side effects include allergic reactions and heartburn.

- Capsules containing peppermint oil are often coated to reduce the likelihood of heartburn. If they are taken at the same time as medicines such as antacids, this coating can break down more quickly, thus increasing the risk of heartburn.

Keep in Mind

Tell all your health care providers about any complementary health approaches you use. Give them a full picture of what you do to manage your health. This will help ensure coordinated and safe care.

Pomegranate

Common Name: pomegranate
Latin Name: *Punica granatum L*

Background

- Since ancient times, the pomegranate has been a symbol of fertility.

259

- The pomegranate fruit has a leathery rind (or husk) with many little pockets of edible seeds and juice inside.

- Researchers have studied all parts of the pomegranate for their potential health benefits. Those parts include the fruit, seed, seed oil, tannin-rich peel, root, leaf, and flower.

- The pomegranate has been used as a dietary supplement for various conditions including wounds, sore throats, and diarrhea

- Pomegranate is made into capsules, extracts, teas, powders, and juice products.

How Much Do We Know?

We don't have a lot of strong scientific evidence on the effects of pomegranate for people's health.

What Have We Learned?

- A 2012 clinical trial of about 100 dialysis patients suggested that pomegranate juice may help ward off infections. In the study, the patients who were given pomegranate juice three times a week for a year had fewer hospitalizations for infections and fewer signs of inflammation, compared with patients who got the placebo.

- Pomegranate extract in mouthwash may help control dental plaque, a small 2011 clinical trial suggested.

- Pomegranate juice may help improve some signs of heart disease but the research is not definitive.

- Compared with a placebo, pomegranate juice did not improve symptoms of chronic obstructive pulmonary disease, a small, 2006 clinical trial showed.

- NCCIH-funded studies are investigating how pomegranate extracts may affect arthritis.

What Do We Know about Safety?

- Some people may be allergic to pomegranate. In rare cases, people who have eaten pomegranate fruit for many years have developed an allergic reaction that causes their tongue or face to swell.

- It is unclear whether pomegranate interacts with the anticoagulant (blood thinning) medicine warfarin or drugs that work similarly in the body to warfarin.

- Federal agencies have taken action against companies selling pomegranate juice and supplements for deceptive advertising and making drug-like claims about the products.

Keep in Mind

Tell all your health care providers about any complementary health approaches you use. Give them a full picture of what you do to manage your health. This will help ensure coordinated and safe care.

Red Clover

Common Names: red clover, cow clover, meadow clover, wild clover
Latin Name: *Trifolium pratense*

Like peas and beans, red clover belongs to the family of plants called legumes. Red clover contains phytoestrogens—compounds similar to the female hormone estrogen. Historically, red clover has been used for cancer and respiratory problems, such as whooping cough, asthma, and bronchitis. Currently, red clover is used as a traditional or folk remedy for menopausal symptoms, breast pain associated with menstrual cycles, high cholesterol, osteoporosis, and symptoms of prostate enlargement.

The flowering tops of the red clover plant are used to prepare extracts available in tablets and capsules, as well as in teas and liquid forms.

What the Science Says

- Several small studies of red clover for menopausal symptoms had mixed results; however, most of these studies had design flaws. A large clinical trial and several reviews of the research literature concluded that red clover had no significant beneficial effects on menopausal symptoms.

- There is not enough scientific evidence to determine whether red clover is effective for any other health conditions.

- NCCIH is studying red clover to learn more about its active components and how they might work in the body, including how

261

red clover isoflavones may affect human prostate cells and the safety and effectiveness of red clover for menopausal symptoms.

Side Effects and Cautions

- Red clover seems to be safe for most adults when used for short periods of time. No serious adverse effects have been reported.

- Because red clover contains estrogen-like compounds, there is a possibility that its long-term use would increase the risk of women developing cancer of the lining of the uterus. However, studies to date have been too brief (less than 6 months) to evaluate whether red clover has estrogen-like effects on the uterus.

- It is unclear whether red clover is safe for women who are pregnant or breastfeeding, or who have breast cancer or other hormone-sensitive cancers.

Keep in Mind

Tell all your health care providers about any complementary health approaches you use. Give them a full picture of what you do to manage your health. This will help ensure coordinated and safe care.

Rhodiola

Common Names: golden root, roseroot, queen's crown
Latin Name: *Rhodiola rosea L*

Background

- Rhodiola grows in cold regions of Europe and Asia, as well as in Alaska.

- Historically, people in northern regions have used rhodiola for anxiety, fatigue, anemia, impotence, infections, headache, and depression related to stress. People also have used it to increase physical endurance, work performance, longevity, and improve resistance to high-altitude sickness.

- Recently, people use rhodiola as a dietary supplement to increase energy, stamina, and strength, to improve attention and memory, and to enhance the ability to cope with stress.

- The root of rhodiola is sometimes brewed and drunk as a tea. Rhodiola root extracts are also available in capsule or tablet form.

How Much Do We Know?

There have been some studies of rhodiola in people; however, the quality of research is limited so firm conclusions about its effectiveness can't be made.

What Have We Learned?

Two review articles—published in 2011 and 2012—looked at 15 studies that tested rhodiola on physical and mental performance in 575 people. Both reviews found evidence that rhodiola may enhance physical performance and ease mental fatigue, but emphasized that the limited quantity and quality of available evidence did not allow firm conclusions to be made.

What Do We Know about Safety?

- When taken orally (by mouth), rhodiola may cause dizziness, dry mouth, and headaches.
- People can have allergic reactions to rhodiola.

Keep in Mind

Tell all your health care providers about any complementary health approaches you use. Give them a full picture of what you do to manage your health. This will help ensure coordinated and safe care.

Sage

Common Names: black sage, broad-leafed sage, common sage
Latin Names: *Salvia officinalis, Salvia lavandulaefolia, Salvia lavandulifolia*

Sage has been used for centuries as a spice and seasoning in cooking and as a folk or traditional remedy for hoarseness, coughs, and sore mouths and throats. In ancient times it even was thought to extend life. Sage was used as a fertility drug in ancient Egypt. Physicians in ancient Greece used a solution of sage and water to stop wounds from bleeding and to clean sores and ulcers.

Recently, sage is used as a folk or traditional remedy for mouth and throat inflammation, indigestion, and excessive sweating; to improve mood; and to boost memory or mental performance.

263

Sage is available as dried leaves, liquid extracts and sprays, and essential oils.

What the Science Says

- Sage has not been well studied as a treatment for sore throat, so there is little scientific evidence to support its use for that ailment.

- Two small studies suggest that sage may improve mood and mental performance in healthy young people and memory and attention in older adults. Results of another small clinical study suggest that a sage extract was better than placebo at enhancing thinking and learning in older adults with mild to moderate Alzheimer's disease.

- Laboratory studies suggest that essential oils from sage may have antimicrobial properties.

Side Effects and Cautions

- Sage is generally regarded as safe by the U.S. Food and Drug Administration and is approved for food use as a spice or seasoning. However, some species of sage contain thujone, which can affect the nervous system. Extended use or taking large amounts of sage leaf or oil may result in restlessness, vomiting, vertigo, rapid heart rate, tremors, seizures, and kidney damage. It also may lead to wheezing. Ingesting 12 drops or more of the essential oil is considered a toxic dose.

- Drug interactions with sage have not been thoroughly studied.

- Sage can stimulate allergic or hypersensitivity reactions. Skin contact may result in inflammation. Ingesting sage powder or dust may cause breathing difficulties.

Keep in Mind

Tell all your health care providers about any complementary health approaches you use. Give them a full picture of what you do to manage your health. This will help ensure coordinated and safe care.

Saw Palmetto

Common Names: saw palmetto, American dwarf palm tree, cabbage palm
Latin Names: *Serenoa repens, Sabal serrulata*

Saw palmetto is a small palm tree native to the eastern United States. Its fruit was used medicinally by the Seminole Tribe of Florida. Saw palmetto is used as a traditional or folk remedy for urinary symptoms associated with an enlarged prostate gland (also called benign prostatic hyperplasia, or BPH), as well as for chronic pelvic pain, bladder disorders, decreased sex drive, hair loss, hormone imbalances, and prostate cancer.

The ripe fruit of saw palmetto is used in several forms, including ground and dried fruit or whole berries. It is available as liquid extracts, tablets, capsules, and as an infusion or a tea.

What the Science Says

- Several small studies suggest that saw palmetto may be effective for treating BPH symptoms. However, a 2011 NCCIH-cofunded study in 369 older men demonstrated that saw palmetto extract administered at up to three times the standard daily dose (320 mg) did not reduce the urinary symptoms associated with BPH more than placebo. In addition, a 2009 review of the research concluded that saw palmetto has not been shown to be more effective than placebo for this use.

- In 2006, an NIH-funded study of 225 men with moderate-to-severe BPH found no improvement with 320 mg of saw palmetto daily for 1 year versus placebo.

- There is not enough scientific evidence to support the use of saw palmetto for reducing the size of an enlarged prostate or for any other conditions.

- Saw palmetto does not appear to affect readings of prostate-specific antigen (PSA) levels. PSA is a protein produced by cells in the prostate. The PSA test is used to screen for prostate cancer and to monitor patients who have had prostate cancer.

- An NCCIH-funded study is looking at the effects of saw palmetto extract on prostate cancer cells.

Side Effects and Cautions

- Saw palmetto appears to be well tolerated by most users. It may cause mild side effects, including stomach discomfort.

Keep in Mind

Tell all your health care providers about any complementary health approaches you use. Give them a full picture of what you do to manage your health. This will help ensure coordinated and safe care.

Soy

Common Name: soy
Latin Name: *Glycine max*

Soy, a plant in the pea family, has been common in Asian diets for thousands of years. It is found in modern American diets as a food or food additive. Soybeans, the high-protein seeds of the soy plant, contain isoflavones—compounds similar to the female hormone estrogen. Traditional or folk uses of soy products include menopausal symptoms, osteoporosis, memory problems, high blood pressure, high cholesterol levels, breast cancer, and prostate cancer.

Soy is available in dietary supplements, in forms such as tablets and capsules. Soy supplements may contain isoflavones or soy protein or both. Soybeans can be cooked and eaten or used to make tofu, soy milk, and other foods. Also, soy is sometimes used as an additive in various processed foods, including baked goods, cheese, and pasta.

What the Science Says

- Research suggests that daily intake of soy protein, may slightly lower levels of LDL ("bad") cholesterol.

- Some studies suggest that soy isoflavone supplements may reduce hot flashes in women after menopause. However, the results have been inconsistent.

- There is not enough scientific evidence to determine whether soy supplements are effective for any other health uses.

- NCCIH supports studies on soy, including its effects in cardiovascular disease and breast cancer, and on menopause-related symptoms and bone loss.

Side Effects and Cautions

- Soy is considered safe for most people when used as a food or when taken for short periods as a dietary supplement.

- Minor stomach and bowel problems such as nausea, bloating, and constipation are possible.

- Allergic reactions such as breathing problems and rash can occur in rare cases.

- The safety of long-term use of soy isoflavones has not been established. Evidence is mixed on whether using isoflavone supplements over time can increase the risk of endometrial hyperplasia (a thickening of the lining of the uterus that can lead to cancer). Studies show no effect of dietary soy on risk for endometrial hyperplasia.

- Soy's possible role in breast cancer risk is uncertain. Until more is known about soy's effect on estrogen levels, women who have or who are at increased risk of developing breast cancer or other hormone-sensitive conditions (such as ovarian or uterine cancer) should be particularly careful about using soy and should discuss it with their health care providers.

Keep in Mind

Tell all your health care providers about any complementary health approaches you use. Give them a full picture of what you do to manage your health. This will help ensure coordinated and safe care.

Tea Tree Oil

Common Names: Australian tea tree oil, tea tree essential oil, melaleuca oil
Latin Name: *Melaleuca alternifolia*

Tea tree oil comes from the leaves of the tea tree and has been used medicinally for centuries by the aboriginal people of Australia. Recently, tea tree oil is often used externally as a folk or traditional remedy for a number of conditions including acne, athlete's foot, nail fungus, wounds, and infections; or for lice, oral candidiasis (thrush), cold sores, dandruff, and skin lesions.

Tea tree oil is primarily used topically (applied to the skin).

What the Science Says

- A 2004 NCCIH-funded review examined the ability of tea tree oil to kill bacteria and found that *in vitro* (in a test tube) studies may provide some preliminary evidence for the use of tea tree oil as an adjunctive (additional) treatment for wounds involving difficult-to-treat bacterial infections such as methicillin-resistant *Staphylococcus aureus* (MRSA). However, large,

267

well-designed clinical trials on tea tree oil are lacking, and it remains unclear whether tea tree oil is effective against these emerging resistant strains of bacteria in people.

• Some smaller-scale clinical studies have had positive results for treating athlete's foot, nail fungus, dandruff, and acne, but more large-scale, well-designed clinical studies are needed.

• Tea tree oil may be effective for acne. One clinical trial compared a 5 percent tea tree oil gel to a 5 percent benzoyl peroxide product for the treatment of acne and found that the benzoyl peroxide worked slightly better but that the tea tree oil had fewer side effects.

Side Effects and Cautions

• Tea tree oil contains varying amounts of 1,8–cineole, a skin irritant. Products with high amounts of this compound may cause skin irritation or contact dermatitis, an allergic reaction, in some individuals. Oxidized tea tree oil (oil that has been exposed to air) may trigger allergies more than fresh tea tree oil.

• Tea tree oil should not be swallowed. Poisonings, mainly in children, have caused drowsiness, disorientation, rash, and ataxia—a loss of muscle control in the arms and legs causing a lack of balance and coordination. One patient went into a coma after drinking half a cup of tea tree oil.

• Topical use of diluted tea tree oil is generally considered safe for most adults. However, one case study did report a young boy who had developed breast growth after using a styling gel and shampoo that contained both lavender oil and tea tree oil.

Keep in Mind

Tell all your health care providers about any complementary health approaches you use. Give them a full picture of what you do to manage your health. This will help ensure coordinated and safe care.

Thunder God Vine

Common Names: thunder god vine, lei gong teng
Latin Name: *Tripterygium wilfordii*

Thunder god vine is a perennial vine native to China, Japan, and Korea. It has been used in China for health purposes for more than

400 years. In traditional Chinese medicine, it has been used for conditions involving inflammation or overactivity of the immune system. Currently, thunder god vine is used as a traditional or folk remedy for excessive menstrual periods and autoimmune diseases, such as rheumatoid arthritis, multiple sclerosis, and lupus.

Extracts are prepared from the skinned root of thunder god vine.

What the Science Says

- Laboratory findings suggest that thunder god vine may fight inflammation, suppress the immune system, and have anti-cancer effects.

- Although early evidence is promising, there have been few high-quality studies of thunder god vine in people. Results from a large study funded by the National Institute of Arthritis and Musculoskeletal and Skin Diseases (NIAMS), which compared an extract of thunder god vine root with a conventional medicine (sulfasalazine) for rheumatoid arthritis, found that participants' symptoms (e.g., joint pain and swelling, inflammation) improved more significantly with thunder god vine than with sulfasalazine.

- A small study on thunder god vine applied to the skin found benefits for rheumatoid arthritis symptoms.

- There is not enough scientific evidence to assess thunder god vine's use for any other health conditions.

Side Effects and Cautions

- Thunder god vine can cause severe side effects and can be poisonous if it is not carefully extracted from the skinned root. Other parts of the plant—including the leaves, flowers, and skin of the root—are highly poisonous and can cause death.

- A number of participants in the NIAMS study experienced gastrointestinal adverse effects such as diarrhea, indigestion, and nausea, as well as upper respiratory tract infections. (The rate of adverse effects was similar in the thunder god vine and sulfasalazine groups.)

- Thunder god vine can also cause hair loss, headache, menstrual changes, and skin rash.

- There are no consistent, high-quality thunder god vine products being manufactured in the United States. Preparations of

269

thunder god vine made outside the United States (for example, in China) can sometimes be obtained, but it is not possible to verify whether they are safe and effective.

• Thunder god vine has been found to decrease bone mineral density in women who take the herb for 5 years or longer. This side effect may be of particular concern to women who have osteoporosis or are at risk for the condition.

• Thunder god vine contains chemicals that might decrease male fertility by changing sperm.

Keep in Mind

Tell all your health care providers about any complementary health approaches you use. Give them a full picture of what you do to manage your health. This will help ensure coordinated and safe care.

Turmeric

Common Names: turmeric, turmeric root, Indian saffron
Latin Name: *Curcuma longa*

Turmeric, a shrub related to ginger, is grown throughout India, other parts of Asia, and Africa. Known for its warm, bitter taste and golden color, turmeric is commonly used in fabric dyes and foods such as curry powders, mustards, and cheeses. It should not be confused with Javanese turmeric.

In traditional Chinese medicine and Ayurvedic medicine, turmeric has been used to aid digestion and liver function, relieve arthritis pain, and regulate menstruation. Historically, turmeric has also been applied directly to the skin for eczema and wound healing. Recently, traditional or folk uses of turmeric include heartburn, stomach ulcers, gallstones, inflammation, and cancer.

Turmeric's finger-like underground stems (rhizomes) are dried and taken by mouth as a powder or in capsules, teas, or liquid extracts. Turmeric can also be made into a paste and used on the skin.

What the Science Says

• There is little reliable evidence to support the use of turmeric for any health condition because few clinical trials have been conducted.

• Preliminary findings from animal and other laboratory studies suggest that a chemical found in turmeric—called curcumin—may have anti-inflammatory, anticancer, and anti-oxidant properties, but these findings have not been confirmed in people.

- NCCIH-funded investigators have studied the active chemicals in turmeric and their effects—particularly anti-inflammatory effects—in human cells to better understand how turmeric might be used for health purposes. NCCIH is also funding basic research studies on the potential role of turmeric in preventing acute respiratory distress syndrome, liver cancer, and post-menopausal osteoporosis.

Side Effects and Cautions

- Turmeric is considered safe for most adults.
- High doses or long-term use of turmeric may cause indigestion, nausea, or diarrhea.
- In animals, high doses of turmeric have caused liver problems. However no cases of liver problems have been reported in people.
- People with gallbladder disease should avoid using turmeric as a dietary supplement, as it may worsen the condition.

Keep in Mind

Tell all your health care providers about any complementary health approaches you use. Give them a full picture of what you do to manage your health. This will help ensure coordinated and safe care.

Valerian

Common Names: valerian, all-heal, garden heliotrope
Latin Name: *Valeriana officinalis*

Valerian is a plant native to Europe and Asia; it is also found in North America. Valerian has been used as a medicinal herb since at least the time of ancient Greece and Rome. Its therapeutic uses were described by Hippocrates, and in the 2nd century, Galen prescribed valerian for insomnia. Recently, valerian is used as a traditional remedy for sleep disorders and anxiety, as well as headaches, depression, irregular heartbeat, and trembling.

The roots and rhizomes (underground stems) of valerian are typically used to make supplements, including capsules, tablets, and liquid extracts, as well as teas.

271

What the Science Says

- Research suggests that valerian may be helpful for insomnia, but there is not enough evidence from well-designed studies to confirm this.

- There is not enough scientific evidence to determine whether valerian works for other conditions, such as anxiety or depression.

- NCCIH-funded research on valerian includes studies on the herb's effects on sleep in healthy older adults and in people with Parkinson's disease. NCCIH-funded researchers are also studying the potential of valerian and other herbal products to relieve menopausal symptoms.

Side Effects and Cautions

- Studies suggest that valerian is generally safe to use for short periods of time (for example, 4 to 6 weeks).

- No information is available about the long-term safety of valerian.

- Valerian can cause mild side effects, such as tiredness the morning after its use, headaches, dizziness, and upset stomach.

Keep in Mind

Tell all your health care providers about any complementary health approaches you use. Give them a full picture of what you do to manage your health. This will help ensure coordinated and safe care.

Yohimbe

Common Names: yohimbe, yohimbe bark
Latin Name: *Pausinystalia yohimbe*

The yohimbe tree is a tall evergreen that is native to western Africa. The bark of the tree contains a chemical called yohimbine. The amount of yohimbine in dietary supplements may vary; some yohimbe products have been found to contain very little yohimbine. A drug form of yohimbine—yohimbine hydrochloride—has been studied for erectile dysfunction.

Yohimbe bark has traditionally been used in Africa as an aphrodisiac (to increase sexual desire). Currently, it is used as a folk or traditional remedy for sexual dysfunction, including erectile dysfunction in men.

As a dietary supplement, the dried bark of the yohimbe tree is made into tea and taken by mouth. An extract of the bark is also put into capsules and tablets.

What the Science Says

It is not known whether yohimbe is effective for any health condition because clinical trials have not been conducted on the bark or its extract.

Side Effects and Cautions

- Yohimbe has been associated with high blood pressure, increased heart rate, headache, anxiety, dizziness, nausea, vomiting, tremors, and sleeplessness. Yohimbe can be dangerous if taken in large doses or for long periods of time.

- People should not combine yohimbe with monoamine oxidase (MAO) inhibitors as effects may be additive. Yohimbe should be used with caution when taken with medicines for high blood pressure, tricyclic antidepressants, or phenothiazines (a group of medicines used mostly for mental health conditions such as schizophrenia).

- People with kidney problems and people with psychiatric conditions should not use yohimbe.

- Women who are pregnant or breastfeeding should not take yohimbe.

Keep in Mind

Tell all your health care providers about any complementary health approaches you use. Give them a full picture of what you do to manage your health. This will help ensure coordinated and safe care.

Chapter 22

Using Dietary Supplements Wisely

Like many Americans, you may take dietary supplements in an effort to stay healthy. With so many dietary supplements available and so many claims made about their health benefits, how can you decide whether a supplement is safe or useful? This chapter provides a general overview of dietary supplements, and discusses safety considerations.

Key Points

- Dietary supplements contain a variety of ingredients, such as vitamins, minerals, amino acids, and herbs or other botanicals. Research has confirmed health benefits of some dietary supplements but not others.

- To use dietary supplements safely, read and follow the label instructions, and recognize that "natural" does not always mean "safe." Be aware that an herbal supplement may contain dozens of compounds and that all of its ingredients may not be known.

- Some dietary supplements may interact with medications or pose risks if you have medical problems or are going to have

Text in this chapter is excerpted from "Using Dietary Supplements Wisely," National Center for Complementary and Integrative Health (NCCIH), February 2014.

275

surgery. Most dietary supplements have not been tested in pregnant women, nursing mothers, or children.

• The U.S. Food and Drug Administration (FDA) regulates dietary supplements, but the regulations for dietary supplements are different and less strict than those for prescription or over-the-counter drugs.

• Tell all your health care providers about any complementary health approaches you use. Give them a full picture of what you do to manage your health. This will help ensure coordinated and safe care.

About Dietary Supplements

Dietary supplements were defined in a law passed by Congress in 1994 called the Dietary Supplement Health and Education Act (DSHEA). According to DSHEA, a dietary supplement is a product that:

• Is intended to supplement the diet

• Contains one or more dietary ingredients (including vitamins, minerals, herbs or other botanicals, amino acids, and certain other substances) or their constituents

• Is intended to be taken by mouth, in forms such as tablet, capsule, powder, softgel, gelcap, or liquid

• Is labeled as being a dietary supplement

Herbal supplements are one type of dietary supplement. An herb is a plant or plant part (such as leaves, flowers, or seeds) that is used for its flavor, scent, and/or potential health-related properties. "Botanical" is often used as a synonym for "herb." An herbal supplement may contain a single herb or mixtures of herbs. The law requires that all of the herbs be listed on the product label.

Research has shown that some uses of dietary supplements are beneficial to health. For example, scientists have found that folic acid (a vitamin) prevents certain birth defects. Other research on dietary supplements has failed to show benefit; for example, several major studies of the herbal supplement echinacea did not find evidence of benefit against the common cold.

Dietary Supplement Use in the United States

According to the 2007 National Health Interview Survey, which included questions on Americans' use of natural products (not including

276

vitamins and minerals), 17.7 percent of American adults had used these types of products in the past 12 months. The most popular of these products used by adults in the past 30 days were fish oil/omega 3/DHA (37.4 percent), glucosamine (19.9 percent), echinacea (19.8 percent), flaxseed oil or pills (15.9 percent), and ginseng (14.1 percent). National Health and Nutrition Examination Survey (NHANES) data collected from 2003 to 2006 that covered all types of dietary supplements indicate that 53 percent of American adults took at least one dietary supplement, most commonly multivitamin/multimineral supplements (taken by 39 percent of all adults). Women were more likely than men to take dietary supplements.

Federal Regulation of Dietary Supplements

The federal government regulates dietary supplements through the FDA. The regulations for dietary supplements are not the same as those for prescription or over-the-counter drugs.

- Manufacturers of dietary supplements are responsible for ensuring that their products are safe and that the label information is truthful and not misleading. However, a manufacturer of a dietary supplement does not have to provide the FDA with data that demonstrate the safety of the product before it is marketed. In contrast, manufacturers of drugs have to provide the FDA with evidence that their products are both safe and effective before the drugs can be sold.

- Manufacturers may make three types of claims for their dietary supplements: health claims, structure/function claims, and nutrient content claims. Some of these claims describe the link between a food substance and a disease or health-related condition; the intended benefits of using the product; or the amount of a nutrient or dietary substance in a product. Different requirements apply to each type of claim. If a dietary supplement manufacturer makes a claim about a product's effects, the manufacturer must have data to support the claim. Claims about how a supplement affects the structure or function of the body must be followed by the words "This statement has not been evaluated by the U.S. Food and Drug Administration (FDA). This product is not intended to diagnose, treat, cure, or prevent any disease."

- Manufacturers must follow "current good manufacturing practices" for dietary supplements to ensure that these products are processed, labeled, and packaged consistently and meet quality standards.

• Once a dietary supplement is on the market, the FDA evaluates safety by doing research and keeping track of any side effects reported by consumers, health care providers, and supplement companies. If the FDA finds a product to be unsafe, it can take action against the manufacturer and/or distributor, and may issue a warning or require that the product be removed from the marketplace.

Also, once a dietary supplement is on the market, the FDA monitors product information, such as label claims and package inserts. The Federal Trade Commission (FTC) is responsible for regulating product advertising; it requires that all information be truthful and not misleading.

The federal government has taken legal action against dietary supplement promoters or Web sites that promote or sell dietary supplements for making false or deceptive statements about their products or because marketed products have proven to be unsafe. In 2010, an investigation by the U.S. Government Accountability Office found instances in which written sales materials for herbal dietary supplements sold through online retailers included illegal claims that the products could treat, prevent, or cure diseases such as diabetes, cancer, or cardiovascular disease.

Sources of Science-Based Information

It's important to look for reliable sources of information on dietary supplements so you can evaluate the claims that are made about them. The most reliable information on dietary supplements is based on the results of rigorous scientific testing.

To get reliable information on a particular dietary supplement:

• Ask your health care providers. Even if they don't know about a specific dietary supplement, they may be able to access the latest medical guidance about its uses and risks.

• Look for scientific research findings on the dietary supplement. The National Center for Complementary and Integrative Health (NCCIH) and the National Institutes of Health (NIH) Office of Dietary Supplements (ODS), as well as other federal agencies, have free publications, clearinghouses, and information on their Web sites.

Safety Considerations

If you're thinking about or currently using a dietary supplement, here are some points to keep in mind.

- **Tell all your health care providers** about any complementary health approaches you use. Give them a full picture of what you do to manage your health. This will help ensure coordinated and safe care.

- It's especially important to talk to your health care providers if you:

  - Take any medications (whether prescription or over-the-counter). Some dietary supplements have been found to interact with medications. For example, the herbal supplement St. John's wort interacts with many medications, making them less effective.

  - Are thinking about replacing your regular medication with one or more dietary supplements.

  - Expect to have surgery. Certain dietary supplements may increase the risk of bleeding or affect the response to anesthesia.

  - Are pregnant, nursing a baby, attempting to become pregnant, or considering giving a child a dietary supplement. Most dietary supplements have not been tested in pregnant women, nursing mothers, or children.

  - Have any medical conditions. Some dietary supplements may harm you if you have particular medical conditions. For example, by taking supplements that contain iron, people with hemochromatosis, a hereditary disease in which too much iron accumulates in the body, could further increase their iron levels and therefore their risk of complications such as liver disease.

- If you're taking a dietary supplement, **follow the label instructions**. Talk to your health care provider if you have any questions, particularly about the best dosage for you to take. If you experience any side effects that concern you, stop taking the dietary supplement, and contact your health care provider.

- Keep in mind that although many dietary supplements (and some prescription drugs) come from natural sources, **"natural"**

279

does not always mean "safe." For example, the herbs comfrey and kava can cause serious harm to the liver. Also, a manufacturer's use of the term "standardized" (or "verified" or "certified") does not necessarily guarantee product quality or consistency.

- Be aware that **an herbal supplement may contain dozens of compounds** and that all of its ingredients may not be known. Researchers are studying many of these products in an effort to identify what ingredients may be active and understand their effects in the body. Also consider the possibility that what's on the label may not be what's in the bottle. Analyses of dietary supplements sometimes find differences between labeled and actual ingredients. For example:

- An herbal supplement may not contain the correct plant species.

- The amounts of the ingredients may be lower or higher than the label states. That means you may be taking less—or more—of the dietary supplement than you realize.

- The dietary supplement may be contaminated with other herbs, pesticides, or metals, or even adulterated with unlabeled, illegal ingredients such as prescription drugs.

For current information from the federal government on the safety of particular dietary supplements, check the "Dietary Supplement Alerts and Safety Information" section of the FDA Web site or the "Alerts and Advisories" section of the NCCIH Web site.

Dietary Supplements Research at the National Institutes of Health (NIH)

NCCIH sponsors an array of research to see how dietary supplements might affect the body and tests their use in clinical trials. In fiscal year 2011, NCCIH supported approximately 200 research projects studying dietary supplements.

Also within NIH, Office of Dietary Supplements (ODS) focuses specifically on dietary supplements, seeking to strengthen knowledge and understanding of these products by supporting and evaluating research, disseminating results, and educating the public.

NCCIH, ODS, and the National Cancer Institute collaborate to fund dietary supplement research centers focused on botanicals, known collectively as the NIH Botanical Research Centers Program. Scientists at the centers conduct basic research, such as exploring mechanisms of action, on botanicals and help to select products to be tested in clinical trials. The centers are advancing the scientific base of knowledge about botanicals, making it possible to better evaluate their safety and effectiveness.

NCCIH also sponsors a number of other research centers that are studying topics in this field, including antioxidant therapies, botanicals for autoimmune and inflammatory diseases, grape-derived polyphenols for Alzheimer's disease, and botanicals for pancreatic diseases and for colorectal cancer.

"New dietary ingredients" (substances that were not used in dietary supplements before 1994) are an exception to this rule; evidence of their safety must be provided to the FDA before they can be used in dietary supplements.

Chapter 23

Dietary Supplements for Children and Teens

Parents should be aware that many complementary health products, including dietary supplements and herbal medicines, have not been tested for safety or effectiveness in children. Because children's metabolism and their immune, digestive, and central nervous systems are still maturing, side effects can differ from those seen in adults. This is especially true for infants and young children.

Nearly 12 percent of children (about 1 in 9) in the United States are using some form of complementary health product or practice, such as dietary or herbal supplements. A dietary or herbal supplement may contain many compounds and its active ingredients may not be known. Also, what's on the label may not be what's in the bottle. Analyses of dietary supplements, including herbal supplements, sometimes find differences between labeled and actual ingredients.

Here are examples of other safety concerns for some supplements that are often given to children:

Text from this chapter is excerpted from "Health info–5 Things To Know About Safety of Dietary Supplements for Children and Teens," National Center for Complementary and Integrative Health (NCCIH), June 4, 2015.

- Dietary supplements, including herbal products, may interact with other products or medications your child is taking or have unwanted side effects on their own. A common combination seen in children is acetaminophen and vitamin C, which slows the body's processing of acetaminophen.

- St. John's wort has been shown to interact with many medications, including antidepressants, birth control pills, seizure control drugs, and certain drugs used to treat cancer.

- Melatonin, a hormone used as a sleep aid, may alter the levels of other hormones in young children and should not be used by children with certain medical conditions such as hormonal disorders, diabetes, liver or kidney disease, cerebral palsy, seizure disorders, migraine, depression, and hypertension.

- Probiotics have been studied for gastrointestinal conditions in children, and studies report that giving probiotics (along with rehydration therapy if needed) is generally safe. However, there is evidence that probiotics should not be given to critically ill patients. Researchers also note that the long-term effects of probiotics and their safety in children have not been well researched.

- The American Academy of Pediatrics does not recommend multivitamins for healthy children and adolescents who eat a varied diet. According to a 2012 report, children who take multivitamins are at greater risk than nonusers of getting too much iron, zinc, copper, selenium, folic acid, and vitamins A and C. However, multivitamins may be needed for those who do not eat a varied diet, and those children who did not take multivitamins were found to have low levels of vitamins D and E and calcium.

Supplements Targeting Body Image

Products such as those advertised to reduce weight or increase strength are popular among teenagers but could be dangerous.

- Several widely marketed bodybuilding products sold as dietary supplements have been found to contain steroids. In 2009, the U.S. Food and Drug Administration issued a warning to consumers to stop using any products that are being marketed for bodybuilding and that claim to contain steroids or steroid-like substances. These products are potentially harmful and could lead to serious liver injury, stroke, kidney failure, or other serious conditions.

- Weight-loss supplements may contain numerous untested ingredients and have not been examined for safety or effectiveness in children. The possibility of product contamination is a main safety concern about dietary supplements for both children and adults, but the danger may be greater for children. Supplements have been found to contain hidden prescription drugs or other compounds, particularly in dietary supplements marketed for weight loss. In addition, herbs are sometimes misused by people with eating disorders such as anorexia nervosa and bulimia nervosa to induce vomiting and control their weight.

- Because of possible health risks, the American College of Sports Medicine recommends against anyone younger than age 18 using creatine, a naturally occurring compound in the body taken to enhance athletic performance.

It's important that parents talk with their child's health care provider about any complementary health approach that is being used or considered, and parents should encourage their teenagers to do the same.

Chapter 24

Dietary Supplements for Seniors

Can Dietary Supplements Help Older Consumers?

Even if you eat a wide variety of foods, how can you be sure that you are getting all the vitamins, minerals, and other nutrients you need as you get older? If you are over 50, your nutritional needs may change. Informed food choices are the first place to start, making sure you get a variety of foods while watching your calorie intake. Supplements and fortified foods may also help you get appropriate amounts of nutrients. To help you make informed decisions, talk to your doctor and/or registered dietitian. They can work together with you to determine if your intake of a specific nutrient might be too low or too high and then decide how you can achieve a balance between the foods and nutrients you personally need.

What Are Dietary Supplements?

The dietary supplements are not only vitamins and minerals. They also include other less-familiar substances, such as herbals, botanicals, amino acids, enzymes, and animal extracts. Some dietary supplements are well understood and established, but others need further study.

Text in this chapter is excerpted from "Tips for Older Dietary Supplement Users," U.S. Food and Drug Administration (FDA), May 11, 2014.

Whatever your choice, supplements should not replace the variety of foods important to a healthful diet.

Unlike drugs, dietary supplements are not pre-approved by the government for safety or effectiveness before marketing. Also, unlike drugs, supplements are not intended to treat, diagnose, prevent, or cure diseases. But some supplements can help assure that you get an adequate dietary intake of essential nutrients; others may help you reduce your risk of disease. Some older people, for example, are tired due to low iron levels. In that case, their doctor may recommend an iron supplement.

At times, it can be confusing to tell the difference between a dietary supplement, a food, or over-the-counter (OTC) medicines. This is because supplements, by law, come in a variety of forms that resemble these products, such as tablets, capsules, powders, energy bars, or drinks. One way to know if a product is a dietary supplement is to look for the Supplement Facts label on the product.

Supplement Facts

Serving Size 1 Capsule

Amount Per Capsule	% Daily Value
Calories 20	
Calories from Fat 20	
Total Fat 2 g	3%•
Saturated Fat 0.5 g	3%•
Polyunsaturated Fat 1 g	†
Monounsaturated Fat 0.5 g	†
Vitamin A 4250 IU	85%
Vitamin D 425 IU	106%
Omega-3 fatty acids 0.5 g	†

• Percent Daily Values are based on a 2,000 calorie diet.
† Daily Value not established.

Ingredients: Cod liver oil, gelatin, water, and glycerin.

Figure 19.1. Supplement Facts

Are There Any Risks, Especially to Older Consumers?

While certain products may be helpful to some older individuals, there may be circumstances when these products may not benefit your health or when they may create unexpected risks. Many supplements contain active ingredients that have strong biological effects in the body. This could make them unsafe in some situations and hurt or complicate your health. For example:

- Are you taking both medicines and supplements? Are you substituting one for the other? Taking a combination of supplements, using these products together with medications (whether prescription or over-the-counter), or substituting them in place of medicines your doctor prescribes could lead to harmful, even life-threatening results. Be alert to any advisories about these products. Coumadin (a prescription medicine), ginkgo biloba (an herbal supplement), aspirin (an over-the-counter drug), and vitamin E (a vitamin supplement) can each thin the blood. Taking any of these products alone or together can increase the potential for internal bleeding or stroke. Another example is St. John's wort that may reduce the effectiveness of prescription drugs for heart disease, depression, seizures, certain cancers, or HIV.

- Are you planning surgery? Some supplements can have unwanted effects before, during, and after surgery. It is important to fully inform your healthcare professional, including your pharmacist, about the vitamins, minerals, herbals, and any other supplements you are taking, especially before surgery. You may be asked to stop taking these products at least 2-3 weeks ahead of the procedure to avoid potentially dangerous supplement/drug interactions - such as changes in heart rate, blood pressure, or bleeding risk that could adversely affect the outcome of your surgery.

- Is taking more of a good thing better? Some people might think that if a little is good, taking a lot is even better. But taking too much of some nutrients, even vitamins and minerals, can also cause problems. Depending on the supplement, your age, and the status of your health, taking more than 100% of the Daily Value (DV) (see the Supplements Facts panel) of certain vitamins and minerals, e.g. Vitamin A, vitamin D, and iron (from supplements and food sources like vitamin-fortified cereals and drinks) may actually harm your health. Large amounts can also interfere with how your medicines work.

Why Speak to My Healthcare Provider about Dietary Supplements?

You and your health professionals (doctors, nurses, registered dietitians, pharmacists, and other caregivers) are a team working toward a common goal -- to develop a personalized health plan for you. Your doctor and other members of the health team can help monitor your medical condition and overall health, especially if any problems develop. Although they may not immediately have answers to your questions, these health professionals have access to the most current research on dietary supplements.

There are numerous resources that provide information about dietary supplements. These include TV, radio, newspapers, magazines, store clerks, friends, family, or the Internet. It is important to question recommendations from people who have no formal training in nutrition, botanicals, or medicine. While some of these sources, like the Web, may seem to offer a wealth of accurate information, these same sources may contain misinformation that may not be obvious. Given the abundance and conflicting nature of information now available about supplements, it is more important than ever to partner with your healthcare team to sort the reliable information from the questionable.

How Will I Be Able to Spot False Claims?

Be savvy! Although the benefits of some dietary supplements have been documented, the claims of others may be unproven. If something sounds too good to be true, it usually is. Here are some signs of a false claim:

Statements that the product is a quick and effective "cure-all." For example: "Extremely beneficial in treatment of rheumatism, arthritis, infections, prostate problems, ulcers, cancer, heart trouble, hardening of the arteries, and more."

Statements that suggest the product can treat or cure diseases. For example: "shrinks tumors" or "cures impotency." Actually, these are drug claims and should not be made for dietary supplements.

Statements that claim the product is "totally safe," "all natural," or has "definitely no side effects."

Promotions that use words like "scientific breakthrough," "miraculous cure," "exclusive product," "secret ingredient," or "ancient remedy." For example: "A scientific breakthrough formulated by using proven principles of natural health-based medical science."

Text that uses overly impressive-sounding terms, like those for a weight-loss product: "hunger stimulation point" and "thermogenesis." Personal testimonials by consumers or doctors claiming amazing results. For example: "My husband has Alzheimer's. He began eating a teaspoonful of this product each day. And now in just 22 days, he mowed the grass, cleaned out the garage, and weeded the flower beds; we take our morning walk together again."

Limited availability and advance payment required. For example: "Hurry. This offer will not last. Send us a check now to reserve your supply." Promises of no-risk "money-back guarantees." For example: "If after 30 days you have not lost at least 4 pounds each week, your uncashed check will be returned to you."

What Are The Key "Points to Ponder" Before I Buy?

Think twice about chasing the latest headline. Sound health advice is generally based on research over time, not a single study. Be wary of results claiming a "quick fix" that depart from scientific research and established dietary guidance. Keep in mind that science does not generally proceed by dramatic breakthroughs, but rather by taking many small steps, slowly building towards scientific agreement.

We may think, "Even if a product may not help me, it at least won't hurt me." It's best not to assume that this will always be true. Some product ingredients, including nutrients and plant components, can be toxic based on their activity in your body. Some products may become harmful when consumed in high enough amounts, for a long enough time, or in combination with certain other substances.

The term 'natural' does not always mean safe. Do not assume this term assures wholesomeness or that these products have milder effects, making them safer to use than prescribed drugs. For example, many weight-loss products claim to be "natural" or "herbal" but this doesn't necessarily make them safe. The products' ingredients may interact with drugs or may be dangerous for people with certain medical conditions.

Spend your money wisely. Some supplement products may be expensive and may not work, given your specific condition. Be wary of substituting a product or therapy for prescription medicines. Be sure to talk with your healthcare team to help you determine what is best for your overall health.

Remember: Safety first. Resist the pressure to decide "on the spot" about trying an untested product or treatment. Ask for more information and consult your doctor, nurse, dietitian, pharmacist, and/or caregiver about whether the product is right for you and safe for you to use.

Who Is Responsible For Ensuring The Safety And Efficacy Of Dietary Supplements?

Unlike prescription and over-the-counter medicines, dietary supplement products are not reviewed by the government before they are marketed. Under the law, manufacturers of dietary supplements are responsible for making sure their products are safe before they go to market. If you want to know more about the product you are purchasing, check with the manufacturer to find out if the firm:

Can supply information to support the claims for their products

Can share information on the safety or efficacy of the ingredients in the product

Has received any adverse event reports from consumers using their products

What is FDA's Responsibility?

FDA has the responsibility to take action against unsafe dietary supplement products after they reach the market. The agency may also take legal action against dietary supplement manufacturers if FDA can prove that claims on marketed dietary supplements are false and misleading.

What If I Think I Have Had A Reaction To A Dietary Supplement?

Adverse effects from the use of dietary supplements should be reported to the FDA's MedWatch Program. You, your healthcare provider, or anyone should report a serious adverse event or illness directly to FDA if you believe it is related to the use of any dietary supplement product by calling FDA at: 1-800-FDA-1088, by fax at: 1-800-FDA-0178 or reporting on-line. FDA would like to know whenever you think a product caused you a serious problem, even if you are not sure that the product was the cause, and even if you do not visit a doctor or clinic.

What's The Bottom Line?

- Dietary supplements are intended to supplement the diet, not to cure, prevent, or treat diseases or replace the variety of foods important to a healthful diet.

- Supplements can help you meet daily requirements for certain nutrients, but when you combine drugs and foods, too much of some nutrients can also cause problems.

- Many factors play a role in deciding if a supplement is right for you, including possible drug interactions and side effects. Do not self-diagnose any health condition. Together, you and your healthcare team can make the best decision for optimal health.

- Ask yourself the following questions and use the checklist below to talk to your doctor, nurse, dietitian, pharmacist, and/or caregiver about dietary supplements.

Ask yourself the following questions and use the checklist below to talk to your doctor, nurse, dietitian, pharmacist, and/or caregiver about dietary supplements.

Questions to Ask:

Is taking a dietary supplement an important part of my total diet?

Are there any precautions or warnings I should know about (e.g. is there an amount or "upper limit" I should not go above)?

Are there any known side effects (e.g., loss of appetite, nausea, headaches, etc.)? Do they apply to me?

Are there any foods, medicines (prescription or over-the counter), or other supplements I should avoid while taking this product?

If I am scheduled for surgery, should I be concerned about the dietary supplements I am taking?

Other Questions to Consider:

What is this product for? What are its intended benefits? How, when and for how long should I take it?

Because many products are marketed as dietary supplements, it is important to remember that supplements include botanical/herbal as well as vitamin/mineral products. The list below gives some examples of products you may see sold as dietary supplements. It is not possible to list them all here. Note: the examples provided do not represent either an endorsement or approval by FDA or any coalition members.

Vitamins, Minerals, Nutrients

Multiple Vitamin/Mineral
Vitamin B Complex
Vitamin C
Vitamin D
Vitamin E
Calcium
Fiber
Folic Acid

Zinc
Iron
Beta-carotene
Omega 3 Fatty Acids

Botanicals and Other Substances

Acidophilus
Black Cohosh
Ginger
Evening Primrose Oil
Echinacea
Garlic
Ginkgo Biloba
Fish Oil
Glucosamine and/or Chondroitin Sulphate
St. John's wort
Saw Palmetto

Chapter 25

Antioxidant Supplements

Chapter Contents

Section 25.1

Antioxidants and Health

Text in this chapter is excerpted from "Antioxidants and Health: An Introduction," National Center for Complementary and Integrative Health (NCCIH), November 2013.

Antioxidants are man-made or natural substances that may prevent or delay some types of cell damage. Diets high in vegetables and fruits, which are good sources of antioxidants, have been found to be healthy; however, research has not shown antioxidant supplements to be beneficial in preventing diseases. Examples of antioxidants include vitamins C and E, selenium, and carotenoids, such as beta-carotene, lycopene, lutein, and zeaxanthin.

Key Points

Vegetables and fruits are rich sources of antioxidants. There is good evidence that eating a diet that includes plenty of vegetables and fruits is healthy, and official U.S. government policy urges people to eat more of these foods. Research has shown that people who eat more vegetables and fruits have lower risks of several diseases; however, it is not clear whether these results are related to the amount of antioxidants in vegetables and fruits, to other components of these foods, to other factors in people's diets, or to other lifestyle choices.

Rigorous scientific studies involving more than 100,000 people combined have tested whether antioxidant supplements can help prevent chronic diseases, such as cardiovascular diseases, cancer, and cataracts. In most instances, antioxidants did not reduce the risks of developing these diseases.

Concerns have not been raised about the safety of antioxidants in food. However, high-dose supplements of antioxidants may be linked to health risks in some cases. Supplementing with high doses of beta-carotene may increase the risk of lung cancer in smokers. Supplementing with high doses of vitamin E may increase risks of prostate cancer and one type of stroke.

Antioxidant supplements may interact with some medicines. Tell all of your health care providers about any complementary and integrative health approaches you use. Give them a full picture of what you do to manage your health. This will help ensure coordinated and safe care.

About Free Radicals, Oxidative Stress, and Antioxidants

Free radicals are highly unstable molecules that are naturally formed when you exercise and when your body converts food into energy. Your body can also be exposed to free radicals from a variety of environmental sources, such as cigarette smoke, air pollution, and sunlight. Free radicals can cause "oxidative stress," a process that can trigger cell damage. Oxidative stress is thought to play a role in a variety of diseases including cancer, cardiovascular diseases, diabetes, Alzheimer's disease, Parkinson's disease, and eye diseases such as cataracts and age-related macular degeneration.

Antioxidant molecules have been shown to counteract oxidative stress in laboratory experiments (for example, in cells or animal studies). However, there is debate as to whether consuming large amounts of antioxidants in supplement form actually benefits health. There is also some concern that consuming antioxidant supplements in excessive doses may be harmful.

Vegetables and fruits are healthy foods and rich sources of antioxidants. Official U.S. Government policy urges people to eat more vegetables and fruits. Concerns have not been raised about the safety of any amounts of antioxidants in food. For more information on antioxidants in foods, visit the U.S. Department of Agriculture Web page on antioxidants and phytonutrients.

Use of Antioxidant Supplements in the United States

A 2009 analysis using data from the National Health and Nutrition Examination Survey (1999–2000 and 2001–2002) estimated the amounts of antioxidants adults in the United States get from foods and supplements. Supplements accounted for 54 percent of vitamin C, 64 percent of vitamin E, 14 percent of alpha- and beta-carotene, and 11 percent of selenium intake.

Safety

- High-dose antioxidant supplements may be harmful in some cases. For example, the results of some studies have

297

linked the use of high-dose beta-carotene supplements to an increased risk of lung cancer in smokers and use of high-dose vitamin E supplements to increased risks of hemorrhagic stroke (a type of stroke caused by bleeding in the brain) and prostate cancer.

- Like some other dietary supplements, antioxidant supplements may interact with certain medications. For example, vitamin E supplements may increase the risk of bleeding in people who are taking anticoagulant drugs ("blood thinners"). There is conflicting evidence on the effects of taking antioxidant supplements during cancer treatment; some studies suggest that this may be beneficial, but others suggest that it may be harmful. The National Cancer Institute recommends that people who are being treated for cancer talk with their health care provider before taking supplements.

What the Science Says

Several decades of dietary research findings suggested that consuming greater amounts of antioxidant-rich foods might help to protect against diseases. Because of these results, there has been a lot of research on antioxidant supplements. Rigorous trials of antioxidant supplements in large numbers of people have not found that high doses of antioxidant supplements prevent disease. This section describes the preliminary research findings, the results of the clinical trials, and possible explanations for the differences in study results.

Observational and Laboratory Studies

Observational studies on the typical eating habits, lifestyles, and health histories of large groups of people have shown that those who ate more vegetables and fruits had lower risks of several diseases, including cardiovascular disease, stroke, cancer, and cataracts. Observational studies can provide ideas about possible relationships between dietary or lifestyle factors and disease risk, but they cannot show that one factor causes another because they cannot account for other factors that may be involved. For example, people who eat more antioxidant-rich foods might also be more likely to exercise and less likely to smoke. It may be that these factors, rather than antioxidants, account for their lower disease risk.

Researchers have also studied antioxidants in laboratory experiments. These experiments showed that antioxidants interacted with free radicals and stabilized them, thus preventing the free radicals from causing cell damage.

Clinical Trials of Antioxidants

Because the results of such research seemed very promising, large, long-term studies—many of which were funded by the National Institutes of Health (NIH)—were conducted to test whether antioxidant supplements, when taken for periods of at least a few years, could help prevent diseases such as cardiovascular diseases and cancer in people. In these studies, volunteers were randomly assigned to take either an antioxidant or a placebo (an identical-looking product that did not contain the antioxidant). The research was conducted in a double-blind manner (neither the study participants nor the investigators knew which product was being taken). Studies of this type—called clinical trials—are designed to provide clear answers to specific questions about how a substance affects people's health.

Among the earliest of these studies were three large NIH-sponsored trials of high-dose supplements of beta-carotene, alone or in combination with other nutrients. These trials, completed in the mid-1990s, all showed that beta-carotene did not protect against cancer or cardiovascular disease. In one trial, beta-carotene supplements increased the risk of lung cancer in smokers, and in another trial, supplements containing both beta-carotene and vitamin A had the same effect.

More recent studies have also found that in most instances antioxidant supplements did not help to prevent disease. For example:

* The Women's Health Study, which included almost 40,000 healthy women at least 45 years of age, found that vitamin E supplements did not reduce the risk of heart attack, stroke, cancer, age-related macular degeneration, or cataracts. Although vitamin E supplements were associated with fewer deaths from cardiovascular causes, they did not reduce the overall death rate of study participants.

* The Women's Antioxidant Cardiovascular Study found no beneficial effects of vitamin C, vitamin E, or beta-carotene supplements on cardiovascular events (heart attack, stroke, or death from cardiovascular diseases) or the likelihood of developing

299

diabetes or cancer in more than 8,000 female health professionals, aged 40 years or older, who were at high risk for cardiovascular disease. Antioxidant supplements also did not slow changes in cognitive function among women in this study who were aged 65 or older.

- The Physicians' Health Study II, which included more than 14,000 male physicians aged 50 or older, found that neither vitamin E nor vitamin C supplements reduced the risk of major cardiovascular events (heart attack, stroke, or death from cardiovascular disease), cancer, or cataracts. In fact, vitamin E supplements were associated with an increased risk of hemorrhagic stroke in this study.

- The Selenium and Vitamin E Cancer Prevention Trial (SELECT)—a study of more than 35,000 men aged 50 or older—found that selenium and vitamin E supplements, taken alone or together, did not prevent prostate cancer. A 2011 updated analysis from this trial, based on a longer followup period of study participants, concluded that vitamin E supplements increased the occurrence of prostate cancer by 17 percent in men who received the vitamin E supplement alone compared with those who received placebo. There was no increase in prostate cancer when vitamin E and selenium were taken together.

Unlike the studies described above, the Age-Related Eye Disease Study (AREDS), led by the National Eye Institute and cosponsored by other components of NIH, including NCCIH, found a beneficial effect of antioxidant supplements. This study showed that a combination of antioxidants (vitamin C, vitamin E, and beta-carotene) and zinc reduced the risk of developing the advanced stage of age-related macular degeneration by 25 percent in people who had the intermediate stage of this disease or who had the advanced stage in only one eye. Antioxidant supplements used alone reduced the risk by about 17 percent. In the same study, however, antioxidants did not help to prevent cataracts or slow their progression.

- A followup study, AREDS2, found that adding omega-3 fatty acids (fish oil) to the combination of supplements did not improve its effectiveness. However, adding lutein and zeaxanthin (two carotenoids found in the eye) improved the supplement's effectiveness in people who were not taking beta-carotene and those who consumed only small amounts of lutein and zeaxanthin in foods.

Why Don't Antioxidant Supplements Work?

Most clinical studies of antioxidant supplements have not found them to provide substantial health benefits. Researchers have suggested several reasons for this, including the following:

- The beneficial health effects of a diet high in vegetables and fruits or other antioxidant-rich foods may actually be caused by other substances present in the same foods, other dietary factors, or other lifestyle choices rather than antioxidants.

- The effects of the large doses of antioxidants used in supplementation studies may be different from those of the smaller amounts of antioxidants consumed in foods.

- Differences in the chemical composition of antioxidants in foods versus those in supplements may influence their effects. For example, eight chemical forms of vitamin E are present in foods. Vitamin E supplements, on the other hand, typically include only one of these forms—alpha-tocopherol. Alpha-tocopherol also has been used in almost all research studies on vitamin E.

- For some diseases, specific antioxidants might be more effective than the ones that have been tested. For example, to prevent eye diseases, antioxidants that are present in the eye, such as lutein, might be more beneficial than those that are not found in the eye, such as beta-carotene.

- The relationship between free radicals and health may be more complex than has previously been thought. Under some circumstances, free radicals actually may be beneficial rather than harmful, and removing them may be undesirable.

- The antioxidant supplements may not have been given for a long enough time to prevent chronic diseases, such as cardiovascular diseases or cancer, which develop over decades.

- The participants in the clinical trials discussed above were either members of the general population or people who were at high risk for particular diseases. They were not necessarily under increased oxidative stress. Antioxidants might help to

301

prevent diseases in people who are under increased oxidative stress even if they don't prevent them in other people.

If You Are Considering Antioxidant Supplements

• Do not use antioxidant supplements to replace a healthy diet or conventional medical care, or as a reason to postpone seeing a health care provider about a medical problem.

• If you have age-related macular degeneration, consult your health care providers to determine whether supplements of the type used in the AREDS trial are appropriate for you.

• If you are considering a dietary supplement, first get information on it from reliable sources. Keep in mind that dietary supplements may interact with medications or other supplements and may contain ingredients not listed on the label. Your health care provider can advise you. If you are pregnant or nursing a child, or if you are considering giving a child a dietary supplement, it is especially important to consult your (or your child's) health care provider.

• Tell all of your health care providers about any complementary health approaches you use. Give them a full picture of what you do to manage your health. This will help ensure coordinated and safe care.

Section 25.2

Coenzyme Q10 (CoQ10)

Text in this section is excerpted from "Coenzyme Q10 (CoQ10): What You Need To Know," National Institute of Complementary and Integrative Health (NCCIH), March 2015.

What Is CoQ10 and Why Is It Important?

Coenzyme Q10 (CoQ10) is an antioxidant that is necessary for cells to function properly. It is found in plants, bacteria, animals, and people. Cells use CoQ10 to make the energy they need to grow and stay

---

What's the Bottom Line?

How much do we know about CoQ10?

There are some information available from high quality studies done in people about the safety and effectiveness of CoQ10 for different conditions.

What do we know about the effectiveness of CoQ10?

CoQ10 supplements may benefit some patients with cardiovascular disorders, but research on other conditions is not conclusive.

What do we know about the safety of CoQ10?

CoQ10 has mild side effects and is generally well tolerated. However, it may make warfarin, an anticoagulant (blood thinner), less effective.

---

healthy. CoQ10 can be found in highest amounts in the heart, liver, kidneys, and pancreas. Levels of CoQ10 decrease as you age.

- A variety of diseases, including some genetic disorders, are associated with low levels of CoQ10.

- Fish, meats, and whole grains all have small amounts of CoQ10, but not enough to significantly boost the levels in your body.

What the Science Says about the Effectiveness of CoQ10

CoQ10 supplements may benefit some patients with cardiovascular disorders. Researchers have also looked at the effects of CoQ10 for drug-induced muscle weakness, reproductive disorders, cancer, and other diseases. However, results from these studies are limited and not conclusive.

The following information highlights the research status on CoQ10 for the conditions for which it has been studied.

Heart Conditions

- For patients with heart failure, taking CoQ10 was associated with improved heart function and also feeling better, according to research reviews published in 2007 and 2009. A 2013

303

meta-analysis also found an association between taking CoQ10 and improved heart function.

- Taking a combination of nutrients including CoQ10 was associated with quicker recovery after bypass and heart valve surgeries, according to a 2011 randomized controlled trial of 117 patients.

- For people with high blood pressure, the results of taking CoQ10 supplements have been mixed.

- Some studies suggest that CoQ10 is associated with blood pressure control, but the findings are limited, a 2009 systematic review showed.

- CoQ10 does not reduce high blood pressure or heart rate in patients with metabolic syndrome (a group of conditions that put you at risk for heart disease and diabetes), a small, randomized clinical trial reported in 2012.

Muscle Weakness from Statins (Cholesterol-lowering Drugs)

- A 2010 review described research showing that CoQ10 may help ease the myopathy (muscle weakness) sometimes associated with taking statins. However, the findings are not definite, the review concluded.

- A 2012 clinical trial of 76 patients who developed muscle pain within 60 days of starting statins found that CoQ10 was no better for pain than a placebo.

Reproductive Disorders

There is evidence that CoQ10 may improve semen quality and sperm count in infertile men, a 2010 review noted. However, it is uncertain whether this improvement affects the likelihood of conception.

Cancer

There is no convincing evidence that CoQ10 prevents or treats cancer, but two large studies from 2010 and 2011 found that women who developed breast cancer were more likely than others to have abnormal CoQ10 levels, either very low or unusually high.

Other Research on CoQ10

Studies have examined CoQ10 for amyotrophic lateral sclerosis (ALS, also known as Lou Gehrig's disease), Down syndrome, diabetes,

Huntington's disease, migraines, Parkinson's disease, neuromuscular diseases, and age-related changes in cells and genes. The research on CoQ10 for these conditions is limited so we can't draw conclusions about its effectiveness.

What the Science Says about the Safety and Side Effects of CoQ10

- Studies have not reported serious side effects related to CoQ10 use.

- The most common side effects of CoQ10 include insomnia, increased liver enzymes, rashes, nausea, upper abdominal pain, dizziness, sensitivity to light, irritability, headaches, heartburn, and fatigue.

- CoQ10 should not be used by women who are pregnant or breastfeeding.

- Statins may lower the levels of CoQ10 in the blood. However, it is unclear what type of health effect this may have on an individual.

- CoQ10 may make warfarin, an anticoagulant (blood thinner), less effective.

More to Consider

- Do not use CoQ10 supplements to replace a healthful diet or conventional medical care, or as a reason to postpone seeing a health care provider about a medical problem.

- If you're thinking about using a dietary supplement, first get information on it from reliable sources. Keep in mind that dietary supplements may interact with medications or other supplements and may contain ingredients not listed on the label. Your health care provider can advise you.

- If you're pregnant or nursing a child, or if you are considering giving a child a dietary supplement, it is especially important to consult your (or your child's) health care provider.

- Look for published research studies on CoQ10 for the health condition that interests you.

- Tell all your health care providers about any complementary health approaches you use. Give them a full picture of what you do to manage your health. This will help ensure coordinated and safe care.

Chapter 26

Multivitamin/Mineral (MVM) Supplements

What are multivitamin/mineral (MVM) dietary supplements?

Multivitamin/mineral (MVM) supplements contain a combination of vitamins and minerals, and sometimes other ingredients as well. They go by many names, including *multis* and *multiples* or simply *vitamins*. The vitamins and minerals in MVMs have unique roles in the body.

What kinds of MVM supplements are available?

There are many types of MVMs in the marketplace. Manufacturers choose which vitamins, minerals, and other ingredients, as well as their amounts, to include in their products.

Among the most common MVMs are basic, once-daily products containing all or most vitamins and minerals, with the majority in amounts that are close to recommended amounts. Higher-potency MVMs often come in packs of two or more pills to take each day. Manufacturers promote other MVMs for special purposes, such as better performance or energy, weight control, or improved immunity.

This chapter includes excerpts from "Multivitamin/mineral Supplements," Office of Dietary Supplements (ODS), National Institutes of Health (NIH), January 7, 2013; and text from "Vitamin A," Office of Dietary Supplements (ODS), National Institutes of Health (NIH), June 5, 2013.

These products usually contain herbal and other ingredients (such as Echinacea and glucosamine) in addition to vitamins and minerals.

The recommended amounts of nutrients people should get vary by age and gender and are known as Recommended Dietary Allowances (RDAs) and Adequate Intakes (AIs). One value for each nutrient, known as the Daily Value (DV), is selected for the labels of dietary supplements and foods. A DV is often, but not always, similar to one's RDA or AI for that nutrient. The label provides the %DV so that you can see how much (what percentage) a serving of the product contributes to reaching the DV.

Who takes MVM supplements?

Research has shown that more than one-third of Americans take MVMs. About one in four young children takes an MVM, but adolescents are least likely to take them. Use increases with age during adulthood so that by age 71 years, more than 40% take an MVM.

Women; the elderly; people with more education, more income, healthier diets and lifestyles, and lower body weights; and people in the western United States use MVMs most often. Smokers and members of certain ethnic and racial groups (such as African Americans, Hispanics, and Native Americans) are less likely to take a daily MVM.

What are some effects of MVMs on health?

People take MVMs for many reasons. Here are some examples of what research has shown about using them to increase nutrient intakes, promote health, and reduce the risk of disease.

Increase nutrient intakes

Taking an MVM increases nutrient intakes and helps people get the recommended amounts of vitamins and minerals when they cannot or do not meet these needs from food alone. But taking an MVM can also raise the chances of getting too much of some nutrients, like iron, vitamin A, zinc, niacin, and folic acid, especially when a person uses more than a basic, once-daily product.

Some people take an MVM as a form of dietary or nutritional "insurance." Ironically, people who take MVMs tend to consume more vitamins and minerals from food than those who don't. Also, the people least likely to get enough nutrients from diet alone who might benefit from MVMs are the least likely to take them.

Health promotion and chronic disease prevention

For people with certain health problems, specific MVMs might be helpful. For example, a study showed that a particular high-dose formula of several vitamins and minerals slowed vision loss in some people with age-related macular degeneration. Although a few studies show that MVMs might reduce the overall risk of cancer in certain men, most research shows that healthy people who take an MVM do not have a lower chance of getting cancer, heart disease, or diabetes. Based on current research, it's not possible to recommend for or against the use of MVMs to stay healthier longer.

One reason we know so little about whether MVMs have health benefits is that studies often use different products, making it hard to compare their results to find patterns. Many MVMs are available, and manufacturers can change their composition at will. It is therefore difficult for researchers to study whether a specific combination of vitamins and minerals affects health. Also, people with healthier diets and lifestyles are more likely to take dietary supplements, making it hard to identify any benefits from the MVMs.

Should I take an MVM?

MVMs cannot take the place of eating a variety of foods that are important to a healthy diet. Foods provide more than vitamins and minerals. They also have fiber and other ingredients that may have positive health effects. But people who don't get enough vitamins and minerals from food alone, are on low-calorie diets, have a poor appetite, or avoid certain foods (such as strict vegetarians and vegans) might consider taking an MVM. Health care providers might also recommend MVMs to patients with certain medical problems.

Some people might benefit from taking certain nutrients found in MVMs. For example:

- Women who might become pregnant should get 400 mcg/day of folic acid from fortified foods and/or dietary supplements to reduce the risk of birth defects of the brain and spine in their newborn babies.

- Pregnant women should take an iron supplement as recommended by their health care provider. A prenatal MVM is likely to provide iron.

- Breastfed and partially breastfed infants should receive vitamin D supplements of 400 IU/day, as should non-breastfed infants who drink less than about 1 quart per day of vitamin D-fortified formula or milk.

- In postmenopausal women, calcium and vitamin D supplements may increase bone strength and reduce the risk of fractures.

- People over age 50 should get recommended amounts of vitamin B12 from fortified foods and/or dietary supplements because they might not absorb enough of the B12 that is naturally found in food.

Can MVMs be harmful?

Taking a basic MVM is unlikely to pose any risks to health. But if you consume fortified foods and drinks (such as cereals or beverages with added vitamins and minerals) or take other dietary supplements, make sure that the MVM you take doesn't cause your intake of any vitamin or mineral to go above the upper levels.

Pay particular attention to the amounts of vitamin A, beta-carotene (which the body can convert to vitamin A), and iron in the MVM.

- Women who get too much vitamin A during pregnancy can increase the risk of birth defects in their babies. This risk does not apply to beta-carotene, however. Smokers, and perhaps former smokers, should avoid MVMs with large amounts of beta-carotene and vitamin A because these ingredients might increase the risk of developing lung cancer.

- Adult men and postmenopausal women should avoid taking MVMs that contain 18 mg or more of iron unless their doctor has told them that they have iron deficiency or inadequacy. When the body takes in much more iron than it can eliminate, the iron can collect in body tissues and organs, such as the liver and heart, and damage them. Iron supplements are a leading cause of poisoning in children under age 6, so keep any products containing iron (such as children's chewable MVMs or adults' iron supplements) out of children's reach.

Are there any interactions with MVMs that I should know about?

MVMs with recommended intake levels of nutrients don't usually interact with medications, with one important exception. If you take medicine to reduce blood clotting, such as warfarin (Coumadin and other brand names), talk to your health care provider before taking any MVM or dietary supplement with vitamin K. Vitamin K lowers the drug's effectiveness and doctors base the medicine dose partly on the amount of vitamin K you usually consume in foods and supplements.

Which kind of MVM should I choose?

Talk to a health care provider to help you figure out whether you should take an MVM and, if so, which one is best for you. Consider basic MVMs whose amounts of most or all vitamins and minerals do not go above the DVs. These MVMs usually have low amounts of calcium and magnesium, so some people might need to take one or both minerals separately. Make sure that the product does not have too much vitamin A and iron.

Also, consider choosing an MVM designed for your age, sex, and other factors (like pregnancy). MVMs for men often contain little or no iron, for example. MVMs for seniors usually provide more calcium and vitamins D and B12 and less iron than MVMs for younger adults. Prenatal MVMs for pregnant women often provide vitamin A as beta-carotene.

What is vitamin A and what does it do?

Vitamin A is a fat-soluble vitamin that is naturally present in many foods. Vitamin A is important for normal vision, the immune system, and reproduction. Vitamin A also helps the heart, lungs, kidneys, and other organs work properly.

There are two different types of vitamin A. The first type, pre-formed vitamin A, is found in meat, poultry, fish, and dairy products. The second type, provitamin A, is found in fruits, vegetables, and other plant-based products. The most common type of provitamin A in foods and dietary supplements is beta-carotene.

How much vitamin A do I need?

The amount of vitamin A you need depends on your age and reproductive status. Recommended intakes for vitamin A for people aged 14 years and older range between 700 and 900 micrograms (mcg) of retinol activity equivalents (RAE) per day. Recommended intakes for women who are nursing range between 1,200 and 1,300 RAE. Lower values are recommended for infants and children younger than 14.

311

However, the vitamin A content of foods and dietary supplements is given on product labels in international units (IU), not mcg RAE. Converting between IU and mcg RAE is not easy. A varied diet with 900 mcg RAE of vitamin A, for example, provides between 3,000 and 36,000 IU of vitamin A depending on the foods consumed.

For adults and children aged 4 years and older, the U.S. Food and Drug Administration has established a vitamin A Daily Value (DV) of 5,000 IU from a varied diet of both plant and animal foods. DVs are not recommended intakes; they don't vary by age and sex, for example. But trying to reach 100% of the DV each day, on average, is useful to help you get enough vitamin A.

What foods provide vitamin A?

Vitamin A is found naturally in many foods and is added to some foods, such as milk and cereal. You can get recommended amounts of vitamin A by eating a variety of foods, including the following:

- Beef liver and other organ meats (but these foods are also high in cholesterol, so limit the amount you eat).

- Some types of fish, such as salmon.

- Green leafy vegetables and other green, orange, and yellow vegetables, such as broccoli, carrots, and squash.

- Fruits, including cantaloupe, apricots, and mangos.

- Dairy products, which are among the major sources of vitamin A for Americans.

- Fortified breakfast cereals.

What kinds of vitamin A dietary supplements are available?

Vitamin A is available in dietary supplements, usually in the form of retinyl acetate or retinyl palmitate (preformed vitamin A), beta-carotene (provitamin A), or a combination of preformed and provitamin A. Most multivitamin-mineral supplements contain vitamin A. Dietary supplements that contain only vitamin A are also available.

Am I getting enough vitamin A?

Most people in the United States get enough vitamin A from the foods they eat, and vitamin A deficiency is rare. However, certain groups of people are more likely than others to have trouble getting enough vitamin A:

- Premature infants, who often have low levels of vitamin A in their first year.

- Infants, young children, pregnant women, and breastfeeding women in developing countries.

- People with cystic fibrosis.

What happens if I don't get enough vitamin A?

Vitamin A deficiency is rare in the United States, although it is common in many developing countries. The most common symptom of vitamin A deficiency in young children and pregnant women is an eye condition called xerophthalmia. Xerophthalmia is the inability to see in low light, and it can lead to blindness if it isn't treated.

What are some effects of vitamin A on health?

Scientists are studying vitamin A to understand how it affects health. Here are some examples of what this research has shown.

Cancer

People who eat a lot of *foods* containing beta-carotene might have a lower risk of certain kinds of cancer, such as lung cancer or prostate cancer. But studies to date have not shown that vitamin A or beta-carotene *supplements* can help prevent cancer or lower the chances of dying from this disease. In fact, studies show that smokers who take high doses of beta-carotene supplements have an *increased* risk of lung cancer.

Age-Related Macular Degeneration

Age-related macular degeneration (AMD), or the loss of central vision as people age, is one of the most common causes of vision loss in older people. Among people with AMD who are at high risk of developing advanced AMD, a supplement containing antioxidants, zinc, and copper with or without beta-carotene has shown promise for slowing down the rate of vision loss.

Measles

When children with vitamin A deficiency (which is rare in North America) get measles, the disease tends to be more severe. In these children, taking supplements with high doses of vitamin A can shorten

313

the fever and diarrhea caused by measles. These supplements can also lower the risk of death in children with measles who live in developing countries where vitamin A deficiency is common.

Can vitamin A be harmful?

Yes, high intakes of some forms of vitamin A can be harmful.

Getting too much preformed vitamin A (usually from supplements or certain medicines) can cause dizziness, nausea, headaches, coma, and even death. High intakes of preformed vitamin A in pregnant women can also cause birth defects in their babies. Women who might be pregnant should not take high doses of vitamin A supplements.

Consuming high amounts of beta-carotene or other forms of provitamin A can turn the skin yellow-orange, but this condition is harmless. High intakes of beta-carotene do not cause birth defects or the other more serious effects caused by getting too much preformed vitamin A.

The upper limits for preformed vitamin A in IU are listed below. These levels do not apply to people who are taking vitamin A for medical reasons under the care of a doctor. Upper limits for beta-carotene and other forms of provitamin A have not been established.

Table 26.1. Upper Limits for Vitamin A

Life Stage	Upper Limit
Birth to 12 months	2,000 IU
Children 1–3 years	2,000 IU
Children 4–8 years	3,000 IU
Children 9–13 years	5,667 IU
Teens 14–18 years	9,333 IU
Adults 19 years and older	10,000 IU

Are there any interactions with vitamin A that I should know about?

Yes, vitamin A supplements can interact or interfere with medicines you take. Here are several examples:

- Orlistat (Alli, Xenical), a weight-loss drug, can decrease the absorption of vitamin A, causing low blood levels in some people.

- Several synthetic forms of vitamin A are used in prescription medicines. Examples are the psoriasis treatment acitretin (Soriatane) and bexarotene (Targretin), used to treat the skin effects of T-cell lymphoma. Taking these medicines in combination with a vitamin A supplement can cause dangerously high levels of vitamin A in the blood.

Tell your doctor, pharmacist, and other health care providers about any dietary supplements and medicines you take. They can tell you if those dietary supplements might interact or interfere with your prescription or over-the-counter medicines or if the medicines might interfere with how your body absorbs, uses, or breaks down nutrients.

Vitamin A and healthful eating

People should get most of their nutrients from food, advises the federal government's *Dietary Guidelines for Americans*. Foods contain vitamins, minerals, dietary fiber and other substances that benefit health. Dietary supplements might help in some situations to increase the intake of a specific vitamin or mineral.

315

Chapter 27

Chromium

What foods provide chromium?

Chromium is widely distributed in the food supply, but most foods provide only small amounts (less than 2 micrograms [mcg] per serving). Meat and whole-grain products, as well as some fruits, vegetables, and spices are relatively good sources. In contrast, foods high in simple sugars (like sucrose and fructose) are low in chromium.

Dietary intakes of chromium cannot be reliably determined because the content of the mineral in foods is substantially affected by agricultural and manufacturing processes and perhaps by contamination with chromium when the foods are analyzed. Therefore, Table 27.1, and food-composition databases generally, provide approximate values of chromium in foods that should only serve as a guide.

Table 27.1. Selected Food Sources of Chromium

Food	Chromium (mcg)
Broccoli, ½ cup	11
Grape juice, 1 cup	8
English muffin, whole wheat, 1	4
Potatoes, mashed, 1 cup	3

Text in this chapter is excerpted from "Health Information – Chromium," Office of Dietary Supplements (ODS), National Institutes of Health (NIH), November 4, 2013.

Table 27.1. Continued

Food	Chromium (mcg)
Garlic, dried, 1 teaspoon	3
Basil, dried, 1 tablespoon	2
Beef cubes, 3 ounces	2
Orange juice, 1 cup	2
Turkey breast, 3 ounces	2
Whole wheat bread, 2 slices	2
Red wine, 5 ounces	1–13
Apple, unpeeled, 1 medium	1
Banana, 1 medium	1
Green beans, ½ cup	1

What are recommended intakes of chromium?

Recommended chromium intakes are provided in the Dietary Reference Intakes (DRIs) developed by the Institute of Medicine of the National Academy of Sciences. Dietary Reference Intakes is the general term for a set of reference values to plan and assess the nutrient intakes of healthy people. These values include the Recommended Dietary Allowance (RDA) and the Adequate Intake (AI). The RDA is the average daily intake that meets a nutrient requirement of nearly all (97 to 98%) healthy individuals. An AI is established when there is insufficient research to establish an RDA; it is generally set at a level that healthy people typically consume.

In 1989, the National Academy of Sciences established an "estimated safe and adequate daily dietary intake" range for chromium. For adults and adolescents that range was 50 to 200 mcg. In 2001, DRIs for chromium were established. The research base was insufficient to establish RDAs, so AIs were developed based on average intakes of chromium from food as found in several studies. Chromium AIs are provided in Table 27.2.

Adult women in the United States consume about 23 to 29 mcg of chromium per day from food, which meets their AIs unless they're pregnant or lactating. In contrast, adult men average 39 to 54 mcg per day, which exceeds their AIs.

The average amount of chromium in the breast milk of healthy, well-nourished mothers is 0.24 mcg per quart, so infants exclusively

Table 27.2. Adequate Intakes (AIs) for chromium

Age	Infants and children (mcg/day)	Males (mcg/day)	Females (mcg/day)	Pregnancy (mcg/day)	Lactation (mcg/day)
0 to 6 months	0.2				
7 to 12 months	5.5				
1 to 3 years	11				
4 to 8 years	15				
9 to 13 years		25	21		
14 to 18 years		35	24	29	44
19 to 50 years		35	25	30	45
>50 years		30	20		

mcg = micrograms

fed breast milk obtain about 0.2 mcg (based on an estimated consumption of 0.82 quarts per day). Infant formula provides about 0.5 mcg of chromium per quart. No studies have compared how well infants absorb and utilize chromium from human milk and formula.

What affects chromium levels in the body?

Absorption of chromium from the intestinal tract is low, ranging from less than 0.4% to 2.5% of the amount consumed, and the remainder is excreted in the feces. Enhancing the mineral's absorption are vitamin C (found in fruits and vegetables and their juices) and the B vitamin niacin (found in meats, poultry, fish, and grain products). Absorbed chromium is stored in the liver, spleen, soft tissue, and bone.

The body's chromium content may be reduced under several conditions. Diets high in simple sugars (comprising more than 35% of calories) can increase chromium excretion in the urine. Infection, acute exercise, pregnancy and lactation, and stressful states (such as physical trauma) increase chromium losses and can lead to deficiency, especially if chromium intakes are already low.

319

When can a chromium deficiency occur?

In the 1960s, chromium was found to correct glucose intolerance and insulin resistance in deficient animals, two indicators that the body is failing to properly control blood-sugar levels and which are precursors of type 2 diabetes. However, reports of actual chromium deficiency in humans are rare. Three hospitalized patients who were fed intravenously showed signs of diabetes (including weight loss, neuropathy, and impaired glucose tolerance) until chromium was added to their feeding solution. The chromium, added at doses of 150 to 250 mcg/day for up to two weeks, corrected their diabetes symptoms. Chromium is now routinely added to intravenous solutions.

Who may need extra chromium?

There are reports of significant age-related decreases in the chromium concentrations of hair, sweat and blood, which might suggest that older people are more vulnerable to chromium depletion than younger adults. One cannot be sure, however, as chromium status is difficult to determine. That's because blood, urine, and hair levels do not necessarily reflect body stores. Furthermore, no chromium-specific enzyme or other biochemical marker has been found to reliably assess a person's chromium status.

There is considerable interest in the possibility that supplemental chromium may help to treat impaired glucose tolerance and type 2 diabetes, but the research to date is inconclusive. No large, randomized, controlled clinical trials testing this hypothesis have been reported in the United States. Nevertheless, this is an active area of research.

What are some current issues and controversies about chromium?

Chromium has long been of interest for its possible connection to various health conditions. Among the most active areas of chromium research are its use in supplement form to treat diabetes, lower blood lipid levels, promote weight loss, and improve body composition.

Type 2 diabetes and glucose intolerance

In type 2 diabetes, the pancreas is usually producing enough insulin but, for unknown reasons, the body cannot use the insulin effectively. The disease typically occurs, in part, because the cells comprising muscle and other tissues become resistant to insulin's action, especially among the obese. Insulin permits the entry of glucose into most cells, where this sugar is used for energy, stored in the liver and muscles (as glycogen), and converted to fat when present in excess. Insulin resistance leads to higher than normal levels of glucose in the blood (hyperglycemia).

Chromium deficiency impairs the body's ability to use glucose to meet its energy needs and raises insulin requirements. It has therefore been suggested that chromium supplements might help to control type 2 diabetes or the glucose and insulin responses in persons at high risk of developing the disease. A review of randomized controlled clinical trials evaluated this hypothesis. This meta-analysis assessed the effects of chromium supplements on three markers of diabetes in the blood: glucose, insulin, and glycated hemoglobin (which provides a measure of long-term glucose levels; also known as hemoglobin A1C). It summarized data from 15 trials on 618 participants, of which 425 were in good health or had impaired glucose tolerance and 193 had type 2 diabetes. Chromium supplementation had no effect on glucose or insulin concentrations in subjects without diabetes nor did it reduce these levels in subjects with diabetes, except in one study. However, that study, conducted in China (in which 155 subjects with diabetes were given either 200 or 1,000 mcg/day of chromium or a placebo) might simply show the benefits of supplementation in a chromium-deficient population.

Overall, the value of chromium supplements for diabetes is inconclusive and controversial. Randomized controlled clinical trials in well-defined, at-risk populations where dietary intakes are known are necessary to determine the effects of chromium on markers of diabetes. The American Diabetes Association states that there is insufficient evidence to support the routine use of chromium to improve glycemic control in people with diabetes. It further notes that there is no clear scientific evidence that vitamin and mineral supplementation benefits people with diabetes who do not have underlying nutritional deficiencies.

Lipid metabolism

The effects of chromium supplementation on blood lipid levels in humans are also inconclusive. In some studies, 150 to 1,000 mcg/day has decreased total and low-density-lipoprotein (LDL or "bad") cholesterol and triglyceride levels and increased concentrations of apolipoprotein A (a component of high-density-lipoprotein cholesterol known as HDL or "good" cholesterol) in subjects with atherosclerosis or elevated

321

cholesterol or among those taking a beta-blocker drug. These findings are consistent with the results of earlier studies.

However, chromium supplements have shown no favorable effects on blood lipids in other studies. The mixed research findings may be due to difficulties in determining the chromium status of subjects at the start of the trials and the researchers' failure to control for dietary factors that influence blood lipid levels.

Body weight and composition

Chromium supplements are sometimes claimed to reduce body fat and increase lean (muscle) mass. Yet a recent review of 24 studies that examined the effects of 200 to 1,000 mcg/day of chromium (in the form of chromium picolinate) on body mass or composition found no significant benefits. Another recent review of randomized, controlled clinical trials did find supplements of chromium picolinate to help with weight loss when compared with placebos, but the differences were small and of debatable clinical relevance. In several studies, chromium's effects on body weight and composition may be called into question because the researchers failed to adequately control for the participants' food intakes. Furthermore, most studies included only a small number of subjects and were of short duration.

What are the health risks of too much chromium?

Few serious adverse effects have been linked to high intakes of chromium, so the Institute of Medicine has not established a Tolerable Upper Intake Level (UL) for this mineral. A UL is the maximum daily intake of a nutrient that is unlikely to cause adverse health effects. It is one of the values (together with the RDA and AI) that comprise the Dietary Reference Intakes (DRIs) for each nutrient.

Chromium and medication interactions

Certain medications may interact with chromium, especially when taken on a regular basis (see Table 27.3). Before taking dietary supplements, check with your doctor or other qualified healthcare provider, especially if you take prescription or over-the-counter medications.

Supplemental sources of chromium

Chromium is a widely used supplement. Estimated sales to consumers were $85 million in 2002, representing 5.6% of the total

Table 27.3. Interactions between chromium and medications

Medications	Nature of interaction
• Antacids	These medications alter stomach acidity and may impair chromium absorption or enhance excretion
• Corticosteroids	
• H2 blockers (such as cimetidine, famotidine, nizatidine, and rantidine)	
• Proton-pump inhibitors (such as omeprazole, lansoprazole, rabeprazole, pantoprazole, and esomeprazole)	
• Beta-blockers (such as atenolol or propanolol)	These medications may have their effects enhanced if taken together with chromium or they may increase chromium absorption
• Corticosteroids	
• Insulin	
• Nicotinic acid	
• Nonsteroidal anti-inflammatory drugs (NSAIDS)	
• Prostaglandin inhibitors (such as ibuprofen, indomethacin, naproxen, piroxicam, and aspirin)	

mineral-supplement market. Chromium is sold as a single-ingredient supplement as well as in combination formulas, particularly those marketed for weight loss and performance enhancement. Supplement doses typically range from 50 to 200 mcg.

The safety and efficacy of chromium supplements need more investigation. Please consult with a doctor or other trained healthcare professional before taking any dietary supplements.

Chromium supplements are available as chromium chloride, chromium nicotinate, chromium picolinate, high-chromium yeast, and chromium citrate. Chromium chloride in particular appears to have poor bioavailability. However, given the limited data on chromium absorption in humans, it is not clear which forms are best to take.

Chromium and Healthful Diets

The federal government's *2010 Dietary Guidelines for Americans* notes that "nutrients should come primarily from foods. Foods in nutri-ent-dense, mostly intact forms contain not only the essential vitamins and minerals that are often contained in nutrient supplements, but also dietary fiber and other naturally occurring substances that may have positive health effects. Dietary supplements may be advantageous in specific situations to increase intake of a specific vitamin or mineral."

The *Dietary Guidelines for Americans* describes a healthy diet as one that:

• Emphasizes a variety of fruits, vegetables, whole grains, and fat-free or low-fat milk and milk products.

• Whole grain products and certain fruits and vegetables like broccoli, potatoes, grape juice, and oranges are sources of chromium. Ready-to-eat bran cereals can also be a relatively good source of chromium.

• Includes lean meats, poultry, fish, beans, eggs, and nuts.

• Lean beef, oysters, eggs, and turkey are sources of chromium.

• Is low in saturated fats, trans fats, cholesterol, salt (sodium), and added sugars.

• Stays within your daily calorie needs.

Chapter 28

Folate (Folic Acid)

What is folate and what does it do?

Folate is a B-vitamin that is naturally present in many foods. A form of folate, called folic acid, is used in dietary supplements and fortified foods.

Our bodies need folate to make DNA and other genetic material. Folate is also needed for the body's cells to divide.

How much folate do I need?

The amount of folate you need depends on your age. Average daily recommended amounts are listed below in micrograms (mcg) of dietary folate equivalents (DFEs).

All women and teen girls who could become pregnant should consume 400 mcg of folic acid daily from supplements, fortified foods, or both in addition to the folate they get naturally from foods.

What foods provide folate?

Folate is naturally present in many foods and food companies add folic acid to other foods, including bread, cereal, and pasta. You can

Text in this chapter is excerpted from "Health information – Folate," Office of Dietary Supplements (ODS), National Institutes of Health (NIH), April 23, 2013.

Table 28.1. Folate – Daily Recommendations

Life Stage	Recommended Amount
Birth to 6 months	65 mcg DFE
Infants 7–12 months	80 mcg DFE
Children 1–3 years	150 mcg DFE
Children 4–8 years	200 mcg DFE
Children 9–13 years	300 mcg DFE
Teens 14–18 years	400 mcg DFE
Adults 19–50 years	400 mcg DFE
Adults 51–70 years	400 mcg DFE
Adults 71+ years	400 mcg DFE
Pregnant teens and women	600 mcg DFE
Breastfeeding teens and women	500 mcg DFE

get recommended amounts by eating a variety of foods, including the following:

- Vegetables (especially asparagus, Brussels sprouts, and dark green leafy vegetables such as spinach and mustard greens).

- Fruits and fruit juices (especially oranges and orange juice).

- Nuts, beans, and peas (such as peanuts, black-eyed peas, and kidney beans).

- Grains (including whole grains; fortified cold cereals; enriched flour products such as bread, bagels, cornmeal, and pasta; and rice).

- Folic acid is added to many grain-based products. To find out whether folic acid has been added to a food, check the product label.

Beef liver is high in folate but is also high in cholesterol, so limit the amount you eat. Only small amounts of folate are found in other animal foods like meats, poultry, seafood, eggs, and dairy products.

What kinds of folic acid dietary supplements are available?

Folic acid is available in multivitamins and prenatal vitamins. It is also available in B-complex dietary supplements and supplements containing only folic acid.

Am I getting enough folate?

Most people in the United States get enough folate. However, certain groups of people are more likely than others to have trouble getting enough folate:

- Teen girls and women aged 14–30 years (especially before and during pregnancy).

- Non-Hispanic Black women.

- People with disorders that lower nutrientabsorption (such as celiac disease and inflammatory bowel disease).

- People with alcoholism.

What happens if I don't get enough folate?

Folate deficiency is rare in the United States, but some people get barely enough. Getting too little folate can result in megaloblastic anemia, which causes weakness, fatigue, trouble concentrating, irritability, headache, heart palpitations, and shortness of breath. Folate deficiency can also cause open sores on the tongue and inside the mouth as well as changes in the color of the skin, hair, or fingernails. Women who don't get enough folate are at risk of having babies with neural tube defects, such as spina bifida. Folate deficiency can also increase the likelihood of having a premature or low-birth-weight baby.

What are some effects of folate on health?

Scientists are studying folate to understand how it affects health. Here are several examples of what this research has shown.

Neural tube defects

Taking folic acid regularly before becoming pregnant and during early pregnancy helps prevent neural tube defects in babies. But about half of all pregnancies are unplanned. Therefore, all women and teen girls who could become pregnant should consume 400 mcg of folic acid daily from supplements, fortified foods, or both in addition to the folate they get naturally from foods.

Since 1998, the U.S. Food and Drug Administration (FDA) has required food companies to add folic acid to enriched bread, cereal, flour, cornmeal, pasta, rice, and other grain products sold in the United States. Because most people in the United States eat these foods on a regular basis, folic acid intakes have increased and the number of babies born with neural tube defects has decreased since 1998.

Preterm birth, congenital heart defects, and other birth defects

Taking folic acid might reduce the risk of having a premature baby and prevent birth defects, such as congenital heart problems. But more research is needed to understand how folic acid affects the risk of these conditions.

Cancer

Folate that is found naturally in food may decrease the risk of several forms of cancer. But folate might have different effects depending on how much is taken and when. Modest amounts of folic acid taken before cancer develops might decrease cancer risk, but high doses taken after cancer (especially colorectal cancer) begins might speed up its progression. For this reason, high doses of folic acid supplements (more than the upper limit of 1,000 mcg) should be taken with caution, especially by people who have a history of colorectal adenomas (which sometimes turn into cancer). More research is needed to understand the roles of dietary folate and folic acid supplements in cancer risk.

Heart disease and stroke

Some scientists used to think that folic acid and other B-vitamins might reduce heart disease risk by lowering levels of homocysteine, an amino acid in the blood. But although folic acid supplements do lower blood homocysteine levels, they don't decrease the risk of heart disease. Some studies have shown that a combination of folic acid with other B-vitamins, however, helps prevent stroke.

Dementia, cognitive function, and Alzheimer's disease

Folic acid supplements with or without other B-vitamins do not seem to improve cognitive function, but more research on this topic is needed.

Depression

People with low blood levels of folate might be more likely to suffer from depression and might not respond as well to treatment with antidepressants as people with normal folate levels.

Folic acid supplements might make antidepressant medications more effective. But it is not clear whether these supplements help people with both normal folate levels and those with folate deficiency. More research is needed to learn about the role of folate in depression and whether folic acid supplements are helpful when used in combination with standard treatment.

Can folate be harmful?

Folate that is naturally present in food is not harmful. Folic acid in supplements and fortified foods, however, should not be consumed in amounts above the upper limit, unless recommended by a health care provider.

Taking large amounts of folic acid might hide a vitamin B12 deficiency. Folic acid can correct the anemia but not the nerve damage caused by vitamin B12 deficiency. This can lead to permanent damage of the brain, spinal cord, and nerves. High doses of folic acid might also increase the risk of colorectal cancer and possibly other cancers in some people.

The upper limits for folic acid are listed below.

Table 28.2. Folic Acid – Upper Limits

Ages	Upper Limit
Birth to 6 months	Not established
Infants 7–12 months	Not established
Children 1–3 years	300 mcg
Children 4–8 years	400 mcg
Children 9–13 years	600 mcg
Teens 14–18 years	800 mcg
Adults	1,000 mcg

Are there any interactions with folate that I should know about?

Folic acid supplements can interact with several medications. Here are some examples:

- Folic acid could interfere with methotrexate (Rheumatrex®, Trexall®) when taken to treat cancer.

- Taking anti-epileptic medications such as phenytoin (Dilantin®), carbamazepine (Carbatrol®, Tegretol®, Equetro®, Epitol®), and

329

valproate (Depacon®) could reduce blood levels of folate. Also, taking folic acid supplements could reduce blood levels of these medications.

*   Taking sulfasalazine (Azulfidine®) for ulcerative colitis could reduce the body's ability to absorb folate and cause folate deficiency.

Tell your doctor, pharmacist, and other health care providers about any dietary supplements and medicines you take. They can tell you if those dietary supplements might interact or interfere with your prescription or over-the-counter medicines or if the medicines might interfere with how your body absorbs, uses, or breaks down nutrients.

Folate and healthful eating

People should get most of their nutrients from food, advises the federal government's *Dietary Guidelines for Americans.* Foods contain vitamins, minerals, dietary fiber and other substances that benefit health. Dietary supplements might help in some situations to increase the intake of a specific vitamin or mineral.

Chapter 29

Magnesium

What is magnesium and what does it do?

Magnesium is a nutrient that the body needs to stay healthy. Magnesium is important for many processes in the body, including regulating muscle and nerve function, blood sugar levels, and blood pressure and making protein, bone, and DNA.

How much magnesium do I need?

The amount of magnesium you need depends on your age and sex. Average daily recommended amounts are listed in Table 29.1 in milligrams (mg):

What foods provide magnesium?

Magnesium is found naturally in many foods and is added to some fortified foods. You can get recommended amounts of magnesium by eating a variety of foods, including the following:

- Legumes, nuts, seeds, whole grains, and green leafy vegetables (such as spinach)

- Fortified breakfast cereals and other fortified foods

- Milk, yogurt, and some other milk products

Text in this chapter is excerpted from "Health Information – Magnesium," Office of Dietary Supplements (ODS), National Institutes of Health (NIH), February 3, 2014.

Table 29.1. Magnesium – Daily Recommendations

Life Stage	Recommended Amount
Birth to 6 months	30 mg
Infants 7–12 months	75 mg
Children 1–3 years	80 mg
Children 4–8 years	130 mg
Children 9–13 years	240 mg
Teen boys 14–18 years	410 mg
Teen girls 14–18 years	360 mg
Men	400–420 mg
Women	310–320 mg
Pregnant teens	400 mg
Pregnant women	350–360 mg
Breastfeeding teens	360 mg
Breastfeeding women	310–320 mg

What kinds of magnesium dietary supplements are available?

Magnesium is available in multivitamin-mineral supplements and other dietary supplements. Forms of magnesium in dietary supplements that are more easily absorbed by the body are magnesium aspartate, magnesium citrate, magnesium lactate, and magnesium chloride.

Magnesium is also included in some laxatives and some products for treating heartburn and indigestion.

Am I getting enough magnesium?

The diets of most people in the United States provide less than the recommended amounts of magnesium. Men older than 70 and teenage girls are most likely to have low intakes of magnesium. When the amount of magnesium people get from food and dietary supplements is combined, however, total intakes of magnesium are generally above recommended amounts.

What happens if I don't get enough magnesium?

In the short term, getting too little magnesium does not produce obvious symptoms. When healthy people have low intakes, the kidneys help retain magnesium by limiting the amount lost in urine. Low magnesium intakes for a long period of time, however, can lead to magnesium deficiency. In addition, some medical conditions and medications interfere with the body's ability to absorb magnesium or increase the amount of magnesium that the body excretes, which can also lead to magnesium deficiency. Symptoms of magnesium deficiency include loss of appetite, nausea, vomiting, fatigue, and weakness. Extreme magnesium deficiency can cause numbness, tingling, muscle cramps, seizures, personality changes, and an abnormal heart rhythm.

The following groups of people are more likely than others to get too little magnesium:

- People with gastrointestinal diseases (such as Crohn's disease and celiac disease)

- People with type 2 diabetes

- People with long-term alcoholism

- Older people

What are some effects of magnesium on health?

Scientists are studying magnesium to understand how it affects health. Here are some examples of what this research has shown.

High blood pressure and heart disease

High blood pressure is a major risk factor for heart disease and stroke. Magnesium supplements might decrease blood pressure, but only by a small amount. Some studies show that people who have more magnesium in their diets have a lower risk of some types of heart disease and stroke. But in many of these studies, it's hard to know how much of the effect was due to magnesium as opposed to other nutrients.

Type 2 diabetes

People with higher amounts of magnesium in their diets tend to have a lower risk of developing type 2 diabetes. Magnesium helps the body break down sugars and might help reduce the risk of insulin resistance (a condition that leads to diabetes). Scientists are studying whether magnesium supplements might help people who already have type 2 diabetes control their disease. More research is needed to better understand whether magnesium can help treat diabetes.

Osteoporosis

Magnesium is important for healthy bones. People with higher intakes of magnesium have a higher bone mineral density, which is important in reducing the risk of bone fractures and osteoporosis. Getting more magnesium from foods or dietary supplements might help older women improve their bone mineral density. More research is needed to better understand whether magnesium supplements can help reduce the risk of osteoporosis or treat this condition.

Migraine headaches

People who have migraine headaches sometimes have low levels of magnesium in their blood and other tissues. Several small studies found that magnesium supplements can modestly reduce the frequency of migraines. However, people should only take magnesium for this purpose under the care of a health care provider. More research is needed to determine whether magnesium supplements can help reduce the risk of migraines or ease migraine symptoms.

Can magnesium be harmful?

Magnesium that is naturally present in food is not harmful and does not need to be limited. In healthy people, the kidneys can get rid of any excess in the urine. But magnesium in dietary supplements and medications should not be consumed in amounts above the upper limit, unless recommended by a health care provider.

The upper limits for magnesium from dietary supplements and/ or medications are listed below. For many age groups, the upper limit appears to be lower than the recommended amount. This occurs because the recommended amounts include magnesium from all sources—food, dietary supplements and medications. The upper limits include magnesium from only dietary supplements and medications; they do not include magnesium found naturally in food.

High intakes of magnesium from dietary supplements and medications can cause diarrhea, nausea, and abdominal cramping. Extremely high intakes of magnesium can lead to irregular heartbeat and cardiac arrest.

Are there any interactions with magnesium that I should know about?

Yes. Magnesium supplements can interact or interfere with some medicines. Here are several examples:

Table 29.2. Magnesium – Upper Limit

Ages	Upper Limit for Magnesium in Dietary Supplements and Medications
Birth to 12 months	Not established
Children 1–3 years	65 mg
Children 4–8 years	110 mg
Children 9–18 years	350 mg
Adults	350 mg

- Bisphosphonates, used to treat osteoporosis, are not well absorbed when taken too soon before or after taking dietary supplements or medications with high amounts of magnesium.

- Antibiotics might not be absorbed if taken too soon before or after taking a dietary supplement that contains magnesium.

- Diuretics can either increase or decrease the loss of magnesium through urine, depending on the type of diuretic.

- Prescription drugs used to ease symptoms of acid reflux or treat peptic ulcers can cause low blood levels of magnesium when taken over a long period of time.

- Very high doses of zinc supplements can interfere with the body's ability to absorb and regulate magnesium.

Tell your doctor, pharmacist, and other health care providers about any dietary supplements and prescription or over-the-counter medicines you take. They can tell you if the dietary supplements might interact with your medicines or if the medicines might interfere with how your body absorbs, uses, or breaks down nutrients.

Magnesium and healthful eating

People should get most of their nutrients from food, advises the federal government's Dietary Guidelines for Americans. Foods contain vitamins, minerals, dietary fiber and other substances that benefit health. Dietary supplements might help in some situations to increase the intake of a specific vitamin or mineral.

Chapter 30

Melatonin

What's the Bottom Line?

How much do we know about melatonin supplements?

Researchers have conducted many studies on whether melatonin supplements may help people with various sleep disorders. However, important questions remain about its usefulness, how much to take, when to take it, and its long-term safety.

What do we know about the usefulness of melatonin supplements?

Melatonin supplements may help some people with certain sleep disorders, including jet lag, sleep problems related to shift work, and delayed sleep phase disorder (one in which people go to bed but can't fall asleep until hours later), and insomnia.

What do we know about the safety of melatonin supplements?

Melatonin supplements appear to be safe when used short-term; less is known about long-term safety.

Text in this chapter is excerpted from "Melatonin: What You Need To Know," National Center for Complementary and Integrative Health (NCCIH), May 2015.

What Is Melatonin?

Melatonin is a natural hormone that plays a role in sleep. Melatonin production and release in the brain is related to time of day, rising in the evening and falling in the morning. Light at night blocks its production. Melatonin dietary supplements have been studied for sleep disorders, such as jet lag, disruptions of the body's internal "clock," insomnia, and problems with sleep among people who work night shifts. It has also been studied for dementia symptoms.

What the Science Says about the Effectiveness of Melatonin

For Sleep Disorders

Studies suggest that melatonin may help with certain sleep disorders, such as jet lag, delayed sleep phase disorder (a disruption of the body's biological clock in which a person's sleep-wake timing cycle is delayed by 3 to 6 hours), sleep problems related to shift work, and some sleep disorders in children. It's also been shown to be helpful for a sleep disorder that causes changes in blind peoples' sleep and wake times. Study results are mixed on whether melatonin is effective for insomnia in adults, but some studies suggest it may slightly reduce the time it takes to fall asleep.

Jet lag

Jet lag is caused by rapid travel across several time zones; its symptoms include disturbed sleep, daytime fatigue, indigestion, and a general feeling of discomfort.

- In a 2009 research review, results from six small studies and two large studies suggested that melatonin may ease jet lag.
- In a 2007 clinical practice guideline, the American Academy of Sleep Medicine supported using melatonin to reduce jet lag symptoms and improve sleep after traveling across more than one time zone.

Delayed Sleep Phase Disorder

Adults and teens with this sleep disorder have trouble falling asleep before 2 a.m. and have trouble waking up in the morning.

- In a 2007 review of the literature, researchers suggested that a combination of melatonin supplements, a behavioral approach to delay sleep and wake times until the desired sleep time is achieved, and reduced evening light may even out sleep cycles in people with this sleep disorder.

- In a 2007 clinical practice guideline, the American Academy of Sleep Medicine recommended timed melatonin supplementation for this sleep disorder.

Shift Work Disorder

Shift work refers to job-related duties conducted outside of morning to evening working hours. About 2 million Americans who work afternoon to nighttime or nighttime to early morning hours are affected by shift work disorder.

- A 2007 clinical practice guideline and 2010 review of the evidence concluded that melatonin may improve daytime sleep quality and duration, but not nighttime alertness, in people with shift work disorder.
- The American Academy of Sleep Medicine recommended taking melatonin prior to daytime sleep for night shift workers with shift work disorder to enhance daytime sleep.

Insomnia

Insomnia is a general term for a group of problems characterized by an inability to fall asleep and stay asleep.

- **In adults.** A 2013 analysis of 19 studies of people with primary sleep disorders found that melatonin slightly improved time to fall asleep, total sleep time, and overall sleep quality. In a 2007 study of people with insomnia, aged 55 years or older, researchers found that prolonged-release melatonin significantly improved quality of sleep and morning alertness.
- **In children.** There's limited evidence from rigorous studies of melatonin for sleep disorders among young people. A 2011 literature review suggested a benefit with minimal side effects in healthy children as well as youth with attention-deficit hyperactivity disorder, autism, and several other populations. There's insufficient information to make conclusions about the safety and effectiveness of long-term melatonin use.

For Other Conditions

While there hasn't been enough research to support melatonin's use for other conditions:

- Researchers are investigating whether adding melatonin to standard cancer care can improve response rates, survival time, and quality of life.

- Results from a few small studies in people (clinical trials) have led investigators to propose additional research on whether melatonin may help to improve mild cognitive impairment in patients with **Alzheimer's disease** (AD) and prevent cell damage associated with **amyotrophic lateral sclerosis** (**ALS,** also known as **Lou Gehrig's disease**). An analysis of the research suggested that adding sustained-release melatonin (but not fast-release melatonin) to high blood pressure management reduced elevated nighttime blood pressure.

Improving Sleep Habits in Children

Sleep problems are one of the most common problems parents encounter with their children. There are some simple steps parents can take to improve their children's sleep, such as having a set bedtime and bedtime routine, avoiding foods or drinks with caffeine, and limiting the amount of screen time. The National Heart, Lung, and Blood Institute has some additional resources for improving sleep habits in both children and adults

What the Science Says about Safety and Side Effects of Melatonin

Melatonin appears to be safe when used short-term, but the lack of long-term studies means we don't know if it's safe for extended use.

- In one study, researchers noted that melatonin supplements may worsen mood in people with dementia.

- In 2011, the U.S. Food and Drug Administration (FDA) issued a warning to a company that makes and sells "relaxation brownies," stating that the melatonin in them hasn't been deemed a safe food additive.

- Side effects of melatonin are uncommon but can include drowsiness, headache, dizziness, or nausea. There have been no reports of significant side effects of melatonin in children.

Keep in Mind

- If you or a family member has trouble sleeping, see your health care provider.

- When you take a melatonin supplement, it may affect your biological clock.

- FDA regulates dietary supplements such as melatonin, but the regulations for dietary supplements are different and less strict than those for prescription or over-the-counter drugs.

- Some dietary supplements may interact with medications or pose risks if you have medical problems or are going to have surgery.

- Most dietary supplements haven't been tested in pregnant women, nursing mothers, or children. If you're pregnant or nursing a child, it's especially important to see your health care provider before taking any medication or supplement, including melatonin.

- To use dietary supplements, such as melatonin safely, read and follow label instructions, and recognize that "natural" does not always mean "safe."

- Tell all your health care providers about any complementary or integrative health approaches you use. Give them a full picture of what you do to manage your health. This will help ensure safe and coordinated care.

Chapter 31

Omega-3 and Flaxseed Supplements

Chapter Contents

Section 31.1

Omega-3 Supplement

Text in this section begins with excerpts from "Omega-3
Supplements: An Introduction," National Center for Complementary
and Integrative Health (NCCIH), August 2015.
Text in this section beginning with "7 Things To Know About
Omega-3 Fatty Acids," is excerpted from "7 Things To Know About
Omega-3 Fatty Acids," National Center for Complementary and
Integrative Health (NCCIH), January 30, 2015.

Omega-3 fatty acids (omega-3s) are a group of polyunsaturated fatty
acids that are important for a number of functions in the body. Some
types of omega-3s are found in foods such as fatty fish and shellfish.
Another type is found in some vegetable oils. Omega-3s are also available as dietary supplements.

Key Facts

* There has been a substantial amount of research on supplements of omega-3s, particularly those found in seafood and fish
  oil, and heart disease. The findings of individual studies have
  been inconsistent. In 2012, two combined analyses of the results
  of these studies did not find convincing evidence these omega-3s
  protect against heart disease.

* There is some evidence that omega-3s found in seafood and fish
  oil may be modestly helpful in relieving symptoms in rheumatoid arthritis. For most other conditions for which omega-3s
  have been studied, definitive conclusions cannot yet be reached,
  or studies have not shown omega-3s to be beneficial.

* Omega-3 supplements may interact with drugs that affect
  blood clotting.

* It is uncertain whether people with fish or shellfish allergies can
  safely consume fish oil supplements.

* Fish liver oils (which are not the same as fish oils) contain vitamins A and D as well as omega-3 fatty acids; these vitamins can
  be toxic in high doses.

- Tell all your health care providers about any complementary health approaches you use. Give them a full picture of what you do to manage your health. This will help ensure coordinated and safe care.

About Omega-3 Fatty Acids

The three principal omega-3 fatty acids are alpha-linolenic acid (ALA), eicosapentaenoic acid (EPA), and docosahexaenoic acid (DHA). The main sources of ALA in the U.S. diet are vegetable oils, particularly canola and soybean oils; flaxseed oil is richer in ALA than soybean and canola oils but is not commonly consumed. ALA can be converted, usually in small amounts, into EPA and DHA in the body. EPA and DHA are found in seafood, including fatty fish (e.g., salmon, tuna, and trout) and shellfish (e.g., crab, mussels, and oysters).

Commonly used dietary supplements that contain omega-3s include fish oil (which provides EPA and DHA) and flaxseed oil (which provides ALA). Algae oils are a vegetarian source of DHA.

Omega-3 fatty acids are important for a number of bodily functions, including muscle activity, blood clotting, digestion, fertility, and cell division and growth. DHA is important for brain development and function. ALA is an "essential" fatty acid, meaning that people must obtain it from food or supplements because the human body cannot manufacture it.

Safety

- Omega-3 fatty acid supplements usually do not have negative side effects. When side effects do occur, they typically consist of minor gastrointestinal symptoms, such as belching, indigestion, or diarrhea.

- It is uncertain whether people with fish or shellfish allergies can safely consume fish oil supplements.

- Omega-3 supplements may extend bleeding time (the time it takes for a cut to stop bleeding). People who take drugs that affect bleeding time, such as anticoagulants ("blood thinners") or nonsteroidal anti-inflammatory drugs (NSAIDs), should discuss the use of omega-3 fatty acid supplements with a health care provider.

- Fish liver oils, such as cod liver oil, are not the same as fish oil. Fish liver oils contain vitamins A and D as well as omega-3 fatty acids. Both of these vitamins can be toxic in large doses. The amounts of vitamins in fish liver oil supplements vary from one product to another.

- There is conflicting evidence about whether omega-3 fatty acids found in seafood and fish oil might increase the risk of prostate cancer. Additional research on the association of omega-3 consumption and prostate cancer risk is under way.

Use of Omega-3 Supplements in the United States

According to the 2007 National Health Interview Survey, which included a comprehensive survey on the use of complementary health approaches by Americans, fish oil/omega-3/DHA supplements are the nonvitamin/nonmineral natural product most commonly taken by adults, and the second most commonly taken by children. Among survey participants who had used selected natural products in the last 30 days, about 37 percent of adults (10.9 million) and 31 percent of children (441,000) had taken an omega-3 supplement for health reasons.

What the Science Says

Moderate evidence has emerged about the health benefits of eating seafood. The health benefits of omega-3 dietary supplements are unclear.

Cardiovascular Disease

- Evidence suggests that seafood rich in omega-3 fatty acids should be included in a heart-healthy diet. However, omega-3s in supplement form have not been shown to protect against heart disease.

- Epidemiological studies done more than 30 years ago noted relatively low death rates due to cardiovascular disease in Eskimo populations with high seafood consumption. Since then, much research has been done on seafood and heart disease. The results provide moderate evidence that people who eat seafood at least once a week are less likely to die of heart disease than those who rarely or never eat seafood.

- The federal government's *Dietary Guidelines for Americans,* includes a new recommendation that adults eat 8 or more ounces of a variety of seafood (fish or shellfish) per week because it provides a range of nutrients, including omega-3 fatty acids. (Smaller amounts are recommended for young children.)

- Many studies have evaluated the effects of supplements rich in EPA and DHA, such as fish oil, on heart disease risk.

- In these studies, researchers compared the number of cardiovascular events (such as heart attacks or strokes) or the number of deaths in people who were given the supplements with those in people who were given inactive substances (placebos) or standard care. Most of these studies involved people who already had evidence of heart disease. A smaller number of studies included people with no history of heart disease.

- The results of individual studies were inconsistent; some indicated that the supplements were protective, but others did not.

- In 2012, two groups of scientists conducted meta-analyses of these studies; one group analyzed only studies in people with a history of heart disease, and the other group analyzed studies in people both with and without a history of heart disease. Neither meta-analysis found convincing evidence of a protective effect.

- In 2014, researchers examined the results of the newest high-quality studies of omega-3s, all of which were completed in 2005 or later. Of nine studies that examined the effects of omega-3s on outcomes related to heart disease, such as heart attacks or abnormal heart rhythms, only one found evidence of a beneficial effect.

- There are several reasons why supplements that contain EPA and DHA may not help to prevent heart disease even though a diet rich in seafood may. Eating seafood a few times a week might provide enough of these omega-3s to protect the heart; more may not be better. Some of the benefits of seafood may result from people eating it in place of less healthful foods. There is also evidence that people who eat seafood have generally healthier lifestyles, and these other lifestyle characteristics may be responsible for the lower incidence of cardiovascular disease.

Rheumatoid Arthritis

A 2012 systematic review concluded that the types of omega-3s found in seafood and fish oil may be modestly helpful in relieving symptoms of rheumatoid arthritis. In the studies included in the review, many of the participants reported that when they were taking fish oil they had briefer morning stiffness, less joint swelling and pain, and less need for anti-inflammatory drugs to control their symptoms.

Infant Development

The nutritional value of seafood is particularly important during early development. The *Dietary Guidelines* recommend that women who are pregnant or breastfeeding consume at least 8 ounces but no more than 12 ounces of seafood each week and not eat certain types of seafood that are high in mercury—a toxin that can harm the nervous system of a fetus or young child.

Diseases of the Brain and the Eye

DHA plays important roles in the functioning of the brain and the eye. Research is being conducted on DHA and other omega-3 fatty acids and diseases of the brain and eye, but there is not enough evidence to draw conclusions about the effectiveness of omega-3s for these conditions.

Research is looking at:

- Diseases of the brain or nervous system, such as cognitive decline and multiple sclerosis.

- Mental and behavioral health problems, such as depression, attention-deficit hyperactivity disorder, autism, bipolar disorder, borderline personality disorder, andschizophrenia.

- Diseases of the eye, such as age-related macular degeneration (AMD; an eye disease that can cause vision loss in older people) and dry eye syndrome. Studies have shown that people who eat diets rich in seafood are less likely to develop the advanced stage of AMD. However, a large National Institutes of Health (NIH)–sponsored study, called Age-Related Eye Disease Study 2 (AREDS2), indicated that supplements containing EPA and DHA did not slow the progression of AMD in people who were at high risk of developing the advanced stage of this disease.

Other Conditions

Omega-3 supplements (primarily fish oil supplements) also have been studied for preventing or treating a variety of other conditions such as allergies, asthma, cachexia (severe weight loss) associated with advanced cancer, Crohn's disease, cystic fibrosis, diabetes, kidney disease, lupus, menstrual cramps, obesity, osteoporosis, and ulcerative colitis, as well as organ transplantation outcomes (e.g., decreasing the likelihood of rejection). No conclusions can be drawn about whether omega-3s are helpful for these conditions based on currently available evidence.

If You Are Considering Omega-3 Supplements

*   Do not use omega-3 supplements to replace conventional care or to postpone seeing a health care provider about a health problem.

*   Consult your health care provider before using omega-3 supplements. If you are pregnant, trying to become pregnant, or breastfeeding; if you take medicine that affects blood clotting; if you are allergic to fish or shellfish; or if you are considering giving a child an omega-3 supplement, it is especially important to consult your (or your child's) health care provider.

*   Look for published research studies on omega-3 supplements for the health condition that interests you.

*   Tell all your health care providers about any complementary health approaches you use. Give them a full picture of what you do to manage your health. This will help ensure coordinated and safe care.

7 Things To Know about Omega-3 Fatty Acids

Omega-3 fatty acids are a group of polyunsaturated fatty acids that are important for a number of functions in the body. The omega-3 fatty acids EPA and DHA are found in seafood, such as fatty fish (e.g., salmon, tuna, and trout) and shellfish (e.g., crab, mussels, and oysters). A different kind of omega-3, called ALA, is found in other foods, including some vegetable oils (e.g., canola and soy). Omega-3s are also available as dietary supplements; for example, fish oil supplements contain EPA and DHA, and flaxseed oil supplements contain ALA. Moderate evidence has emerged about the health benefits of consuming seafood. The health benefits of omega-3 dietary supplements are unclear.

1. **Results of studies on diets rich in seafood (fish and shellfish) and heart disease provide moderate evidence that people who eat seafood at least once a week are less likely to die of heart disease than those who rarely**

or never eat seafood. The *Dietary Guidelines for Americans*, includes a new recommendation that adults eat 8 or more ounces of a variety of seafood per week because it provides a range of nutrients, including omega-3 fatty acids.

2. **Evidence suggests that seafood rich in EPA and DHA should be included in a heart-healthy diet; however, supplements of EPA and DHA have not been shown to protect against heart disease.** In 2012, two groups of scientists analyzed the research on the effects of EPA/DHA supplements on heart disease risk. One group analyzed only studies in people with a history of heart disease, and the other group analyzed studies in people both with and without a history of heart disease. Neither review found strong evidence of a protective effect of the supplements.

3. **A 2012 review of the scientific literature concluded that EPA and DHA, the types of omega-3s found in seafood and fish oil, may be modestly helpful in relieving symptoms of rheumatoid arthritis.** In the studies included in the review, many of the participants reported that when they were taking fish oil they had briefer morning stiffness, less joint swelling and pain, and less need for anti-inflammatory drugs to control their symptoms.

4. **The nutritional value of seafood is of particular importance during fetal growth and development, as well as in early infancy and childhood.** Women who are pregnant or breastfeed should consume 8 to 12 ounces of seafood per week from a variety of seafood types that are low in methyl mercury as part of a healthy eating pattern and while staying within their calorie needs. Pregnant or breastfeeding women should limit the amount of white tuna (labeled as "albacore") to no more than 6 ounces per week. They should not eat tilefish, shark, swordfish, and king mackerel because they are high in methyl mercury.

5. **There is ongoing research on omega-3 fatty acids and diseases of the brain and eye, but there is not enough evidence to draw conclusions about the effectiveness of omega-3s for these conditions.** DHA plays important roles in the functioning of the brain and the eye. Researchers are actively investigating the possible benefits of DHA and other omega-3 fatty acids in preventing or treating a variety of brain- and eye-related conditions.

6. **There is conflicting evidence about whether a link might exist between the omega-3 fatty acids found in seafood and fish oil (EPA/DHA) and an increased risk of prostate cancer.** Additional research on the association of omega-3 consumption and prostate cancer risk is under way.

7. **The bottom line: Including seafood in your diet is healthful. Whether omega-3 supplements are beneficial is uncertain.** If you are considering omega-3 supplements, talk to your health care provider. It's especially important to consult your (or your child's) health care provider if you are pregnant or breastfeeding, if you take medicine that affects blood clotting, if you are allergic to seafood, or if you are considering giving a child an omega-3 supplement.

Section 31.2

Flaxseed and Flaxseed Oils

Text in this section is excerpted from "Flaxseed and Flaxseed Oil," National Center for Complementary and Integrative Health (NCCIH), April 2012.

Common Names: flaxseed, linseed
Latin Name: *Linum usitatissimum*

Flaxseed is the seed of the flax plant, which is believed to have originated in Egypt. It grows throughout Canada and Northwestern United States. Flaxseed oil comes from flaxseeds. The most common folk or traditional use of flaxseed is as a laxative; it is also used for hot flashes and breast pain. Flaxseed oil has different folk or traditional uses, including arthritis. Both flaxseed and flaxseed oil have been used for high cholesterol levels and in an effort to prevent cancer.

Whole or crushed flaxseed can be mixed with water or juice and taken by mouth. Flaxseed is also available in powder form. Flaxseed oil is available in liquid and capsule forms. Flaxseed contains lignans (phytoestrogens, or plant estrogens), while flaxseed oil preparations lack lignans.

What the Science Says

• Flaxseed contains soluble fiber, like that found in oat bran, and may have a laxative effect.

• Studies of flaxseed preparations to lower cholesterol levels report mixed results. A 2009 review of the clinical research found that cholesterol-lowering effects were more apparent in postmenopausal women and in people with high initial cholesterol concentrations.

• Some studies suggest that alpha-linolenic acid (a substance found in flaxseed and flaxseed oil) may benefit people with heart disease. But not enough reliable data are available to determine whether flaxseed is effective for heart conditions.

• Study results are mixed on whether flaxseed decreases hot flashes.

• Although some population studies suggest that flaxseed might reduce the risk of certain cancers, there is not enough research to support a recommendation for this use.

• NCCIH is funding studies on flaxseed. Recent studies are looking at its potential role in preventing or treating atherosclerosis (hardening of the arteries), breast cancer, and ovarian cysts.

Side Effects and Cautions

• Flaxseed and flaxseed oil supplements seem to be well tolerated. Few side effects have been reported.

• Flaxseed, like any supplemental fiber source, should be taken with plenty of water; otherwise, it could worsen constipation or, in rare cases, even cause intestinal blockage. Both flaxseed and flaxseed oil can cause diarrhea.

• The fiber in flaxseed may lower the body's ability to absorb medications that are taken by mouth. Flaxseed should not be taken at the same time as any conventional oral medications or other dietary supplements.

Keep in Mind

Tell all your health care providers about any complementary health approaches you use. Give them a full picture of what you do to manage your health. This will help ensure coordinated and safe care.

Chapter 32

Selenium

What is selenium and what does it do?

Selenium is a nutrient that the body needs to stay healthy. Selenium is important for reproduction, thyroid gland function, DNA production, and protecting the body from damage caused by free radicals and from infection.

How much selenium do I need?

The amount of selenium that you need each day depends on your age. Average daily recommended amounts are listed below in micrograms (mcg).

What foods provide selenium?

Selenium is found naturally in many foods. The amount of selenium in plant foods depends on the amount of selenium in the soil where they were grown. The amount of selenium in animal products depends on the selenium content of the foods that the animals ate. You can get recommended amounts of selenium by eating a variety of foods, including the following:

- Seafood
- Meat, poultry, eggs, and dairy products
- Breads, cereals, and other grain products

Text in this chapter is excerpted from "Selenium," Office of Dietary Supplements (ODS), National Institutes of Health (NIH), November 22, 2013.

Table 32.1. Selenium – Daily Recommendations

Life Stage	Recommended Amount
Birth to 6 months	15 mcg
Infants 7–12 months	20 mcg
Children 1–3 years	20 mcg
Children 4–8 years	30 mcg
Children 9–13 years	40 mcg
Teens 14–18 years	55 mcg
Adults 19–50 years	55 mcg
Adults 51–70 years	55 mcg
Adults 71 years and older	55 mcg
Pregnant teens and women	60 mcg
Breastfeeding teens and women	70 mcg

What kinds of selenium dietary supplements are available?

Selenium is available in many multivitamin-mineral supplements and other dietary supplements. It can be present in several different forms, including selenomethionine and sodium selenate.

Am I getting enough selenium?

Most Americans get enough selenium from their diet because they eat food grown or raised in many different areas, including areas with soil that is rich in selenium.

Certain groups of people are more likely than others to have trouble getting enough selenium:

- People undergoing kidney dialysis
- People living with HIV
- People who eat only local foods grown in soils that are low in selenium

What happens if I don't get enough selenium?

Selenium deficiency is very rare in the United States and Canada. Selenium deficiency can cause Keshan disease (a type of heart disease) and male infertility. It might also cause Kashin-Beck disease, a type of arthritis that produces pain, swelling, and loss of motion in your joints.

What are some effects of selenium on health?

Scientists are studying selenium to understand how it affects health. Here are some examples of what this research has shown.

Cancer

Studies suggest that people who consume lower amounts of selenium could have an increased risk of developing cancers of the colon and rectum, prostate, lung, bladder, skin, esophagus, and stomach. But whether selenium supplements reduce cancer risk is not clear. More research is needed to understand the effects of selenium from food and dietary supplements on cancer risk.

Cardiovascular disease

Scientists are studying whether selenium helps reduce the risk of cardiovascular disease. Some studies show that people with lower blood levels of selenium have a higher risk of heart disease, but other studies do not. More studies are needed to better understand how selenium in food and dietary supplements affects heart health.

Cognitive decline

Blood selenium levels decrease as people age, and scientists are studying whether low selenium levels contribute to a decline in brain function in the elderly. Some studies suggest that people with lower blood selenium levels are more likely to have poorer mental function. But a study of elderly people in the United States found no link between selenium levels and memory. More research is needed to find out whether selenium dietary supplements might help reduce the risk of or treat cognitive decline in elderly people.

Thyroid disease

The thyroid gland has high amounts of selenium that play an important role in thyroid function. Studies suggest that people—especially women—who have low blood levels of selenium (and iodine) might develop problems with their thyroid. But whether selenium dietary supplements can help treat or reduce the risk of thyroid disease is not clear. More research is needed to understand the effects of selenium on thyroid disease.

Can selenium be harmful?

Yes, if you get too much. Brazil nuts, for example, contain very high amounts of selenium (68–91 mcg per nut) and can cause you to go over the upper limit if you eat too many. Getting too much selenium over time can cause the following:

- Garlic breath

- Nausea

- Diarrhea

- Skin rashes

- Irritability

- Metallic taste in the mouth

- Brittle hair or nails

- Loss of hair or nails

- Discolored teeth

- Nervous system problems

Extremely high intakes of selenium can cause severe problems, including difficulty breathing, tremors, kidney failure, heart attacks, and heart failure.

The upper limits for selenium from foods and dietary supplements are listed below.

Table 32.2. Selenium – Upper Limits

Ages	Upper Limit
Birth to 6 months	45 mcg
Infants 7–12 months	60 mcg
Children 1–3 years	90 mcg
Children 4–8 years	150 mcg
Children 9–13 years	280 mcg
Teens 14–18 years	400 mcg
Adults	400 mcg

Are there any interactions with selenium that I should know about?

Yes, some of the medications you take may interact with selenium. For example, cisplatin, a chemotherapy drug used to treat cancer, can lower selenium levels, but the effect this has on the body is not clear.

Tell your doctor, pharmacist, and other health care providers about any dietary supplements and prescription or over-the-counter medicines you take. They can tell you if the dietary supplements might interact with your medicines or if the medicines might interfere with how your body absorbs, uses, or breaks down nutrients.

Selenium and healthful eating

People should get most of their nutrients from food, advises the federal government's *Dietary Guidelines for Americans.* Foods contain vitamins, minerals, dietary fiber and other substances that benefit health. Dietary supplements might help in some situations to increase the intake of a specific vitamin or mineral.

Chapter 33

Bone and Joint Health Supplements

Chapter Contents

Section 33.1

Calcium Supplements and Bone Health

Text in this section is excerpted from "Health
Information – Calcium," Office of Dietary Supplements (ODS),
National Institutes of Health (NIH), March 19, 2013.

What is calcium and what does it do?

Calcium is a mineral found in many foods. The body needs calcium
to maintain strong bones and to carry out many important functions.
Almost all calcium is stored in bones and teeth, where it supports their
structure and hardness.

The body also needs calcium for muscles to move and for nerves to
carry messages between the brain and every body part. In addition,
calcium is used to help blood vessels move blood throughout the body
and to help release hormones and enzymes that affect almost every
function in the human body.

How much calcium do I need?

The amount of calcium you need each day depends on your age. Average daily recommended amounts are listed below in milligrams (mg):

Table 33.1. Calcium – Daily Recommendations

Life Stage	Recommended Amount
Birth to 6 months	200 mg
Infants 7–12 months	260 mg
Children 1–3 years	700 mg
Children 4–8 years	1,000 mg
Children 9–13 years	1,300 mg
Teens 14–18 years	1,300 mg
Adults 19–50 years	1,000 mg
Adult men 51–70 years	1,000 mg
Adult women 51–70 years	1,200 mg
Adults 71 years and older	1,200 mg

Table 33.1. Continued

Life Stage	Recommended Amount
Pregnant and breastfeeding teens	1,300 mg
Pregnant and breastfeeding adults	1,000 mg

What foods provide calcium?

Calcium is found in many foods. You can get recommended amounts of calcium by eating a variety of foods, including the following:

• Milk, yogurt, and cheese are the main food sources of calcium for the majority of people in the United States.

• Kale, broccoli, and Chinese cabbage are fine vegetable sources of calcium.

• Fish with soft bones that you eat, such as canned sardines and salmon, are fine animal sources of calcium.

• Most grains (such as breads, pastas, and unfortified cereals), while not rich in calcium, add significant amounts of calcium to the diet because people eat them often or in large amounts.

• Calcium is added to some breakfast cereals, fruit juices, soy and rice beverages, and tofu. To find out whether these foods have calcium, check the product labels.

What kinds of calcium dietary supplements are available?

Calcium is found in many multivitamin-mineral supplements, though the amount varies by product.Dietary supplements that contain only calcium or calcium with other nutrients such as vitamin D are also available. Check the Supplement Facts label to determine the amount of calcium provided.

The two main forms of calcium dietary supplements are carbonate and citrate. Calcium carbonate is inexpensive, but is absorbed best when taken with food. Some over-the-counter antacid products, such as Tums and Rolaids, contain calcium carbonate. Each pill or chew provides 200–400 mg of calcium. Calcium citrate, a more expensive form of the supplement, is absorbed well on an empty or a full stomach. In addition, people with low levels of stomach acid (a condition more common in people older than 50) absorb calcium citrate more easily than calcium carbonate. Other forms of calcium in supplements and fortified foods include gluconate, lactate, and phosphate.

Calcium absorption is best when a person consumes no more than 500 mg at one time. So a person who takes 1,000 mg/day of calcium from supplements, for example, should split the dose rather than take it all at once.

Calcium supplements may cause gas, bloating, and constipation in some people. If any of these symptoms occur, try spreading out the calcium dose throughout the day, taking the supplement with meals, or changing the supplement brand or calcium form you take.

Am I getting enough calcium?

Many people don't get recommended amounts of calcium from the foods they eat, including:

- Boys aged 9 to 13 years

- Girls aged 9 to 18 years

- Women older than 50 years

- Men older than 70 years

When total intakes from both food and supplements are considered, many people—particularly adolescent girls—still fall short of getting enough calcium, while some older women likely get more than the upper limit.

Certain groups of people are more likely than others to have trouble getting enough calcium:

- Postmenopausal women because they experience greater bone loss and do not absorb calcium as well. Sufficient calcium intake from food, and supplements if needed, can slow the rate of bone loss.

- Women of childbearing age whose menstrual periods stop (amenorrhea) because they exercise heavily, eat too little, or both. They need sufficient calcium to cope with the resulting decreased calcium absorption, increased calcium losses in the urine, and slowdown in the formation of new bone.

- People with lactose intolerance cannot digest this natural sugar found in milk and experience symptoms like bloating, gas, and diarrhea when they drink more than small amounts at a time. They usually can eat other calcium-rich dairy products that are low in lactose, such as yogurt and many cheeses, and drink lactose-reduced or lactose-free milk.

- Vegans (vegetarians who eat no animal products) and ovo-vegetarians (vegetarians who eat eggs but no dairy products), because they avoid the dairy products that are a major source of calcium in other people's diets.

Many factors can affect the amount of calcium absorbed from the digestive tract, including:

- Age. Efficiency of calcium absorption decreases as people age. Recommended calcium intakes are higher for people over age 70.

- Vitamin D intake. This vitamin, present in some foods and produced in the body when skin is exposed to sunlight, increases calcium absorption.

- Other components in food. Both oxalic acid (in some vegetables and beans) and phytic acid (in whole grains) can reduce calcium absorption. People who eat a variety of foods don't have to consider these factors. They are accounted for in the calcium recommended intakes, which take absorption into account.

Many factors can also affect how much calcium the body eliminates in urine, feces, and sweat. These include consumption of alcohol- and caffeine-containing beverages as well as intake of other nutrients (protein, sodium, potassium, and phosphorus). In most people, these factors have little effect on calcium status.

What happens if I don't get enough calcium?

Insufficient intakes of calcium do not produce obvious symptoms in the short term because the body maintains calcium levels in the blood by taking it from bone. Over the long term, intakes of calcium below recommended levels have health consequences, such as causing low bone mass (osteopenia) and increasing the risks of osteoporosis and bone fractures.

Symptoms of serious calcium deficiency include numbness and tingling in the fingers, convulsions, and abnormal heart rhythms that can lead to death if not corrected. These symptoms occur almost always in people with serious health problems or who are undergoing certain medical treatments.

What are some effects of calcium on bone health?

Scientists are studying calcium to understand how it affects bone health.

Bones need plenty of calcium and vitamin D throughout childhood and adolescence to reach their peak strength and calcium content by about age 30. After that, bones slowly lose calcium, but people can help reduce these losses by getting recommended amounts of calcium throughout adulthood and by having a healthy, active lifestyle that includes weight-bearing physical activity (such as walking and running). Osteoporosis is a disease of the bones in older adults (especially women) in which the bones become porous, fragile, and more prone to fracture. Osteoporosis is a serious public health problem for more than 10 million adults over the age of 50 in the United States. Adequate calcium and vitamin D intakes as well as regular exercise are essential to keep bones healthy throughout life.

What are some effects of calcium on other parts of the body?

Cardiovascular disease

Whether calcium affects the risk of cardiovascular disease is not clear. Some studies show that getting enough calcium might protect people from heart disease and stroke. But other studies show that some people who consume high amounts of calcium, particularly from supplements, might have an increased risk of heart disease. More research is needed in this area.

High blood pressure

Some studies have found that getting recommended intakes of calcium can reduce the risk of developing high blood pressure (hypertension). One large study in particular found that eating a diet high in fat-free and low-fat dairy products, vegetables, and fruits lowered blood pressure.

Cancer

Studies have examined whether calcium supplements or diets high in calcium might lower the risks of developing cancer of the colon or rectum or increase the risk of prostate cancer. The research to date provides no clear answers. Given that cancer develops over many years, longer term studies are needed.

Kidney stones

Most kidney stones are rich in calcium oxalate. Some studies have found that higher intakes of calcium from dietary supplements are linked to a greater risk of kidney stones, especially among older adults. But calcium from foods does not appear to cause kidney stones. For most people, other factors (such as not drinking enough fluids) probably have a larger effect on the risk of kidney stones than calcium intake.

Weight loss

Although several studies have shown that getting more calcium helps lower body weight or reduce weight gain over time, most studies have found that calcium—from foods or dietary supplements—has little if any effect on body weight and amount of body fat.

Can calcium be harmful?

Getting too much calcium can cause constipation. It might also interfere with the body's ability to absorb iron and zinc, but this effect is not well established. In adults, too much calcium (from dietary supplements but not food) might increase the risk of kidney stones. Some studies show that people who consume high amounts of calcium might have increased risks of prostate cancer and heart disease, but more research is needed to understand these possible links.

The upper limits for calcium are listed below. Most people do not get amounts above the upper limits from food alone; excess intakes usually come from the use of calcium supplements. Surveys show that some older women in the United States probably get amounts somewhat above the upper limit since the use of calcium supplements is common among these women.

Table 33.2. Calcium – Upper Limits

Life Stage	Upper Limit
Birth to 6 months	1,000 mg
Infants 7–12 months	1,500 mg
Children 1–8 years	2,500 mg
Children 9–18 years	3,000 mg
Adults 19–50 years	2,500 mg
Adults 51 years and older	2,000 mg
Pregnant and breastfeeding teens	3,000 mg
Pregnant and breastfeeding adults	2,500 mg

Are there any interactions with calcium that I should know about?

Calcium dietary supplements can interact or interfere with certain medicines that you take, and some medicines can lower or raise calcium levels in the body. Here are some examples:

- Calcium can reduce the absorption of these drugs when taken together:

- Bisphosphonates (to treat osteoporosis)

- Antibiotics of the fluoroquinolone and tetracycline families

- Levothyroxine (to treat low thyroid activity)

- Phenytoin (an anticonvulsant)

- Tiludronate disodium (to treat Paget's disease).

- Diuretics differ in their effects. Thiazide-type diuretics (such as Diuril and Lozol) reduce calcium excretion by the kidneys which in turn can raise blood calcium levels too high. But loop diuretics (such as Lasix and Bumex) increase calcium excretion and thereby lower blood calcium levels.

- Antacids containing aluminum or magnesium increase calcium loss in the urine.

- Mineral oil and stimulant laxatives reduce calcium absorption.

- Glucocorticoids (such as prednisone) can cause calcium depletion and eventually osteoporosis when people use them for months at a time.

Tell your doctor, pharmacist, and other health care providers about any dietary supplements and medicines you take. They can tell you if those dietary supplements might interact or interfere with your prescription or over-the-counter medicines or if the medicines might interfere with how your body absorbs, uses, or breaks down nutrients.

Calcium and healthful eating

People should get most of their nutrients from food, advises the federal government's *Dietary Guidelines for Americans*. Foods contain vitamins, minerals, dietary fiber and other substances that benefit health. Dietary supplements might help in some situations to increase the intake of a specific vitamin or mineral.

Section 33.2

Glucosamine/Chondroitin Supplements and Joint Health

Text in this section is excerpted from "Glucosamine and Chondroitin for Osteoarthritis: What You Need To Know," National Center for Complementary and Integrative Health (NCCIH), January 2015.

What's the Bottom Line?

How much do we know about glucosamine and chondroitin supplements?

There are some information available about the safety and usefulness of glucosamine and chondroitin from large, high-quality studies in people.

What do we know about the effectiveness of glucosamine and chondroitin supplements?

- Research results suggest that chondroitin isn't helpful for pain from osteoarthritis of the knee or hip.
- It's unclear whether glucosamine helps with osteoarthritis knee pain or whether either supplement lessens osteoarthritis pain in other joints.

What do we know about the safety of glucosamine and chondroitin supplements?

- Studies have found that glucosamine and chondroitin supplements may interact with the anticoagulant (blood-thinning) drug warfarin (Coumadin). Overall, studies have not shown any other serious side effects.
- If you take glucosamine or chondroitin supplements, tell your health care providers. They can do a better job caring for you if they know what dietary supplements you use.

What Are Glucosamine and Chondroitin?

Glucosamine and chondroitin are structural components of cartilage, the tissue that cushions the joints. Both are produced naturally in the body. They are also available as dietary supplements. Researchers have studied the effects of these supplements, individually or in combination, on osteoarthritis, a common type of arthritis that destroys cartilage in the joints.

Cartilage is the connective tissue that cushions the ends of bones within the joints. In osteoarthritis, the surface layer of cartilage between the bones of a joint wears down. This allows the bones to rub together, which can cause pain and swelling and make it difficult to move the joint. The knees, hips, spine, and hands are the parts of the body most likely to be affected by osteoarthritis.

What the Science Says about Glucosamine and Chondroitin for Osteoarthritis

For the Knee or Hip

Glucosamine

Major studies of glucosamine for osteoarthritis of the knee have had conflicting results.

- A large National Institutes of Health (NIH) study, called the Glucosamine/chondroitin Arthritis Intervention Trial (GAIT), compared glucosamine hydrochloride, chondroitin, both supplements together, celecoxib (a prescription drug used to manage osteoarthritis pain), or a placebo (an inactive substance) in patients with knee osteoarthritis. Most participants in the study had mild knee pain.

- Those who received the prescription drug had better short-term pain relief (at 6 months) than those who received a placebo.

- Overall, those who received the supplements had no significant improvement in knee pain or function, although the investigators saw evidence of improvement in a small subgroup of patients with moderate-to-severe pain who took glucosamine and chondroitin together.

- In several European studies, participants reported that their knees felt and functioned better after taking glucosamine. The study participants took a large, once-a-day dose of a preparation of glucosamine sulfate sold as a prescription drug in Europe.

- Researchers don't know why the results of these large, well-done studies differ. It may be because of differences in the types of glucosamine used (glucosamine hydrochloride in the NIH study vs. glucosamine sulfate in the European studies), differences in the way they were administered (one large daily dose in the European studies vs. three smaller ones in the NIH study), other differences in the way the studies were done, or chance.

Joint Structure

A few studies have looked at whether glucosamine or chondroitin can have beneficial effects on joint structure. Some but not all studies found evidence that chondroitin might help, but the improvements may be too small to make a difference to patients. There is little evidence that glucosamine has beneficial effects on joint structure.

Experts' Recommendations

Experts disagree on whether glucosamine and chondroitin may help knee and hip osteoarthritis. The American College of Rheumatology (ACR) has recommended that people with knee or hip osteoarthritis not use glucosamine or chondroitin. But the recommendation was not a strong one, and the ACR acknowledged that it was controversial.

For Other Parts of the Body

Only a small amount of research has been done on glucosamine and chondroitin for osteoarthritis of joints other than the knee and hip. Because there have been only a few relatively small studies, no definite conclusions can be reached.

- **Chondroitin for osteoarthritis of the hand**

  A 6-month trial of chondroitin in 162 patients with severe osteoarthritis of the hand showed that it may improve pain and function.

- **Glucosamine for osteoarthritis of the jaw**

  One study of 45 patients with osteoarthritis of the jaw showed that those given glucosamine had less pain than those given ibuprofen. But another study, which included 59 patients with osteoarthritis of the jaw, found that those taking glucosamine did no better than those taking a placebo (pills that don't contain the active ingredient).

- **Glucosamine for chronic low-back pain and osteoarthritis of the spine**

A Norwegian trial involving 250 people with chronic low-back pain and osteoarthritis of the lower spine found that participants who received glucosamine fared the same at 6 months as those who received placebo.

What the Science Says about Safety and Side Effects

- No serious side effects have been reported in large, well-conducted studies of people taking glucosamine, chondroitin, or both for up to 3 years.

- However, glucosamine or chondroitin may interact with the anticoagulant (blood-thinning) drug warfarin (Coumadin).

- A study in rats showed that long-term use of moderately large doses of glucosamine might damage the kidneys. Although results from animal studies don't always apply to people, this study does raise concern.

- Glucosamine might affect the way your body handles sugar, especially if you have diabetes or other blood sugar problems, such as insulin resistance or impaired glucose tolerance.

If you use dietary supplements, such as glucosamine and chondroitin, read and follow the label instructions, and recognize that "natural" does not always mean "safe."

The U.S. Food and Drug Administration (FDA) regulates dietary supplements, but the regulations for dietary supplements are different and less strict than those for prescription or over-the-counter drugs.

Some dietary supplements may interact with medications or pose risks if you have medical problems or are going to have surgery. Most dietary supplements have not been tested in pregnant women, nursing mothers, or children.

Keep in Mind

- If your joints hurt, see your health care provider. It's important to find out what's causing your joint pain. Some diseases that cause joint pain—such as rheumatoid arthritis—may need immediate treatment.

- If you take warfarin or have blood sugar problems, make sure you talk to your doctor about potential side effects if you are considering or taking glucosamine or chondroitin supplements.

- If you're pregnant or nursing a child, it's especially important to see your health care provider before taking any medication or supplement, including glucosamine or chondroitin.

- Help your health care providers give you better coordinated and safe care by telling them about all the health approaches you use. Give them a full picture of what you do to manage your health.

Chapter 34

Supplements to Support the Immune System

Chapter Contents

Section 34.1

Astragalus

Text in this section is excerpted from "Astragalus," National Center for Complementary and Integrative Health (NCCIH), April 2012.

Common Names: astragalus, *bei qi*, *huang qi*, *ogi*, *hwanggi*, milk vetch

Latin Names: *Astragalus membranaceus*, *Astragalus mongholicus*

Native to China, astragalus has been used for centuries in traditional Chinese medicine. In the United States, the herb gained popularity in the 1980s. There are actually over 2,000 species of astragalus; however, the two related species *Astragalus membranaceus* and *Astragalus mongholicus* are the ones primarily used for health purposes.

Historically, astragalus has been used in traditional Chinese medicine, usually in combination with other herbs, to support and enhance the immune system. It is still widely used in China for chronic hepatitis and as an adjunctive therapy for cancer. It is also used as a folk or traditional remedy for colds and upper respiratory infections, and for heart disease.

The root of the astragalus plant is typically used in soups, teas, extracts, or capsules. Astragalus is generally used with other herbs, such as ginseng, angelica, and licorice.

What the Science Says

- The evidence for using astragalus for any health condition is limited. High-quality clinical trials (studies in people) are generally lacking. There is some preliminary evidence to suggest that astragalus, either alone or in combination with other herbs, may have potential benefits for the immune system, heart, and liver, and as an adjunctive therapy for cancer.

- NCCIH-funded investigators are studying the effects of astragalus on the body, particularly on the immune system.

Side Effects and Cautions

- Astragalus is considered safe for most adults. Its possible side effects are not well known because astragalus is generally used in combination with other herbs.

- Astragalus may interact with medications that suppress the immune system, such as the drug cyclophosphamide taken by cancer patients and similar drugs taken by organ transplant recipients. It may also affect blood sugar levels and blood pressure.

- People should be aware that some astragalus species, usually not found in dietary supplements used by humans, can be toxic. For example, several species that grow in the United States contain the neurotoxin swainsonine and have caused "locoweed" poisoning in animals. Other species contain potentially toxic levels of selenium.

Keep in Mind

Tell all your health care providers about any complementary health approaches you use. Give them a full picture of what you do to manage your health. This will help ensure coordinated and safe care.

Section 34.2

Echinacea

Text in this section is excerpted from "Echinacea," National Center for Complementary and Integrative Health (NCCIH), April 2012.

Common Names: echinacea, purple coneflower, coneflower, American coneflower

Latin Names: *Echinacea purpurea, Echinacea angustifolia, Echinacea pallida*

There are nine known species of echinacea, all of which are native to the United States and southern Canada. The most commonly used is *Echinacea purpurea.* Echinacea has traditionally been used for colds, flu, and other infections, based on the idea that it might stimulate the immune system to more effectively fight infection. Less common folk or traditional uses of echinacea include for wounds and skin problems, such as acne or boils.

The above ground parts of the plant and roots of echinacea are used fresh or dried to make teas, squeezed (expressed) juice, extracts, or preparations for external use.

What the Science Says

- Study results are mixed on whether echinacea can prevent or effectively treat upper respiratory tract infections such as the common cold. For example, two NCCIH-funded studies did not find a benefit from echinacea, either as *Echinacea purpurea* fresh-pressed juice for treating colds in children, or as an unrefined mixture of *Echinacea angustifolia* root and *Echinacea purpurea* root and herb in adults. However, other studies have shown that echinacea may be beneficial in treating upper respiratory infections.

- NCCIH is continuing to support the study of echinacea for the treatment of upper respiratory infections. NCCIH is also studying echinacea for its potential effects on the immune system.

Side Effects and Cautions

- When taken by mouth, echinacea usually does not cause side effects. However, some people experience allergic reactions, including rashes, increased asthma, and anaphylaxis (a life-threatening allergic reaction). In clinical trials, gastrointestinal side effects were most common.

- People are more likely to experience allergic reactions to echinacea if they are allergic to related plants in the daisy family, which includes ragweed, chrysanthemums, marigolds, and daisies. Also, people with asthma or atopy (a genetic tendency toward allergic reactions) may be more likely to have an allergic reaction when taking echinacea.

Keep in Mind

Tell all your health care providers about any complementary health approaches you use. Give them a full picture of what you do to manage your health. This will help ensure coordinated and safe care.

Section 34.3

European Elder

Text in this section is excerpted from "European Elder," National Center for Complementary and Integrative Health (NCCIH), April 2012.

Common Names: European elder, black elder, elder, elderberry, elder flower, sambucus

Latin Name: *Sambucus nigra*

European elder is a tree native to Europe and parts of Asia and Africa, and it also grows in the United States. There are several different types of elder, such as American elder, but European elder is the type most often used as a supplement. Parts of the elder tree—such as the berries and flowers—have historically been used for pain, swelling, infections, coughs, and skin conditions. Current folk or traditional uses of elderberry and elder flower include flu, colds, fevers, constipation, and sinus infections.

The dried flowers (elder flower) and the cooked blue/black berries (elderberry) of the European elder tree are used in teas, liquid extracts, and capsules.

What the Science Says

- Although some small studies show that elderberry may relieve flu symptoms, the evidence is not strong enough to support this use of the berry.

379

- A few studies have suggested that a product containing elder flower and other herbs can help treat sinus infections when used with antibiotics, but further research is needed to confirm any benefit.

- No reliable information is available on the effectiveness of elderberry and elder flower for other uses.

Side Effects and Cautions

- Uncooked or unripe elderberries are toxic and cause nausea, vomiting, or severe diarrhea. Only the blue/black berries of elder are edible.

- Because of elder flower's possible diuretic effects, use caution if taking it with drugs that increase urination.

Keep in Mind

Tell all your health care providers about any complementary health approaches you use. Give them a full picture of what you do to manage your health. This helps to ensure coordinated and safe care.

Section 34.4

Zinc

Text in this section is excerpted from "Health Information - Zinc," Office of Dietary Supplements (ODS), National Institutes of Health (NIH), June 5, 2013.

Zinc is an essential mineral that is naturally present in some foods, added to others, and available as a dietary supplement. Zinc is also found in many cold lozenges and some over-the-counter drugs sold as cold remedies.

Zinc is involved in numerous aspects of cellular metabolism. It is required for the catalytic activity of approximately 100 enzymes and it plays a role in immune function, protein synthesis, wound healing,

DNA synthesis, and cell division. Zinc also supports normal growth and development during pregnancy, childhood, and adolescence and is required for proper sense of taste and smell. A daily intake of zinc is required to maintain a steady state because the body has no specialized zinc storage system.

Recommended Intakes

Intake recommendations for zinc and other nutrients are provided in the Dietary Reference Intakes (DRIs) developed by the Food and Nutrition Board (FNB) at the Institute of Medicine of the National Academies (formerly National Academy of Sciences). DRI is the general term for a set of reference values used for planning and assessing nutrient intakes of healthy people. These values, which vary by age and gender, include the following:

- Recommended Dietary Allowance (RDA): average daily level of intake sufficient to meet the nutrient requirements of nearly all (97%–98%) healthy individuals.

- Adequate Intake (AI): established when evidence is insufficient to develop an RDA and is set at a level assumed to ensure nutritional adequacy.

- Tolerable Upper Intake Level (UL): maximum daily intake unlikely to cause adverse health effects.

The current RDAs for zinc are listed in Table 34.1. For infants aged 0 to 6 months, the FNB established an AI for zinc that is equivalent to the mean intake of zinc in healthy, breastfed infants.

Table 34.1. Recommended Dietary Allowances (RDAs) for Zinc

Age	Male	Female	Pregnancy	Lactation
0–6 months	2 mg*	2 mg*		
7–12 months	3 mg	3 mg		
1–3 years	3 mg	3 mg		
4–8 years	5 mg	5 mg		
9–13 years	8 mg	8 mg		
14–18 years	11 mg	9 mg	12 mg	13 mg
19+ years	11 mg	8 mg	11 mg	12 mg

Adequate Intake (AI)

Sources of Zinc

Food

A wide variety of foods contain zinc (Table 34.2.). Oysters contain more zinc per serving than any other food, but red meat and poultry provide the majority of zinc in the American diet. Other good food sources include beans, nuts, certain types of seafood (such as crab and lobster), whole grains, fortified breakfast cereals, and dairy products.

Phytates—which are present in whole-grain breads, cereals, legumes, and other foods—bind zinc and inhibit its absorption. Thus, the bioavailability of zinc from grains and plant foods is lower than that from animal foods, although many grain- and plant-based foods are still good sources of zinc.

Table 34.2. Selected Food Sources of Zinc

Food	Milligrams (mg) per serving	Percent DV*
Oysters, cooked, breaded and fried, 3 ounces	74	493
Beef chuck roast, braised, 3 ounces	7	47
Crab, Alaska king, cooked, 3 ounces	6.5	43
Beef patty, broiled, 3 ounces	5.3	35
Breakfast cereal, fortified with 25% of the DV for zinc, ¾ cup serving	3.8	25
Lobster, cooked, 3 ounces	3.4	23
Pork chop, loin, cooked, 3 ounces	2.9	19
Baked beans, canned, plain or vegetarian, ½ cup	2.9	19
Chicken, dark meat, cooked, 3 ounces	2.4	16
Yogurt, fruit, low fat, 8 ounces	1.7	11
Cashews, dry roasted, 1 ounce	1.6	11
Chickpeas, cooked, ½ cup	1.3	9
Cheese, Swiss, 1 ounce	1.2	8
Oatmeal, instant, plain, prepared with water, 1 packet	1.1	7
Milk, low-fat or non fat, 1 cup	1	7
Almonds, dry roasted, 1 ounce	0.9	6

Table 34.2. Continued

Food	Milligrams (mg) per serving	Percent DV*
Kidney beans, cooked, ½ cup	0.9	6
Chicken breast, roasted, skin removed, ½ breast	0.9	6
Cheese, cheddar or mozzarella, 1 ounce	0.9	6
Peas, green, frozen, cooked, ½ cup	0.5	3
Flounder or sole, cooked, 3 ounces	0.3	2

* DV = Daily Value. DVs were developed by the U.S. Food and Drug Administration to help consumers compare the nutrient contents of products within the context of a total diet. The DV for zinc is 15 mg for adults and children age 4 and older. Food labels, however, are not required to list zinc content unless a food has been fortified with this nutrient. Foods providing 20% or more of the DV are considered to be high sources of a nutrient.

The U.S. Department of Agriculture's (USDA's) Nutrient Database Web site lists the nutrient content of many foods and provides a comprehensive list of foods containing zinc arranged by nutrient content and by food name.

Dietary supplements

Supplements contain several forms of zinc, including zinc gluconate, zinc sulfate, and zinc acetate. The percentage of elemental zinc varies by form. For example, approximately 23% of zinc sulfate consists of elemental zinc; thus, 220 mg of zinc sulfate contains 50 mg of elemental zinc. The elemental zinc content appears in the Supplement Facts panel on the supplement container. Research has not determined whether differences exist among forms of zinc in absorption, bioavailability, or tolerability.

In addition to standard tablets and capsules, some zinc-containing cold lozenges are labeled as dietary supplements.

Other sources

Zinc is present in several products, including some labeled as homeopathic medications, sold over the counter for the treatment and prevention of colds. Numerous case reports of anosmia (loss of the sense of smell), in some cases long-lasting or permanent, have been associated with the use of zinc-containing nasal gels or sprays. In June 2009, the FDA warned consumers to stop using three zinc-containing intranasal products because they might cause anosmia. The manufacturer recalled these products from the marketplace. Currently, these safety concerns have not been found to be associated with cold lozenges containing zinc.

Zinc is also present in some denture adhesive creams at levels ranging from 17–34 mg/g. While use of these products as directed (0.5–1.5 g/day) is not of concern, chronic, excessive use can lead to zinc toxicity, resulting in copper deficiency and neurologic disease. Such toxicity has been reported in individuals who used 2 or more standard 2.4 oz tubes of denture cream per week. Many denture creams have now been reformulated to eliminate zinc.

Zinc Intakes and Status

Most infants (especially those who are formula fed), children, and adults in the United States consume recommended amounts of zinc according to two national surveys, the 1988–1991 National Health and Nutrition Examination Survey (NHANES III) and the 1994 Continuing Survey of Food Intakes of Individuals (CSFII).

However, some evidence suggests that zinc intakes among older adults might be marginal. An analysis of NHANES III data found that 35%–45% of adults aged 60 years or older had zinc intakes below the estimated average requirement of 6.8 mg/day for elderly females and 9.4 mg/day for elderly males. When the investigators considered intakes from both food and dietary supplements, they found that 20%–25% of older adults still had inadequate zinc intakes.

Zinc intakes might also be low in older adults from the 2%–4% of U.S. households that are food insufficient (sometimes or often not having enough food). Data from NHANES III indicate that adults aged 60 years or older from food-insufficient families had lower intakes of zinc and several other nutrients and were more likely to have zinc intakes below 50% of the RDA on a given day than those from food-sufficient families.

Zinc Deficiency

Zinc deficiency is characterized by growth retardation, loss of appetite, and impaired immune function. In more severe cases, zinc deficiency causes hair loss, diarrhea, delayed sexual maturation, impotence, hypogonadism in males, and eye and skin lesions. Weight loss, delayed healing of wounds, taste abnormalities, and mental lethargy can also occur. Many of these symptoms are non-specific and often associated with other health conditions; therefore, a medical examination is necessary to ascertain whether a zinc deficiency is present.

Zinc nutritional status is difficult to measure adequately using laboratory tests due to its distribution throughout the body as a component of various proteins and nucleic acids. Plasma or serum zinc levels are the most commonly used indices for evaluating zinc deficiency, but these levels do not necessarily reflect cellular zinc status due to tight homeostatic control mechanisms. Clinical effects of zinc deficiency can be present in the absence of abnormal laboratory indices. Clinicians consider risk factors (such as inadequate caloric intake, alcoholism, and digestive diseases) and symptoms of zinc deficiency (such as impaired growth in infants and children) when determining the need for zinc supplementation.

Groups at Risk of Zinc Inadequacy

In North America, overt zinc deficiency is uncommon. When zinc deficiency does occur, it is usually due to inadequate zinc intake or absorption, increased losses of zinc from the body, or increased requirements for zinc. People at risk of zinc deficiency or inadequacy need to include good sources of zinc in their daily diets. Supplemental zinc might also be appropriate in certain situations.

People with gastrointestinal and other diseases

Gastrointestinal surgery and digestive disorders (such as ulcerative colitis, Crohn's disease, and short bowel syndrome) can decrease zinc absorption and increase endogenous zinc losses primarily from the gastrointestinal tract and, to a lesser extent, from the kidney. Other diseases associated with zinc deficiency include malabsorption syndrome, chronic liver disease, chronic renal disease, sickle cell disease, diabetes, malignancy, and other chronic illnesses. Chronic diarrhea also leads to excessive loss of zinc.

Vegetarians

The bioavailability of zinc from vegetarian diets is lower than from non-vegetarian diets because vegetarians do not eat meat, which is high in bioavailable zinc and may enhance zinc absorption. In addition, vegetarians typically eat high levels of legumes and whole grains, which contain phytates that bind zinc and inhibit its absorption.

Vegetarians sometimes require as much as 50% more of the RDA for zinc than non-vegetarians. In addition, they might benefit from using certain food preparation techniques that reduce the binding of zinc by phytates and increase its bioavailability. Techniques to increase zinc bioavailability include soaking beans, grains, and seeds in water for several hours before cooking them and allowing them to sit after soaking until sprouts form. Vegetarians can also increase their zinc intake by consuming more leavened grain products (such as bread) than unleavened products (such as crackers) because leavening partially breaks down the phytate; thus, the body absorbs more zinc from leavened grains than unleavened grains.

Pregnant and lactating women

Pregnant women, particularly those starting their pregnancy with marginal zinc status, are at increased risk of becoming zinc insufficient due, in part, to high fetal requirements for zinc. Lactation can also deplete maternal zinc stores. For these reasons, the RDA for zinc is higher for pregnant and lactating women than for other women (see Table 34.1.)

Older infants who are exclusively breastfed

Breast milk provides sufficient zinc (2 mg/day) for the first 4–6 months of life but does not provide recommended amounts of zinc for infants aged 7–12 months, who need 3 mg/day. In addition to breast milk, infants aged 7–12 months should consume age-appropriate foods or formula containing zinc. Zinc supplementation has improved the growth rate in some children who demonstrate mild-to-moderate growth failure and who have a zinc deficiency.

People with sickle cell disease

Results from a large cross-sectional survey suggest that 44% of children with sickle cell disease have a low plasma zinc concentration, possibly due to increased nutrient requirements and/or poor nutritional status. Zinc deficiency also affects approximately 60%–70% of adults with sickle cell disease. Zinc supplementation has been shown to improve growth in children with sickle cell disease.

Alcoholics

Approximately 30%–50% of alcoholics have low zinc status because ethanol consumption decreases intestinal absorption of zinc and increases urinary zinc excretion. In addition, the variety and amount of food consumed by many alcoholics is limited, leading to inadequate zinc intake.

Zinc and Health

Immune function

Severe zinc deficiency depresses immune function, and even mild to moderate degrees of zinc deficiency can impair macrophage and neutrophil functions, natural killer cell activity, and complement activity. The body requires zinc to develop and activate T-lymphocytes. Individuals with low zinc levels have shown reduced lymphocyte proliferation response to mitogens and other adverse alterations in immunity that can be corrected by zinc supplementation. These alterations in immune function might explain why low zinc status has been associated with increased susceptibility to pneumonia and other infections in children in developing countries and the elderly.

Wound healing

Zinc helps maintain the integrity of skin and mucosal membranes. Patients with chronic leg ulcers have abnormal zinc metabolism and low serum zinc levels, and clinicians frequently treat skin ulcers with zinc supplements. The authors of a systematic review concluded that zinc sulfate might be effective for treating leg ulcers in some patients who have low serum zinc levels. However, research has not shown that the general use of zinc sulfate in patients with chronic leg ulcers or arterial or venous ulcers is effective.

Diarrhea

Acute diarrhea is associated with high rates of mortality among children in developing countries. Zinc deficiency causes alterations in immune response that probably contribute to increased susceptibility to infections, such as those that cause diarrhea, especially in children.

Studies show that poor, malnourished children in India, Africa, South America, and Southeast Asia experience shorter courses of infectious diarrhea after taking zinc supplements. The children in these studies received 4–40 mg of zinc a day in the form of zinc acetate, zinc gluconate, or zinc sulfate.

In addition, results from a pooled analysis of randomized controlled trials of zinc supplementation in developing countries suggest that zinc helps reduce the duration and severity of diarrhea in zinc-deficient or otherwise malnourished children. Similar findings were reported in a meta-analysis published in 2008 and a 2007 review of zinc supplementation for preventing and treating diarrhea. The effects of zinc supplementation on diarrhea in children with adequate zinc status, such as most children in the United States, are not clear.

The World Health Organization and UNICEF now recommend short-term zinc supplementation (20 mg of zinc per day, or 10 mg for infants under 6 months, for 10–14 days) to treat acute childhood diarrhea.

Common cold

Researchers have hypothesized that zinc could reduce the severity and duration of cold symptoms by directly inhibiting rhinovirus binding and replication in the nasal mucosa and suppressing inflammation. Although studies examining the effect of zinc treatment on cold symptoms have had somewhat conflicting results, overall zinc appears to be beneficial under certain circumstances. Several studies are described below in which zinc is administered as a lozenge or zinc-containing syrup that temporarily "sticks" in the mouth and throat. This allows zinc to make contact with the rhinovirus in those areas.

In a randomized, double-blind, placebo-controlled clinical trial, 50 subjects (within 24 hours of developing the common cold) took a zinc acetate lozenge (13.3 mg zinc) or placebo every 2–3 wakeful hours. Compared with placebo, the zinc lozenges significantly reduced the duration of cold symptoms (cough, nasal discharge, and muscle aches).

In another clinical trial involving 273 participants with experimentally induced colds, zinc gluconate lozenges (providing 13.3 mg zinc) significantly reduced the duration of illness compared with placebo but had no effect on symptom severity. However, treatment with zinc acetate lozenges (providing 5 or 11.5 mg zinc) had no effect on either cold duration or severity. Neither zinc gluconate nor zinc acetate lozenges affected the duration or severity of cold symptoms in 281 subjects with natural (not experimentally induced) colds in another trial.

In 77 participants with natural colds, a combination of zinc gluconate nasal spray and zinc orotate lozenges (37 mg zinc every 2–3 wakeful hours) was also found to have no effect on the number of asymptomatic patients after 7 days of treatment.

In September 2007, Caruso and colleagues published a structured review of the effects of zinc lozenges, nasal sprays, and nasal gels on the common cold. Of the 14 randomized, placebo-controlled studies included, 7 (5 using zinc lozenges, 2 using a nasal gel) showed that the zinc treatment had a beneficial effect and 7 (5 using zinc lozenges, 1 using a nasal spray, and 1 using lozenges and a nasal spray) showed no effect.

More recently, a Cochrane review concluded that "zinc (lozenges or syrup) is beneficial in reducing the duration and severity of the common cold in healthy people, when taken within 24 hours of onset of symptoms". The author of another review completed in 2004 also concluded that zinc can reduce the duration and severity of cold symptoms. However, more research is needed to determine the optimal dosage, zinc formulation and duration of treatment before a general recommendation for zinc in the treatment of the common cold can be made.

As previously noted, the safety of intranasal zinc has been called into question because of numerous reports of anosmia (loss of smell), in some cases long-lasting or permanent, from the use of zinc-containing nasal gels or sprays.

Age-related macular degeneration (AMD)

Researchers have suggested that both zinc and antioxidants delay the progression of age-related macular degeneration (AMD) and vision loss, possibly by preventing cellular damage in the retina. In a population-based cohort study in the Netherlands, high dietary intake of zinc as well as beta carotene, vitamin C, and vitamin E was associated with reduced risk of AMD in elderly subjects. However, the authors of a systematic review and meta-analysis published in 2007 concluded that zinc is not effective for the primary prevention of early AMD, although zinc might reduce the risk of progression to advanced AMD.

The Age-Related Eye Disease Study (AREDS), a large, randomized, placebo-controlled, clinical trial (n = 3,597), evaluated the effect of high doses of selected antioxidants (500 mg vitamin C, 400 IU vitamin E, and 15 mg beta-carotene) with or without zinc (80 mg as zinc oxide) on the development of advanced AMD in older individuals with varying degrees of AMD. Participants also received 2 mg copper to prevent the copper deficiency associated with high zinc intakes. After an average follow-up period of 6.3 years, supplementation with antioxidants plus zinc (but not antioxidants alone) significantly reduced the risk of developing advanced AMD and reduced visual acuity loss. Zinc supplementation alone significantly reduced the risk of developing

389

advanced AMD in subjects at higher risk but not in the total study population. Visual acuity loss was not significantly affected by zinc supplementation alone. A follow-up AREDS2 study confirmed the value of this supplement in reducing the progression of AMD over a median follow-up period of 5 years. Importantly, AREDS2 revealed that a formulation providing 25 mg zinc (about one-third the amount in the original AREDS formulation) provided the same protective effect against developing advanced AMD.

Two other small clinical trials evaluated the effects of supplementation with 200 mg zinc sulfate (providing 45 mg zinc) for 2 years in subjects with drusen or macular degeneration. Zinc supplementation significantly reduced visual acuity loss in one of the studies but had no effect in the other.

A Cochrane review concluded that the evidence supporting the use of antioxidant vitamins and zinc for AMD comes primarily from the AREDS study. Individuals who have or are developing AMD should talk to their health care provider about taking a zinc-containing AREDS supplement.

Interactions with iron and copper

Iron-deficiency anemia is a serious world-wide public health problem. Iron fortification programs have been credited with improving the iron status of millions of women, infants, and children. Fortification of foods with iron does not significantly affect zinc absorption. However, large amounts of supplemental iron (greater than 25 mg) might decrease zinc absorption. Taking iron supplements between meals helps decrease its effect on zinc absorption.

High zinc intakes can inhibit copper absorption, sometimes producing copper deficiency and associated anemia. For this reason, dietary supplement formulations containing high levels of zinc, such as the one used in the AREDS study, sometimes contain copper.

Health Risks from Excessive Zinc

Zinc toxicity can occur in both acute and chronic forms. Acute adverse effects of high zinc intake include nausea, vomiting, loss of appetite, abdominal cramps, diarrhea, and headaches. One case report cited severe nausea and vomiting within 30 minutes of ingesting 4 g of zinc gluconate (570 mg elemental zinc). Intakes of 150–450 mg of zinc per day have been associated with such chronic effects as low copper status, altered iron function, reduced immune function,

Table 34.3. Tolerable Upper Intake Levels (ULs) for Zinc

Age	Male	Female	Pregnant	Lactating
0–6 months	4 mg	4 mg		
7–12 months	5 mg	5 mg		
1–3 years	7 mg	7 mg		
4–8 years	12 mg	12 mg		
9–13 years	23 mg	23 mg		
14–18 years	34 mg	34 mg	34 mg	34 mg
19+ years	40 mg	40 mg	40 mg	40 m

and reduced levels of high-density lipoproteins. Reductions in a copper-containing enzyme, a marker of copper status, have been reported with even moderately high zinc intakes of approximately 60 mg/day for up to 10 weeks. The doses of zinc used in the AREDS study (80 mg per day of zinc in the form of zinc oxide for 6.3 years, on average) have been associated with a significant increase in hospitalizations for genitourinary causes, raising the possibility that chronically high intakes of zinc adversely affect some aspects of urinary physiology.

The FNB has established ULs for zinc (Table 34.3.). Long-term intakes above the UL increase the risk of adverse health effects. The ULs do not apply to individuals receiving zinc for medical treatment, but such individuals should be under the care of a physician who monitors them for adverse health effects.

Interactions with Medications

Zinc supplements have the potential to interact with several types of medications. A few examples are provided below. Individuals taking these medications on a regular basis should discuss their zinc intakes with their healthcare providers.

Antibiotics

Both quinolone antibiotics (such as Cipro®) and tetracycline antibiotics (such as Achromycin® and Sumycin®) interact with zinc in the gastrointestinal tract, inhibiting the absorption of both zinc and the antibiotic. Taking the antibiotic at least 2 hours before or 4–6 hours after taking a zinc supplement minimizes this interaction.

Penicillamine

Zinc can reduce the absorption and action of penicillamine, a drug used to treat rheumatoid arthritis. To minimize this interaction, individuals should take zinc supplements at least 2 hours before or after taking penicillamine.

Diuretics

Thiazide diuretics such as chlorthalidone (Hygroton®) and hydrochlorothiazide (Esidrix® and HydroDIURIL®) increase urinary zinc excretion by as much as 60%. Prolonged use of thiazide diuretics could deplete zinc tissue levels, so clinicians should monitor zinc status in patients taking these medications.

Zinc and Healthful Diets

The federal government's 2010 *Dietary Guidelines for Americans* notes that "nutrients should come primarily from foods. Foods in nutrient-dense, mostly intact forms contain not only the essential vitamins and minerals that are often contained in nutrient supplements, but also dietary fiber and other naturally occurring substances that may have positive health effects. Dietary supplements...may be advantageous in specific situations to increase intake of a specific vitamin or mineral."

The *Dietary Guidelines for Americans* describes a healthy diet as one that:

- Emphasizes a variety of fruits, vegetables, whole grains, and fat-free or low-fat milk and milk products.

- Whole grains and milk products are good sources of zinc. Many ready-to-eat breakfast cereals are fortified with zinc.

- Includes lean meats, poultry, fish, beans, eggs, and nuts.

- Oysters, red meat, and poultry are excellent sources of zinc. Baked beans, chickpeas, and nuts (such as cashews and almonds) also contain zinc.

- Is low in saturated fats, trans fats, cholesterol, salt (sodium), and added sugars.

- Stays within your daily calorie needs.

Chapter 35

Supplements for Mood and Brain Health

Chapter Contents

Section 35.1

Ginkgo Biloba

Text in this section is excerpted from "Ginkgo Biloba," National
Center for Complementary and Integrative Health (NCCIH),
January 27, 2015.

Common Names: ginkgo, *Ginkgo biloba*, fossil tree, maidenhair
tree, Japanese silver apricot, *baiguo, bai guo ye*, kew tree, yinhsing
(yin-hsing)
Latin Name: *Ginkgo biloba*

The ginkgo tree is one of the oldest types of trees in the world.
Ginkgo seeds have been used in traditional Chinese medicine for
thousands of years, and cooked seeds are occasionally eaten. Historically, ginkgo leaf extract has been used to treat a variety of ailments
and conditions, including asthma, bronchitis, fatigue, and tinnitus
(ringing or roaring sounds in the ears). Recently, folk uses of ginkgo
leaf extracts include attempts to improve memory; to treat or help
prevent Alzheimer's disease and other types of dementia; to decrease
intermittent claudication (leg pain caused by narrowing arteries);
and to treat sexual dysfunction, multiple sclerosis, tinnitus, and other
health conditions.

Extracts are usually taken from the ginkgo leaf and are used to
make tablets, capsules, or teas. Occasionally, ginkgo extracts are used
in skin products.

What the Science Says

- Numerous studies of ginkgo have been done for a variety of conditions. Among the most widely researched are dementia, memory impairment, intermittent claudication, and tinnitus.

- An NCCIH-funded study of the well-characterized ginkgo
  product EGb–761 found it ineffective in lowering the overall
  incidence of dementia and Alzheimer's disease in the elderly.

Further analysis of the same data also found ginkgo to be ineffective in slowing cognitive decline, lowering blood pressure, or reducing the incidence of hypertension. In this clinical trial, known as the Ginkgo Evaluation of Memory study, researchers recruited more than 3,000 volunteers age 75 and over who took 240 mg of ginkgo daily. Participants were followed for an average of approximately 6 years.

• Some smaller studies of ginkgo for memory enhancement have had promising results, but a trial sponsored by the National Institute on Aging of more than 200 healthy adults over age 60 found that ginkgo taken for 6 weeks did not improve memory.

• Overall, the evidence on ginkgo for symptoms of intermittent claudication has not yet shown a significant benefit for this condition, although several small studies have found modest improvements. There is conflicting evidence on the efficacy of ginkgo for tinnitus.

• Other NCCIH-funded research includes studies of ginkgo for symptoms of multiple sclerosis, intermittent claudication, cognitive decline, sexual dysfunction due to antidepressants, insulin resistance, and short-term memory loss associated with electroconvulsive therapy for depression.

Side Effects and Cautions

• Side effects of ginkgo may include headache, nausea, gastrointestinal upset, diarrhea, dizziness, or allergic skin reactions. More severe allergic reactions have occasionally been reported.

• There are some data to suggest that ginkgo can increase bleeding risk, so people who take anticoagulant drugs, have bleeding disorders, or have scheduled surgery or dental procedures should use caution and talk to a health care provider if using ginkgo.

• Fresh (raw) ginkgo seeds contain large amounts of a chemical called ginkgotoxin, which can cause serious adverse reactions— even seizures and death. Roasted seeds can also be dangerous. Products made from standardized ginkgo leaf extracts contain little ginkgotoxin and appear to be safe when used orally and appropriately.

- National Toxicology Program (NTP) studies showed that rats and mice developed tumors after being given a specific ginkgo extract for up to 2 years. Further studies are needed to find out what substances in ginkgo caused the tumors and whether taking ginkgo as a dietary supplement affects the risk of cancer in people.

Keep in Mind

Tell all your health care providers about any complementary health approaches you use. Give them a full picture of what you do to manage your health. This will help ensure coordinated and safe care.

Section 35.2

St. John's Wort

Text in this section is excerpted from "St. John's Wort," National
Center for Complementary and Integrative Health (NCCIH),
April 2012.

Common Names: St. John's wort, hypericum, Klamath weed, goatweed
Latin Name: *Hypericum perforatum*

St. John's wort is a plant with yellow flowers whose medicinal uses were first recorded in ancient Greece. The name St. John's wort apparently refers to John the Baptist, as the plant blooms around the time of the feast of St. John the Baptist in late June. Historically, St. John's wort has been used for centuries to treat mental disorders and nerve pain. St. John's wort has also been used for malaria, as a sedative, and as a balm for wounds, burns, and insect bites. Recently, St. John's wort is used as a folk or traditional remedy for depression, anxiety, and/or sleep disorders.

The flowering tops of St. John's wort are used to prepare teas, tablets, and capsules containing concentrated extracts. Liquid extracts and topical preparations are also used.

What the Science Says

Although some studies of St. John's wort have reported benefits for depression, others have not. For example, a large study sponsored by NCCIH found that the herb was no more effective than placebo in treating major depression of moderate severity, and a study co-funded by NCCIH and the National Institute of Mental Health found that neither St. John's wort nor a standard antidepressant medication relieved symptoms of minor depression better than a placebo.

Side Effects and Cautions

- Research has shown that St. John's wort interacts with many medications in ways that can interfere with their intended effects. Examples of medications that can be affected include:

  - Antidepressants
  - Birth control pills
  - Cyclosporine, which prevents the body from rejecting transplanted organs
  - Digoxin, a heart medication
  - Indinavir and possibly other drugs used to control HIV infection
  - Irinotecan and possibly other drugs used to treat cancer
  - Seizure-control drugs, such as phenytoin and phenobarbital
  - Warfarin and related anticoagulants.

- St. John's wort may cause increased sensitivity to sunlight. Other side effects can include anxiety, dry mouth, dizziness, gastrointestinal symptoms, fatigue, headache, or sexual dysfunction.

- Taking St. John's wort with certain antidepressants may lead to increased serotonin-related side effects, which may be potentially serious.

- St. John's wort is not a proven therapy for depression. If depression is not adequately treated, it can become severe. Anyone who may have depression should see a health care provider. There are effective proven therapies available.

Keep in Mind

- Tell all your health care providers about any complementary health approaches you use. Give them a full picture of what you do to manage your health. This will help ensure coordinated and safe care.

Chapter 36

Probiotics: Supplements for Gastrointestinal Health

What's the Bottom Line

How much do we know about probiotics?

Although a great deal of research has been done on probiotics, much remains to be learned.

What do we know about the usefulness of probiotics?

Some probiotics may help to prevent diarrhea that is caused by infections or antibiotics. They may also help with symptoms of irritable bowel syndrome. However, benefits have not been conclusively demonstrated, and not all probiotics have the same effects.

What do we know about the safety of probiotics?

In healthy people, probiotics usually have only minor side effects, if any. However, in people with underlying health problems (for example, weakened immune systems), serious complications such as infections have occasionally been reported,

Text in this chapter is excerpted from "Probiotics," National Center for Complementary and Integrative Health (NCCIH), July 22, 2015.

What Are Probiotics?

Probiotics are live microorganisms that are intended to have health benefits. Products sold as probiotics include foods (such as yogurt), dietary supplements, and products that are not used orally, such as skin creams.

Although people often think of bacteria and other microorganisms as harmful "germs," many microorganisms help our bodies function properly. For example, bacteria that are normally present in our intestines help digest food, destroy disease-causing microorganisms, and produce vitamins. Large numbers of microorganisms live on and in our bodies. In fact, microorganisms in the human body outnumber human cells by 10 to 1. Many of the microorganisms in probiotic products are the same as or similar to microorganisms that naturally live in our bodies.

The History of Probiotics

The concept behind probiotics was introduced in the early 20th century, when Nobel laureate Elie Metchnikoff, known as the "father of probiotics," proposed that consuming beneficial microorganisms could improve people's health. Researchers continued to investigate this idea, and the term "probiotics"—meaning "for life"—eventually came into use.

What Kinds of Microorganisms Are in Probiotics?

Probiotics may contain a variety of microorganisms. The most common are bacteria that belong to groups called *Lactobacillus* and *Bifidobacterium*. Each of these two broad groups includes many types of bacteria. Other bacteria may also be used as probiotics, and so may yeasts such as *Saccharomyces boulardii*.

Probiotics, Prebiotics, and Synbiotics

Prebiotics are not the same as probiotics. The term "prebiotics" refers to dietary substances that favor the growth of beneficial bacteria over harmful ones. The term "synbiotics" refers to products that combine probiotics and prebiotics.

How Popular Are Probiotics?

Data from the 2012 National Health Interview Survey (NHIS) show that about 4 million (1.6 percent) U.S. adults had used probiotics or prebiotics in the past 30 days. Among adults, probiotics or prebiotics were the third most commonly used dietary supplement other than vitamins and minerals, and the use of probiotics quadrupled between 2007 and 2012. The 2012 NHIS also showed that 300,000 children age 4 to 17 (0.5 percent) had used probiotics or prebiotics in the 30 days before the survey.

What the Science Says about the Effectiveness of Probiotics

Researchers have studied probiotics to find out whether they might help prevent or treat a variety of health problems, including:

- Digestive disorders such as diarrhea caused by infections, antibiotic-associated diarrhea, irritable bowel syndrome, and inflammatory bowel disease

- Allergic disorders such as atopic dermatitis (eczema) and allergic rhinitis (hay fever)

- Tooth decay, periodontal disease, and other oral health problems

- Colic in infants

- Liver disease

- The common cold

- Prevention of necrotizing enterocolitis in very low birth weight infants.

There's preliminary evidence that some probiotics are helpful in preventing diarrhea caused by infections and antibiotics and in improving symptoms of irritable bowel syndrome, but more needs to be learned. We still don't know which probiotics are helpful and which are not. We also don't know how much of the probiotic people would have to take or who would most likely benefit from taking probiotics. Even for the conditions that have been studied the most, researchers are still working toward finding the answers to these questions.

Probiotics are not all alike. For example, if a specific kind of *Lactobacillus* helps prevent an illness, that doesn't necessarily mean that another kind of *Lactobacillus* would have the same effect or that any of the *Bifidobacterium* probiotics would do the same thing.

Although some probiotics have shown promise in research studies, strong scientific evidence to support specific uses of probiotics for most health conditions is lacking. The U.S. Food and Drug Administration (FDA) has not approved any probiotics for preventing or treating any health problem. Some experts have cautioned that the rapid growth in marketing and use of probiotics may have outpaced scientific research for many of their proposed uses and benefits.

What is the Government Regulation of Probiotics?

Many probiotics are sold as dietary supplements, which do not require FDA approval before they are marketed. Dietary supplement labels may make claims about how the product affects the structure or function of the body without FDA approval, but they cannot make health claims (claims that the product reduces the risk of a disease) without the FDA's consent.

If a probiotic is marketed as a drug for specific treatment of a disease or disorder in the future, it will be required to meet more stringent requirements. It must be proven safe and effective for its intended use through clinical trials and be approved by the FDA before it can be sold.

What the Science Says about the Safety and Side Effects of Probiotics?

Whether probiotics are likely to be safe for you depends on the state of your health.

- In people who are generally healthy, probiotics have a good safety record. Side effects, if they occur at all, usually consist only of mild digestive symptoms such as gas.

- On the other hand, there have been reports linking probiotics to severe side effects, such as dangerous infections, in people with serious underlying medical problems.

- The people who are most at risk of severe side effects include critically ill patients, those who have had surgery, very sick infants, and people with weakened immune systems

- The people who are most at risk of severe side effects include critically ill patients, those who have had surgery, very sick infants, and people with weakened immune systems

Even for healthy people, there are uncertainties about the safety of probiotics. Because many research studies on probiotics haven't looked closely at safety, there isn't enough information right now to answer some safety questions. Most of our knowledge about safety comes from studies of *Lactobacillus* and *Bifidobacterium*; less is known about other probiotics. Information on the long-term safety of probiotics is limited, and safety may differ from one type of probiotic to another. For example, even though a National Center for Complementary and Integrative Health (NCCIH)-funded study showed that a particular kind of *Lactobacillus* appears safe in healthy adults age 65 and older, this does not mean that all probiotics would necessarily be safe for people in this age group.

Keep in Mind

- Don't replace scientifically proven treatments with unproven products and practices. Don't use a complementary health product, such as probiotics, as a reason to postpone seeing your health care provider about any health problem.

- If you're considering a probiotic dietary supplement, consult your health care provider first. This is especially important if you have health problems. Anyone with a serious underlying health condition should be monitored closely while taking probiotics.

- If you're pregnant or nursing a child, or if you're considering giving a child a dietary supplement, such as probiotics, it's especially important to consult your (or your child's) health care provider.

- Tell all your health care providers about any complementary or integrative health approaches you use. Give them a full picture of what you do to manage your health. This will help ensure coordinated and safe care.

Chapter 37

Supplements for Bodybuilding and Energy

Chapter Contents

Section 37.1

Bodybuilding

Text in this section is excerpted from "Bodybuilding," National
Center for Complementary and Integrative Health (NCCIH),
June 10, 2015

Some bodybuilders and athletes turn to dietary supplements to help
them increase muscle size and definition. However, many bodybuilding
products marketed as dietary supplements have been found to contain
other ingredients that can be harmful. Use caution and talk with your
health care provider before you begin taking any supplement to gain
strength or muscle size.

Bottom Line

- Multivitamin and mineral supplements are unnecessary for athletes or other physically active people who eat a well-balanced
  diet and enough calories. The safety of supplements used for
  bodybuilding remains an issue of concern (see Safety section
  below).

- There is no scientific evidence that other dietary supplements,
  such as choline, methoxyisoflavone, zinc/magnesium aspartate,
  nitric oxide precursors, and chromium, are effective for building
  strength and muscle mass.

- Evidence suggests that creatine, a popular dietary supplement,
  may enhance the effects of vigorous exercise on strength, muscle
  mass, and endurance, but it may also cause fluid weight gain,
  nausea, cramping, and diarrhea.

Safety

- Many bodybuilding products marketed as dietary supplements
  have been found to be deceptively labeled and to contain hidden ingredients that can be harmful, such as anabolic steroids,

compounds chemically similar to them, or other substances that don't qualify as dietary ingredients.

- In April 2013, the U.S. Food and Drug Administration issued a warning to consumers to avoid products containing the stimulant dimethylamylamine (DMAA). DMAA can elevate blood pressure and lead to other problems, such as a heart attack.

- Evidence suggests that creatine (an amino acid produced by the body) supplements may be safe for short-term use in healthy adults, but the American College of Sports Medicine recommends against anyone younger than age 18 using it to enhance athletic performance.

- Some dietary supplements may have side effects and some may interact with drugs or other supplements. Some vitamins and minerals are harmful at high doses. Talk with your health care provider before using a dietary supplement to increase muscle size and strength.

Section 37.2

Energy Drinks

Text in this section is excerpted from "Energy Drinks," National Center for Complementary and Integrative Health (NCCIH), August 31, 2015.

Energy drinks are widely promoted as products that increase alertness and enhance physical and mental performance. Marketing targeted at young people has been quite effective. Next to multivitamins, energy drinks are the most popular dietary supplement consumed by American teens and young adults. Males between the ages of 18 and 34 years consume the most energy drinks, and almost one-third of teens between 12 and 17 years drink them regularly.

Caffeine is the major ingredient in most energy drinks—a 24-oz energy drink may contain as much as 500 mg of caffeine (similar to that in four or five cups of coffee). Energy drinks also may contain guarana (another source of caffeine sometimes called Brazilian cocoa), sugars, taurine, ginseng, B vitamins, glucuronolactone, yohimbe, carnitine, and bitter orange.

Consuming energy drinks also increases important safety concerns. Between 2007 and 2011, the overall number of energy-drink related visits to emergency departments doubled, with the most significant increase (279 percent) in people aged 40 and older. A growing trend among young adults and teens is mixing energy drinks with alcohol. About 25 percent of college students consume alcohol with energy drinks, and they binge-drink significantly more often than students who don't mix them. In 2011, 42 percent of all energy-drink related emergency department visits involved combining these beverages with alcohol or drugs (including illicit drugs, like marijuana, as well as central nervous system stimulants, like Ritalin or Adderall).

Bottom Line

- Although there's very limited data that caffeine-containing energy drinks may temporarily improve alertness and physical endurance, evidence that they enhance strength or power is lacking. More important, they can be dangerous because large amounts of caffeine may cause serious heart rhythm, blood flow, and blood pressure problems.

- There's not enough evidence to determine the effects of additives other than caffeine in energy drinks.

- The amounts of caffeine in energy drinks vary widely, and the actual caffeine content may not be identified easily.

Safety

- Large amounts of caffeine may cause serious heart and blood vessel problems such as heart rhythm disturbances and increases in heart rate and blood pressure. Caffeine also may harm children's still-developing cardiovascular and nervous systems.

- Caffeine use may be associated with palpitations, anxiety, sleep problems, digestive problems, elevated blood pressure, and dehydration.

- Guarana, commonly added to energy drinks, contains caffeine. Therefore, the addition of guarana increases the drink's total caffeine content.

- Young adults who combine caffeinated drinks with alcohol may not be able to tell how intoxicated they are.

- Excessive energy drink consumption may disrupt teens' sleep patterns and may fuel risk-taking behavior.

- Many energy drinks contain as much as 25–50 g of simple sugars; this may be problematic for people who are diabetic or prediabetic.

Chapter 38

Supplements for Weight Loss

Chapter Contents

Section 38.1

Green Tea

Text in this section is excerpted from "Green Tea," National Center for Complementary and Integrative Health (NCCIH), April 2012.

Common Names: green tea, Chinese tea, Japanese tea
Latin Name: *Camellia sinensis*

All types of tea (green, black, and oolong) are produced from the Camellia sinensis plant using different methods. Fresh leaves from the plant are steamed to produce green tea. Green tea and green tea extracts, such as its component EGCG (Epigallocatechin gallate), have traditionally been used to prevent and treat a variety of cancers, including breast, stomach, and skin cancers, and for mental alertness, weight loss, lowering cholesterol levels, and protecting skin from sun damage.

Green tea is usually brewed and drunk as a beverage. Green tea extracts can be taken in capsules and are sometimes used in skin products.

What the Science Says

- Laboratory studies suggest that green tea may help protect against or slow the growth of certain cancers, but studies in people have shown mixed results.

- Some evidence suggests that the use of green tea preparations improves mental alertness, most likely because of its caffeine content. There are not enough reliable data to determine whether green tea can aid in weight loss, lower blood cholesterol levels, or protect the skin from sun damage.

- NCCIH supports studies to learn more about the components in green tea and their effects on conditions such as cancer, diabetes, and heart disease.

Side Effects and Cautions

- Green tea is safe for most adults when used in moderate amounts.

- There have been some case reports of liver problems in people taking concentrated green tea extracts. The problems do not seem to be connected with green tea infusions or beverages. Although these cases are very rare and the evidence is not definitive, experts suggest that concentrated green tea extracts be taken with food, and that people discontinue use and consult a health care practitioner if they have a liver disorder or develop symptoms of liver trouble, such as abdominal pain, dark urine, or jaundice.

- Green tea and green tea extracts contain caffeine. Caffeine can cause insomnia, anxiety, irritability, upset stomach, nausea, diarrhea, or frequent urination in some people.

- Green tea contains small amounts of vitamin K, which can make anticoagulant drugs, such as warfarin, less effective.

Keep in Mind

Tell all your health care providers about any complementary health approaches you use. Give them a full picture of what you do to manage your health. This will help ensure coordinated and safe care.

Section 38.2

Hoodia

Text in this section is excerpted from "Hoodia," National Center for Complementary and Integrative Health (NCCIH), April 2012.

Common Names: hoodia, Kalahari cactus, Xhoba
Latin Name: *Hoodia gordonii*

Hoodia is a flowering, cactus-like plant native to the Kalahari Desert in southern Africa. Its harvest is protected by conservation laws. Historically, Kalahari Bushmen ate hoodia stems to reduce their hunger and thirst during long hunts. Recently, the main folk use of hoodia is as an appetite suppressant for weight loss.

Dried extracts of hoodia stems and roots are used to make capsules, powders, and chewable tablets. Hoodia can also be used to make liquid extracts and teas. Hoodia products often contain other herbs or minerals, such as green tea or chromium picolinate.

What the Science Says

There is no reliable scientific evidence to support hoodia's use. No studies of the herb in people have been published.

Side Effects and Cautions

- Hoodia's safety is unknown. Its potential risks, side effects, and interactions with medicines and other supplements have not been studied.

- The quality of hoodia products varies widely. News reports suggest that some products sold as hoodia do not contain any hoodia.

Keep in Mind

Tell all your health care providers about any complementary health approaches you use. Give them a full picture of what you do to manage your health. This will help ensure coordinated and safe care.

Part Five

Alternative Treatments for Specific Diseases and Conditions

Chapter 39

Arthritis and CAM

Rheumatoid Arthritis and Complementary Health Approaches

Rheumatoid arthritis (RA) is a health condition that causes pain, swelling, stiffness, and loss of function in the joints. Conventional medical treatments are highly effective for RA; however, researchers are also studying complementary health approaches as possible additions to RA treatments. Some complementary health approaches for RA are intended to reduce joint inflammation, and some are intended to reduce symptoms such as pain. This chapter provides basic information on RA; summarizes scientific research on the effectiveness and safety of selected mind and body practices, dietary supplements, and other approaches that have been studied for RA.

Key Points

- In general, there is not enough scientific evidence to prove that any complementary health approaches are beneficial for RA,

---

This chapter includes excerpts from "Rheumatoid Arthritis and Complementary Health Approaches," National Center for Complementary and Integrative Health (NCCIH), July 2013; and text from "Osteoarthritis and Complementary Health Approaches," National Center for Complementary and Integrative Health (NCCIH), May 2014.

and there are safety concerns about some of them. Some mind and body practices and dietary supplements may help people with RA manage their symptoms and therefore may be beneficial additions to conventional RA treatments, but there is not enough evidence to draw conclusions.

- Some complementary health approaches—particularly dietary supplements—may have side effects or may interact with conventional medical treatments or each other. Although many dietary supplements (and some prescription drugs) come from natural sources, "natural" does not always mean "safe." In particular, the herb thunder god vine *(Tripterygium wilfordii)* can have serious side effects.

- Conventional treatments are highly effective in slowing or stopping permanent joint damage in RA. Do not replace conventional medical therapy for RA with an unproven health product or practice.

- Tell all your health care providers about any complementary health approaches you use. Give them a full picture of what you do to manage your health. This will help ensure coordinated and safe care.

About Rheumatoid Arthritis

Rheumatoid arthritis is an inflammatory autoimmune disease—a type of condition in which the immune system, which normally protects the body by fighting infections and diseases, instead targets the body. RA is different from other types of arthritis such as osteoarthritis, a wear-and-tear condition that most commonly occurs as people age. In RA, the immune system attacks the tissues that line the joints, causing pain, swelling, and stiffness in the joints and affecting their ability to work properly. Over time, RA may damage bone and cartilage within the joints and weaken muscles, ligaments, and tendons that support the joints.

RA often begins in middle age and occurs more frequently in women than in men. Although RA primarily affects the joints, particularly the wrists and fingers, some people with RA may have other health problems, such as anemia, dry eyes or mouth, and heart or lung problems. People with RA may have fatigue, occasional fevers, or a general sense of not feeling well. They may also experience other symptoms such as depression, anxiety, a feeling of helplessness, and low self-esteem.

Early treatment to avoid permanent joint damage is key for preventing disability and progression of RA. Treatment for RA combines a variety of approaches and is aimed at relieving pain, reducing joint swelling, slowing or preventing joint damage, and improving physical function and well-being. Conventional medicines used for RA include:

- Disease-modifying antirheumatic drugs (DMARDs) to slow the progress of the disease.

- Biologic response modifiers to reduce inflammation and structural damage to the joints.

- Nonsteroidal anti-inflammatory drugs (NSAIDs) and corticosteroids to reduce inflammation.

Other treatments include surgery, physical therapy, modified exercise programs, and devices that ease physical stress on the joints (such as splints). People with RA are also encouraged to make lifestyle changes such as balancing activity with rest, eating a healthy diet, and reducing emotional stress.

To find out more about RA, contact the National Institute of Arthritis and Musculoskeletal and Skin Diseases (NIAMS).

About Scientific Evidence on Complementary Health Approaches

Scientific evidence on complementary health approaches includes results from laboratory research as well as clinical trials (studies in people). It provides information on whether an approach is helpful and safe. Scientific journals publish study results, as well as review articles that evaluate the evidence as it accumulates; fact sheets from the National Center for Complementary and Integrative Health (NCCIH)—8 base information about research findings primarily on the most rigorous review articles, known as systematic reviews and meta-analyses.

What the Science Says

In general, there is not enough scientific evidence to prove that any complementary health approaches are beneficial for RA, and there are

419

safety concerns about some of them. Some mind and body practices and dietary supplements may be beneficial additions to conventional RA treatments, but there is not enough evidence to draw conclusions. This section describes the scientific evidence on several complementary health approaches studied for RA.

Mind and Body Practices

Results from clinical trials suggest that some mind and body practices—such as relaxation,mindfulness meditation, tai chi, and yoga—help people with RA manage their symptoms and therefore may be beneficial additions to conventional treatments.

- **Acupuncture** has been studied for a variety of pain conditions, but very little acupunctureresearch has focused on RA. Reviews of the research on acupuncture have found conflicting evidence regarding its usefulness for RA.

- A 2010 systematic review looked at the benefits of mind and body techniques such as **mindfulness meditation** (which involves nonjudgmental attention to experiences in the present moment), **biofeedback**, and **relaxation training** on the physical and psychological symptoms associated with RA. There was some evidence that these techniques may be helpful, but overall, the research results have been mixed.

- A 2008 study compared cognitive-behavioral therapy that emphasizes pain management with **mindfulness meditation** for RA. The researchers found that mindfulness meditation, which helps regulate emotions, improved participants' ability to cope with pain. The researchers noted that participants with a history of depression responded better than others to mindfulness meditation.

- A few small studies have been conducted on **tai chi** for RA. In general, tai chi has not been shown to be effective for joint pain, swelling, and tenderness, although improvements in mood, quality of life, and overall physical function have been reported.

  - A 2010 study examined the effect of practicing tai chi on 15 patients with RA. The researchers found that tai chi improved muscle strength and endurance, but there was no evidence that it reduced disease activity or pain.

  - A 2007 systematic review of the research concluded that the value of tai chi for treating RA is still unproven. Many factors—including differences in tai chi styles, number of movements, length of the practice, and qualifications of instructors—add to the challenge of designing quality tai chi studies. Some people have reported soreness, but most studies have found that tai chi is relatively safe for people with RA.

- **Yoga** incorporates several elements of exercise that may be beneficial for arthritis, including activities that may help improve strength and flexibility. However, only a few studies have examined yoga for RA. Preliminary studies have found that yoga may improve physical function and decrease the number of tender and swollen joints. Yoga exercises should be performed with caution by people with RA who have limited mobility or spinal problems. People with RA may need assistance in modifying some yoga postures to minimize joint stress and may need to use props to help with balance.

Dietary Supplements

No dietary supplement has shown clear benefits for RA, but there is preliminary evidence for a few, particularly fish oil, gamma-linolenic acid, and the herb thunder god vine. Dosage and safety issues and potential interactions with conventional medicines need to be more thoroughly evaluated.

Fish oil contains high levels of omega-3 fatty acids—substances the body needs to perform a number of important functions. Types of fish high in omega-3s include herring, mackerel, salmon, and tuna. Fish oil supplements are available as capsules or oils.

- Clinical trials on RA have found that fish oil supplements may help to relieve tender joints and morning stiffness. Studies have also found that fish oil may reduce the need for NSAIDs and other conventional RA medicines. For example, the results of a randomized, controlled clinical trial published in 2008 found that people who received a blend of cod liver oil and fish oil over a 9-month period reduced their NSAID intake by more than one-third, compared with those who took a placebo.

- Because the omega-3 fatty acids in fish oil may make blood clot more slowly, people who take medications that affect clotting, such as anticoagulants, should discuss the use of fish oil supplements with a health care provider. Products made from fish liver oils (for example, cod liver oil) may contain vitamins A and D as well as omega-3 fatty acids; these vitamins can be toxic in large doses.

Gamma-linolenic acid (GLA) is an omega-6 fatty acid found in the oils of some plant seeds, including evening primrose *(Oenothera biennis)*, borage *(Borago officinalis)*, and black currant *(Ribes nigrum)*. In the body, GLA may be converted into substances that reduce inflammation.

- There is some preliminary evidence that GLA may be beneficial for RA; however, the quality of the studies on GLA has been inconsistent. The more rigorous studies suggest that GLA may relieve symptoms such as joint pain, stiffness, and tenderness; in some cases, GLA led to a decreased need for NSAID medication.

- Side effects of GLA may include headache, soft stools, constipation, gas, and belching. Some borage oil preparations contain chemicals called pyrrolizidine alkaloids that may harm the liver.

Thunder god vine *(Tripterygium wilfordii)* has been used for centuries in traditional Chinese medicine. Extracts are prepared from the skinned root of the herb, as other parts of the plant are highly poisonous. **Thunder god vine can cause severe side effects.**

- Findings from laboratory and animal studies suggest that thunder god vine may fight inflammation and suppress the immune system. A 2011 systematic review looked at three human studies of oral (taken by mouth) thunder god vine and one study of topical (applied to the skin) thunder god vine for RA. The data showed that both oral and topical thunder god vine may improve some RA symptoms, but the study methods were not consistent among the trials.

- **A systematic review of the research on thunder god vine for RA concluded that serious side effects occurred frequently enough that the risk of using it outweighs its benefits.** Depending on the dose and type of extract, thunder god vine may cause serious side effects. Thunder god vine can affect the reproductive system, possibly causing menstrual changes in women and infertility in men. Long-term use may decrease bone mineral density in women, potentially increasing the risk of osteoporosis. Other side effects can include diarrhea, upset stomach, hair loss, headache, and skin rash.

Research on **other supplements** for RA symptoms is still in the early stages. For example:

- Varieties of **boswellia** (*Boswellia serrata, Boswellia carterii,* also known as frankincense) produce a resin that has shown anti-inflammatory and immune system effects in laboratory and animal studies, but no rigorous clinical trials in people with RA have been conducted.

- Laboratory studies have identified anti-inflammatory compounds in **ginger** (*Zingiber officinale*). Most of this research has focused on the anti-inflammatory properties of gingerol compounds—the components of ginger that give it flavor. A 2009 study funded in part by NCCIH examined whether nongingerol compounds had an antiarthritic effect in rats. The researchers found that ginger extract with both gingerol and nongingerol components prevented joint inflammation and destruction better than ginger extract containing only gingerols. They concluded that the nongingerol compounds may play a role in the anti-arthritic properties of ginger. Although these laboratory and animal studies show some promise, studies regarding ginger extracts for RA symptoms in people are lacking.

- A 2010 NCCIH-funded review has found evidence that substances found in **green tea** might be useful for RA and osteo-arthritis, but the effects of these substances in either type of arthritis have not been fully tested in people.

- In animal studies, extracts of **turmeric** (*Curcuma longa*) containing the chemical curcumin were found to protect joints from inflammation. Building on previous laboratory research that examined turmeric's anti-arthritic properties, a 2010 study, funded in part by NCCIH, looked at whether turmeric essential oils (TEO) protected joints in rats. The researchers found that an oral dose of TEO had an anti-inflammatory effect specific to the joints. There may be a potential role for turmeric or its components in preventing or slowing RA disease, but this has not yet been demonstrated in people.

Other Types of Complementary Health Approaches Studied for Rheumatoid Arthritis

Other complementary health approaches have been studied for RA:

- An NCCIH-funded preliminary study of **Ayurvedic medicine**, a system of healing that originated in India and involves using individually prescribed combinations of herbs, found that classic, individualized Ayurvedic approaches, methotrexate (a conventional medication frequently used to treat RA), or a combination of both were equally effective in reducing symptoms of RA. Because this was a small, preliminary study, its results, although promising, are insufficient to show definitively that Ayurvedic medicine is helpful for RA.

- **Balneotherapy** is the technique of bathing in tap or mineral water for health purposes. Preliminary research on balneotherapy for RA has been conducted in areas where it is most popular, such as Europe and Israel's Dead Sea region. Although some benefits have been reported, there is not enough reliable evidence to draw conclusions.

- Some people with RA may try following **special diets**—such as vegetarian and vegan diets, the Mediterranean diet, and periods of fasting—to control symptoms. Research on these diets has been inconclusive. Although a few studies suggest that decreasing or eliminating meat, dairy, or foods likely to cause allergies may help in some cases, others do not. One drawback is that special diets may be difficult for people to follow over time. In addition, some diets could put people at risk for nutritional deficiencies.

- **Traditional Chinese medicine (TCM)** encompasses multiple practices, including acupuncture, Chinese herbal medicine, and others. Several practices that are part of TCM, including acupuncture, tai chi, and the herb thunder god vine, have been studied individually for RA, as described above. Some research has also been done on TCM as a whole for RA symptoms and for relief of side effects from conventional RA treatments, but no conclusions can be reached because of the poor quality of some of the research, variations in study design, and insufficient data on safety.

If You Are Considering Complementary Health Approaches for Rheumatoid Arthritis

- Do not replace proven conventional treatments for RA with unproven health products and practices. Do not change your use of prescribed RA medications without consulting your health care provider. Going without effective treatment for RA could lead to permanent joint damage.

• Be aware that some complementary health approaches—particularly dietary supplements—may interact with conventional medical treatments. Also consider the possibility that what's on the label of a dietary supplement may not be what's in the bottle; for example, some tests of dietary supplements have found that the contents did not match the dose on the label, and some herbal supplements have been found to be contaminated.

• Women who are pregnant or nursing or people who are thinking of using a complementary health approach to treat a child should consult their (or their child's) health care provider before using any complementary health approach.

• Tell all your health care providers about any complementary health approaches you use. Give them a full picture of what you do to manage your health. This will help ensure coordinated and safe care.

Osteoarthritis and Complementary Health Approaches

Osteoarthritis (OA) is a disease that causes pain and difficulty in moving joints, particularly in the knees, hips, hands, and spine. This section provides basic information on OA, summarizes scientific research on selected dietary supplements, mind and body practices, and other complementary health approaches that have been studied for OA.

Key Points

• It is important **not** to replace conventional medical treatments for OA with an unproven complementary health approach.

• Some research has shown that acupuncture may help to reduce pain and improve joint mobility, and a small number of studies on massage and tai chi for OA symptoms suggest that both practices may help to reduce pain and improve physical function (the ability to walk and move).

- There is little conclusive evidence that dietary supplements help with OA symptoms or the underlying course of the disease.

- Tell all your health care providers about any complementary health approaches you use. Give them a full picture of what you do to manage your health. This will help ensure coordinated and safe care.

About Osteoarthritis

Osteoarthritis is the most common type of arthritis—affecting nearly 27 million Americans—and is an increasing problem among older adults. OA occurs when the cartilage (protective tissue) between the bones of a joint is worn down. As a result, the bones rub together, causing pain and loss of function—such as stiffness or reduced range of motion—in the joints.

OA is different from rheumatoid arthritis, which is an autoimmune disease that affects other tissues in the body in addition to joints, including the eyes, heart, and lungs. Risk factors for OA include aging, joint injuries, or genetic problems that specifically affect the joint cartilage. Both men and women are affected by OA; although after the age of 45 women tend to be more at risk of developing the disease.

Treatments for OA address the symptoms, such as pain, swelling, and reduced function in the joints. Non-drug approaches involve lifestyle changes such as exercise, weight control, and rest. Conventional drug treatments for OA include nonsteroidal anti-inflammatory drugs (NSAIDs), acetaminophen (a class of pain reliever), and injections of corticosteroids (anti-inflammatory hormones). While important and very helpful for many, these drugs are not always effective and they sometimes result in serious side effects. For example, NSAIDs may cause liver damage, ulcers, and gastrointestinal bleeding and can increase your risk of having a heart attack or stroke.

Use of Complementary Health Approaches for Osteoarthritis in the United States

According to the 2007 National Health Interview Survey, which included a comprehensive survey on the use of complementary health approaches by Americans, 5.2 percent of U.S. adults used complementary approaches for joint pain or stiffness, and 3.5 percent used them for arthritis.

What the Science Says

Dietary Supplements

Researchers have found little conclusive evidence that dietary supplements work for OA symptoms or the underlying course of the disease.

Glucosamine and Chondroitin Sulfate

Glucosamine and chondroitin sulfate—taken separately or together—are marketed for supporting joint health and have also been widely used for OA. Both are produced naturally in the body. They are also available as dietary supplements.

Experts Disagree

Experts disagree on whether glucosamine and chondroitin may help knee and hip osteoarthritis. The American College of Rheumatology (ACR) has recommended that people with hip or knee osteoarthritis not use glucosamine or chondroitin. But the recommendation was not a strong one, and the ACR acknowledged that it was controversial.

- NCCIH funded a study that examined the use of glucosamine and chondroitin sulfate for knee pain from OA. The Glucosamine/chondroitin Arthritis Intervention Trial (GAIT) enrolled close to 1,600 participants. Results indicated that overall, a 6-month treatment with the dietary supplements was no better than placebo. While there was some evidence suggesting that participants with moderate-to-severe pain had modest reductions in pain with the combined supplements, this has not been confirmed. In a followup study of GAIT participants, researchers examined whether glucosamine and chondroitin could prevent the progression of OA—an evaluation based on measuring joint space width. Results showed no significant change in joint space width or improvement in pain and function.

- A 2010 meta-analysis that looked at 10 glucosamine and chondroitin trials involving 3,803 patients with knee or hip OA published similar results. Compared with placebo, glucosamine, chondroitin, or a combination of both did not significantly reduce pain or change joint space.

- However, in several European studies, participants reported that their knees felt and functioned better after taking a large, daily dose of glucosamine sulfate.

- Glucosamine and chondroitin appear to be relatively safe and well tolerated when used in suggested doses over a 2-year period. In a few specific situations, however, there are concerns that side effects or drug interactions might occur:

  - Glucosamine may interact with the anticoagulant (blood-thinning) drug warfarin.

  - There is conflicting evidence about whether glucosamine might have negative effects on glucose metabolism, especially in people with insulin resistance or impaired glucose tolerance.

  - Although recent animal studies conducted by the U.S. Food and Drug Administration show that high doses of glucosamine hydrochloride may promote cartilage regeneration and repair, this dose was also found to cause severe kidney problems in the rats.

Dimethyl Sulfoxide (DMSO) and Methylsulfonylmethane (MSM)

DMSO and MSM are two chemically related dietary supplements that have been used for arthritic conditions. A 2009 meta-analysis of a small number of studies looked at topical (applied to skin) DMSO and oral (taken by mouth) MSM as potential products for OA of the knee. There was no evidence of significant reductions in pain compared to placebo. Although there is limited safety data available, some side effects from topical DMSO have been reported, including upset stomach, skin irritation, and garlic taste, breath, and body odor. Only minor side effects are associated with MSM including allergy, upset stomach, and skin rashes.

S-Adenosyl-L-methionine (SAMe)

SAMe is a molecule that is naturally produced in the body and is often taken as a dietary supplement. A 2009 systematic review concluded that there was not enough evidence to support the use of SAMe for OA of the knee or hip. The reviewers did indicate that small improvements in pain and function were seen in some but not all studies. SAMe is generally considered safe. Common side effects include gastrointestinal problems, dry mouth, headache, sweating, dizziness, and nervousness.

Herbal Remedies

Although some results suggest that a few herbs may be beneficial for OA symptoms, the overall evidence is weak. In addition, not all herbs have been studied or prepared in a consistent way, and conclusions among reviews of the literature provide conflicting interpretations. There is also a general lack of safety data available for many herbal medicines.

Be aware that **an herbal supplement may contain dozens of compounds** and that its composition may not be well characterized or fully understood. Researchers are studying many of these products in an effort to identify active ingredients and understand their effects in the body. It is also important to keep in mind that although many dietary supplements (and some prescription drugs) come from natural sources, **"natural does not always mean safe."**

Mind and Body Practices

Mind and body practices—such as acupuncture, massage, tai chi, qi gong, and yoga—have been studied for OA. Results from clinical trials suggest that acupuncture may be beneficial for some OA symptoms. There are a limited number of quality studies for tai chi, qi gong, and yoga.

In 2012, the American College of Rheumatology issued recommendations for using drug and non-drug approaches for OA of the hand, hip, and knee. The guidelines conditionally (cautiously) recommend tai chi, along with other non-drug approaches such as self-management programs and walking aids, for managing knee OA. Acupuncture is also conditionally recommended for those who have chronic moderate-to-severe knee pain and are candidates for total knee replacement but can't or won't undergo the procedure. It is important to talk with your health care provider before beginning any new conventional or complementary health approach.

Acupuncture has been studied in clinical trials for pain in a number of conditions including OA. Studies focused primarily on OA of the knee. There is also evidence that acupuncture may help to lessen pain and improve function in other joints such as the hip.

- A 2009 NCCIH-funded literature review examined acupuncture for chronic back pain, OA, and headache. The authors concluded that acupuncture typically appears better than standard, or conventional, care or wait list controls for people with OA but may not provide additional benefit for people with OA who are receiving advice and exercise.

- In a 2008 NCCIH-funded systematic review of randomized controlled trials of acupuncture for OA of the knee, researchers examined 10 trials involving 1,456 participants. The authors concluded that these studies provide evidence that acupuncture is effective for pain and improving mobility in people with OA.

- Authors of a 2007 meta-analysis suggested that although some large, high-quality trials have shown that acupuncture may be effective for osteoarthritis of the knee, differences in the design, size, and protocol of the studies make it hard to draw any definite conclusions from the body of research. These authors concluded that it is too soon to recommend acupuncture as a routine part of care for patients with osteoarthritis.

- Authors of a 2010 systematic review looked at the effects of acupuncture in people with OA in peripheral joints of the body— knee, hip, or hand. The reviewers examined 16 trials involving 3,498 people and found that although acupuncture, when compared to a sham treatment, showed statistically significant, short-term improvements in osteoarthritis pain, the benefits were small and not clinically relevant (useful in a clinical setting). In contrast, the reviewers also found that acupuncture, when compared to a waiting list control, showed statistically significant and clinically relevant benefits in people with peripheral joint osteoarthritis. The researchers suggest the beneficial effects in the latter studies were due in part to expectation or placebo effects.

There are few complications associated with acupuncture, but adverse effects such as minor bruising or bleeding can occur; infections can result from the use of nonsterile needles or poor technique from an inexperienced practitioner.

Massage therapy has been studied for pain; however, there are very few studies that look at massage therapy and OA specifically. The results of one clinical trial, which did examine massage on adults with OA of the knee, indicated that massage may reduce pain and improve function.

Tai chi is an ancient meditative practice that originated in China as a martial art.

- A small, 2009 NCCIH-funded randomized controlled trial showed that participants who practiced tai chi had improvement in pain and physical function as well as in depression and health-related quality of life when compared to participants enrolled in an education and stretching program. Although previous tai chi studies have shown an improvement in balance, this study did not find a statistically significant improvement in participants' balance tests.

- Tai chi is considered to be a relatively safe practice.

Qi gong is a group of traditional Chinese exercises, breathing techniques, and meditation practices. There are studies on qi gong and pain, but there is very little research specifically on qi gong and OA.

- A randomized controlled trial funded by NCCIH studied the effects of practitioner-led qi gong on OA of the knee. The results from this study were inconclusive.

- Qi gong is generally considered to be a safe practice.

Yoga—while numerous studies have been published on yoga for anxiety and stress, little research has been done on yoga and OA. Yoga is generally low-impact and safe for healthy people when practiced appropriately under the guidance of a well-trained instructor; however, overstretching can occur, particularly in diseased joints and ligaments. If you have a medical condition, consult your health care provider before starting yoga.

Mind and Body Practices and Placebo

Researching mind and body interventions for pain management presents many challenges. One such challenge is the role of placebo effects—a term which describes improvements that are not related specifically to the treatment being studied. Placebo effects can be quite large in pain studies. A "placebo control" pill (which is identical in appearance but contains no active ingredient) can be useful in separating product-related effects from placebo effects when researching a dietary supplement. However, it is much more difficult—and often impossible—to conceal the nature of mind and body practices from study participants because they involve activities in which the person must engage. They also often involve interactions with providers that are known to activate placebo effects (e.g., touch). In studies of mind and body practices for pain, investigators must give very careful attention to study design and steps to ensure that measurements of improvement are as objective as possible.

Other Complementary Health Approaches for Osteoarthritis

Homeopathy. A 2006 literature review concluded that there is little evidence to support homeopathy as an effective approach for OA symptoms, particularly pain. There has been no recent research studying the effects of homeopathy on OA.

Magnets. The available scientific evidence does not support the use of magnets for pain relief.

If You Are Considering Complementary Health Approaches for Osteoarthritis

- Do not replace conventional treatments for osteoarthritis with unproven products or practices. Do not use complementary health approaches to postpone seeing your health care provider about any health problem.

- Keep in mind that dietary supplements may interact with medications or other supplements and may contain ingredients not listed on the label. Your health care provider can advise you.

- Women who are pregnant or nursing should consult their health care provider before using any complementary health approach.

- Tell all your health care providers about any complementary health approaches you use. Give them a full picture of what you do to manage your health. This will help ensure coordinated and safe care.

Chapter 40

Asthma and Allergies and CAM

Asthma is a chronic lung disease that affects people of all ages. It causes episodes of wheezing, coughing, shortness of breath, and chest tightness. Although there is no cure, most people with asthma are able to manage the disease with medications and behavioral changes.

Researchers also are studying various complementary health approaches for asthma relief. This chapter provides basic information about asthma, summarizes scientific research on the effectiveness and safety of complementary health approaches for asthma.

Key Points

- Conventional medical treatments are very effective for managing asthma symptoms. See your health care provider to discuss a comprehensive medical treatment plan for your asthma.
- There is not enough evidence to support the use of any complementary health approaches for the relief of asthma.

About Asthma

In asthma, the airways that carry air into and out of the lungs become irritated, inflamed, and narrowed. The muscles around the

This chapter includes excerpts from "Asthma and Complementary Health Approaches," National Center for Complementary and Integrative Health (NCCIH), April 2013; and text from "5 Things To Know About Complementary Health Approaches for Seasonal Allergy Relief," National Center for Complementary and Integrative Health (NCCIH), January 30, 2015.

airways tighten and the cells in the airway produce more mucus than normal. This makes it difficult for air to flow into and out of the lungs and causes wheezing, shortness of breath, and other symptoms.

More than 24 million people in the United States have been diagnosed with asthma, including approximately 7 million children. It is not known why some people develop asthma, but the tendency runs in families and the chance of having the disease appears to be increasing, especially among children.

Conventional treatment for asthma focuses on preventing attacks and relieving symptoms once an attack is underway. Prevention may include avoiding "asthma triggers" (the things that can set off or worsen symptoms) or taking medicine every day to prevent symptoms.

Once an asthma attack is underway, quick-relief medications may be used to relax muscles around the airways and open up airways so air can flow through them. Prevention techniques are generally preferred over quick-relief medications.

Complementary Health Approaches for Asthma

Most people are able to control their asthma with conventional therapies and by avoiding the substances that can set off asthma attacks. Even so, some people turn to complementary health approaches in their efforts to relieve symptoms. According to the 2002 National Health Interview Survey (NHIS), which included a comprehensive survey on the use of complementary health approaches by Americans, asthma ranked 13th as a condition prompting use of complementary health approaches by adults; 1.1 percent of respondents (an estimated 788,000 adults) said they had used a complementary approach for asthma in the past year. In the 2007 NHIS survey, which included adults and children, asthma ranked eighth among conditions prompting use of complementary health approaches by children, but did not appear in a similar ranking for adults.

What the Science Says about Complementary Health Approaches and Asthma

According to reviewers who have assessed the research, there is not enough evidence to support the use of any complementary health approaches for the relief of asthma.

- Several studies have looked at actual or true **acupuncture**— stimulation of specific points on the body with thin metal needles—for asthma. Although a few studies showed some reduction in medication use and improvements in symptoms and quality of life, the majority showed no difference between actual acupuncture and simulated or sham acupuncture on asthma symptoms. At this point, there is little evidence that acupuncture is an effective treatment for asthma.

- There has been renewed patient interest in **breathing exercises** or **retraining** to reduce hyperventilation, regulate breathing, and achieve a better balance of carbon dioxide and oxygen in the blood. A review of seven randomized controlled trials found a trend toward improvement in symptoms with breathing techniques but not enough evidence for firm conclusions.

- A 2011 study examined the placebo response in patients with chronic asthma and found that patients receiving a placebo (placebo inhaler and simulated acupuncture) reported significant improvement in symptoms such as chest tightness and perception of difficulty breathing. However, lung function did not improve in these patients. This is an important distinction because although the patients felt better, their risk for becoming very sick from untreated asthma was not lessened.

If You Are Considering Complementary Health Approaches for Asthma

- Conventional medical treatments are very effective for managing asthma symptoms. See your health care provider to discuss a comprehensive medical treatment plan for your asthma.

- Do not use any complementary approaches to postpone seeing your health care provider about asthma-like symptoms or any health problem.

- Do not replace conventional treatments for asthma with unproven products or practices.

- Keep in mind that dietary supplements can act in the same way as drugs. They can cause health problems if not used correctly or if used in large amounts, and some may interact with medications you take. Your health care provider can advise you. If you are pregnant or nursing a child, or if you are considering giving a child a dietary supplement, it is especially important to consult your (or your child's) health care provider.

- Tell all your health care providers about any complementary health approaches you use. Give them a full picture of what you

do to manage your health. This will help ensure coordinated and safe care.

5 Things To Know about Complementary Health Approaches for Seasonal Allergy Relief

Seasonal allergies, also called "hay fever," are triggered each spring, summer, and fall when trees, weeds, and grasses release pollen into the air. When the pollen ends up in your nose and throat, it can bring on sneezing, runny nose, coughing, and itchy eyes and throat. Pollen counts tend to be the highest early in the morning on warm, dry, breezy days and the lowest during chilly, wet periods. People manage seasonal allergies by taking medication, avoiding exposure to the substances that trigger their allergic reactions, or having a series of "allergy shots" (a form of immunotherapy).

People also try various complementary approaches to manage their allergies. According to the 2007 National Health Interview Survey, "respiratory allergy" is among the 15 conditions for which children in the United States most often use complementary approaches. If you are considering any complementary health approach for the relief of seasonal allergy symptoms, here are some things you need to know.

1. **Nasal saline irrigation.** There is reasonably good evidence that saline nasal irrigation (putting salt water into one nostril and draining it out the other) can be useful for modest improvement of allergy symptoms. Nasal irrigation is generally safe; however, neti pots and other rinsing devices must be used and cleaned properly. According to the U.S. Food and Drug Administration, tap water that is not filtered, treated, or processed in specific ways is not safe for use as a nasal rinse.

2. **Butterbur extract.** There are hints that the herb butterbur may decrease the symptoms associated with nasal allergies. However, there are concerns about its safety.

3. **Honey.** Only a few studies have looked at the effects of honey on seasonal allergy symptoms, and there is no convincing scientific evidence that honey provides symptom relief. Eating honey is generally safe; however, children under 1 year of age should not eat honey. People who are allergic to pollen or bee stings may also be allergic to honey.

4. **Acupuncture.** Only a few small studies have been conducted on acupuncture for relief of seasonal allergy symptoms, and

the limited scientific evidence currently available has not shown acupuncture to be beneficial in treating seasonal allergies.

5. **Talk to your health care provider.** If you suffer from seasonal allergies and are considering a complementary health approach, talk to your health care provider about the best ways to manage your symptoms. You may find that when the pollen count is high, staying indoors, wearing a mask, or rinsing off when you come inside can help.

Chapter 41

Cancer and CAM

People with cancer want to do everything they can to combat the disease, manage its symptoms, and cope with the side effects of treatment. Many turn to complementary health approaches, including natural products, such as herbs (botanicals) and other dietary supplements, and mind and body practices, such as acupuncture, massage, and yoga.

This section was produced through a collaboration between the National Center for Complementary and Integrative Health (NCCIH) and the National Cancer Institute (NCI). It provides an introductory overview of complementary health approaches that have been studied for cancer prevention, treatment of the disease, or symptom management, including what the science says about their effectiveness and any concerns that have been raised about their safety.

Key Facts

- **Symptom management.** A substantial amount of scientific evidence suggests that some complementary health approaches may help to manage some symptoms of cancer and side effects of treatment. For other complementary approaches, the evidence is more limited.

Text in this chapter is excerpted from "Cancer and Complementary Health Approaches," National Center for Complementary and Integrative Health (NCCIH), July 2014.

- **Disease treatment.** At present, there is no convincing evidence that any complementary health approach is effective in curing cancer or causing it to go into remission.

- **Cancer prevention.** A 2012 study indicated that taking a multivitamin/mineral supplement may slightly reduce the risk of cancer in older men. No other complementary health approach has been shown to be helpful in preventing cancer.

Keep in Mind

- **Unproven products or practices should not be used to replace or delay conventional medical treatment for cancer.**

- Some complementary approaches can interfere with standard cancer treatments or have special risks for people who've been diagnosed with cancer. **Before using any complementary health approach, people who've been diagnosed with cancer should talk with their health care providers to make sure that all aspects of their care work together.**

- Tell all your health care providers about any complementary health approaches you use. Give them a full picture of what you do to manage your health. This will help ensure coordinated and safe care.

About Cancer

Cancer is a term for diseases in which abnormal cells divide without control. Cancer cells can invade nearby tissues and spread to other parts of the body through the bloodstream and the lymph system. Although cancer is the second leading cause of death in the United States, improvements in screening, detection, treatment, and care have increased the number of cancer survivors, and experts expect the number of survivors to continue to increase in the coming years.

About Complementary Health Approaches

Complementary health approaches are a group of diverse medical and health care systems, practices, and products whose origins come from outside of mainstream medicine. They include such products and practices as herbal supplements, other dietary supplements, meditation, spinal manipulation, and acupuncture.

The same careful scientific evaluation that is used to assess conventional therapies should be used to evaluate complementary approaches. Some complementary approaches are beginning to find a place in cancer treatment—not as cures, but as additions to treatment plans that may help patients cope with disease symptoms and side effects of treatment and improve their quality of life.

Use of Complementary Health Approaches for Cancer

Many people who've been diagnosed with cancer use complementary health approaches.

- According to the 2007 National Health Interview Survey (NHIS), which included a comprehensive survey on the use of complementary health approaches by Americans, 65 percent of respondents who had ever been diagnosed with cancer had used complementary approaches, as compared to 53 percent of other respondents. Those who had been diagnosed with cancer were more likely than others to have used complementary approaches for general wellness, immune enhancement, and pain management.

- Other surveys have also found that use of complementary health approaches is common among people who've been diagnosed with cancer, although estimates of use vary widely. Some data indicate that the likelihood of using complementary approaches varies with the type of cancer and with factors such as sex, age, and ethnicity. The results of surveys from 18 countries show that use of complementary approaches by people who had been diagnosed with cancer was more common in North America than in Australia/New Zealand or Europe and that use had increased since the 1970s and especially since 2000.

- Surveys have also shown that many people with cancer don't tell their health care providers about their use of complementary health approaches. In the NHIS, survey respondents who had been diagnosed with cancer told their health care providers about 15 percent of their herb use and 23 percent of their total use of complementary approaches. In other studies, between 32 and 69 percent of cancer patients and survivors who used dietary supplements or other complementary approaches reported that they discussed these approaches with their physicians. The differences in the reported percentages may reflect differences in the definitions of complementary approaches used in the studies, as well as differences in the communication practices of different groups of patients.

What the Science Says about the Safety and Side Effects of Complementary Health Approaches for Cancer

- **Delaying conventional cancer treatment can decrease the chances of remission or cure.** Don't use unproven products or practices to postpone or replace conventional medical treatment for cancer.

- Some complementary health approaches may interfere with cancer treatments or be unsafe for cancer patients. For example, the herb St. John's wort, which is sometimes used for depression, can make some cancer drugs less effective.

- Other complementary approaches may be harmful if used inappropriately. For example, to make massage therapy safe for people with cancer, it may be necessary to avoid massaging places on the body that are directly affected by the disease or its treatment (for example, areas where the skin is sensitive following radiation therapy).

- People who've been diagnosed with cancer should consult the health care providers who are treating them for cancer before using any complementary health approach for any purpose— whether or not it's cancer-related.

What the Science Says about the Effectiveness of Complementary Health Approaches for Cancer

No complementary health product or practice has been proven to cure cancer. Some complementary approaches may help people manage cancer symptoms or treatment side effects and improve their quality of life.

Incorporating Complementary Health Approaches into Cancer Care

In 2009, the Society for Integrative Oncology issued evidence-based clinical practice guidelines for health care providers to consider when incorporating complementary health approaches in the care of cancer patients. The guidelines point out that, when used in addition to conventional therapies, some of these approaches help to control symptoms and enhance patients' well-being. The guidelines warn, however, that unproven methods shouldn't be used in place of conventional treatment because delayed treatment of cancer reduces the likelihood of a remission or cure.

A comprehensive summary of research on complementary health approaches for cancer is beyond the scope of this chapter. The following sections provide an overview of the research status of some commonly used complementary approaches, highlighting results from a few reviews and studies focusing on preventing and treating the disease, as well as managing cancer symptoms and treatment side effects.

Talking with Your Health Care Providers about Complementary Approaches and Cancer

The National Institutes of Health (NIH) has resources that can help you talk with your health care providers about complementary approaches and cancer.

- NCI's Office of Cancer Complementary and Alternative Medicine has a workbook to help cancer patients and their health care providers talk about and keep track of complementary approaches that patients are using.
- NCCIH has tips to help both patients and health care providers discuss complementary health approaches.

Complementary Health Approaches for Cancer Symptoms and Treatment Side Effects

Some complementary health approaches, such as acupuncture, massage therapy, mindfulness-based stress reduction, and yoga, may help people manage cancer symptoms or the side effects of treatment. However, some approaches may interfere with conventional cancer treatment or have other risks. **People who have been diagnosed with cancer should consult their health care providers before using any complementary health approach.**

- There is substantial evidence that **acupuncture** can help to manage treatment-related nausea and vomiting in cancer patients. There isn't enough evidence to judge whether acupuncture relieves cancer pain or other symptoms such as treatment-related hot flashes. Complications from acupuncture are rare, as long as the acupuncturist uses sterile needles and proper procedures. Chemotherapy and radiation therapy weaken the body's immune system, so it's especially important for acupuncturists to follow strict clean-needle procedures when treating cancer patients.

- Recent studies suggest that the herb **ginger** may help to control nausea related to cancer chemotherapy when used in addition to conventional anti-nausea medication.

- Studies suggest that **massage therapy** may help to relieve symptoms experienced by people with cancer, such as pain, nausea, anxiety, and depression. However, investigators haven't reached any conclusions about the effects of massage therapy because of the limited amount of rigorous research in this field. People with cancer should consult their health care providers before having massage therapy to find out if any special precautions are needed. The massage therapist shouldn't use deep or intense pressure without the health care providers' approval and may need to avoid certain sites, such as areas directly over a tumor or those where the skin is sensitive following radiation therapy.

- There is evidence that **mindfulness-based stress reduction,** a type of meditation training, can help cancer patients relieve anxiety, stress, fatigue, and general mood and sleep disturbances, thus improving their quality of life. Most participants in mindfulness studies have been patients with early-stage cancer, primarily breast cancer, so the evidence favoring mindfulness training is strongest for this group of patients.

- Preliminary evidence indicates that **yoga** may help to improve anxiety, depression, distress, and stress in people with cancer. It also may help to lessen fatigue in breast cancer patients and survivors. However, only a small number of yoga studies in cancer patients have been completed, and some of the research hasn't been of the highest quality. Because yoga involves physical activities, it's important for people with cancer to talk with their health care providers in advance to find out whether any aspects of yoga might be unsafe for them.

- Various studies suggest possible benefits of **hypnosis, relaxation therapies,** and **biofeedback** to help patients manage cancer symptoms and treatment side effects.

- A 2008 review of the research literature on **herbal supplements** and cancer concluded that although several herbs have shown promise for managing side effects and symptoms such as nausea and vomiting, pain, fatigue, and insomnia, *the scientific evidence is limited,* and many clinical trials haven't been well designed. Use of herbs for managing symptoms also raises concerns about potential negative interactions with conventional cancer treatments.

Coping with Cancer

People who have cancer, or who've been treated for cancer, may have physical or emotional difficulties as a result of the disease or its treatment. Many conventional approaches can help people cope with these problems. For example, counseling may help people who are distressed about being diagnosed with cancer, medicines can control nausea related to chemotherapy, and exercise may help decrease treatment-related fatigue. Some people find that complementary approaches also help them cope with cancer and improve their quality of life. In addition, using complementary approaches can help people feel they are playing an active part in their own care. If you have cancer or if you've been treated for cancer, be sure to tell your health care providers about all approaches—both conventional and complementary—that you're using. Your health care providers need this information so they can make sure that all aspects of your care work well together.

Complementary Health Approaches for Cancer Treatment

This section discusses complementary health approaches to directly treat cancer (that is, to try to cure the disease or cause a remission).

No complementary approach has cured cancer or caused it to go into remission. Some products or practices that have been advocated for cancer treatment may interfere with conventional cancer treatments or have other risks. **People who've been diagnosed with cancer should consult their health care providers before using any complementary health approach.**

- Studies on whether **herbal supplements** or substances derived from them might be of value in cancer treatment are in their early stages, and *scientific evidence is limited.* Herbal supplements may have side effects, and some may interact in harmful ways with drugs, including drugs used in cancer treatment.

- The effects of taking **vitamin and mineral supplements,** including **antioxidant supplements,** during cancer treatment are *uncertain*. NCI advises cancer patients to talk to their health care providers before taking any supplements.

- A 2010 NCCIH-supported trial of a standardized **shark cartilage** extract, taken in addition to chemotherapy and radiation therapy, *showed no benefit* in patients with advanced lung cancer. An earlier, smaller study in patients with advanced breast or colorectal cancers also showed no benefit from the addition of shark cartilage to conventional treatment.

- A 2011 systematic review of research on **laetrile** found *no evidence that it's effective* as a cancer treatment. Laetrile can be toxic, especially if taken orally, because it contains cyanide.

Beware of Cancer Treatment Frauds

The U.S. Food and Drug Administration (FDA) and the Federal Trade Commission (FTC) have warned the public to be aware of fraudulent cancer treatments. Cancer treatment frauds aren't new, but in recent years it has become easier for the people who market them to reach the public using the Internet.

Some fraudulent cancer treatments are harmful by themselves, and others can be indirectly harmful because people may delay seeking medical care while they try them, or because the fraudulent product interferes with the effectiveness of proven cancer treatments.

The people who sell fraudulent cancer treatments often market them with claims such as "scientific breakthrough," "miraculous cure," "secret ingredient," "ancient remedy," "treats all forms of cancer," or "shrinks malignant tumors." The advertisements may include personal stories from people who've taken the product, but such stories—whether or not they're real—aren't reliable evidence that a product is effective. Also, a money-back guarantee isn't proof that a product works.

If you're considering using any anticancer product that you've seen in an advertisement, talk to your health care provider first.

Complementary Health Approaches for Cancer Prevention

A large 2012 clinical trial has shown that taking a multivitamin/mineral supplement may slightly reduce the risk of cancer in older men. No other complementary health approach has been shown to be helpful in preventing cancer, and some have been linked with increased health risks.

Vitamin and Mineral Supplements. The results of a study of older men completed in 2012 indicate that taking a multivitamin/mineral supplement slightly reduces the risk of cancer. In this study, which was part of the Physicians' Health Study II (a complex trial that tested several types of supplements), more than 14,000 male U.S. physicians were randomly assigned to take a multivitamin/mineral supplement or a placebo (an identical-appearing product that did not contain vitamins and minerals) for 11 years. Those who took the supplement had 8 percent fewer total cancers than those who took the placebo.

Other studies of vitamins and minerals—most of which evaluated supplements containing only one or a few nutrients—haven't found protective effects against cancer. Some of these studies identified possible risks of supplementing with high doses of certain vitamins or related substances. Examples of research results include the following:

- In another part of the Physicians' Health Study II (not the part described above), supplementing with relatively high doses of either vitamin E or vitamin C did not reduce the risks of prostate cancer or total cancer in men aged 50 or older. Men taking vitamin E had an *increased* risk of hemorrhagic stroke (a type of stroke caused by bleeding in the brain).

- A 2010 meta-analysis of 22 clinical trials found no evidence that antioxidant supplements (vitamins A, C, and E; beta-carotene; and selenium) help to prevent cancer.

- Two large-scale studies found evidence that supplements containing beta-carotene *increased* the risk of lung cancer among smokers.

- The Selenium and Vitamin E Cancer Prevention Trial (SELECT), funded by NCI, NCCIH, and other agencies at NIH, showed that selenium and vitamin E supplements, taken either alone or together, did not prevent prostate cancer. It also showed that vitamin E supplements, taken alone, *increased* the risk of prostate cancer in healthy men. There was no increase in prostate cancer risk when vitamin E and selenium were taken together. The doses of selenium and vitamin E used in this study were much higher than those typically included in multivitamin/mineral supplements.

- Although substantial evidence suggests that calcium may help protect against colorectal cancer, the evidence of potential benefit from calcium in supplement form is limited and inconsistent. Therefore, NCI doesn't recommend the use of calcium supplements to reduce the risk of colorectal cancer.

Other Natural Products. A 2009 systematic review of 51 studies with more than 1.6 million participants found "insufficient and conflicting" evidence regarding an association between consuming **green tea** and cancer prevention. Several other natural products, including *Ginkgo biloba,* **isoflavones, noni, pomegranate,** and **grape seed extract,** have been investigated for possible cancer-preventive effects, but the evidence on these substances is too limited for any conclusions to be reached.

Do You Want To Learn More about Cancer Prevention?

People can reduce their risk of cancer in many ways. They include avoiding exposure to agents that cause cancer (such as cigarette smoke), having tests (such as colonoscopies) that find precancerous conditions early, and, for some people who are at high risk, taking medicines to reduce cancer risk (chemoprevention).

If You Have Been Diagnosed with Cancer and Are Considering a Complementary Health Approach

- Cancer patients need to make informed decisions about complementary health approaches. NCCIH and NCI have written a brochure that can help: *Thinking About Complementary and Alternative Medicine: A Guide for People With Cancer.*

- Gather information about the complementary health product or practice that interests you, and then discuss it with your health care providers. If you've been diagnosed with cancer, it's especially important to talk with your health care providers before

448

you start using any new complementary health approach. If you're already using a complementary approach, tell your health care providers about it, even if your reason for using it has nothing to do with cancer. Some approaches may interfere with standard cancer treatment or may be harmful when used along with standard treatment. Examples of questions to ask include:

- What is known about the benefits and risks of this product or practice? Do the benefits outweigh the risks?

- What are the potential side effects?

- Will this approach interfere with conventional treatment?

- Can you refer me to a practitioner?

- Do not use any health product or practice that has not been proven safe and effective to replace conventional cancer care or as a reason to postpone seeing your health care provider about any health problem.

- Tell all your health care providers about any complementary health approaches you use. Give them a full picture of what you do to manage your health. This will help ensure coordinated and safe care.

Chapter 42

Chronic Pain and CAM

What's the Bottom Line?

Are complementary health approaches for chronic pain safe?

There's no simple answer to this question. Although many of the complementary approaches studied for chronic pain have good safety records, that doesn't mean that they're risk-free for everyone. Your age, health, special circumstances (such as pregnancy), and medicines or supplements that you take may affect the safety of complementary approaches.

Are any complementary health approaches for chronic pain effective?

The currently available evidence is not strong enough to allow definite conclusions to be reached about whether any complementary approach is effective for chronic pain. However, a growing body of scientific evidence suggests that several of these approaches, including spinal manipulation, acupuncture, massage, and yoga, may help to manage some painful conditions.

Text in this chapter is excerpted from "Chronic Pain," National Center for Complementary and Integrative Health (NCCIH), August 2015.

What Is Chronic Pain and Why Is It Important?

Chronic pain is pain that lasts a long time. It's a very common problem. Results from the 2012 National Health Interview Survey show that

- About 25.3 million U.S. adults (11.2 percent) had pain every day for the previous 3 months.

- Nearly 40 million adults (17.6 percent) had severe pain.

- Individuals with severe pain had worse health, used more health care, and had more disability than those with less severe pain.

Chronic pain becomes more common as people grow older, at least in part because health problems that can cause pain, such as osteoarthritis, become more common with advancing age. Not all people with chronic pain have a physician-diagnosed health problem, but among those who do, the most frequent conditions by far are low-back pain or osteoarthritis, according to a national survey. Other common diagnoses include rheumatoid arthritis, migraine, carpal tunnel syndrome, and fibromyalgia. The annual economic cost of chronic pain in the United States, including both treatment and lost productivity, has been estimated at nearly $635 billion.

Chronic pain may result from an underlying disease or health condition, an injury, medical treatment (such as surgery), inflammation, or a problem in the nervous system (in which case it is called "neuropathic pain"), or the cause may be unknown. Pain can affect quality of life and productivity, and it may be accompanied by difficulty in moving around, disturbed sleep, anxiety, depression, and other problems.

What the Science Says about Safety and Side Effects

Although many of the complementary approaches studied for chronic pain have good safety records, that doesn't mean that they're risk-free for everyone. Your age, health, special circumstances (such as pregnancy), and other treatments (such as medication) may affect the safety of complementary approaches. If you are considering or using a complementary approach for pain, check with your health care providers to make sure that it is safe for you and compatible with your conventional treatment.

Here are some safety considerations for specific approaches:

Spinal manipulation

Side effects from spinal manipulation—a technique performed by trained practitioners that involves using their hands or a device to apply a controlled force to a joint of the spine—can include physical discomfort in the parts of the body that were treated, temporary headaches, or tiredness. There have been rare reports of more serious problems.

Acupuncture

Acupuncture is generally considered safe when performed by an experienced, well-trained practitioner using sterile needles. Improperly performed acupuncture can cause serious side effects.

Yoga

Yoga, a mind and body practice that combines physical activity or postures, breathing exercises, and meditation, has been studied for pain conditions such as chronic low-back pain and arthritis. Overall, those who practice yoga have a low rate of side effects. However, injuries from yoga, some of them serious, have been reported. People with health conditions may need to modify or avoid some yoga poses to prevent side effects. If you have a health condition, you should talk with your health care provider before starting yoga, and inform your yoga instructor about your health issues.

Herbal Products

Some **herbal products** studied for painful conditions (in particular, thunder god vine *(Tripterygium wilfordii)*, which is sometimes used for rheumatoid arthritis) may have serious side effects. NCCIH's *Herbs at a Glance* fact sheets have information about the potential side effects and drug interactions of specific herbs.

Glucosamine and chondroitin

Studies in people have not found safety issues with the dietary supplements **glucosamine** or **chondroitin**. They also indicate that glucosamine or chondroitin may interact with the anticoagulant (blood-thinning) drug warfarin.

What the Science Says about Complementary Health Approaches for Chronic Pain

The scientific evidence suggests that some complementary health approaches may help people manage chronic pain. In most instances, though, the amount of evidence is too small to clearly show whether an approach is useful.

A comprehensive description of scientific research on all the complementary approaches that have been studied for chronic pain is beyond the scope of this chapter. This section highlights the research status of some approaches used for common kinds of pain.

Low-back pain

- A 2007 comprehensive evaluation of studies in people found fair evidence that *acupuncture* is helpful in chronic low-back pain. Based on this finding, clinical practice guidelines recommend considering acupuncture as one of several non-drug treatment options when patients with chronic low-back pain do not respond to self-care. A 2012 combined analysis of data from several studies also supports the conclusion that acupuncture is a reasonable option to consider. How acupuncture works to relieve pain is unclear. Current evidence suggests that many factors—like expectation and belief—that are unrelated to acupuncture needling may play important roles in the beneficial effects of acupuncture on pain.

- *Massage* may be helpful for chronic low-back pain.

- There is some evidence that *progressive relaxation* may help relieve low-back pain, but studies on this topic have not been of the highest quality.

- *Spinal manipulation* can provide relief from low-back pain and appears to work at least as well as other treatments.

- Studies have shown that *yoga* can be helpful for low-back pain.

- A 2006 systematic review of research on *herbal remedies* for low-back pain found preliminary evidence that short-term use of three herbs—devil's claw and white willow bark (taken by mouth) and cayenne (applied on the skin)—might be helpful for low-back pain, but it is not known whether these herbs are safe or effective when used for longer periods of time.

* Studies of *prolotherapy* (a treatment involving repeated injections of irritant solutions) for low-back pain have had inconsistent results.

Osteoarthritis

* A 2012 combined analysis of data from several studies indicated that *acupuncture* can be helpful and a reasonable option to consider for osteoarthritis pain. After that analysis was completed, a 2014 Australian study showed that both needle and laser acupuncture were modestly better at relieving knee pain from osteoarthritis than no treatment but not better than simulated (sham) laser acupuncture. These results are generally consistent with previous studies, which showed that acupuncture is consistently better than no treatment but not necessarily better than simulated acupuncture at relieving osteoarthritis pain.

* A small amount of research on *massage* and *tai chi* suggests that both practices might help to reduce osteoarthritis pain.

* Numerous natural products, including *glucosamine, chondroitin, dimethyl sulfoxide (DMSO), methylsulfonylmethane (MSM), S-adenosyl-L-methionine (SAMe),* and a variety of *herbs,* have been studied for osteoarthritis, but there is little conclusive evidence of benefit for symptoms.

Rheumatoid arthritis

* Research results suggest that some mind and body practices, such as *relaxation, mindfulness meditation, tai chi,* and *yoga,* may be beneficial additions to treatment plans, but some studies indicate that these practices may do more to improve other aspects of patients' health than to relieve pain.

* Omega-3 fatty acids of the types found in *fish oil* may have modest benefits in relieving symptoms in rheumatoid arthritis. No other dietary supplement has shown clear benefits for rheumatoid arthritis, but there is preliminary evidence for a few, particularly *gamma-linolenic acid* and the herb *thunder god vine*. However, serious safety concerns have been raised about thunder god vine.

Headache

- *Relaxation training* may help to relieve chronic headaches and prevent migraines.

- *Biofeedback* may be helpful for migraines and tension-type headaches.

- A 2012 combined analysis of data from several studies indicates that *acupuncture* can be helpful and a reasonable option to consider for headache pain. How acupuncture works to relieve pain is unclear. Current evidence suggests that many factors—like expectation and belief—that are unrelated to acupuncture needling may play important roles in the beneficial effects of acupuncture on pain.

- *Spinal manipulation* may help people suffering from chronic tension-type or cervicogenic (neck-related) headaches and may also be helpful in preventing migraines.

- Several dietary supplements, including *riboflavin, coenzyme Q10,* and the herbs *butterbur* and *feverfew,* have been studied for migraine, with some promising results in preliminary studies.

Neck pain

- *Acupuncture* hasn't been studied as extensively for neck pain as for some other conditions. A large randomized clinical trial in Germany found that people who received acupuncture for neck pain had better pain relief than those who didn't receive acupuncture. Several small studies have compared actual acupuncture with simulated acupuncture, but the amount of research is limited. No current guidelines recommend acupuncture for neck pain.

- There is some evidence that *spinal manipulation* or *mobilization* (movement imposed on joints and muscles) may help to relieve neck pain, but much of the research on these techniques has been of low quality.

Fibromyalgia

- It is uncertain whether *acupuncture* is helpful for fibromyalgia.

- Some evidence suggests that *tai chi* may be helpful for fibromyalgia pain and other symptoms, but the amount of research on tai chi has been small.

- Studies have found improvements in fibromyalgia symptoms from various *meditation* techniques, but much of the research on this topic has not been of the highest quality.

- There is insufficient evidence that any *natural products* can help to relieve fibromyalgia pain.

- Studies of *homeopathy* have not demonstrated that it is beneficial for fibromyalgia.

Irritable bowel syndrome

- Although no complementary health approach has definitely been shown to be helpful for irritable bowel syndrome, some research results for *hypnotherapy* and *probiotics* have been promising.

- A study of *mindfulness meditation* has indicated that it may help reduce the severity of irritable bowel syndrome in women.

- Studies on *peppermint oil* have suggested that it may be helpful, but the quality of much of the research is poor.

- Studies of *acupuncture* for irritable bowel syndrome have not found actual acupuncture to be more helpful than simulated acupuncture.

Other types of pain

- Various complementary approaches have also been studied for other types of chronic pain, such as **facial pain, nerve pain, chronic prostatitis/chronic pelvic pain syndrome, menstrual cramps, elbow pain, pain associated with endometriosis, carpal tunnel syndrome,** and **cancer pain.** There is promising evidence that some complementary approaches may be helpful for some of these types of pain, but the evidence is insufficient to clearly establish the effectiveness of any of the approaches.

Other complementary approaches

- It has been suggested that *vitamin D* may be helpful for chronic pain, but there has been only a small amount of research on this topic, and much of the research has been of poor quality.

- *Music* may help to relieve pain and decrease the need for pain-relieving drugs, but research indicates that its effects are small.

- There is a lack of high-quality research to definitively evaluate whether *Reiki* is of value for pain relief.

- Although *static magnets* are widely marketed for pain control, the evidence does not support their use.

Guidelines for the Treatment of Chronic Pain Conditions

National health professional organizations have issued guidelines for treating several chronic pain conditions. Some mention ways in which certain complementary health approaches can be incorporated into treatment plans. Others discourage the use of certain complementary approaches.

For example, the guideline for treating back pain issued by the American College of Physicians and the American Pain Society states that nondrug approaches should be considered in patients who do not improve with self-care. Some of the suggested nondrug approaches, such as exercise therapy and cognitive-behavioral therapy, are conventional; others, including acupuncture, massage therapy, spinal manipulation, and progressive relaxation, are complementary.

Another example is the guideline for treating osteoarthritis of the knee and hip issued by the American College of Rheumatology. For osteoarthritis of the knee, the guidelines mention tai chi as one of several nondrug approaches that might be helpful. The same guidelines, however, discourage using the dietary supplements glucosamine and chondroitin for osteoarthritis of the hip or knee.

If You Are Considering Complementary Health Approaches for Chronic Pain

- Do not use an unproven product or practice to replace conventional care or to postpone seeing a health care provider about chronic pain or any other health problem.

- Learn about the product or practice you are considering, especially the scientific evidence on its safety and whether it works.

- Talk with the health care providers you see for chronic pain. Tell them about the product or practice you are considering and ask any questions you may have. They may be able to advise you on its safety, use, and likely effectiveness.

- If you are considering a practitioner-provided complementary health practice such as spinal manipulation, massage, or acupuncture, ask a trusted source (such as your health care provider or a nearby hospital) to recommend a practitioner. Find out about the training and experience of any practitioner you are considering. Ask whether the practitioner has experience working with your pain condition.

- If you are considering dietary supplements, keep in mind that they can cause health problems if not used correctly, and some may interact with prescription or nonprescription medications or other dietary supplements you take. Your health care provider can advise you. If you are pregnant or nursing a child, or if you are considering giving a child a dietary supplement, it is especially important to consult your (or your child's) health care provider.

- Tell all your health care providers about any complementary or integrative health approaches you use. Give them a full picture of what you do to manage your health. This will help ensure coordinated and safe care.

Chapter 43

Cognitive Decline and CAM

Cognitive Functions, Dementia, and Alzheimer's Disease

Thinking, reasoning, and remembering are cognitive functions. Dementia is when those functions decrease much more significantly than what occurs with normal aging. In older people the most common cause of dementia is Alzheimer's disease. An incurable disease, it slowly impairs your memory and thinking skills and, eventually, the ability to care for yourself.

Bottom Line:

- Researchers are investigating a variety of complementary health approaches, as well as diets, for preventing or slowing the progression of dementia, including Alzheimer's disease. There is no strong evidence that any complementary health approach or diet can prevent cognitive impairment.

- Researchers are also looking at approaches to help reduce the behavioral and emotional symptoms of Alzheimer's disease.

This chapter includes excerpts from "Cognitive Function, Dementia, and Alzheimer's Disease," National Center for Complementary and Integrative Health (NCCIH), January 27, 2015; text from "Alzheimer's Disease at a Glance," National Center for Complementary and Integrative Health (NCCIH), November 2014; and text from "5 Things To Know About Complementary Health Practices for Cognitive Function, Dementia, and Alzheimer's Disease," National Center for Complementary and Integrative Health (NCCIH), January 30, 2015.

- For caregivers, taking a mindfulness meditation class may reduce stress more than just getting time off from providing care.

Safety:

- Don't use complementary health approaches as a reason to postpone seeing a health care provider about memory loss. Treatable conditions, such as depression, bad reactions to medications, or thyroid, liver, or kidney problems, can impair memory.

- Some complementary health approaches interact with medications and can have serious side effects. If you are considering replacing conventional medications with other approaches, talk to your health care provider.

Alzheimer's Disease at a Glance

Researchers have explored many complementary health approaches for preventing or slowing dementia, including Alzheimer's disease. Currently, there is no strong evidence that any complementary health approach or diet can prevent cognitive impairment.

What the Science Says

Following are some of the complementary health approaches that have been studied in recent years.

- **Fish Oil/Omega-3s.** Among the nutritional and dietary factors studied to prevent cognitive decline in older adults, the most consistent positive research findings are for omega-3 fatty acids, often measured as how much fish people ate. However, taking omega-3 supplements did not have any beneficial effects on the cognitive functioning of older people without dementia.

- **Ginkgo.** An NCCIH-funded study of the well-characterized ginkgo supplement EGb-761 found that it didn't lower the incidence of dementia, including Alzheimer's disease, in older adults. Further analysis of the same data showed that ginkgo did not slow cognitive decline, lower blood pressure, or reduce the incidence of hypertension. In this clinical trial, known as the Ginkgo Evaluation of Memory study, researchers recruited more than 3,000 volunteers age 75 and older who took 240 mg of ginkgo daily. Participants were followed for an average of approximately 6 years.

- **B-vitamins**. Results of short-term studies suggest that B-vitamin supplements do not help cognitive functioning in adults age 50 or older with or without dementia. The vitamins studied were B12, B6, and folic acid, taken alone or in combination.

- **Curcumin,** which comes from turmeric, has anti-inflammatory and antioxidant properties that might affect chemical processes in the brain associated with Alzheimer's disease, laboratory studies have suggested. However, the few clinical trials (studies done in people) that have looked at the effects of curcumin on Alzheimer's disease have not found a benefit.

- **Melatonin**. People with dementia can become agitated and have trouble sleeping. Supplements ofmelatonin, which is a naturally occurring hormone that helps regulate sleep, are being studied to see if they improve sleep in some people with dementia. However, in one study researchers noted that melatonin supplements may worsen mood in people with dementia.

- For caregivers, taking a mindfulness meditation class or a caregiver education class reduced stress more than just getting time off from providing care, a small, 2010 NCCIH-funded study showed.

Side Effects and Risks

Don't use complementary approaches as a reason to postpone seeing a health care provider about memory loss. Treatable conditions, such as depression, bad reactions to medications, or thyroid, liver, or kidney problems, can cause memory impairment.

Keep in mind that although many dietary supplements (and some prescription drugs) come from natural sources, "natural" does not always mean "safe."

Some dietary supplements have been found to interact with medications, whether prescription or over-the-counter. For example, the herbal supplement St. John's wort interacts with many medications, making them less effective. Your health care provider can advise you.

5 Things To Know about Complementary Health Practices for Cognitive Function, Dementia, and Alzheimer's Disease

Many people, particularly older individuals, worry about forgetfulness and whether it is the first sign of dementia or Alzheimer's disease. In fact, forgetfulness has many causes. It can also be a normal part of aging, or related to various treatable health issues or to emotional problems, such as stress, anxiety, or depression. The National Institute on Aging has a lot of information on the aging brain as well as cognitive function, dementia, and Alzheimer's disease. Although no treatment is proven to stop dementia or Alzheimer's disease, some conventional drugs may limit worsening of symptoms for a period of time in the early stages of the disease.

Many dietary supplements are marketed with claims that they enhance memory or improve brain function and health. To date, research has yielded no convincing evidence that any dietary supplement can reverse or slow the progression of dementia or Alzheimer's disease. Additional research on dietary supplements, as well as several mind and body practices such as music therapy and mental imagery, which have shown promise in basic research or preliminary clinical studies, is underway.

Here are 5 things to know about current research on complementary health approaches for cognitive function, dementia, and Alzheimer's disease.

1. **To date there is no convincing evidence from a large body of research that any dietary supplement can prevent worsening of cognitive impairment associated with dementia or Alzheimer's disease.** This includes studies of ginkgo, omega-3 fatty acids/fish oil, vitamins B and E, Asian ginseng, grape seed extract, and curcumin. Additional research on some of these supplements is underway.

2. **Preliminary studies of some mind and body practices such as music therapy suggest they may be helpful for some of the symptoms related to dementia, such as agitation and depression.** Several studies on music therapy in people with Alzheimer's disease have shown improvement in agitation, depression, and quality of life.

3. **Mindfulness-based stress reduction programs may be helpful in reducing stress among caregivers of patients with dementia.** To reduce caregiver stress, studies suggest that a mindfulness-based stress reduction program is more helpful for improving mental health than attending an education and support program or just taking time off from providing care.

4. **Don't use complementary health approaches as a reason to postpone seeing a health care provider about**

memory loss. Treatable conditions, such as depression, bad reactions to medications, or thyroid, liver, or kidney problems, can impair memory.

5. **Some complementary health approaches interact with medications and can have serious side effects.** If you are considering replacing conventional medications with other approaches, talk to your health care provider.

Chapter 44

Diabetes and CAM

Diabetes is a group of chronic diseases that affect metabolism—the way the body uses food for energy and growth. Millions of people have diabetes, which can lead to serious health problems if it is not managed well. Conventional medical treatments and following a healthy lifestyle, including watching your weight, can help you prevent, manage, and control many complications of diabetes. Researchers are studying several complementary health approaches, including dietary supplements, to see if they can help people manage type 2 diabetes—the focus of this chapter—or lower their risk of developing the disease.

Key Facts

A healthy diet, physical activity, and blood glucose testing are the basic tools for managing type 2 diabetes. Your health care providers will help you learn to manage your diabetes and track how well you are controlling it. It is very important **not** to replace proven conventional medical treatment for diabetes with an unproven health product or practice.

Text in this chapter is excerpted from "Diabetes and Dietary Supplements," National Center for Complementary and Integrative Health (NCCIH), November 2014.

Are dietary supplements for diabetes safe?

Some dietary supplements may have side effects, including interacting with your diabetes treatment or increasing your risk of kidney problems.

Are any dietary supplements for diabetes effective?

There is not enough scientific evidence to suggest that any dietary supplements can help prevent or manage type 2 diabetes.

Keep in Mind

Tell all your health care providers about any complementary health approaches you use. Give them a full picture of what you do to manage your health. This will help ensure coordinated and safe care.

About Diabetes

There are three different types of diabetes—type 1, type 2, and gestational. All three types of diabetes involve problems with how our bodies respond to the hormone insulin. Most of the food we eat is broken down into glucose, a type of sugar and the main fuel for our bodies. To use glucose, our bodies need insulin. People with type 1 diabetes produce little or no insulin. People with type 2 diabetes do not respond normally to the insulin their bodies make.

About 90 to 95 percent of people diagnosed with diabetes have type 2 diabetes. Only about 5 percent have type 1 diabetes, which is usually diagnosed in childhood or early adulthood and requires treatment with insulin. Gestational diabetes affects only pregnant women. It usually goes away after the birth, but it increases the risk of the mother developing diabetes later in life.

Side Effects and Risks

There are multiple case reports linking dietary supplement use to kidney disease, which is of particular concern because diabetes is the leading cause of chronic kidney disease and kidney failure in the United States. Supplement use should be monitored closely in patients who have or are at risk for kidney disease.

What the Science Says

Overall, there is not enough scientific evidence to show that any dietary supplement can help manage or prevent type 2 diabetes. This chapter addresses some of the many supplements studied for diabetes, with a focus on those that have undergone clinical trials (studies in people).

Alpha-Lipoic Acid

Alpha-lipoic acid is an antioxidant (a substance that may protect against cell damage). Studies have examined the effects of alpha-lipoic acid supplements on complications of diabetes.
For example:

- A 2011 clinical trial of 467 participants with type 2 diabetes found that supplements of 600 milligrams of alpha-lipoic acid daily did not prevent diabetic macular edema, an eye condition that causes blurred vision.

- Alpha-lipoic acid and vitamin E supplements taken separately or in combination did not improve cholesterol levels or the body's response to insulin in a 2011 clinical trial of 102 people with type 2 diabetes.

Safety

High doses of alpha-lipoic acid supplements can cause gastrointestinal problems.

Chromium

Found in many foods, chromium is an essential trace mineral. If you have too little chromium in your diet, your body can't use glucose efficiently. Studies, including a 2007 systematic review, have found few or no benefits of chromium supplements for controlling diabetes or reducing the risk of developing it. Many of the studies used for the review were small or not high quality.

Safety

Chromium supplements may cause stomach pain and bloating, and there have been a few reports of kidney damage, muscular problems, and skin reactions following large doses.

Herbal Supplements

There is no strong evidence that herbal supplements can help to control diabetes or its complications.

469

- Researchers have found some risks but no clear benefits of **cinnamon** for people with diabetes.

  - A 2012 systematic review of 10 randomized controlled trials did not support using cinnamon for type 1 or type 2 diabetes.

  - A trial of 59 people with type 2 diabetes found that a combination of cinnamon, calcium, and zinc didn't improve their blood pressure.

  - When researchers tested samples of the common spice cassia cinnamon for sale at grocery stores in Europe, they found many samples contained coumarin, a substance that may cause or worsen liver disease in people who are sensitive. Also, eating large amounts of cinnamon containing coumarin may be especially risky for people taking blood-thinning drugs; the interaction of coumarin and blood thinners can increase the likelihood of bleeding.

- Researchers are studying whether **Asian ginseng** and **American ginseng** may help control glucose levels. Currently, research reviews and clinical trials show that there is not enough evidence to support their use.

- Other herbal supplements studied for diabetes include **aloe vera, bitter melon, Chinese herbal medicines, fenugreek, garlic,** *Gymnema sylvestre,* **milk thistle, nettle, prickly pear cactus,** and **sweet potato.** None have been proven to be effective.

Safety

Information on the safety of herbal supplements for people with diabetes is generally inconclusive or unavailable. Interactions between herbs and conventional diabetes drugs have not been well studied and could be a health risk. For example, in some people cinnamon might worsen liver disease and interact with blood thinners.

Magnesium

Found in many foods, including whole grains, nuts, and green leafy vegetables, magnesium is essential to the body's ability to process glucose. Magnesium deficiency may increase the risk of developing diabetes.

- There is no evidence from clinical trials that magnesium helps to manage diabetes.

- A 2011 meta-analysis reviewed the results of 13 studies that looked at how much magnesium people got in their diets, either through supplements or food, and their risk of diabetes. The review found that people who had lower magnesium intake had a greater risk of developing diabetes.

- One of the studies in the 2011 research review mentioned above, a large 2007 clinical trial, found that people who ate more cereal fiber and magnesium-rich food had a lower risk of developing type 2 diabetes.

- People who had a diet rich in magnesium had a 15 percent reduced risk of developing type 2 diabetes, according to a 2007 meta-analysis of studies that looked at magnesium from foods or supplements.

Safety

No serious side effects were reported in studies where people with diabetes were given magnesium supplements for up to 16 weeks. However, the long-term safety of magnesium supplements for people with diabetes has not been established. Large doses of magnesium in supplements can cause diarrhea and abdominal cramping. Very large doses—more than 5,000 mg/day per day—can be deadly.

Omega-3s

Omega-3s supplements don't help people with diabetes control their blood sugar levels, a 2008 systematic review found. A 2012 study that combined a meta-analysis and a systematic review looked at the possible link between eating seafood or plants with omega-3s and the risk of developing type 2 diabetes. The study found little evidence that these dietary sources of omega-3s affected the risk of developing diabetes.

Safety

- Omega-3 supplements usually do not have negative side effects. When side effects do occur, they typically consist of minor gastrointestinal symptoms, such as belching, indigestion, or diarrhea.

- Omega-3 supplements may extend bleeding time (the time it takes for a cut to stop bleeding). People who take drugs that affect bleeding time, such as anticoagulants ("blood thinners") or nonsteroidal anti-inflammatory drugs (NSAIDs), should discuss the use of omega-3 fatty acid supplements with a health care provider.

Vitamins

- Studies (including a 2010 research review and 2009 clinical trial) have found no evidence that taking **vitamin C** supplements is helpful for diabetes.

- The research on diabetes and **vitamin D** and **calcium** supplements is not conclusive.

  - Supplementing with vitamin D combined with calcium appears to lower the risk of developing type 2 diabetes, according to a 2007 systematic review and meta-analysis.

  - In a 2008 clinical trial studying 33,951 post-menopausal women over 7 years, calcium plus vitamin D supplements did no better than a placebo at reducing the risk of developing diabetes.

  - The lower risk seen in some studies in people who consume more calcium may be because those individuals are also getting more magnesium, a 2012 meta-analysis reported.

Safety

Getting too much calcium may interfere with the body's ability to absorb iron and zinc. Also, calcium supplements can interact with certain medicines.

Other Supplements

- There is no strong evidence that supplements of the trace mineral **vanadium** improve blood sugar control in people with type 2 diabetes.

- The evidence is still preliminary on the effects on diabetes of supplements and foods rich in **polyphenols**—antioxidants found in fruits, grains, and vegetables, a 2010 research review concluded.

The Importance of Healthy Behaviors

Along with taking oral medications or insulin if needed, healthy eating, physical activity, and blood glucose testing are basic tools for managing type 2 diabetes. Managing your stress is also important, as stress can raise your blood glucose.

Diet

The National Diabetes Education Program (NDEP) recommends that you develop a diabetes meal plan with help from your health care providers. A healthy diet can help you feel better, lose weight if you need to, and lower your risk for heart disease, stroke, and other diabetes-related conditions.

Physical Activity

The NDEP recommends that people with diabetes set a goal to be more active most days of the week. Start slow by taking 10 minute walks, three times a day. Twice a week, work to increase your muscle strength. Your goal is 30 to 60 minutes of physical activity, such as brisk walking, on most days of the week, but always talk with your doctor before you start a new physical activity program.

Research has shown that being physically active can:

- Improve your blood sugar, blood pressure, and cholesterol levels;
- Improve your body's ability to use insulin;
- Strengthen your heart and bones;
- Keep your joints flexible; and
- Lower your risk of falling.

If You Have Diabetes and Are Thinking about Using a Dietary Supplement

- Talk to a health care provider before considering any dietary supplement for yourself, particularly if you are pregnant or nursing, or for a child. Many supplements have not been tested in pregnant women, nursing mothers, or children.

- Do not replace scientifically proven treatments for diabetes with unproven health products or practices. The consequences of not following your prescribed medical regimen for diabetes can be very serious.

- Keep in mind that dietary supplements may interact with medications or other dietary supplements and may contain ingredients not listed on the label.

- Tell all your health care providers about any complementary health approaches you use. Give them a full picture of what you do to manage your health. This will help ensure coordinated and safe care.

Chapter 45

Eye Conditions and CAM

Eye conditions that can lead to permanent visual impairment or blindness—including age-related macular degeneration (AMD), cataracts, diabetic retinopathy, and glaucoma—are serious public health problems. Researchers are working to find better ways to prevent and treat these conditions, including the use of dietary supplements.

Bottom Line:

Supplements containing antioxidants and zinc have been shown to reduce the likelihood that AMD will progress to the advanced stage in people who already have the intermediate stage of this disease. However, no dietary supplements have been shown to help prevent or treat cataracts, glaucoma, or diabetic retinopathy.

Safety

- Don't replace scientifically proven medical treatments for an eye condition with dietary supplements that are unproven. To preserve your vision, it is very important to follow the prescribed treatment for your eye condition.

- "Natural" does not necessarily mean "safe."

Text in this chapter begins with excerpts from "Eye Conditions," National Center for Complementary and Integrative Health (NCCIH), January 27, 2015. Text in this chapter beginning with "Eye Conditions at a Glance" is excerpted from "Eye Conditions at a Glance," National Center for Complementary and Integrative Health (NCCIH), July 2013.

Eye Conditions at a Glance

More than 19 million Americans have visual impairment—meaning impairment that cannot be corrected by eyeglasses or contact lenses—and about 700,000 are blind. AMD, cataract, diabetic retinopathy, and glaucoma are the main causes of visual impairment and blindness in older Americans.

What the Science Says

- **Age-Related Macular Degeneration (AMD).** AMD is a common eye condition among people age 50 and older. It is a leading cause of vision loss in older adults. It gradually destroys the macula, the part of the eye that provides sharp, central vision needed for seeing objects clearly. Treatment is only partially effective. The National Institutes of Health sponsored a major study called the Age-Related Eye Disease Study (AREDS), which looked at whether a dietary supplement could reduce the risk of developing AMD, and a second study, called Age-Related Eye Disease Study 2 (AREDS2), which tested changes to this dietary supplement.

  - AREDS showed that a dietary supplement containing high doses of vitamins C and E, beta carotene, and zinc may delay the development of advanced AMD in people who are at high risk because they either have (1) intermediate-stage AMD in one or both eyes or (2) advanced AMD in one eye but not the other.

  - AREDS2 investigated several modifications of the original AREDS supplement formula in people with AMD who were at risk for progressing to the advanced stage of the disease. The results of this study showed that

  - Adding omega-3 fatty acids (fish oil) did not improve the effectiveness of the supplement combination.

  - Reducing the amount of zinc or omitting beta-carotene from the supplements did not decrease their effectiveness.

  - Adding lutein and zeaxanthin (two carotenoids found in the eye) to the supplements improved their effectiveness in people who were not taking beta-carotene and those who consumed only small amounts of lutein and zeaxanthin in foods. The results also suggested that the supplements might be improved by substituting lutein and zeaxanthin for beta-carotene.

- **Cataracts.** A cataract occurs when the lens of the eye becomes clouded, causing blurring or discoloration of vision. If vision loss from a cataract becomes severe enough to interfere with normal activities, surgery to remove the lens and replace it with an artificial one may be needed. Studies on supplements of antioxidants (vitamins C and E and beta-carotene) indicate that these supplements do not prevent cataracts or slow their progression.

- **Diabetic Retinopathy.** In diabetic retinopathy, an eye disease that occurs as a complication of diabetes, the blood vessels of the retina become damaged. This can cause blurring of vision and vision loss. No dietary supplements have been shown to be helpful for diabetic retinopathy.

- **Glaucoma.** Glaucoma can damage the optic nerve, resulting in a loss of vision, starting with peripheral (side) vision. Early detection and treatment of glaucoma are important. Researchers have studied several dietary supplements for glaucoma, including *Ginkgo biloba,* coenzyme Q10, melatonin, resveratrol, and antioxidants. However, the amount of evidence is limited, and none of these supplements has been proven to be helpful.

Side Effects and Risks

- It's important to follow your eye care professional's instructions for treating eye conditions. Don't use unproven approaches to replace conventional medical treatments.

- Antioxidant and zinc supplements are recommended only for some people who have AMD, not all. For example, if you have early-stage AMD, they are not recommended for you. If you have AMD, ask your eye care professional whether taking supplements is advisable.

- Keep in mind that dietary supplements can cause health problems if not used correctly or if used in large amounts, and some may interact with medications you take.

Chapter 46

Fibromyalgia and CAM

Fibromyalgia is a disorder that causes widespread pain and fatigue. Researchers are evaluating a variety of complementary health approaches as possible additions to conventional treatment for fibromyalgia. This chapter provides basic information about fibromyalgia, and summarizes scientific research on complementary approaches for fibromyalgia.

Key Points

- Some mind and body practices, such as tai chi, qi gong, and massage therapy, may be helpful for fibromyalgia symptoms.

- There is not enough evidence to support the use of natural products, such as topical creams containing capsaicin or dietary supplements like S-adenosyl-L-methionine (SAMe), soy, or magnesium, for fibromyalgia.

- Be aware that some complementary approaches—particularly dietary supplements—may interact with conventional medical treatments. Although many dietary supplements (and some prescription drugs) come from natural sources, "natural" does not always mean "safe."

- Tell all your health care providers about any complementary health approaches you use. Give them a full picture of what you

Text in this chapter is excerpted from "Fibromyalgia and Complementary Health Approaches," National Center for Complementary and Integrative Health (NCCIH), August 2013.

do to manage your health. This will help ensure coordinated and safe care.

About Fibromyalgia

People with fibromyalgia have widespread pain and "tender points" on their bodies that hurt when slight pressure is put on them. People with fibromyalgia may also have other problems, such as:

- Trouble sleeping

- Morning stiffness

- Headaches

- Painful menstrual periods

- Tingling or numbness in hands or feet

- Problems with thinking and memory (sometimes called "fibro fog")

Fibromyalgia may also be associated with depression and anxiety.

The causes of fibromyalgia are unknown, but current research is looking at how different parts of the nervous system may contribute to fibromyalgia pain.

It is estimated that fibromyalgia affects 5 million American adults. Most people with fibromyalgia—between 80 and 90 percent—are women. However, men and children also can have the disorder.

A person with fibromyalgia may have other, coexisting chronic pain conditions. Such conditions may include chronic fatigue syndrome, endometriosis, interstitial cystitis (painful bladder syndrome), irritable bowel syndrome, temporomandibular joint dysfunction, and vulvodynia (chronic vulvar pain). It is not known whether these disorders share a common cause.

About Scientific Evidence on Complementary Health Approaches

Scientific evidence on complementary health approaches includes results from laboratory research as well as clinical trials (studies in people). It provides information on whether an approach is helpful and safe. Scientific journals publish study results, as well as review articles that evaluate the evidence as it accumulates; fact sheets from the National Center for Complementary and Integrative Health (NCCIH)—base information about research findings primarily on the most rigorous review articles, known as systematic reviews and meta-analyses.

What the Science Says

Much of the research on complementary health approaches for fibromyalgia is still preliminary, and evidence of effectiveness is limited. However, some studies have shown that practices such as tai chi, qi gong, and massage therapy may help relieve fibromyalgia symptoms.

- Research suggests that **tai chi**—a practice originating in China that involves moving the body slowly, gently, and with awareness—may provide a benefit to patients with fibromyalgia. A 2010 NCCIH-funded study compared the effects of a tai chi program with a wellness education and stretching program for managing fibromyalgia over a 12-week period. The researchers found that the participants in the tai chi group had significant improvements in symptoms such as pain, sleep quality, depression, and quality of life, and maintained these benefits for up to 24 weeks. A larger followup study of tai chi for fibromyalgia is underway. A 2009 review examined the use of **qi gong**—another Chinese practice involving physical movement, mental focus, and breathing techniques—for fibromyalgia. The reviewers found that qi gong may improve symptoms related to fibromyalgia.

- A 2009 study compared the effects of manual lymph drainage therapy (a **massage** technique used to move fluid away from areas where lymph vessels are blocked or damaged) and connective tissue massage in women with fibromyalgia. The researchers found that both types of massage helped to reduce pain, improve quality of life, and increase the pain pressure threshold. Manual lymph drainage therapy had a greater effect on the participants' overall health.

- A 2010 systematic review of **acupuncture** for fibromyalgia concluded that acupuncture had a small pain-relieving effect.

However, this effect might have been due to biases in the acupuncture studies.

- Studies have examined the use of **balneotherapy**—bath therapy for health purposes—for fibromyalgia. A 2009 systematic review found that balneotherapy may provide some benefit to patients with fibromyalgia, particularly for improving pain. However, because of variations in the study designs and small sample sizes, definite conclusions about the value of balneotherapy cannot be reached based on the current evidence.

- Researchers have looked at whether various types of **biofeedback** may be helpful for fibromyalgia. However, because studies have been small and because not all studies used rigorous methods (such as comparing true and simulated [sham] biofeedback), it is not yet possible to reach definite conclusions.

- A 2010 systematic review concluded that **homeopathy** has not been proven beneficial in relieving fibromyalgia symptoms.

- Small studies have examined various **natural products**—such as topical creams containing capsaicin (the substance that gives chili peppers their heat) or dietary supplements like S-adenosyl-L-methionine (SAMe) or soy—for fibromyalgia. A 2010 systematic review concluded that there is not enough evidence to determine whether these products provide a health benefit. Researchers are investigating whether low magnesium levels contribute to fibromyalgia and if magnesium supplements might help to reduce symptoms.

- An NCCIH-funded study examined the use of **Reiki**, a practice based on an Eastern idea that an energy supports the body's natural healing abilities, for fibromyalgia-related pain. The study showed no effect of Reiki on pain or any of the other outcomes measured in the study (physical and mental functioning, medication use, and visits to health care providers).

- Research evidence is insufficient to draw conclusions about the effectiveness of **chiropractic care**, **hypnosis**, or **magnet therapy** for fibromyalgia.

If You Are Considering Complementary Health Approaches for Fibromyalgia

- Be aware that some complementary health approaches—particularly dietary supplements—may interact with conventional medical treatments.

- If you are considering a practitioner-provided complementary health approach such as acupuncture, check with your insurer to see if the services will be covered, and ask a trusted source (like your fibromyalgia health care provider or a nearby hospital or medical school) to recommend a practitioner.

- Tell all your health care providers about any complementary health approaches you use. Give them a full picture of what you do to manage your health. This will help ensure coordinated and safe care.

Chapter 47

Headache and CAM

What's the Bottom Line?

What do we know about the usefulness of complementary approaches for headaches?

Mind and Body Approaches

- **Acupuncture** can be helpful for headaches. Much of its benefit may be due to nonspecific factors including expectation, beliefs, and placebo responses rather than specific effects of needling.
- Some studies indicate that **biofeedback**-based techniques may be helpful for tension headaches and migraines, but not all research results agree.
- For **massage, relaxation techniques, spinal manipulation,** and **tai chi**, the evidence is too limited or inconsistent to allow conclusions to be reached.

Text in this chapter is excerpted from "Headaches and Complementary Health Approaches: What You Need To Know," National Center for Complementary and Integrative Health (NCCIH), October 2014.

Dietary Supplements

- Guidelines from the American Academy of Neurology and the American Headache Society classify **butterbur** as effective; **feverfew, magnesium,** and **riboflavin** as probably effective; and **coenzyme Q10** as possibly effective for preventing migraines.

What do we know about the safety of complementary approaches for headaches?

In general, the complementary approaches discussed in this chapter have good safety records. However, that doesn't mean that they're risk-free for everyone. Your age, health, special circumstances (such as pregnancy), and medicines or supplements that you take may affect the safety of complementary approaches.

Some Basics about Headaches

Headaches are the most common form of pain. They're a major reason why people miss work or school or visit a health care provider. This chapter focuses on two types of headache: tension headaches and migraines. Researchers have studied complementary health approaches for both.

Tension Headaches and Migraines: What's the Difference?

- **Tension headaches**—the most common type of headache—are caused by tight muscles in the shoulders, neck, scalp, and jaw. They may be related to stress, depression, or anxiety and may occur more often in people who work too much, sleep too little, miss meals, or drink alcoholic beverages.

- **Migraine headaches**—which affect about 12 percent of Americans—involve moderate to severe throbbing pain, often on one side of the head. During a migraine, people are sensitive to light and sound and may feel nauseated. Some people have visual disturbances before a migraine—like seeing zigzag lines or flashing lights, or temporarily losing their vision. Anxiety, stress, lack of food or sleep, exposure to light, or hormonal changes (in women) can trigger migraines. Genes that control the activity of some brain cells may play a role in causing migraines.

What the Science Says about Complementary Health Approaches for Headache

Research has produced promising results for some complementary health approaches for tension headache or migraine. For other approaches, evidence of effectiveness is limited or conflicting.

Mind and Body Approaches

Mind and body approaches that have been studied for headache include acupuncture, biofeedback, massage, relaxation techniques, spinal manipulation, and tai chi.

Acupuncture

Acupuncture is a technique in which practitioners stimulate specific points on the body, most often by inserting thin needles through the skin.

There have been many studies of acupuncture for headache. The combined results from these studies indicate that acupuncture may help relieve headache pain, but that much of its benefit may be due to nonspecific effects including expectation, beliefs, and placebo responses rather than specific effects of needling.

Acupuncture is generally considered safe when performed by an experienced practitioner using sterile needles. Improperly performed acupuncture can cause potentially serious side effects.

Biofeedback

Biofeedback measures body functions and gives you information about them so that you can become more aware of those functions and learn to control them. For example, a biofeedback device may show you measurements of muscle tension. By watching how these measurements change, you can become more aware of when your muscles are tense and learn to relax them.

Several types of biofeedback have been studied for headaches, including techniques that help people learn to relax and more specific techniques that focus on changes that occur during headaches.

- **Tension headaches.** Many studies have tested biofeedback for tension headaches, and several evaluations of this research have concluded that biofeedback may be helpful. However, an evaluation that included only the highest quality studies concluded that there is conflicting evidence about whether biofeedback is helpful for tension headaches.

- **Migraines.** Studies have shown decreases in the frequency of migraines in people who were using biofeedback. However, it's unclear whether biofeedback is better than a placebo for migraines.

Biofeedback generally does not have harmful side effects.

Massage

Massage therapy includes a variety of techniques in which practitioners manipulate the soft tissues of the body.

Limited evidence from two small studies suggests massage therapy is possibly helpful for migraines, but clear conclusions cannot be drawn.

Massage therapy appears to have few risks when performed by a trained practitioner. However, people with health conditions and pregnant women may need to avoid some types of massage and should consult their health care providers before having massage therapy.

Relaxation Techniques

Relaxation techniques—such as progressive muscle relaxation, guided imagery, and breathing exercises—are practices that can produce the body's natural relaxation response. (Some types of biofeedback are also designed to help people learn relaxation; biofeedback is discussed in a separate section above.)

Although some experts consider relaxation techniques to be promising for tension headaches, there isn't much evidence to support their effectiveness. An evaluation of high-quality studies on relaxation techniques found conflicting evidence on whether they're better than no treatment or a placebo. Some studies suggest that relaxation techniques are less helpful than biofeedback.

Relaxation techniques generally don't have side effects. However, rare harmful effects have been reported in people with serious physical or mental health conditions.

Spinal Manipulation

Spinal manipulation is a technique in which practitioners use their hands or a device to apply a controlled force to a joint of the spine. Chiropractors or other health professionals may use this technique.

Spinal manipulation is frequently used for headaches. However, it's uncertain whether manipulation is helpful because studies have had contradictory results.

Side effects from spinal manipulation can include temporary headaches, tiredness, or discomfort in the area that was manipulated. There have been rare reports of strokes occurring after manipulation of the upper (cervical) spine, but whether manipulation actually caused the strokes is unclear.

Tai Chi

Tai chi, which originated in China, combines meditation with slow, graceful movements, deep breathing, and relaxation.

One small randomized study has evaluated tai chi for tension headaches. Some evidence of improvements in headache status and health-related quality of life was found among patients on the tai chi program compared to others on a wait list. These data are too limited to draw meaningful conclusions about whether this practice is helpful for tension headaches.

Tai chi is generally considered to be a safe practice.

Dietary Supplements

Several dietary supplements have been studied for headaches, particularly for migraine prevention. In 2012, the American Academy of Neurology and the American Headache Society issued evidence-based guidelines that classified certain dietary supplements as "effective," "probably effective," or "possibly effective" in preventing migraines. Their findings regarding effectiveness of specific supplements are summarized in the next sections. Also included are brief summaries of evidence on the safety and side effects of each supplement.

Butterbur

In their guidelines for migraine prevention, the American Academy of Neurology and the American Headache Society concluded that butterbur is effective and should be offered to patients with migraine to reduce the frequency and severity of migraine attacks.

The most common side effects of butterbur are belching and other mild digestive tract symptoms. Raw butterbur extracts contain pyrrolizidine alkaloids, which can cause liver damage and cancer. Extracts of butterbur that are almost completely free from these alkaloids are available. It is uncertain whether butterbur products, including reduced-alkaloid products, are safe for prolonged use.

Coenzyme Q10

Coenzyme Q10 is an antioxidant that cells need to function properly. It's available as a dietary supplement and has been studied for a variety of purposes. The guidelines from the American Academy of Neurology and the American Headache Society say that coenzyme Q10 is possibly effective and may be considered for migraine prevention.

No serious side effects of coenzyme Q10 have been reported. It may interact with some medications, including the anticoagulant (blood-thinning) medication warfarin (Coumadin).

Feverfew

The guidelines from the American Academy of Neurology and the American Headache Society say that a specific feverfew extract called MIG-99 is probably effective and should be considered for migraine prevention.

Side effects of feverfew may include joint aches, digestive disturbances, and mouth ulcers. It may interact with anticoagulants (blood thinners) and some other medications. Feverfew is not safe for use during pregnancy. Its long-term safety has not been established.

Magnesium

Magnesium deficiency is related to factors that promote headaches, and people who get migraines may have lower levels of magnesium in their bodies than those who do not. The guidelines from the American Academy of Neurology and the American Headache Society say that magnesium is probably effective and should be considered for migraine prevention.

Magnesium supplements can cause diarrhea and may interact with some medications. Because the amounts of magnesium people take for migraines are greater than the Tolerable Upper Intake Level for this mineral (the largest amount that's likely to be safe for almost everyone), magnesium supplements for migraine should be used only under the supervision of a health care provider.

Riboflavin

The American Academy of Neurology and American Headache Society's guidelines say that riboflavin is probably effective and should be considered for migraine prevention.

Riboflavin has minimal side effects, but it can cause an intense yellow discoloration of the urine.

More to Consider

* Most dietary supplements have not been tested in pregnant women, nursing mothers, or children. If you're pregnant or nursing a child, or if you're considering giving a child a dietary supplement, consult your (or your child's) health care provider.

* Be aware that some dietary supplements may interact with conventional medical treatments.

* If you're considering a practitioner-provided complementary health practice such as biofeedback or acupuncture, ask a trusted source (such as your health care provider or nearby hospital) to recommend a practitioner. Find out about the training and experience of any complementary health practitioner you're considering.

* Tell all your health care providers about any complementary health approaches you use. Give them a full picture of what you do to manage your health. This will help ensure coordinated and safe care.

Chapter 48

Heart Disease and Chelation Therapy

Coronary heart disease is the number-one killer of men and women in the United States. Lifestyle changes (such as quitting smoking), medicines, and medical and surgical procedures are among the mainstays of conventional treatment. Some heart patients also turn to chelation therapy using disodium EDTA (ethylene diamine tetra-acetic acid), a controversial complementary health approach. The use of disodium EDTA for heart disease has not been approved by the U.S. Food and Drug Administration. Use of this therapy to treat heart disease and other diseases grew, however, in the United States from 2002 to 2007 by nearly 68 percent, to an estimated 111,000 people using it annually.

Chelation is a chemical process in which a substance is used to bind molecules, such as metals or minerals, and hold them tightly so that they can be removed from the body. Chelation has been used to rid the body of excess or toxic metals. It has some uses in conventional medicine, such as treating lead poisoning or iron overload. When used as a complementary treatment for heart disease, a health care provider typically administers a solution of disodium EDTA, a man-made amino

Text in this chapter is excerpted from "Chelation for Coronary Heart Disease," National Center for Complementary and Integrative Health (NCCIH), August 20, 2015.

acid, in a series of infusions through the veins. A course of treatment can require 30 or more infusions of several hours each, taken weekly until the maintenance phase. Patients also typically take high-dose pills of vitamins and minerals.

To determine whether chelation therapy, with or without high-dose vitamins and minerals, may be useful, National Center for Complementary and Integrative Health (NCCIH) and the National Heart, Lung, and Blood Institute sponsored the first large-scale, multicenter clinical trial on chelation therapy in people with coronary heart disease. Results of the Trial to Assess Chelation Therapy (TACT) began to be released in 2013.

Bottom Line

- Overall, TACT showed that infusions of EDTA chelation therapy produced a modest but statistically significant reduction in cardiovascular events in EDTA-treated participants. However, further examination of the data showed that patients with diabetes were significantly impacted by chelation therapy while patients without diabetes were not.

- Patients with diabetes, who made up approximately one third of the 1,708 TACT participants, had a 41 percent overall reduction in the risk of any cardiovascular event; a 40 percent reduction in the risk of death from heart disease, nonfatal stroke, or nonfatal heart attack; a 52 percent reduction in recurrent heart attacks; and a 43 percent reduction in death from any cause. In contrast, there was no significant benefit of EDTA treatment in participants who did not have diabetes.

- The TACT study team also looked at the impact of taking high-dose vitamins and minerals in addition to the chelation therapy. They found that chelation plus high-dose vitamins and minerals produced the greatest reduction in risk of cardiovascular events versus placebo.

- Further research is needed to fully understand the TACT results. Since this is the first clinical trial to show a benefit, these results are not, by themselves, sufficient to support the routine use of chelation as post-heart attack therapy.

Safety

- In the TACT study, which had extensive safety monitoring, 16 percent of people receiving chelation and 15 percent of people receiving the placebo stopped their infusions because of an adverse event. Four of those events were serious; two were in the chelation group (one death) and two in the placebo group (one death).

- The most common side effect of EDTA chelation is a burning sensation at the site where EDTA is administered. Rare side effects can include fever, headache, nausea, and vomiting. Even more rare are serious and potentially fatal side effects that can include heart failure, a sudden drop in blood pressure, abnormally low calcium levels in the blood (hypocalcemia), permanent kidney damage, and bone marrow depression (meaning that blood cell counts fall). Hypocalcemia and death may occur particularly if disodium EDTA is infused too rapidly. Reversible injury to the kidneys, although infrequent, has been reported with EDTA chelation therapy. Other serious side effects can occur if EDTA is not administered by a trained health professional.

- If you're considering chelation therapy, discuss it first with your cardiologist or other health care provider for your heart care. Seek out and consider information available from scientific studies on the therapy.

- If you decide to use chelation, choose the practitioner carefully. Do not take over-the-counter products marketed for "chelation" purposes.

- Give all your health care providers a full picture of what you do to manage your health. This will help ensure coordinated and safe care.

Chapter 49

Hepatitis C and CAM

Hepatitis C is a liver disease caused by a virus. It's usually chronic (long-lasting), but most people don't have any symptoms until the virus causes liver damage, which can take 10 or more years to happen. Without medical treatment, chronic hepatitis C can eventually cause liver cancer or liver failure. Conventional medical treatments are available for chronic hepatitis C. Some people with hepatitis C also try complementary health approaches, especially dietary supplements. This chapter provides basic information on hepatitis C and summarizes scientific research on selected supplements.

Key Points

Are Dietary Supplements for Hepatitis C Safe?

- Colloidal silver is not safe; it can cause irreversible side effects.

- Data on the safety of other supplements is limited. However, some can have side effects or may interact in harmful ways with medications, and some may be unsafe for people with certain health problems.

- If you have hepatitis C, check with your health care provider before using any dietary supplement to make sure that it is safe

Text in this chapter is excerpted from "Hepatitis C: A Focus on Dietary Supplements," National Center for Complementary and Integrative Health (NCCIH), November 2014.

for you and compatible with any medical treatment that you're receiving for hepatitis C or any other health problem.

Are Dietary Supplements for Hepatitis C Effective?

- No dietary supplement has been shown to be effective for hepatitis C or its complications.

- The results of research supported by the National Center for Complementary and Integrative Health (NCCIH) and National Institute of Diabetes and Digestive and Kidney Diseases (NIDDK) have shown that silymarin, the active extract of milk thistle and the most popular complementary health product taken by people with liver disease, was no more effective than placebo in people with hepatitis C.

- Research on other dietary supplements for hepatitis C, such as zinc, licorice root (or its extract glycyrrhizin), S-adenosyl-L-methionine (SAMe), and lactoferrin, is in its early stages, and no firm conclusions can be reached about the potential effectiveness of these supplements.

Keep in Mind

- It's important not to replace conventional medical therapy for hepatitis C with dietary supplements or other approaches that haven't been shown to be effective.

- Tell all your health care providers about any complementary health approaches you use. Give them a full picture of what you do to manage your health. This will help ensure coordinated and safe care.

What Is Hepatitis C?

Hepatitis C is a contagious liver disease. It's caused by the hepatitis C virus. People can get hepatitis C through contact with blood from a person who's already infected or, less commonly, through having sex with an infected person. The infection usually becomes chronic. Chronic hepatitis C often is treated with drugs that can eliminate the virus. This may slow or stop liver damage, but the drugs may cause side effects, and for some people, treatment is ineffective. An estimated 3.2 million Americans have chronic hepatitis C.

Use of Herbal Supplements and Other Complementary Approaches for Hepatitis C

Several herbal supplements have been studied for hepatitis C, and substantial numbers of people with hepatitis C have tried herbal supplements. For example, a survey of 1,145 participants in the Hepatitis C Antiviral Long-Term Treatment Against Cirrhosis (HALT-C) trial, a study supported by the National Institutes of Health (NIH), found that 23 percent of the participants were using herbal products. Although participants reported using many different herbal products, silymarin (milk thistle) was by far the most common. Another study, which surveyed 120 adults with hepatitis C, found that many used a variety of complementary health approaches, including multivitamins, herbal remedies, massage, deep breathing exercises, meditation, progressive relaxation, and yoga.

What the Science Says

No dietary supplement has been shown to be effective for hepatitis C. This section summarizes what's known about the safety and effectiveness of milk thistle and some of the other dietary supplements studied for hepatitis C.

- **Milk thistle** (scientific name *Silybum marianum*) is a plant from the aster family. Silymarin is an active component of milk thistle believed to be responsible for the herb's health-related properties. Milk thistle has been used in Europe for treating liver disease and jaundice since the 16th century. In the United States, silymarin is the most popular dietary supplement taken by people with liver disease. However, two rigorously designed studies of silymarin in people with hepatitis C didn't show any benefit.

- A 2012 controlled clinical trial, cofunded by NCCIH and NIDDK, showed that two higher-than-usual doses of silymarin were no better than placebo in reducing the high blood levels of an enzyme that indicates liver damage. In the study, 154 people who hadn't responded to standard antiviral treatment for chronic hepatitis C were randomly assigned to receive 420 mg of silymarin, 700 mg of silymarin, or placebo three times per day for 24 weeks. At the end of the treatment period, blood levels of the enzyme were similar in all three groups.

- Results of the HALT-C study mentioned above suggested that silymarin use by hepatitis C patients was associated with fewer and milder symptoms of liver disease and somewhat better quality of life, but there was no change in virus activity or liver inflammation. The researchers emphasized that this was a retrospective study (one that examined the medical and lifestyle histories of the participants). Its finding of improved quality of life in patients taking silymarin wasn't confirmed in the more rigorous 2012 study described above.

Safety. Available evidence from clinical trials in people with liver disease suggests that milk thistle is generally well-tolerated. Side effects can include a laxative effect, nausea, diarrhea, abdominal bloating and pain, and occasional allergic reactions. In NIH-funded studies of silymarin in people with hepatitis C that were completed in 2010 and 2012, the frequency of side effects was similar in people taking silymarin and those taking placebos. However, these studies were not large enough to show with certainty that silymarin is safe for people with chronic hepatitis C.

Other supplements have been studied for hepatitis C, but overall, no benefits have been clearly demonstrated. These supplements include the following:

- Probiotics are live microorganisms that are intended to have a health benefit when consumed. Research hasn't produced any clear evidence that probiotics are helpful in people with hepatitis C. Most people can use probiotics without experiencing any side effects—or with only mild gastrointestinal side effects such as intestinal gas—but there have been some case reports of serious adverse effects in people with underlying serious health conditions.

- Preliminary studies, most of which were conducted outside the United States, have examined the use of zinc for hepatitis C. Zinc supplements might help to correct zinc deficiencies associated with hepatitis C or reduce some symptoms, but the evidence for these possible benefits is limited. Zinc is generally considered to be safe when used appropriately, but it can be toxic if taken in excessive amounts.

- A few preliminary studies have looked at the effects of combining supplements such as lactoferrin, SAMe, or zinc with conventional drug therapy for hepatitis C. The evidence isn't sufficient to draw clear conclusions about benefit or safety.

- Glycyrrhizin—a compound found in licorice root—has been tested in a few clinical trials in hepatitis C patients, but there's currently not enough evidence to determine if it's helpful. In large amounts, glycyrrhizin or licorice can be dangerous in people with a history of hypertension (high blood pressure), kidney failure, or cardiovascular diseases.

- Preliminary studies have examined the potential of the following products for treating chronic hepatitis C: TJ-108 (a mixture of herbs used in Japanese Kampo medicine), schisandra, oxymatrine (an extract from the sophora root), and thymus extract. The limited research on these products hasn't produced convincing evidence that they're helpful for hepatitis C.

- Colloidal silver has been suggested as a treatment for hepatitis C, but there's currently no research to support its use for this purpose. Colloidal silver is known to cause serious side effects, including a permanent bluish discoloration of the skin called argyria.

If You're Considering Taking a Dietary Supplement for Hepatitis C

- Do not use any complementary health approach to replace conventional treatments for hepatitis C or as a reason to postpone seeing your health care provider about any medical problem.

- Be aware that dietary supplements may have side effects or interact with conventional medical treatments.

- If you're pregnant or nursing a child, or if you're considering giving a child a dietary supplement, it's especially important to consult your (or your child's) health care provider. Supplements can act like drugs, and many have not been tested in pregnant women, nursing mothers, or children.

- Tell all your health care providers about any complementary health approaches you use. Give them a full picture of what you do to manage your health. This will help ensure coordinated and safe care.

Chapter 50

Hormones, Aging, and CAM

For decades, hormone replacement therapy (HRT)—more recently known as menopausal hormone therapy (MHT)—was conventional medicine's main treatment for menopausal symptoms. In 2002, findings from a large study called the Women's Health Initiative raised serious concerns about the long-term safety of MHT. These concerns are one reason that many women are turning to complementary health approaches.

Bio-Identical Hormones: Sorting Myths from Facts

"A natural, safer alternative to dangerous prescription drugs"
"Can slim you down by reducing hormonal imbalances"
"Prevents Alzheimer's disease and senility"

All of these claims have been made by marketers of compounded "bio-identical" hormones, also known as "bio-identical hormone replacement therapy" (BHRT). But these claims are unproven. FDA is concerned that claims like these mislead women and health care

This chapter includes excerpts from "Hormones (Bio-identicals)," National Center for Complementary and Integrative Health (NCCIH), January 27, 2015; text from "Bio-Identicals: Sorting Myths from Facts," U.S. Food and Drug Administration (FDA), February 27, 2015; and text from "Can We Prevent Aging?," National Institute on Aging (NIH), July 20, 2015.

professionals, giving them a false sense of assurance about using potentially dangerous hormone products.

FDA is providing the facts about "BHRT" drugs and the uncertainties surrounding their safety and effectiveness so that women and their doctors can make informed decisions about their use.

"BHRT" is a marketing term not recognized by FDA. Sellers of compounded "bio-identical" hormones often claim that their products are identical to hormones made by the body and that these "all-natural" pills, creams, lotions, and gels are without the risks of drugs approved by FDA for menopausal hormone therapy (MHT). FDA-approved MHT drugs provide effective relief of the symptoms of menopause such as hot flashes and vaginal dryness. They also can prevent thinning of bones. FDA has not approved compounded "BHRT" drugs and cannot assure their safety or effectiveness.

During menopause, a woman's body produces less of the hormone estrogen, which may lead to hot flashes, vaginal dryness, and thin bones. MHT drugs contain estrogen or a combination of estrogen and another hormone, a progestin. FDA-approved MHT drugs are sold by prescription only, and FDA advises women who choose to use hormones to use them at the lowest dose that helps, for the shortest time needed.

Some "BHRT" drugs are compounded in pharmacies. Traditional compounding involves combining, mixing, or altering ingredients by a pharmacist, according to a prescription from a licensed health care professional, to produce a drug that meets an individual's special medical needs. FDA considers traditional compounding to be a valuable service when used appropriately, such as customizing a drug for someone who is allergic to a dye or preservative in an FDA-approved medicine. But some pharmacies that compound "BHRT" drugs make unsupported claims that these drugs are more effective and safer than FDA-approved MHT drugs.

FDA is taking action against pharmacies that make false and misleading claims about "BHRT" drugs and is encouraging consumers to become informed about these products and their risks. Here is some information to help sort the myths from the facts:

Myth: "Bio-identical" hormones are safer and more effective than FDA-approved MHT drugs.

Fact: FDA is not aware of any credible scientific evidence to support claims made regarding the safety and effectiveness of compounded "BHRT" drugs. "They are not safer just because they are 'natural,'" says Kathleen Uhl, M.D., Director of FDA's Office of Women's Health.

Drugs that are approved by FDA must undergo the agency's rigorous evaluation process, which scrutinizes everything about the drug to ensure its safety and effectiveness—from early testing, to the design and results of large clinical trials, to the severity of side effects, to the conditions under which the drug is manufactured. FDA-approved MHT drugs have undergone this process and met all federal standards for approval. No compounded "BHRT" drug has met these standards.

Pharmacies that compound these "BHRT" drugs may not follow good drug manufacturing requirements that apply to commercial drug manufacturers. Compounding pharmacies custom-mix these products according to a health care professional's order. The mix contains not only the active hormone, but other inactive ingredients that help hold a pill together or give a cream, lotion, or gel its form and thickness so that it can be applied to the body. It is unknown whether these mixtures, which are not FDA-approved, are properly absorbed or provide the appropriate levels of hormones needed in the body. It is also unknown whether the amount of drug delivered is consistent from pill to pill or each time a cream or gel is applied.

Myth: "Bio-identical" hormone products can prevent or cure heart disease, Alzheimer's disease, and breast cancer.

Fact: Compounded "BHRT" drugs have not been shown to prevent or cure any of these diseases. In fact, like FDA-approved MHT drugs, they may increase the risk of heart disease, breast cancer, and dementia in some women. No large, long-term study has been done to determine the adverse effects of "bio-identical" hormones.

Myth: "Bio-identical" hormone products that contain estriol, a weak form of estrogen, are safer than FDA-approved estrogen products.

Fact: FDA has not approved any drug containing estriol. The safety and effectiveness of estriol are unknown. "No data have been submitted to FDA that demonstrate that estriol is safe and effective," according to Daniel Shames, M.D., a senior official in the FDA office that oversees reproductive products.

Myth: If "bio-identical" products were unsafe, there would be a lot of reports of bad side effects.

Fact: "Bio-identical" products are typically compounded in pharmacies. "Unlike commercial drug manufacturers, pharmacies aren't required to report adverse events associated with compounded drugs," says Steve Silverman, Assistant Director of the Office of Compliance in FDA's Center for Drug Evaluation and Research. "Also, while some health risks associated with 'BHRT' drugs may arise after a relatively short period of use, others may not occur for many years. One of the big problems is that we just don't know what risks are associated with these so-called 'bio-identicals.'"

Myth: A pharmacy can make a "BHRT" drug just for you based on hormone levels in a saliva sample.

Fact: "Advertisements that a drug can be created 'just for you' based on saliva testing are appealing," says Uhl, "but unrealistic." Hormone levels in saliva do not accurately reflect the amount of hormones a woman has in her body for the purpose of adjusting hormone therapy dose levels. A woman's hormone levels change throughout the day, and from day to day. FDA-approved tests can tell a woman's hormone level in a specific body fluid, such as saliva, blood, or urine, at that particular point in time. "These tests are useful to tell if a woman is menopausal or not," says Uhl, "but they have not been shown to be useful for adjusting hormone therapy dosages."

Myth: FDA wants all compounded hormone therapies off the market.

Fact: "We are not trying to pull all compounded hormone therapies off the market," says Silverman. "We believe that, like all traditionally compounded drugs, a woman should be able to get a compounded hormone therapy drug when her physician decides that it will best serve her specific medical needs. But we also want women to be informed and careful about choosing products that have not been proven safe and effective. And pharmacies cannot promote compounded drugs with false or misleading claims."

In addition, FDA has not approved any drug containing the hormone estriol. Pharmacies should not compound drugs containing estriol unless the prescriber has a valid investigational new drug (IND) application. INDs provide benefits that include allowing physicians to treat individual patients with drugs that are not FDA-approved, while also providing additional safeguards for patients.

Myth: All women who take FDA-approved MHT drugs are going to get blood clots, heart attacks, strokes, breast cancer, or gall bladder disease.

Fact: Like all medicines, hormone therapy has risks and benefits. For some women, hormone therapy may increase their chances of getting these conditions. However, there are no convincing data that there is less risk of developing a blood clot, heart attack, stroke, breast cancer, or gall bladder disease with a "BHRT" product. Women should talk to their health care professional about taking hormones. If you decide to use MHT drugs for menopause

- use at the lowest dose that helps

- use for the shortest time needed

If you are taking a compounded "BHRT" drug now, talk to your health care professional about treatment options to determine if compounded drugs are the best option for your particular medical needs.

Can We Prevent Aging?

People are living longer. In 1970, the average life expectancy at birth in the United States was 70.8 years; in 2008, it was 78.0 years; and by 2020, the U.S. Census Bureau projects life expectancy will reach 79.5 years.

Views on aging are also changing. Disease and disability were once considered an inevitable part of growing older, but that is no longer true. While aging does put us at greater risk for health issues, many older adults can be healthy and active well into their advancing years.

The National Institute on Aging (NIA), part of the Federal Government's National Institutes of Health (NIH), investigates ways to support healthy aging and prevent or delay the onset of age-related disease and decline. We have already gained important insights, and what we learn from ongoing and future studies may not only help to increase longevity, but may also promote what is known as "active life expectancy"—the time in late life free of disability. We already know, for example, that healthy eating and exercise and physical activity help promote healthy aging. Are there other interventions that can help? NIA-supported and other studies are taking a look at the possible benefits and risks of a number of approaches, including antioxidants, calorie restriction, and hormone supplements. This text provides an overview of what we know about these interventions and the research needed to learn more. Until we have a better understanding, it is a good idea to be skeptical of claims that any supplements can solve your age-related problems.

Antioxidants

Antioxidants protect the body from the harmful effects of by-products known as free radicals, made normally when the body changes oxygen and food into energy. The discovery of antioxidants raised hopes that people could slow aging simply by adding them to the diet. So far, studies of antioxidant-laden foods and supplements in humans have yielded little support for this conclusion. Further research, including large-scale epidemiological studies, might clarify whether dietary antioxidants can help people live longer, healthier lives. For now, although the effectiveness of dietary antioxidant supplementation remains controversial, there is positive evidence for the health benefits of fruits and vegetables.

Calorie Restriction, Intermittent Fasting, Resveratrol, and Rapamycin

Scientists are discovering that what you eat, how frequently, and how much may have an effect on quality and years of life. Of particular interest has been calorie restriction, a diet that is lower by a specific percent of calories than the normal diet but includes all needed nutrients. Research in some animals has shown calorie restriction of up to 40 percent fewer calories than normal to have an impressive positive effect on disease, markers of aging, and, perhaps, life span.

Even though calorie restriction appears to work in a variety of species, its effects on longevity are far from universal. It has been found to extend the life of protozoa (very small, one-celled organisms), yeast, fruit flies, some strains of mice, and rats, as well as other species. However, several animal models, including wild mice, show no lifespan extension by calorie restriction. In some strains of mice, calorie restriction even appears to shorten lifespan. Studies in nonhuman primates have also had conflicting results.

Calorie restriction studies with humans and other primates, such as monkeys, are ongoing. Some studies in nonhuman primates have shown that calorie restriction reduces the incidence of certain diseases such as cancer. Other studies in primates have not yet reached final conclusions.

Findings of the Comprehensive Assessment of Long-term Effects of Reducing Intake of Energy (CALERIE) pilot study in humans showed that overweight adults who cut their calorie consumption by 20 to 30 percent lowered their fasting insulin levels and core body temperature. Both of these changes correlate with increased longevity in animal models. The lower calorie intake also reduced their risk for major causes of mortality such as heart disease and diabetes. CALERIE is currently evaluating a 2-year, 25 percent reduction in caloric intake for feasibility, safety, and effects on factors influencing longevity and health.

Scientists do not yet know if long-term calorie restriction is safe, beneficial, or practical for humans. However, the study of calorie restriction offers new insights into the aging process and biological mechanisms that could influence healthy aging. This research may also provide clues about how to prevent or delay diseases that become more prevalent with age and inform the development of treatments for such diseases.

Some studies focus on identifying chemicals that somehow mimic calorie restriction's benefits. Resveratrol, a compound found naturally in foods like grapes and nuts, is of interest. In one study, scientists compared two groups of overweight mice on a high-fat diet. One group was given a high dose of resveratrol together with the high-fat diet. The overweight mice receiving resveratrol were healthier and lived longer than the overweight mice that did not get resveratrol.

In a follow-up study, researchers found that, when started at middle age, resveratrol slowed age-related deterioration and functional decline of mice on a standard diet, but did not increase longevity. A recent study in humans reported that resveratrol may have some similar health benefits to those in animals; however, it is still too early to make any definitive conclusions about how resveratrol affects human health and aging. More research is needed before scientists know if there is a proper and safe dose of resveratrol or if it has any clinical applicability in people.

Rapamycin is also being investigated. This compound is used to help suppress the immune system in transplant patients so that the body does not reject the new organ. Rapamycin has been found to extend median and maximum lifespan of mice, even when fed to the animals beginning at early-old age. This finding suggests that an intervention started later in life may still increase longevity. Researchers are now looking for rapamycin's effects on health span of animal models. Since rapamycin treatment in people is associated with serious toxicities, its potential for human long-term use is uncertain. Researchers do not know if rapamycin has any effect on human aging or if any potential benefit would outweigh risks. But, this discovery in mice has led to an exciting new research direction.

Scientists are also looking at the effect of intermittent fasting or reduced meal frequency. In animals, like mice, reduced meal frequency appears to have a protective effect on the brain and may also help with heart function and regulation of sugar content in the blood. However, here, too, the influence of intermittent fasting on human health and longevity is currently unclear.

While research into these types of approaches continues, it is important to remember there is already plenty of research supporting the value of a healthy, balanced diet and physical activity to help delay or prevent age-related health problems.

Hormones

Hormones are chemical messengers that set in motion different processes to keep our bodies working properly. For example, they are involved in regulating our metabolism, immune function, sexual reproduction, and growth. Hormones are made by specialized groups of cells within the body's glands. The glands—such as the pituitary, thyroid, adrenals, ovaries, and testes—release hormones into the body as needed to stimulate, regulate, and control the function of other tissues and organs involved in biological processes. Most hormones are typically found in very low concentrations in the bloodstream. But a hormone's concentration will fluctuate depending on the body's activity or time of day.

We cannot survive without hormones. As children, hormones help us grow up. In our teenage years, they drive puberty. As we get older, some hormone levels naturally decline. But what does that mean? Scientists do not know exactly.

In order to learn more, NIA is investigating how the administration of hormones to older people affects frailty and function. Many of these studies focus on hormones that naturally decline with age, including:

- Human growth hormone

- Testosterone

- Estrogen and progesterone (as part of menopausal hormone therapy)

- Dehydroepiandrosterone (DHEA)

How Hormones Work

A hormone acts upon a cell much like a key unlocking a door. After being released by a gland, a hormone molecule travels through the blood until it finds a cell with the right fit. The hormone latches onto a cell via the cell's receptor. When this happens a signal is sent into the cell. These signals may instruct the cell to multiply, make proteins or enzymes, or perform other vital tasks. Some hormones can even cause a cell to release other hormones.

A hormone may fit with many types of cells but may not affect all cells in the same way. For example, one hormone may stimulate one cell to perform a task, but it might also turn off a different cell. Additionally, how a cell responds to a hormone may change throughout life.

Hormone Therapy

Levels of some hormones change naturally over the lifespan. Some hormones increase with age, like parathyroid hormone that helps regulate the amount of calcium in the blood and bone. Some tend to decrease over time, such as testosterone in men and estrogen in women. When the body fails to make enough of a hormone because of a disease or disorder, a doctor may prescribe hormone supplements. These come in many forms such as pills, shots, topicals (gels, creams, and sprays applied to the skin), and medicated skin patches.

You may have read magazine articles or seen television programs suggesting that treatment with hormones can make people feel young again or can slow or prevent aging. That's because finding a "fountain of youth" is a captivating story. The truth is that, to date, no research has shown that hormone therapies add years to life or prevent age-related frailty. And, while some drugs have real health benefits for people with clinical hormone deficiencies due to a disease or disorder, they also can cause harmful side effects. That's why people who have a diagnosed hormone deficiency should still only take hormones prescribed by a doctor and under a doctor's supervision.

In some cases, the U.S. Food and Drug Administration (FDA) may have approved a hormone (or hormone therapy) for one purpose, but it is prescribed by physicians for another. This off-label use may occur when physicians believe that research, such as clinical studies, demonstrates a drug's usefulness for another condition. However, consumers should be aware that off-label use of any drug may not have been tested and verified to the same degree as the original use of the drug.

Some Dangers of Hormone Therapy and "Anti-Aging" Supplements

Higher concentrations of hormones in your body are not necessarily better. And, a decrease in hormone concentration with age is not necessarily a bad thing. The body maintains a delicate balance between how much hormone it produces and how much it needs to function properly. Natural hormone production fluctuates throughout the day. That means that the amount of hormone in your blood when you wake up may be different 2, 12, or 20 hours later.

If you take hormone supplements, especially without medical supervision, you can adversely affect this tightly controlled, regulated system. Replacement or supplemental hormones cannot replicate your body's natural variation. Because hormonal balance is so intricate, too much of a hormone in your system may actually cause the opposite of the intended effect. For example, taking a hormone supplement can cause your own hormone regulation to stop working. Or, your body may process the supplements differently than the naturally produced hormone, causing an alternate, undesired effect. It is also possible that a supplement could amplify negative side effects of the hormone naturally produced by the body. At this point, scientists do not know all the consequences.

Some hormone-like products are sold over the counter without a prescription. Using them can be dangerous. Products that are marketed as dietary supplements are not approved or regulated by the FDA. That is, companies making dietary supplements do not need to provide any proof that their products are safe and effective before selling them. There is no guarantee that the "recommended" dosage is safe, that the same amount of active ingredients is in every bottle, or that the substance is what the company claims. What you bought over the counter may not have been thoroughly studied, and potential negative side effects may not be understood or defined. In addition, these over-the-counter products may interfere with your other medications. NIA does not recommend taking any supplement touted as an "anti-aging" remedy because there is no proof of effectiveness and the health risks of short- and long-term use are largely unknown.

Human Growth Hormone

Growth hormone is important for normal growth and development, as well as for maintaining tissues and organs. It is made by the pituitary gland, a pea-sized structure located at the base of the brain.

Research supports supplemental use of human growth hormone (hGH) injections in certain circumstances. For instance, hGH injections can help children who do not produce enough growth hormone. Sometimes hGH injections may be prescribed for young adults whose obesity is the result of having had their pituitary gland surgically removed. These uses are different from taking hGH as an "anti-aging" strategy. As with other hormones, growth hormone levels often decline with age, but this decrease is not necessarily bad. At least one epidemiological study suggests that people who have high levels of naturally produced growth hormone are more apt to die at younger ages than those with lower levels of the hormone. Researchers have also studied animals with genetic disorders that suppress growth hormone production and secretion. They found that reduced growth hormone secretion actually promotes longevity in the tested species.

Although there is no conclusive evidence that hGH can prevent aging or halt age-related physical decline, some clinics market hGH for that purpose, and some people spend a great deal of money on such supplements. Shots can cost more than $15,000 a year. These shots are only available by prescription and should be administered by a doctor. But, because of the unknown risks—and the evidence suggests that side effects strongly overcome any possible benefits—it is hard to find a doctor who will prescribe hGH shots. Over-the-counter dietary supplements, known as human growth hormone releasers, are currently being marketed as low-cost alternatives to hGH shots. But claims of their anti-aging effects, like all those regarding hGH, are unsubstantiated.

Research is starting to paint a fuller picture of the effects of hGH, but there is still much to learn. For instance, study findings indicate that injections of hGH can increase muscle mass; however, it seems to have little impact on muscle strength or function. Questions about potential side effects, such as diabetes, joint pain, and fluid buildup leading to high blood pressure or heart failure, remain unanswered, too. A report that children who were treated with pituitary growth hormone have an increased risk of cancer created a heightened concern about the dangers of hGH injections. Whether or not older people treated with hGH for extended periods have an increased risk of cancer is unknown. To date, only small, short-term studies have looked specifically at hGH as an "anti-aging" therapy for older people. Additional research is necessary to assess the potential risks and benefits of hGH.

Testosterone

Testosterone is a vital sex hormone that plays an important role in puberty. In men, testosterone not only regulates sex drive (libido), it also helps regulate bone mass, fat distribution, muscle mass and strength, and the production of red blood cells and sperm. Testosterone isn't exclusively a male hormone—women produce small amounts as well.

As men age, they often produce somewhat less testosterone, especially compared to years of peak testosterone production during adolescence and early adulthood. Normal testosterone production ranges widely, and it is unclear what amount of decline or how low a level of testosterone will cause adverse effects.

In recent years, the popular press has increasingly reported about "male menopause," a condition supposedly caused by diminishing testosterone levels in aging men. There is very little scientific evidence that this condition, also known as andropause or viropause, exists. The likelihood that an aging man will experience a major shutdown of testosterone production similar to a woman's menopause is very remote. In fact, many of the changes that take place in older men often are incorrectly attributed to decreasing testosterone levels. For instance, some men experiencing erectile difficulty (impotence) may be tempted to blame it on lowered testosterone, but many cases of erectile problems are due to circulatory problems.

For men whose bodies make very little or no testosterone, testosterone replacement may offer benefits. FDA-approved testosterone drugs come in different forms, including patches, injections, and topical gels. Men whose testes (the reproductive glands that make testosterone and sperm) have been damaged or whose pituitary glands have been harmed or destroyed by trauma, infections, or tumors may also be prescribed testosterone. Treatment with testosterone drugs can help men with exceptionally low testosterone levels maintain strong muscles and bones and increase their sex drive. It is unclear if men who are at the lower end of the normal range for testosterone production would benefit from treatment.

More research is needed to learn what effects testosterone drug therapy may have in healthy older men without these extreme deficiencies. National Institute on Aging (NIA) is investigating the role of testosterone therapy in delaying or preventing frailty and helping with other age-related health issues. Results from preliminary studies involving small groups of men are inconclusive. Specifically, it remains unclear to what degree testosterone supplements can help men maintain strong muscles and sturdy bones, sustain robust sexual activity, or sharpen memory.

There are also concerns about the long-term, harmful effects that testosterone drugs might have on the aging body. Most epidemiological studies suggest that higher natural levels of testosterone are not associated with a higher incidence of prostate cancer—the second leading cause of cancer death among men. However, scientists do not know if taking testosterone drugs increases men's risk for developing prostate cancer or promoting the growth of an existing tumor. There is also uncertainty about effects of testosterone treatment on the cardiovascular system in older men, especially men with mobility limitations and other diseases. Future studies will address this issue to ensure that older men receiving testosterone treatment are not exposed to unnecessary risks.

Bottom Line

There is no scientific proof that testosterone treatment in healthy men will help them age better. Until more scientifically rigorous studies are conducted, it is not known if the possible benefits of testosterone therapy outweigh any of its potential risks. NIA continues to conduct research to gather more evidence about the effects of testosterone treatment in aging men.

Hormones in Women

Estrogen and progesterone are two hormones that play an important part in women's menstrual cycle and pregnancy. Estrogen also helps maintain bone strength and may reduce the risk of heart disease and memory problems before menopause. Both estrogen and progesterone are produced naturally by the ovaries. However, after menopause, the ovaries make much less of these hormones. For more than 60 years, millions of women have used estrogen to relieve their menopausal symptoms, especially hot flashes and vaginal dryness. Some women may also be prescribed estrogen to prevent or treat osteoporosis—loss of bone strength—that often happens after menopause. The use of estrogen (by a woman whose uterus has been removed) or estrogen with progesterone or a progestin, a synthetic form of progesterone (by a woman with a uterus), to treat the symptoms of menopause is called menopausal hormone therapy (MHT), formerly known as hormone replacement therapy (HRT).

There is a rich research base investigating estrogen. Many large, reliable long-term studies of estrogen and its effects on the body have been conducted. Yet, much remains unknown. In fact, the history of estrogen research demonstrates why it is important to examine both the benefits and risks of any hormone therapy before it becomes widely used. Here's what scientists know:

- **Endometrial problems**—While estrogen helps some women with symptom management during and after menopause, it can raise the risk of certain problems. Estrogen may cause a thickening of the lining of the uterus (endometrium) and increase the risk of endometrial cancer. To lessen these risks, doctors now prescribe progesterone or a progestin, in combination with estrogen, to women with a uterus to protect the lining.

- **Heart disease**—The role of estrogen in heart disease is complex. Early studies suggested MHT could lower postmenopausal women's risk for heart disease—the number one killer of women in the United States. But results from the NIH Women's Health Initiative (WHI) suggest that using estrogen with or without a progestin after menopause does not protect women from heart disease and may even increase their risk.

In 2002, WHI scientists reported that using estrogen plus progestin actually elevates some postmenopausal women's chance of developing heart disease, stroke, blood clots, and breast cancer, but women also experienced fewer hip fractures and cases of colorectal cancer. In 2004, WHI scientists published another report, this time on postmenopausal women who used estrogen alone, which had some similar findings: women had an increased risk of stroke and blood clots, but fewer hip fractures. Then, in 2007, a closer analysis of the WHI results indicated that younger women, ages 50 to 59 at the start of the trial, who used estrogen alone, had significantly less calcified plaque in their coronary arteries than women not using estrogen. Increased plaque in coronary arteries is a risk factor for heart attacks. Scientists also noted that the risk of heart attack increased in women who started MHT more than 10 years after menopause (especially if these women had menopausal symptoms). There was no evidence of increased risk of heart attack in women who began MHT within 10 years of going through menopause.

- **Dementia**—Some observational studies have suggested that estrogen may protect against Alzheimer's disease. However, testing in clinical trials in older, postmenopausal women has challenged that view. In 2003, researchers leading the WHI Memory Study (WHIMS), a substudy of the WHI, reported that women age 65 and older who took one kind of estrogen combined with progestin were at twice the risk for developing dementia compared to women who did not take any hormones.

- In 2004, WHIMS scientists reported that using the same kind of estrogen alone also increased the risk of developing dementia in women age 65 and older compared to women not taking any hormones. What possibly accounts for the different findings between the observational and clinical studies? One central issue may be timing. The women in the WHIMS trial started treatment a decade or more after menopause. In observational studies that reported estrogen's positive effects on cognition, the majority of women began treatment soon after menopause.

This has led researchers to wonder if it may be advantageous to begin treatment earlier, at a time closer to menopause. Additionally, it appears that progesterone and progestins (progesterone-like compounds) differ in their impact on brain health.

Despite research thus far, there are still many unknowns about the risks and benefits of MHT. For instance, because women in their early 50's were only a small part of the WHI, scientists do not yet know if certain risks are applicable to younger women who use estrogen to relieve their symptoms during the menopausal transition.

You may also have heard about another approach to hormone therapy for women—"bio-identical hormones." These are hormones derived from plants, such as soy or yams, that have identical chemical structures to hormones produced by the human body. The term "bio-identical hormones" is now also being applied to the use of compounded hormones. Large clinical trials of these compounded hormones have not been done, and many bio-identical hormones that are available without a prescription are not regulated or approved for safety and efficacy by the FDA. FDA-regulated bio-identical hormones, such as estradiol and progesterone, are available by prescription for women considering MHT.

For middle-age and older women, the decision to take hormones is far more complex and difficult than ever before. Questions about MHT remain. Would using a different estrogen and/or progestin or different dose change the risks? Would the results be different if the hormones were given as a patch or cream, rather than a pill? Would taking progestin less often be as effective and safe? Does starting MHT around the time of menopause, compared to years later, change the risks? Can we predict which women will benefit or be harmed by using MHT? As these and other questions are addressed by research, women should continue to review the pros and cons of MHT with their doctors. They should assess the benefits as well as personal risks to make an informed decision about whether or not this therapy is right for them.

DHEA

Dehydroepiandrosterone, or DHEA, is made from cholesterol by the adrenal glands, which sit on top of each kidney. It is converted by the body into two other important hormones: testosterone and estrogen.

For most people, DHEA production peaks in the mid-20's and then gradually declines with age. The effects of this decline, including its role in the aging process, are unclear. Even so, some proponents claim that over-the-counter DHEA supplements can improve energy and strength and boost immunity. Claims are also made that supplements increase muscle and decrease fat. To date, there is no conclusive scientific evidence that DHEA supplements have any of these benefits.

The conversion of naturally produced DHEA into estrogen and testosterone is highly individualized. There is no way to predict who will make more or less of these hormones. Having an excess of testosterone or estrogen in your body could be risky.

Scientists do not yet know the effects of long-term (defined as over 1 year) use of DHEA supplements. Early indications are that these supplements, even when taken briefly, may have detrimental effects on the body, including liver damage. But the picture is not clear. Two short-term studies showed that taking DHEA supplements has no harmful effects on blood, prostate, or liver function. However, these studies were too small to lead to broader conclusions about the safety or efficacy of DHEA supplementation.

Researchers are working to find more definite answers about DHEA's effects on aging, muscles, and the immune system. In the meantime, if you are thinking about taking DHEA supplements, be aware that the effects are not fully known and might turn out to cause more harm than good.

Many Questions, Seeking Answers

NIA supports research that seeks to learn more about aging and the risks and benefits of potential interventions such as antioxidants, calorie restriction, hormone therapies, and supplements. These studies take time. A great deal of basic animal and clinical research remains to be done. And, because research is an incremental process, results can move knowledge forward, but it can also take scientists back to basics. Although one goal of NIA research is to determine whether these interventions improve the health of older people, have no effect, or are harmful, don't be surprised if the results of these studies open the door to more questions.

Until more is known about antioxidants, resveratrol, and hormone supplements, consumers should view these types of supplements with a good deal of caution and doubt. Despite what advertisements on television, the internet, and magazines may claim, there are no specific therapies proven to prevent aging. Some harmful side effects already have been discovered; additional research may uncover others.

People with genuine deficiencies in specific hormones should consult their doctors about appropriate treatments. Talk with your doctor if you are interested in any form of hormone therapy or "anti-aging" approaches beyond a healthy diet and physical activity. Meanwhile, people who choose to take any hormone supplement without a doctor's supervision should be aware that these supplements appear to have few clear-cut benefits for healthy individuals and no proven influence on the aging process.

Chapter 51

Hypertension (High Blood Pressure) and CAM

Hypertension (high blood pressure) is a common disease in which blood flows through blood vessels (arteries) at higher than normal pressures.

Measuring Blood Pressure

Blood pressure is the force of blood pushing against the walls of the arteries as the heart pumps blood. High blood pressure, sometimes called hypertension, happens when this force is too high. Health care workers check blood pressure readings the same way for children, teens, and adults. They use a gauge, stethoscope or electronic sensor, and a blood pressure cuff. With this equipment, they measure:

- **Systolic Pressure:** blood pressure when the heart beats while pumping blood

- **Diastolic Pressure:** blood pressure when the heart is at rest between beats

This chapter includes excerpts from "Hypertension (High Blood Pressure)," National Center for Complementary and Integrative Health (NCCIH), August 20, 2015; and text from "Description of High Blood Pressure," National Heart, Lung, and Blood Institute (NHLBI), September 10, 2015.

Health care workers write blood pressure numbers with the systolic number above the diastolic number. For example:

118/76 mmHg

People read "118 over 76"

millimeters of mercury.

Normal Blood Pressure

Normal blood pressure for adults is defined as a systolic pressure below 120 mmHg and a diastolic pressure below 80 mmHg. It is normal for blood pressures to change when you sleep, wake up, or are excited or nervous. When you are active, it is normal for your blood pressure to increase. However, once the activity stops, your blood pressure returns to your normal baseline range.

Blood pressure normally rises with age and body size. Newborn babies often have very low blood pressure numbers that are considered normal for babies, while older teens have numbers similar to adults.

Abnormal Blood Pressure

Abnormal increases in blood pressure are defined as having blood pressures higher than 120/80 mmHg. The following table outlines and defines high blood pressure severity levels.

The ranges in the table are blood pressure guides for adults who do not have any short-term serious illnesses. **People with diabetes or chronic kidney disease should keep their blood pressure below 130/80 mmHg.**

Table 51.1. Stages of High Blood Pressure in Adults

Stages	Systolic (top number)		Diastolic (bottom number)
Prehypertension	120–139	OR	80–89
High blood pressure Stage 1	140–159	OR	90–99
High blood pressure Stage 2	160 or higher	OR	100 or higher

Although blood pressure increases seen in prehypertension are less than those used to diagnose high blood pressure, prehypertension can progress to high blood pressure and should be taken seriously. Over time, consistently high blood pressure weakens and damages your blood vessels, which can lead to complications.

Types of High Blood Pressure

There are two main types of high blood pressure: primary and secondary high blood pressure.

Primary High Blood Pressure

Primary, or essential, high blood pressure is the most common type of high blood pressure. This type of high blood pressure tends to develop over years as a person ages.

Secondary High Blood Pressure

Secondary high blood pressure is caused by another medical condition or use of certain medicines. This type usually resolves after the cause is treated or removed.

Causes of High Blood Pressure

Changes, either from genes or the environment, in the body's normal functions may cause high blood pressure, including changes to kidney fluid and salt balances, the renin-angiotensin-aldosterone system, sympathetic nervous system activity, and blood vessel structure and function.

Biology and High Blood Pressure

Researchers continue to study how various changes in normal body functions cause high blood pressure. The key functions affected in high blood pressure include:

- Kidney fluid and salt balances
- Renin-angiotensin-aldosterone system
- Sympathetic nervous system activity
- Blood vessel structure and function

Kidney Fluid and Salt Balances

The kidneys normally regulate the body's salt balance by retaining sodium and water and excreting potassium. Imbalances in this kidney function can expand blood volumes, which can cause high blood pressure.

Renin-Angiotensin-Aldosterone System

The renin-angiotensin-aldosterone system makes angiotensin and aldosterone hormones. Angiotensin narrows or constricts blood vessels, which can lead to an increase in blood pressure. Aldosterone controls how the kidneys balance fluid and salt levels. Increased aldosterone levels or activity may change this kidney function, leading to increased blood volumes and high blood pressure.

Sympathetic Nervous System Activity

The sympathetic nervous system has important functions in blood pressure regulation, including heart rate, blood pressure, and breathing rate. Researchers are investigating whether imbalances in this system cause high blood pressure.

Blood Vessel Structure and Function

Changes in the structure and function of small and large arteries may contribute to high blood pressure. The angiotensin pathway and the immune system may stiffen small and large arteries, which can affect blood pressure.

Genetic Causes of High Blood Pressure

Much of the understanding of the body systems involved in high blood pressure has come from genetic studies. High blood pressure often runs in families. Years of research have identified many genes and other mutations associated with high blood pressure, some in the renal salt regulatory and renin-angiotensin-aldosterone pathways. However, these known genetic factors only account for 2 to 3 percent of all cases. Emerging research suggests that certain DNA changes during fetal development also may cause the development of high blood pressure later in life.

Environmental Causes of High Blood Pressure

Environmental causes of high blood pressure include unhealthy lifestyle habits, being overweight or obese, and medicines.

Unhealthy Lifestyle Habits

Unhealthy lifestyle habits can cause high blood pressure, including:

- High dietary sodium intake and sodium sensitivity
- Drinking excess amounts of alcohol
- Lack of physical activity

Overweight and Obesity

Research studies show that being overweight or obese can increase the resistance in the blood vessels, causing the heart to work harder and leading to high blood pressure.

Medicines

Prescription medicines such as asthma or hormone therapies, including birth control pills and estrogen, and over-the-counter medicines such as cold relief medicines may cause this form of high blood pressure. This happens because medicines can change the way your body controls fluid and salt balances, cause your blood vessels to constrict, or impact the renin-angiotensin-aldosterone system leading to high blood pressure.

Other Medical Causes of High Blood Pressure

Other medical causes of high blood pressure include other medical conditions such as chronic kidney disease, sleep apnea, thyroid problems, or certain tumors. This happens because these other conditions change the way your body controls fluids, sodium, and hormones in your blood, which leads to secondary high blood pressure.

Risk Factors for High Blood Pressure

Anyone can develop high blood pressure; however, age, race or ethnicity, being overweight, gender, lifestyle habits, and a family history of high blood pressure can increase your risk for developing high blood pressure.

Age

Blood pressure tends to rise with age. About 65 percent of Americans age 60 or older have high blood pressure. However, the risk for prehypertension and high blood pressure is increasing for children and teens, possibly due to the rise in the number of overweight children and teens.

Race/Ethnicity

High blood pressure is more common in African American adults than in Caucasian or Hispanic American adults. Compared with these ethnic groups, African Americans:

- Tend to get high blood pressure earlier in life.
- Often, on average, have higher blood pressure numbers.
- Are less likely to achieve target blood pressure goals with treatment.

Overweight

You are more likely to develop prehypertension or high blood pressure if you're overweight or obese. The terms "overweight" and "obese" refer to body weight that's greater than what is considered healthy for a certain height.

Gender

Before age 55, men are more likely than women to develop high blood pressure. After age 55, women are more likely than men to develop high blood pressure.

Lifestyle Habits

Unhealthy lifestyle habits can raise your risk for high blood pressure, and they include:

- Eating too much sodium or too little potassium
- Lack of physical activity
- Drinking too much alcohol
- Stress

Family History

A family history of high blood pressure raises the risk of developing prehypertension or high blood pressure. Some people have a high sensitivity to sodium and salt, which may increase their risk for high blood pressure and may run in families. Genetic causes of this condition are why family history is a risk factor for this condition.

Signs, Symptoms, and Complications of High Blood Pressure

Because diagnosis is based on blood pressure readings, this condition can go undetected for years, as symptoms do not usually appear until the body is damaged from chronic high blood pressure.

Complications of High Blood Pressure

When blood pressure stays high over time, it can damage the body and cause complications. Some common complications and their signs and symptoms include:

- **Aneurysms:** When an abnormal bulge forms in the wall of an artery. Aneurysms develop and grow for years without causing signs or symptoms until they rupture, grow large enough to press on nearby body parts, or block blood flow. The signs and symptoms that develop depend on the location of the aneurysm.

- **Chronic Kidney Disease:** When blood vessels narrow in the kidneys, possibly causing kidney failure.

- **Cognitive Changes:** Research shows that over time, higher blood pressure numbers can lead to cognitive changes. Signs and symptoms include memory loss, difficulty finding words, and losing focus during conversations.

- **Eye Damage:** When blood vessels in the eyes burst or bleed. Signs and symptoms include vision changes or blindness.

- **Heart Attack:** When the flow of oxygen-rich blood to a section of heart muscle suddenly becomes blocked and the heart doesn't get oxygen. The most common warning symptoms of a heart attack are chest pain or discomfort, upper body discomfort, and shortness of breath.

- **Heart Failure:** When the heart can't pump enough blood to meet the body's needs. Common signs and symptoms of heart failure include shortness of breath or trouble breathing; feeling tired; and swelling in the ankles, feet, legs, abdomen, and veins in the neck.

- **Peripheral Arterial Disease:** A disease in which plaque builds up in leg arteries and affects blood flow in the legs. When people have symptoms, the most common are pain, cramping, numbness, aching, or heaviness in the legs, feet, and buttocks after walking or climbing stairs.

- **Stroke:** When the flow of oxygen-rich blood to a portion of the brain is blocked. The symptoms of a stroke include sudden onset of weakness; paralysis or numbness of the face, arms, or legs; trouble speaking or understanding speech; and trouble seeing.

Diagnosis of High Blood Pressure

For most patients, health care providers diagnose high blood pressure when blood pressure readings are consistently 140/90 mmHg or above.

Confirming High Blood Pressure

A blood pressure test is easy and painless and can be done in a health care provider's office or clinic. To prepare for the test:

- Don't drink coffee or smoke cigarettes for 30 minutes prior to the test.

- Go to the bathroom before the test.

- Sit for 5 minutes before the test.

To track blood pressure readings over a period of time, the health care provider may ask you to come into the office on different days and at different times to take your blood pressure. The health care provider also may ask you to check readings at home or at other locations that have blood pressure equipment and to keep a written log of all your results.

Whenever you have an appointment with the health care provider, be sure to bring your log of blood pressure readings. Every time you visit the health care provider, he or she should tell you what your blood pressure numbers are; if he or she does not, you should ask for your readings.

Blood Pressure Severity and Type

Your health care provider usually takes 2–3 readings at several medical appointments to diagnose high blood pressure. Using the results of your blood pressure test, your health care provider will diagnose prehypertension or high blood pressure if:

- Your systolic or diastolic readings are consistently higher than 120/80 mmHg.
- Your child's blood pressure numbers are outside average numbers for children of the same age, gender, and height.

Once your health care provider determines the severity of your blood pressure, he or she can order additional tests to determine if your blood pressure is due to other conditions or medicines or if you have primary high blood pressure. Health care providers can use this information to develop your treatment plan.

Some people have "white coat hypertension." This happens when blood pressure readings are only high when taken in a health care provider's office compared with readings taken in any other location. Health care providers diagnose this type of high blood pressure by reviewing readings in the office and readings taken anywhere else. Researchers believe stress, which can occur during the medical appointment, causes white coat hypertension.

How Is High Blood Pressure Treated?

Based on your diagnosis, health care providers develop treatment plans for high blood pressure that include lifelong lifestyle changes and medicines to control high blood pressure; lifestyle changes such as weight loss can be highly effective in treating high blood pressure.

Treatment Plans

Health care providers work with you to develop a treatment plan based on whether you were diagnosed with primary or secondary high blood pressure and if there is a suspected or known cause. Treatment plans may evolve until blood pressure control is achieved.

If your health care provider diagnoses you with secondary high blood pressure, he or she will work to treat the other condition or change the medicine suspected of causing your high blood pressure. If high blood pressure persists or is first diagnosed as primary high blood pressure, your treatment plan will include lifestyle changes. When lifestyle changes alone do not control or lower blood pressure, your health care provider may change or update your treatment plan by prescribing medicines to treat the disease. Health care providers prescribe children and teens medicines at special doses that are safe and effective in children.

If your health care provider prescribes medicines as a part of your treatment plan, keep up your healthy lifestyle habits. The combination of the medicines and the healthy lifestyle habits helps control and lower your high blood pressure.

Some people develop "resistant" or uncontrolled high blood pressure. This can happen when the medications they are taking do not work well for them or another medical condition is leading to uncontrolled blood pressure. Health care providers treat resistant or uncontrolled high blood pressure with an intensive treatment plan that can include a different set of blood pressure medications or other special treatments.

To achieve the best control of your blood pressure, follow your treatment plan and take all medications as prescribed. Following your prescribed treatment plan is important because it can prevent or delay complications that high blood pressure can cause and can lower your risk for other related problems.

Healthy Lifestyle Changes

Healthy lifestyle habits can help you control high blood pressure. These habits include:

- Healthy eating

- Being physically active

- Maintaining a healthy weight

- Limiting alcohol intake

- Managing and coping with stress

To help make lifelong lifestyle changes, try making one healthy lifestyle change at a time and add another change when you feel that you have successfully adopted the earlier changes. When you practice several healthy lifestyle habits, you are more likely to lower your blood pressure and maintain normal blood pressure readings.

Healthy Eating

To help treat high blood pressure, health care providers recommend that you limit sodium and salt intake, increase potassium, and eat foods that are heart healthy.

Limiting Sodium and Salt

A low-sodium diet can help you manage your blood pressure. You should try to limit the amount of sodium that you eat. This means choosing and preparing foods that are lower in salt and sodium. Try to use low-sodium and "no added salt" foods and seasonings at the table or while cooking. Food labels tell you what you need to know about choosing foods that are lower in sodium. Try to eat no more than 2,300 mg sodium a day. If you have high blood pressure, you may need to restrict your sodium intake even more.

Your health care provider may recommend the Dietary Approaches to Stop Hypertension (DASH) eating plan if you have high blood pressure. The DASH eating plan focuses on fruits, vegetables, whole grains, and other foods that are heart healthy and low in fat, cholesterol, and salt.

The DASH eating plan is a good heart-healthy eating plan, even for those who don't have high blood pressure. Read more about the DASH eating plan.

Heart-Healthy Eating

Your health care provider also may recommend heart-healthy eating, which should include:

- Whole grains

- Fruits, such as apples, bananas, oranges, pears, and prunes

- Vegetables, such as broccoli, cabbage, and carrots

- Legumes, such as kidney beans, lentils, chick peas, black-eyed peas, and lima beans

- Fat-free or low-fat dairy products, such as skim milk

- Fish high in omega-3 fatty acids, such as salmon, tuna, and trout, about twice a week

When following a heart-healthy diet, you should avoid eating:

- A lot of red meat

- Palm and coconut oils

- Sugary foods and beverages

In the National Heart, Lung, and Blood Institute (NHLBI)-sponsored Hispanic Community Health Study/Study of Latinos, which studied Hispanics living in the United States, Cubans ate more sodium and Mexicans ate less sodium than other Hispanic groups in the study. All Hispanic Americans should follow these healthy eating recommendations even when cooking traditional Latino dishes. Try some of these popular Hispanic American heart-healthy recipes.

Being Physically Active

Routine physical activity can lower high blood pressure and reduce your risk for other health problems. Talk with your health care provider before you start a new exercise plan. Ask him or her how much and what kinds of physical activity are safe for you.

Everyone should try to participate in moderate-intensity aerobic exercise at least 2 hours and 30 minutes per week, or vigorous-intensity aerobic exercise for 1 hour and 15 minutes per week. Aerobic exercise, such as brisk walking, is any exercise in which your heart beats harder and you use more oxygen than usual. The more active you are, the more you will benefit. Participate in aerobic exercise for at least 10 minutes at a time, spread throughout the week.

Maintaining a Healthy Weight

Maintaining a healthy weight can help you control high blood pressure and reduce your risk for other health problems. If you're overweight or obese, try to lose weight. A loss of just 3 to 5 percent can lower your risk for health problems. Greater amounts of weight loss can improve blood pressure readings, lower LDL cholesterol, and increase HDL cholesterol. However, research shows that no matter your weight, it is important to control high blood pressure to maintain good health.

A useful measure of overweight and obesity is body mass index (BMI). BMI measures your weight in relation to your height. To figure out your BMI, check out NHLBI's online BMI calculator or talk to your health care provider.

A BMI:

- Below 18.5 is a sign that you are underweight.

- Between 18.5 and 24.9 is in the healthy range.

- Between 25 and 29.9 is considered overweight.

- Of 30 or more is considered obese.

A general goal to aim for is a BMI below 25. Your health care provider can help you set an appropriate BMI goal.

Measuring waist circumference helps screen for possible health risks. If most of your fat is around your waist rather than at your hips, you're at a higher risk for heart disease and type 2 diabetes. This risk may be high with a waist size that is greater than 35 inches for women or greater than 40 inches for men. To learn how to measure your waist, visit Assessing Your Weight and Health Risk.

Limiting Alcohol Intake

Limit alcohol intake. Too much alcohol will raise your blood pressure and triglyceride levels, a type of fat found in the blood. Alcohol also adds extra calories, which may cause weight gain.

Men should have no more than two drinks containing alcohol a day. Women should have no more than one drink containing alcohol a day. One drink is:

- 12 ounces of beer

- 5 ounces of wine

- 1½ ounces of liquor

Managing and Coping with Stress

Learning how to manage stress, relax, and cope with problems can improve your emotional and physical health and can lower high blood pressure. Stress management techniques include:

- Being physically active

- Listening to music or focusing on something calm or peaceful

- Performing yoga or tai chi

- Meditating

Medicines

Blood pressure medicines work in different ways to stop or slow some of the body's functions that cause high blood pressure. Medicines to lower blood pressure include:

- **Diuretics (Water or Fluid Pills):** Flush excess sodium from your body, which reduces the amount of fluid in your blood and helps to lower your blood pressure. Diuretics are often used with other high blood pressure medicines, sometimes in one combined pill.

- **Beta Blockers:** Help your heart beat slower and with less force. As a result, your heart pumps less blood through your blood vessels, which can help to lower your blood pressure.

- **Angiotensin-Converting Enzyme (ACE) Inhibitors:** Angiotensin-II is a hormone that narrows blood vessels, increasing blood pressure. ACE converts Angiotensin I to Angiotensin II. ACE inhibitors block this process, which stops the production of Angiotensin II, lowering blood pressure.

- **Angiotensin II Receptor Blockers (ARBs):** Block angiotensin II hormone from binding with receptors in the blood vessels. When angiotensin II is blocked, the blood vessels do not constrict or narrow, which can lower your blood pressure.

- **Calcium Channel Blockers:** Keep calcium from entering the muscle cells of your heart and blood vessels. This allows blood vessels to relax, which can lower your blood pressure.

- **Alpha Blockers:** Reduce nerve impulses that tighten blood vessels. This allows blood to flow more freely, causing blood pressure to go down.

- **Alpha-Beta Blockers:** Reduce nerve impulses the same way alpha blockers do. However, like beta blockers, they also slow the heartbeat. As a result, blood pressure goes down.

- **Central Acting Agents:** Act in the brain to decrease nerve signals that narrow blood vessels, which can lower blood pressure.

- **Vasodilators:** Relax the muscles in blood vessel walls, which can lower blood pressure.

To lower and control blood pressure, many people take two or more medicines. If you have side effects from your medicines, don't stop taking your medicines. Instead, talk with your health care provider about the side effects to see if the dose can be changed or a new medicine prescribed.

Future Treatments

Scientists, doctors, and researchers continue to study the changes that cause high blood pressure, to develop new medicines and treatments to control high blood pressure. Possible future treatments under investigation include new combination medicines, vaccines, and interventions aimed at the sympathetic nervous system, such as kidney nerve ablation.

Prevention of High Blood Pressure

Healthy lifestyle habits, proper use of medicines, and regular medical care can prevent high blood pressure or its complications.

Preventing High Blood Pressure Onset

Healthy lifestyle habits can help prevent high blood pressure from developing. It is important to check your blood pressure regularly. Children should have their blood pressure checked starting at 3 years of age. If prehypertension is detected, it should be taken seriously to avoid progressing to high blood pressure.

Preventing Worsening High Blood Pressure or Complications

If you have been diagnosed with high blood pressure, it is important to obtain regular medical care and to follow your prescribed treatment plan, which will include healthy lifestyle habit recommendations and possibly medicines. Not only can healthy lifestyle habits prevent high blood pressure from occurring, but they can reverse pre-hypertension and help control existing high blood pressure or prevent complications and long-term problems associated with this condition, such as coronary heart disease, stroke, or kidney disease.

Complementary Approaches

Some complementary health approaches are showing promise as elements of a program of lifestyle change that can help lower blood pressure.

- Research results show that some mind and body practices, such as meditation and yoga, may help reduce blood pressure in people with hypertension. A 2008 analysis also found evidence that qi gong can be a useful addition in controlling high blood pressure.

- In 2013, the American Heart Association suggested that biofeedback and Transcendental Meditation, in addition to conventional medication, can help people lower their blood pressure.

- Several studies suggest that certain dietary supplements including cocoa, coenzyme Q10, garlic, and fish oil (omega-3 fatty acids) may help reduce blood pressure in people being treated for hypertension. However, the evidence is very limited and sometimes conflicting.

Safety

- Lifestyle changes and, if necessary, conventional medicines can safely help most people control their blood pressure. If you're considering a complementary or integrative approach, you should discuss the decision with your health care provider. Do not replace your conventional treatment with an unproven product or practice.

- If you're considering a dietary supplement, remember that "natural" does not necessarily mean "safe." Some dietary supplements may have side effects including raising blood pressure, and some may interact with medications or other dietary supplements. Some vitamins and minerals are toxic at high doses.

- Relaxation techniques are generally considered safe for healthy people. There have been rare reports that certain relaxation techniques might cause or worsen symptoms in people with epilepsy or certain psychiatric conditions, or with a history of abuse or trauma. If you have heart disease, you should talk to your health care provider before doing progressive muscle relaxation.

Chapter 52

Irritable Bowel Syndrome and CAM

What's the Bottom Line?

What do we know about the effectiveness of complementary health approaches for Irritable Bowel Syndrome (IBS)?

- Although there isn't firm evidence, some studies suggest that mind and body practices, including **hypnotherapy**, may help.
- Researchers have investigated probiotics and a variety of dietary supplements for IBS. Some may improve IBS symptoms, but the quality of many of the studies is weak, so we can't draw conclusions about their effectiveness.

What do we know about the safety of complementary health approaches for IBS?

- Mind and body practices appear to be safe for IBS.
- Some dietary supplements studied for IBS can cause side effects, may interact with medications or other supplements, or contain ingredients not listed on the label.

Text in this chapter is excerpted from "Irritable Bowel Syndrome and Complementary Health Approaches: What You Need To Know," National Center for Complementary and Integrative Health (NCCIH), March 2015.

What Is IBS?

IBS is a chronic disorder that affects the large intestine and causes symptoms such as abdominal pain, cramping, constipation, and diarrhea.

As many as one in five Americans have symptoms of IBS. The cause of IBS isn't well understood but stress, large meals, certain foods, and alcohol may trigger symptoms in people with this disorder.

What the Science Says about the Effectiveness of Complementary Health Approaches for IBS

Some evidence is emerging that a few complementary health approaches may be helpful for IBS. However, the research is limited so we don't know for sure.

Mind and Body Practices for IBS

Acupuncture. For easing the severity of IBS, actual acupuncture wasn't better than simulated acupuncture, a 2012 systematic review reported. A 2009 clinical trial included in the review found that of the 230 participants with IBS, those who received either actual or simulated acupuncture did better than those who received no acupuncture.

Hypnotherapy (hypnosis). Researchers are studying gut-directed hypnotherapy (GDH), which focuses on improving bowel symptoms. Several IBS studies have found an association between hypnotherapy and long-term improvement in gastrointestinal symptoms, anxiety, depression, disability, and quality of life. The American College of Gastroenterology stated in a 2014 paper that there is some evidence that hypnosis helps with IBS symptoms, but the research is very uncertain.

- Just more than half of study participants who had 10 GDH sessions over 12 weeks felt better, compared with 25 percent of participants not assigned to undergo GDH, a 2013 study of 90 adults with IBS showed. The benefits lasted for at least 15 months. The non-GDH group had the same number of sessions of supportive talks with a physician who was trained in diseases related to stress and other factors.

- A research review suggested that children with IBS who underwent GDH had greater reductions in abdominal pain than children who received standard treatment. This was true whether the children underwent GDH with a therapist or listened to an audio recording. However, the result may not be reliable, as the researchers found only three small studies that met their standards.

- Many children and adolescents with mild symptoms of IBS who get only reassurance from their health care provider improve over time.

Mindfulness meditation training. Some studies suggest that mindfulness training helps people with IBS, but there's not enough evidence to draw firm conclusions.

- The American College of Gastroenterology stated in a 2014 paper that the few studies that have looked at mindfulness meditation training for IBS found no significant effects. But the authors noted that given the limited number of studies, they can't be sure it doesn't help. A 2013 review that included the same studies plus others concluded that mindfulness training improved IBS patients' pain and quality of life but not their depression or anxiety. The amount of improvement was small.

- A 2011 NCCIH-supported clinical trial (which was in the 2013 review) of 75 women with IBS showed that mindfulness training may decrease the severity of IBS symptoms, including psychological distress, compared to attending a support group. The benefits lasted for at least 3 months after the training ended.

Yoga. In a small 2014 NCCIH-supported study, young adults (18 to 26 years old) reported generally feeling better and having less pain, constipation, and nausea after completing a series of yoga classes, compared with a waitlist control group. They were still feeling better at the study's 2-month followup.

There's too little evidence to draw conclusions about the effectiveness of **meditation, relaxation training,** and **reflexology** for IBS.

Placebos, Placebo Effects, and IBS

To understand the usefulness of any intervention, rigorous studies are needed to compare the approach being tested with comparable but inactive products or practices, called placebos. The placebo effect describes improvements that aren't related specifically to the treatment being studied but to other factors, such as the patients' belief that they're taking something helpful. Even how a clinician talks with patients may lead to a positive response unrelated to the treatment. Placebo effects are often seen in IBS treatment studies.

In a 2008 clinical trial on placebos, 262 adults with IBS were given simulated acupuncture, simulated acupuncture with added positive attention from the health practitioners, or no intervention. None of the groups received actual acupuncture. The group that received the added positive attention improved the most, and the simulated acupuncture group fared better than the group who received no intervention.

Normally, researchers tell study participants that they'll receive either a placebo or the treatment being tested, but they won't know which they received until after the study. However, in a 2010 study, funded in part by NCCIH, which tested the placebo effect, the researchers told half of the members of a group of 80 IBS patients that that they were getting a placebo and that placebos have been shown to help patients. The others received no intervention. The practitioner interacted with the participants in both groups a similar amount. The placebo recipients' symptoms improved more than those of the no-treatment group.

About Dietary Supplements for IBS

A variety of dietary supplements, many of which are Chinese herbs and herb combinations, have been investigated for IBS, but we can't draw any conclusions about them because of the poor quality of many of the studies.

- **Chinese herbs.** In a 2008 systematic review, a combination of Chinese herbs was associated with improved IBS symptoms, but extracts of three single herbs had no beneficial effect.

- **Peppermint oil.** Peppermint oil capsules may be modestly helpful in reducing several common symptoms of IBS, including abdominal pain and bloating. It's superior to placebo in improving IBS symptoms, the American College of Gastroenterology stated in a 2014 paper.

- **Probiotics.** Generally, probiotics improve IBS symptoms, bloating, and flatulence, the American College of Gastroenterology stated in a 2014 paper. However, it noted that the quality of existing studies is limited. It's not possible to draw firm conclusions about specific probiotics for IBS in part because studies have used different species, strains, preparations, and doses.

- IBS patients given probiotics did no better than those who got a placebo, a 2013 clinical trial of 131 patients found. The group received either the placebo or probiotics for 6 months.

- In a 2012 review, 34 of 42 studies of probiotics for IBS symptoms found greater improvement in people taking probiotics than a placebo. However, the difference in improvement between the probiotic and placebo groups varied a lot among the studies.

- A 2011 review of studies on a strain of probiotic bacteria showed associations between taking probiotics and a decrease in symptoms in children with IBS.

More to Consider

- Unproven products or practices should not be used to replace conventional treatments for IBS or as a reason to postpone seeing a health care provider about IBS symptoms or any other health problem.

- If you're considering a practitioner-provided complementary practice such as hypnotherapy or acupuncture, ask a trusted source (such as the health care provider who treats your IBS or a nearby hospital) to recommend a practitioner. Find out about the training and experience of any practitioner you're considering.

- Keep in mind that dietary supplements may interact with medications or other supplements and may contain ingredients not listed on the label. Your health care provider can advise you. If you're pregnant or nursing a child, or if you're considering giving a child a dietary supplement, it's especially important to consult your (or your child's) health care provider.

• Tell all of your health care providers about any complementary health approaches you use. Give them a full picture of what you do to manage your health. This will help ensure coordinated and safe care.

Chapter 53

Low-Back Pain and CAM

Low-back pain (often referred to as "lower back pain") is a common condition that usually improves with self-care (practices that people can do by themselves, such as remaining active, applying heat, and taking pain-relieving medications). However, it is occasionally difficult to treat. Some health care professionals are trained to use a technique called spinal manipulation to relieve low-back pain and improve physical function (the ability to walk and move). This chapter provides basic information about low-back pain, summarizes research on spinal manipulation for low-back pain, and suggests sources for additional information.

Key Points

- Spinal manipulation is one of several options—including exercise, massage, and physical therapy—that can provide mild-to-moderate relief from low-back pain. Spinal manipulation appears to work as well as conventional treatments such as applying heat, using a firm mattress, and taking pain-relieving medications.

Text in this chapter is excerpted from "Spinal Manipulation for Low-Back Pain," National Center for Complementary and Integrative Health (NCCIH), April 2013.

- Spinal manipulation appears to be a generally safe treatment for low-back pain when performed by a trained and licensed practitioner. The most common side effects (e.g., discomfort in the treated area) are minor and go away within 1 to 2 days. Serious complications are very rare.

- Cauda equina syndrome (CES), a significant narrowing of the lower part of the spinal canal in which nerves become pinched and may cause pain, weakness, loss of feeling in one or both legs, and bowel or bladder problems, may be an extremely rare complication of spinal manipulation. However, it is unclear if there is actually an association between spinal manipulation and CES.

- Tell all your health care providers about any complementary health practices you use. Give them a full picture of what you do to manage your health. This will help ensure coordinated and safe care.

About Low-Back Pain

Back pain is one of the most common health complaints, affecting 8 out of 10 people at some point during their lives. The lower back is the area most often affected. For many people, back pain goes away on its own after a few days or weeks. But for others, the pain becomes chronic and lasts for months or years. Low-back pain can be debilitating, and it is a challenging condition to diagnose, treat, and study. The total annual costs of low-back pain in the United States—including lost wages and reduced productivity—are more than $100 billion.

About Spinal Manipulation

Spinal manipulation—sometimes called "spinal manipulative therapy"—is practiced by health care professionals such as chiropractors, osteopathic physicians, naturopathic physicians, physical therapists, and some medical doctors. Practitioners perform spinal manipulation by using their hands or a device to apply a controlled force to a joint of the spine. The amount of force applied depends on the form of manipulation used. The goal of the treatment is to relieve pain and improve physical functioning.

Side Effects and Risks

Reviews have concluded that spinal manipulation for low-back pain is relatively safe when performed by a trained and licensed practitioner. The most common side effects are generally minor and include feeling tired or temporary soreness.

Reports indicate that cauda equina syndrome (CES), a significant narrowing of the lower part of the spinal canal in which nerves become pinched and may cause pain, weakness, loss of feeling in one or both legs, and bowel or bladder problems, may be an extremely rare complication of spinal manipulation. However, it is unclear if there is actually an association between spinal manipulation and CES, since CES usually occurs without spinal manipulation. In people whose pain is caused by a herniated disc, manipulation of the low back appears to have a very low chance of worsening the herniation.

What the Science Says about Spinal Manipulation for Low-Back Pain

Overall, studies have shown that spinal manipulation is one of several options—including exercise, massage, and physical therapy—that can provide mild-to-moderate relief from low-back pain. Spinal manipulation also appears to work as well as conventional treatments such as applying heat, using a firm mattress, and taking pain-relieving medications.

In 2007 guidelines, the American College of Physicians and the American Pain Society included spinal manipulation as one of several treatment options for practitioners to consider when low-back pain does not improve with self-care. More recently, a 2010 Agency for Healthcare Research and Quality (AHRQ) report noted that complementary health therapies, including spinal manipulation, offer additional options to conventional treatments, which often have limited benefit in managing back and neck pain. The AHRQ analysis also found that spinal manipulation was more effective than placebo and as effective as medication in reducing low-back pain intensity. However, the researchers noted inconsistent results when they compared spinal manipulation with massage or physical therapy to reduce low-back pain intensity or disability.

Researchers continue to study spinal manipulation for low-back pain.

- A 2011 review of 26 clinical trials looked at the effectiveness of different treatments, including spinal manipulation, for chronic low-back pain. The authors concluded that spinal manipulation is as effective as other interventions for reducing pain and improving function.

- A 2010 review that looked at various manual therapies, such as spinal manipulation and massage, for a range of conditions found strong evidence that spinal manipulation is effective for chronic low-back pain and moderate evidence of its effectiveness for acute low-back pain.

- A 2009 analysis looked at the evidence from 76 trials that studied the effects of several conventional and complementary health practices for low-back pain. The researchers found that the pain-relieving effects of many treatments, including spinal manipulation, were small and were similar in people with acute or chronic pain.

- A 2008 review that focused on spinal manipulation for chronic low-back pain found strong evidence that spinal manipulation works as well as a combination of medical care and exercise instruction, moderate evidence that spinal manipulation combined with strengthening exercises works as well as prescription nonsteroidal anti-inflammatory drugs combined with exercises, and limited-to-moderate evidence that spinal manipulation works better than physical therapy and home exercise.

Researchers are investigating whether the effects of spinal manipulation depend on the length and frequency of treatment. In one study funded by National Center for Complementary and Integrative Health (NCCIH) that examined long-term effects in more than 600 people with low-back pain, results suggested that chiropractic care involving spinal manipulation was at least as effective as conventional medical care for up to 18 months. However, less than 20 percent of participants in this study were pain free at 18 months, regardless of the type of treatment used.

Researchers are also exploring how spinal manipulation affects the body. In an NCCIH-funded study of a small group of people with low-back pain, spinal manipulation affected pain perception in specific ways that other therapies (stationary bicycle and low-back extension exercises) did not.

Managing Low-Back Pain

A review of evidence-based clinical guidelines for managing low-back pain resulted in several recommendations for primary care physicians and pointed to potential benefits of nondrug therapies including spinal manipulation, as well as exercise, massage, and physical therapy:

- **Acute low-back pain:** Routine imaging (X-rays or MRIs) generally is not necessary for patients who have had non-specific low-back pain for a short time. These patients often improve on their own and usually should remain active, learn about back pain and self-care options, and consider nondrug therapies, including spinal manipulation, if pain persists longer than 4 weeks.
- **Chronic low-back pain:** Long-term use of opioid drugs usually does not improve functioning for patients with chronic low-back pain. However, these patients may benefit from nondrug therapies, including spinal manipulation. Psychological and social factors also may play a role in chronic low-back pain. Most patients will not become pain free; a realistic outlook focuses on improving function in addition to reducing pain.

Chapter 54

Mental Health Disorders and CAM

Chapter Contents

Section 54.1

Attention Deficit Hyperactivity Disorder (ADHD) and CAM

This section includes excerpts from "Attention-Deficit Hyperactivity Disorder – Facts about ADHD," Centers for Disease Control (CDC), June 26, 2015; text from "Attention-Deficit Hyperactivity Disorder," National Center for Complementary and Integrative Health (NCCIH), July 21, 2015; and text from "Attention-Deficit Hyperactivity Disorder at a Glance," National Center for Complementary and Integrative Health (NCCIH), June 2013.

Attention-deficit hyperactivity disorder (ADHD) is one of the most common neurodevelopmental disorders of childhood. It is usually first diagnosed in childhood and often lasts into adulthood. Children with ADHD may have trouble paying attention, controlling impulsive behaviors (may act without thinking about what the result will be), or be overly active.

Signs and Symptoms

It is normal for children to have trouble focusing and behaving at one time or another. However, children with ADHD do not just grow out of these behaviors. The symptoms continue and can cause difficulty at school, at home, or with friends.

A child with ADHD might:

- daydream a lot
- forget or lose things a lot
- squirm or fidget
- talk too much
- make careless mistakes or take unnecessary risks
- have a hard time resisting temptation
- have trouble taking turns
- have difficulty getting along with others

Types

There are three different types of ADHD, depending on which types of symptoms are strongest in the individual:

- **Predominantly Inattentive Presentation:** It is hard for the individual to organize or finish a task, to pay attention to details, or to follow instructions or conversations. The person is easily distracted or forgets details of daily routines.

- **Predominantly Hyperactive-Impulsive Presentation:** The person fidgets and talks a lot. It is hard to sit still for long (e.g., for a meal or while doing homework). Smaller children may run, jump or climb constantly. The individual feels restless and has trouble with impulsivity. Someone who is impulsive may interrupt others a lot, grab things from people, or speak at inappropriate times. It is hard for the person to wait their turn or listen to directions. A person with impulsiveness may have more accidents and injuries than others.

- **Combined Presentation:** Symptoms of the above two types are equally present in the person.

Because symptoms can change over time, the presentation may change over time as well.

Causes of ADHD

Scientists are studying cause(s) and risk factors in an effort to find better ways to manage and reduce the chances of a person having ADHD. The cause(s) and risk factors for ADHD are unknown, but current research shows that genetics plays an important role. Recent studies of twins link genes with ADHD.

In addition to genetics, scientists are studying other possible causes and risk factors including:

- Brain injury

- Environmental exposures (e.g., lead)

- Alcohol and tobacco use during pregnancy

- Premature delivery

- Low birth weight

Research does not support the popularly held views that ADHD is caused by eating too much sugar, watching too much television, parenting, or social and environmental factors such as poverty or family chaos. Of course, many things, including these, might make symptoms worse, especially in certain people. But the evidence is not strong enough to conclude that they are the main causes of ADHD.

Treatment

Bottom Line

Conventional treatment, which may include medication, behavior therapy, or a combination of both, is helpful for the majority of children with ADHD and for adults, too. Many complementary health approaches have been studied for ADHD, but none has been conclusively shown to be helpful. Approaches studied include omega-3 fatty acids and other dietary supplements, special diets, neurofeedback, and several mind and body practices. Research is continuing on some of these approaches.

Safety

- If you are considering a dietary supplement for ADHD, remember that "natural" does not necessarily mean "safe." Some dietary supplements may have side effects, and some may interact with medications or other dietary supplements. Some vitamins and minerals are toxic at high doses.

- Before using dietary supplements or other complementary approaches for ADHD, consult your health care provider.

People with attention-deficit hyperactivity disorder (ADHD) may have trouble paying attention or controlling impulsive behavior, and they may be overly active. Difficulty paying attention is the main problem for some people, hyperactivity and impulsiveness for others. Surveys estimate that as many as 9 percent of American children and 4 percent of adults have ADHD. Conventional treatment for ADHD includes medication, behavior therapy, or a combination of both. Stimulant medication (the most commonly used type of medication) has been shown to be helpful for at least 70 percent of children with ADHD.

What the Science Says

Although conventional treatment has been proven helpful for ADHD symptoms in children and adults, complementary approaches have not. Complementary health approaches studied for ADHD include the following:

Dietary supplements

- The possibility that omega-3 fatty acids could be helpful for ADHD is being investigated, but the evidence is inconclusive.

- Correcting deficiencies in the minerals zinc, iron, or magnesium may improve ADHD symptoms, but this does not mean that supplements of these minerals would be helpful for people with ADHD who are not deficient, and all three minerals can be toxic if taken in excessive amounts.

- Melatonin has not been shown to relieve ADHD symptoms, but it may help children with ADHD who have sleep problems to fall asleep sooner.

- Research on L-carnitine/acetyl-L-carnitine and various herbs, such as St. John's wort, French maritime pine bark extract (also known as Pycnogenol), and *Ginkgo biloba*, has not demonstrated that these supplements are helpful for ADHD.

- *Special diets.* Despite much research, the role of foods and food ingredients (such as color additives) in ADHD remains controversial. Some evidence suggests that only a small number of people with ADHD are affected by substances in food, and that different individuals may react to different foods or food components.

- *Neurofeedback.* Some research has suggested that neurofeedback, a technique in which people are trained to alter their brain wave patterns, may improve ADHD symptoms, but several small studies that compared neurofeedback with a simulated (sham) version of the procedure did not find differences between the two treatments.

- *Other complementary health approaches.* An assessment of research on homeopathy concluded that there is no evidence that it is helpful for ADHD symptoms. Several mind and body practices, including acupuncture, chiropractic care, massage therapy, meditation, and yoga, have been studied for ADHD. However, the amount of evidence on each of these practices is small, and no conclusions can be reached about whether they are helpful.

Side Effects and Risks

- Dietary supplements may have side effects and may interact with drugs. In particular, St. John's wort can speed up the process by which the body breaks down many drugs, thus making the drugs less effective. Zinc, iron, and magnesium can all be toxic in high doses.

- If you're interested in trying a special diet, consult your health care provider and consider getting guidance from a registered dietitian. Planning, evaluating, and following special diets can be challenging, and it is important to ensure that the diet meets nutritional needs.

- If you're considering using any of the approaches discussed here for ADHD, discuss this decision with your (or your child's) health care provider.

Section 54.2

Stress and CAM

Text in this section begins with excerpts from "Stress Fact Sheet,"
U.S. Department of Veteran Affairs (VA), July 2013.

Text in this section beginning with "5 Things To Know About
Relaxation Techniques for Stress," is excerpted from "5 Things
To Know About Relaxation Techniques for Stress," National
Center for Complementary and Integrative Health (NCCIH),
January 30, 2015.

What is Stress?

- Stress is a normal psychological and physical reaction to demands in our lives. It is the way our bodies react physically, emotionally, mentally, and behaviorally to any change in the status quo. Even imagined change can cause stress.

- Stress is highly individual. A situation that one person may find stressful may not bother another person. Stress occurs when something happens that we feel imposes a demand on us. When we perceive that we cannot cope, or feel inadequate to meet the demand, we begin to feel stress.

- Stress is not entirely bad. We need a certain amount of stress in our lives because it is stimulating and motivating. It gives us the energy to try harder and keeps us alert.

- When we find ourselves in situations that challenge us too much, we react with the "fight or flight" stress response.

- Stress actually begins in our brains and it is expressed in our body. Once we perceive stress, our body sends out chemical messengers in the form of stress hormones to help our bodies handle the stress.

What are Possible Symptoms of Stress?

- **Mental Symptoms:** forgetfulness, nervousness, confusion, poor concentration, lethargy, negativity, overly busy mind

- **Physical Symptoms:** tension, fatigue, insomnia, muscle aches, digestive upset, appetite change, headaches, restlessness

- **Emotional Symptoms:** anxiety, mood swings, irritability, depression, resentment, anger, impatience, worrying, feeling pressured

- **Social or Behavioral Symptoms:** lashing out, decreased sex drive, lack of intimacy, isolation, intolerance, loneliness, avoiding social situations, overuse of alcohol, tobacco, and/or drugs

- **Spiritual Symptoms:** apathy, loss of direction, emptiness, loss of life's meaning, unforgiving, no sense of purpose

How Does Stress Affect Our Health and Our Lives?

- 75 to 90% of all medical office visits are for stress-related ailments and complaints

- Stress is linked to the 6 leading causes of death in America – heart disease, cancer, lung ailments, accidents, cirrhosis of the liver, and suicide

- Stress is also implicated in hypertension, smoking, obesity, alcoholism, drug abuse, gastrointestinal problems, arthritis, immune system disturbances, skin disorders, neurological conditions, etc.

What Can You Do about Stress?

Your reaction to stress is determined by a combination of factors including your physiology, past successes/failures in coping with stress, and interpretations of stressful events in your life. Managing stress effectively is a complex skill – one you can learn with time and active participation. Cultivating constructive thinking, maintaining an optimistic and hopeful outlook, and altering patterns of negative thinking are some of the more important strategies.

The following strategies also can be of value:

Physical techniques:

- Exercise regularly and aim for 20 to 30 minutes at least 3 times each week
- Eat in moderation and choose a healthy diet
- Stop smoking
- Reduce alcohol
- Limit caffeine
- Get adequate rest

Psychological techniques:

- Learn to relax both mind and body – try deep/abdominal breathing, progressive muscle relaxation, and visualizing positive outcomes
- Build some fun into your routine
- Use humor
- Learn to look differently at situations that cause stress
- Learn to get along better with others
- Find ways to manage your time effectively
- Establish realistic expectations for yourself and others

Environmental techniques:

- Develop a social support network
- Maintain a neat, clean, and comfortable work area
- Improve lighting
- Reduce noise

- Open windows if possible

- Ban smoking

- Consider a humidifier

- Maintain indoor plants

When Is It Time to Ask for Help?

- If you feel trapped, as though there's nowhere to turn

- If you worry excessively and can't concentrate

Relaxation Techniques for Stress

When you're under stress, your body reacts by releasing hormones that produce the "fight-or-flight" response. Your heart rate and breathing rate go up and blood vessels narrow (restricting the flow of blood). Occasional stress is a normal coping mechanism. But over the long-term, stress may contribute to or worsen a range of health problems including digestive disorders, headaches, sleep disorders, and other symptoms.

In contrast to the stress response, the relaxation response slows the heart rate, lowers blood pressure, and decreases oxygen consumption and levels of stress hormones. In theory, voluntarily creating the relaxation response through regular use of relaxation techniques could counteract the negative effects of stress.

- **Relaxation techniques are generally safe, but there is limited evidence of usefulness for specific health conditions.** Research is under way to find out more about relaxation and health outcomes.

- **Relaxation techniques include a number of practices such as progressive relaxation, guided imagery, biofeedback, self-hypnosis, and deep breathing exercises.** The goal is similar in all: to consciously produce the body's natural relaxation response, characterized by slower breathing, lower blood pressure, and a feeling of calm and well-being.

- **Relaxation techniques often combine breathing and focused attention to calm the mind and the body.** These techniques may be most effective when practiced regularly and combined with good nutrition, regular exercise, and a strong social support system.

- **Most relaxation techniques can be self-taught and self-administered.** Most methods require only brief instruction from a book or experienced practitioner before they can be done without assistance.

- **Do not use relaxation techniques as a replacement for conventional care or to postpone seeing a doctor about a medical problem.** Talk to your health care providers if you are considering using a relaxation technique for a particular health condition. This will help ensure coordinated and safe care.

Chapter 55

Sleep Disorders and CAM

What's the Bottom Line?

What do we know about the usefulness of complementary approaches for sleep disorders?

- **Relaxation techniques** can be helpful for insomnia.
- **Melatonin** supplements may be helpful for sleep problems caused by shift work or jet lag. Melatonin may also be helpful for people with insomnia, but its effect is small.

What do we know about the safety of complementary approaches for sleep disorders?

- **Relaxation techniques** are generally considered safe.
- **Melatonin** appears to be relatively safe for short-term use, but its long-term safety has not been established.
- There are serious safety concerns about **kava** products (which have been linked to severe liver damage) and **L-tryptophan supplements** (which may be associated with a potentially serious disorder called eosinophilia-myalgia syndrome).

Text in this chapter is excerpted from "Sleep Disorders and Complementary Health Approaches: What You Need To Know," National Center for Complementary and Integrative Health (NCCIH), April 2014.

What Are Sleep Disorders and How Important Are They?

There are more than 80 different sleep disorders. This chapter focuses on insomnia—difficulty falling asleep or difficulty staying asleep. Insomnia is one of the most common sleep disorders.

Chronic, long-term sleep disorders affect millions of Americans each year. These disorders and the sleep deprivation they cause can interfere with work, driving, social activities, and overall quality of life, and can have serious health implications. Sleep disorders account for an estimated $16 billion in medical costs each year, plus indirect costs due to missed days of work, decreased productivity, and other factors.

Is It a Sleep Disorder or Not Enough Sleep?

Some people who feel tired during the day have a true sleep disorder, but for others, the real problem is not allowing enough time for sleep. Adults need at least 7 to 8 hours of sleep each night to be well rested, but the average adult sleeps for less than 7 hours a night. Sleep is a basic human need, like eating, drinking, and breathing, and is vital to good health and well-being. Shortchanging yourself on sleep slows your thinking and reaction time, makes you irritable, and increases your risk of injury. It may even decrease your resistance to infections, increase your risk of obesity, and increase your risk of heart disease.

What the Science Says about Complementary Health Approaches and Insomnia

Research has produced promising results for some complementary health approaches for insomnia, such as relaxation techniques. However, evidence of effectiveness is still limited for most products and practices, and safety concerns have been raised about a few.

Mind and Body Practices

- There is evidence that relaxation techniques can be effective in treating chronic insomnia.

- Progressive relaxation may help people with insomnia and nighttime anxiety.

- Music-assisted relaxation may be moderately beneficial in improving sleep quality in people with sleep problems, but the number of studies has been small.

- Various forms of relaxation are sometimes combined with components of cognitive-behavioral therapy (such as sleep restriction and stimulus control), with good results.

- Using relaxation techniques before bedtime can be part of a strategy to improve sleep habits that also includes other steps, such as maintaining a consistent sleep schedule; avoiding caffeine, alcohol, heavy meals, and strenuous exercise too close to bedtime; and sleeping in a quiet, cool, dark room.

- Relaxation techniques are generally safe. However, rare side effects have been reported in people with serious physical or mental health conditions. If you have a serious underlying health problem, it would be a good idea to consult your health care provider before using relaxation techniques.

- In a preliminary study, mindfulness-based stress reduction, a type of meditation, was as effective as a prescription drug in a small group of people with insomnia.

- Several other studies have also reported that mindfulness-based stress reduction improved sleep, but the people who participated in these studies had other health problems, such as cancer.

- Preliminary studies in postmenopausal women and women with osteoarthritis suggest that **yoga** may be helpful for insomnia.

- Some practitioners who treat insomnia have reported that **hypnotherapy** enhanced the effectiveness of cognitive-behavioral therapy and relaxation techniques in their patients, but very little rigorous research has been conducted on the use of hypnotherapy for insomnia.

- A small 2012 study on **massage therapy** showed promising results for insomnia in postmenopausal women. However, conclusions cannot be reached on the basis of a single study.

- Most of the studies that have evaluated **acupuncture** for insomnia have been of poor scientific quality. The current evidence is not rigorous enough to show whether acupuncture is helpful for insomnia.

Dietary Supplements

Melatonin and Related Supplements

- Melatonin may help with jet lag and sleep problems related to shift work.

561

- A 2013 evaluation of the results of 19 studies concluded that melatonin may help people with insomnia fall asleep faster, sleep longer, and sleep better, but the effect of melatonin is small compared to that of other treatments for insomnia.

- Studies of melatonin in children with sleep problems suggest that it may be helpful, both in generally healthy children and in those with conditions such as autism or attention-deficit hyperactivity disorder. However, both the number of studies and the number of children who participated in the studies are small, and all of the studies tested melatonin only for short periods of time.

- Melatonin supplements appear to be relatively safe for short-term use, although the use of melatonin was linked to bad moods in elderly people (most of whom had dementia) in one study.

- The long-term safety of melatonin supplements has not been established.

- Dietary supplements containing substances that can be changed into melatonin in the body—L-tryptophan and 5-hydroxytryptophan (5-HTP)—have been researched as sleep aids.

- Studies of L-tryptophan supplements as an insomnia treatment have had inconsistent results, and the effects of 5-HTP supplements on insomnia have not been established.

- The use of L-tryptophan supplements may be linked to eosinophilia-myalgia syndrome (EMS), a complex, potentially fatal disorder with multiple symptoms including severe muscle pain. It is uncertain whether the risk of EMS associated with L-tryptophan supplements is due to impurities in L-tryptophan preparations or to L-tryptophan itself.

Herbs

- Although chamomile has traditionally been used for insomnia, often in the form of a tea, there is no conclusive evidence from clinical trials showing whether it is helpful. Some people, especially those who are allergic to ragweed or related plants, may have allergic reactions to chamomile.

- Although kava is said to have sedative properties, very little research has been conducted on whether this herb is helpful for insomnia. More importantly, kava supplements have been linked to a risk of severe liver damage.

- Clinical trials of valerian (another herb said to have sedative properties) have had inconsistent results, and its value for insomnia has not been demonstrated. Although few people have reported negative side effects from valerian, it is uncertain whether this herb is safe for long-term use.

- Some "sleep formula" dietary supplements combine valerian with other herbs such as hops, lemon balm, passionflower, and kava or other ingredients such as melatonin and 5-HTP. There is little evidence on these preparations from studies in people.

Other Complementary Health Approaches

- Aromatherapy is the therapeutic use of essential oils from plants. It is uncertain whether aromatherapy is helpful for treating insomnia because little rigorous research has been done on this topic.

- A 2010 systematic review concluded that current evidence does not demonstrate significant effects of homeopathic medicines for insomnia.

Could You Have Sleep Apnea?

Do you snore loudly? Does your bed partner say that you make gasping or snorting sounds during the night? Do you fight off sleepiness during the day?

If you have any of these symptoms, talk to your health care provider. You might have sleep apnea—a condition in which sleep is disrupted because of pauses in breathing. For more information, visit the NHLBI Web site (www.nhlbi.nih.gov).

If You Are Considering Complementary Health Approaches for Sleep Problems

- Talk to your health care providers. Tell them about the complementary health approach you are considering and ask any questions you may have. Because trouble sleeping can be an indication of a more serious condition, and because some prescription and over-the-counter drugs can contribute to sleep problems, it is important to discuss your sleep-related symptoms with your health care providers before trying any complementary health product or practice.

- Be cautious about using any sleep product—prescription medications, over-the-counter medications, dietary supplements, or homeopathic remedies. Find out about potential side effects and any risks from long-term use or combining products.

- Keep in mind that "natural" does not always mean safe. For example, kava products can cause serious harm to the liver. Also, a manufacturer's use of the term "standardized" (or "verified" or "certified") does not necessarily guarantee product quality or consistency. Natural products can cause health problems if not used correctly. The health care providers you see about your sleep problems can advise you.

- If you are pregnant, nursing a child, or considering giving a child a dietary supplement or other natural health product, it is especially important to consult your (or your child's) health care provider.

- If you are considering a practitioner-provided complementary health practice, check with your insurer to see if the services will be covered, and ask a trusted source (such as your health care provider or a nearby hospital or medical school) to recommend a practitioner.

- Tell all your health care providers about any complementary health approaches you use. Give them a full picture of what you do to manage your health. This will help ensure coordinated and safe care.

Chapter 56

Women-Related Health Conditions and CAM

Pelvic Pain, Natural Child Birth, and Menopausal Symptoms

What is pelvic pain?

"Pelvic pain" is a general term used to describe pain that occurs mostly or only in the region below a woman's belly button. This region includes the lower stomach, lower back, bottom, and genital area.

Pelvic pain is chronic if it lasts for more than 6 months and affects a woman's quality of life. This condition is a common reason why women seek medical care.

This chapter includes excerpts from "Pelvic Pain: Condition Information," National Institute of Child Health and Human Development (NICHD), April 12, 2013; text from "What is natural childbirth?" National Institute of Child Health and Human Development (NICHD), August 14, 2014; text from "Menopausal Symptoms and Complementary Health Practices: What the Science Says," National Center for Complementary and Integrative Health (NCCIH), September 23, 2013; and text from "4 Things To Know About Menopausal Symptoms and Complementary Health Practices," National Center for Complementary and Integrative Health (NCCIH), January 30, 2015.

What are the symptoms of pelvic pain?

The symptoms of pelvic pain vary from woman to woman. Pelvic pain can be severe enough that it interferes with normal activities, such as going to work, exercising, or having sex.

Women describe pelvic pain in many ways. Pelvic pain can be steady, or it can come and go. It can be a sharp and stabbing pain felt in a specific spot, or a dull pain that is spread out. Some women have pain that occurs only during their menstrual periods. Some women feel pain when they need to use the bathroom, and some feel pain when lifting something heavy. Some women have pain in the vulva (the external genitals), which is called vulvodynia, during sex or when inserting a tampon.

How many women have pelvic pain?

About 15% of women of childbearing age in the United States report having pelvic pain that lasts at least 6 months. Among them, about 15% of employed women have pain that is severe enough to cause them to miss work.

What causes pelvic pain?

Researchers do not know the exact causes of pelvic pain. Often, pelvic pain signals that there may be a problem with one of the organs in the pelvic area. This organ could be a reproductive organ, such as the uterus (also called the womb), or other organs like the intestine or the bladder. Pain also can be a symptom of an infection.

The extent of a woman's pelvic pain is not always the same as the extent of the related condition. For example, if a woman has a physical abnormality that is associated with the pain, the size of the abnormality may be small, but she may still experience a lot of pain.

The following health problems can cause or contribute to pelvic pain:

- **Adhesions.** Adhesions are bands of tissue that form between internal tissues and organs and keep them from shifting easily as the body moves. They can form as a result of surgery or infections, such as pelvic inflammatory disease.

- **Endometriosis.** This condition occurs when tissues that normally grow inside the uterus grow somewhere else in the pelvis, such as on the outside of the uterus, ovaries, or fallopian tubes. The two most common symptoms of endometriosis are pain and infertility.

- **Interstitial cystitis/painful bladder syndrome.** This syndrome causes bladder pain and a need to urinate often and right away. This pain may be a burning or sharp pain in the bladder or at the opening where urine leaves the body.

- **Irritable bowel syndrome.** This syndrome is a digestive problem that can cause pain, bloating, constipation, or diarrhea. Researchers have yet to find a specific cause for irritable bowel syndrome but stress or certain foods can trigger symptoms in some people.

- **Pelvic floor disorders.** These disorders occur when the muscles and connective tissues that hold all the pelvic organs in place weaken or are injured. Sometimes the condition is caused by spasms or an increase in pelvic floor muscles tone. Pelvic floor disorders can cause discomfort and pain as well as functional problems, such as trouble with bladder control.

- **Uterine fibroids.** Uterine fibroids are noncancerous tumors made of muscle cells and other tissues that grow within and around the wall of the uterus. Symptoms can include heavy or painful periods, pain during sex, and lower back pain.

- **Vulvodynia.** This condition involves pain or discomfort of the vulva (the parts of the female sex organs that are on the outside of the body). This condition can cause burning, stinging, itching, or rawness of the vulva.

A woman may have more than one cause of pelvic pain at the same time. In some cases, a person with one chronic pain condition has an increased risk for other types of chronic pain. Sometimes, a woman's health care provider may not be able to find the cause of the pelvic pain.

What is natural childbirth?

Natural childbirth can refer to many different ways of giving birth without using pain medication, either in the home or at the hospital or birthing center.

Natural Forms of Pain Relief

Women who choose natural childbirth can use a number of natural ways to ease pain. These include:

- Emotional support

- Relaxation techniques

- A soothing atmosphere

- Moving and changing positions frequently

- Using a birthing ball

- Using soothing phrases and mental images

- Placing a heating pad or ice pack on the back or stomach

- Massage

- Taking a bath or shower

- Hypnosis

- Aromatherapy

- Acupuncture or acupressure

- Applying small doses of electrical stimulation to nerve fibers to activate the body's own pain-relieving substances (called transcutaneous electrical nerve stimulation, or TENS)

- Injecting sterile water into the lower back, which can relieve the intense discomfort and pain in the lower back known as back labor

A woman should discuss the many aspects of labor with her health care provider well before labor begins to ensure that she understands all of the options, risks, and benefits of pain relief during labor and delivery. It might also be helpful to put all the decisions in writing to clarify the options chosen.

Menopausal Symptoms and Complementary Health Practices : What the Science Says

Since the 2005 National Institutes of Health (NIH) panel's findings, scientists are continuing to build an evidence base on complementary therapies for menopausal symptoms. Results of research suggest that some mind and body approaches may be promising for reducing menopausal symptoms, while there is little evidence that natural products have any additional beneficial effects.

Mind and Body Therapies for Menopausal Symptoms

A growing body of evidence suggests that mind and body practices such as yoga, tai chi, qi gong, hypnosis, and acupuncture may benefit women during menopause. Research is under way to explore these preliminary findings.

- A 2010 review of 21 papers assessed mind and body therapies for menopausal symptoms. The researchers found that yoga, tai chi, and meditation-based programs may be helpful in reducing common menopausal symptoms including the frequency and intensity of hot flashes, sleep and mood disturbances, stress, and muscle and joint pain.

- Another 2010 review assessed studies that examined the use of acupuncture for hot flashes related to natural or induced menopause. The studies that the researchers included in their review were limited to acupuncture studies performed using needles stimulated by hand or electrically. The researchers found that acupuncture may reduce the frequency and severity of hot flashes; they also concluded that the effect may occur regardless of where the acupuncture needle is placed on the body. However, some studies did not provide sufficient evidence to support the use of acupuncture for hot flashes due to their small size and poor quality. Further research is needed in order to provide more conclusive results.

- A study funded by NCCAM found that hypnosis significantly improved various measures of hot flashes in a group of post-menopausal women. Although the mechanism of how clinical hypnosis works is unknown, the women in this same study who practiced hypnosis had significantly greater levels of satisfaction than the control group. An earlier study found that hypnosis appears to reduce perceived hot flashes in breast cancer survivors and may have additional benefits such as improved mood and sleep.

Natural Products and Menopausal Symptoms

Many natural products have been studied for their effects on menopausal symptoms, but scientists have found little evidence that they are helpful. While some herbs and botanicals are often found in over-the-counter formulas and combinations, many of these combination products have not been studied. Further, because natural products used for menopausal symptoms can have side effects and can interact with other botanicals or supplements or with medications, research in this area is addressing safety as well as efficacy. Some findings from this research are highlighted below.

Black Cohosh (Actaea racemosa, Cimicifuga racemosa)

Strength of Evidence

- Black cohosh has received more scientific attention for its possible effects on menopausal symptoms than have other botanicals.

Research Results

- A 2012 Cochrane systematic review on black cohosh for menopausal symptoms concludes that its efficacy has yet to be demonstrated.

- Other research suggests that black cohosh does not act like estrogen, as once was thought.

Safety

- United States Pharmacopeia experts suggest that **women should discontinue use of black cohosh and consult a health care practitioner if they have a liver disorder or develop symptoms of liver trouble,** such as abdominal pain, dark urine, or jaundice.

- There have been several case reports of hepatitis (inflammation of the liver), as well as liver failure, in women who were taking black cohosh. It is not known if black cohosh was responsible for these problems. Although these cases are very rare and the evidence is not definitive, scientists are concerned about the possible effects of black cohosh on the liver.

Soy

Strength of Evidence
There have been many studies on the effects of soy isoflavone supplements for menopausal symptoms.

Research Results

- The scientific literature includes mixed results on soy extracts for hot flashes. Some studies find benefits, but others do not.

Safety

- Although information on adverse effects is limited, soy extracts appear to be generally safe when taken for short periods of time. However, long-term use of soy extracts (which also contain phytoestrogens) has been associated with thickening of the lining of the uterus.

Dehydroepiandrosterone (DHEA)

DHEA is a naturally occurring substance that is changed in the body to the hormones estrogen and testosterone. DHEA is manufactured and sold as a dietary supplement.

Strength of Evidence

- There have been several small studies of DHEA for menopausal symptoms.

Research Results

- A few small studies have suggested that DHEA might possibly have some benefit for hot flashes and decreased sexual arousal, although small randomized controlled trials have shown no benefit.

Safety

- Concerns have been raised about the safety of DHEA because it is converted in the body to hormones, which are known to carry risks. Its long-term effects, risks, and benefits have not been well studied, and it remains unclear whether it might increase the risk for breast or prostate cancer.

- There is the possibility that even short-term use of DHEA supplements might have detrimental effects on the body.

Other Natural Products

- Other natural products have been studied for their effects on menopausal symptoms. The 2005 NIH panel found no consistent or conclusive evidence that red clover, Asian ginseng, or *kava* decreases hot flashes. Very few studies of dong quai have been done, but findings from one trial demonstrated no benefit.

- A review of the research literature of red clover also found no apparent evidence of adverse events from short-term use (up

571

to 16 weeks). However, the same review noted the lack of data on the safety of long-term use. There are some concerns that red clover, which contains phytoestrogens, might have harmful effects on hormone-sensitive tissue.

- Short-term use of Asian ginseng at recommended doses appears to be safe for most people; however, some sources suggest that prolonged use might cause side effects. Asian ginseng may lower levels of blood sugar; this effect may be seen more in people with diabetes. Therefore, people with diabetes should use extra caution with Asian ginseng, especially if they are using medicines to lower blood sugar or taking other herbs, such as bitter melon and fenugreek, that are also thought to lower blood sugar.

- **It is important to note that kava has been associated with liver disease.** The U.S. Food and Drug Administration (FDA) has issued a warning to patients and providers about *kava* because of its potential to damage the liver.

- *Dong quai* is known to interact with, and increase the activity in the body of, the blood-thinning medicine warfarin. This can lead to bleeding complications in women who take dong quai.

Bio-Identical Hormone Replacement Therapy

"Bio-identical hormone replacement therapy," or BHRT, is a marketing term that is not recognized by the FDA. It is a term used to describe medications that are prepared in specialized pharmacies. BHRT may contain any variation of hormones including estrone, estradiol, estriol, progesterone, and testosterone.

Compounded bio-identical hormones are often marketed as natural and safe alternatives to conventional hormone therapy prescription medications. However, compounded formulas are often inconsistent and can vary depending on the batch or the pharmacist. While FDA-approved hormone preparations have been tested for efficacy, purity, safety, and potency, there is a lack of scientific evidence surrounding BHRT and the safety and efficacy of these compounds. As a result, compounded bio-identical hormones are not approved by the FDA.

4 Things To Know about Menopausal Symptoms and Complementary Health Practices

Menopause is the permanent end of a woman's menstrual periods. Menopause can occur naturally or be caused by surgery, chemotherapy, or radiation. A woman is said to have completed natural menopause when she has not had a period for 12 consecutive months. For American women, this typically happens at around age 51 or 52.

Some symptoms that women experience as they age are related to menopause and decreased activity of the ovaries. Other symptoms may be related to aging in general. For decades, menopausal hormone therapy was a widely used treatment for menopausal symptoms, but findings from the Women's Health Initiative raised serious concerns about the long-term safety of menopausal hormone therapy. Natural products or mind and body practices are sometimes used in an effort to relieve menopausal symptoms such as hot flashes and night sweats. Here are 4 things to know if you are considering a complementary health practice for menopausal symptoms:

1. **Mind and body practices such as yoga, tai chi, qi gong, hypnosis, and acupuncture may help reduce the severity of menopausal symptoms.** Researchers looked at mind and body therapies for menopausal symptoms and found that yoga, tai chi, and meditation-based programs may be helpful in reducing common menopausal symptoms including the frequency and intensity of hot flashes, sleep and mood disturbances, stress, and muscle and joint pain.

2. **Many natural products, such as black cohosh, soy isoflavone supplements, and DHEA, have been studied for their effects on menopausal symptoms, but scientists have found little evidence that they are helpful.** There is also no conclusive evidence that the herbs red clover, kava, or dong quai reduce hot flashes.

3. **Natural products used for menopausal symptoms can have side effects and can interact with other botanicals or supplements or with medications.** For example, United States Pharmacopeia experts suggest that women should discontinue use of black cohosh and consult a health care provider if they have a liver disorder or develop symptoms of liver trouble, such as abdominal pain, dark urine, or jaundice. Also, concerns have been raised about the safety of DHEA because

it is converted in the body to hormones, which are known to carry risks.

4. **Tell all your health care providers about any complementary health practices you use.** Give them a full picture of what you do to manage your health. This will help ensure coordinated and safe care.

Part Six

Additional Help and Information

Chapter 57

Glossary of Terms Related to Complementary and Alternative Medicine

acupuncture: A family of procedures that originated in traditional Chinese medicine. Acupuncture is the stimulation of specific points on the body by a variety of techniques, including the insertion of thin metal needles through the skin. It is intended to remove blockages in the flow of qi and restore and maintain health.

Alexander technique: Alexander technique is a movement therapy that uses guidance and education on ways to improve posture and movement. The intent is to teach a person how to use muscles more efficiently in order to improve the overall functioning of the body. Examples of the Alexander technique as CAM are using it to treat low-back pain and the symptoms of Parkinson's disease.

aromatherapy: Aromatherapy is the use of essential oils from plants to support and balance the mind, body, and spirit. Aromatherapy may be combined with other complementary treatments like massage therapy and acupuncture, as well as with standard treatments.

Ayurvedic medicine: Ayurvedic medicine (also called Ayurveda) is one of the world's oldest medical systems. It originated in India and has evolved there over thousands of years. In the United States, Ayurvedic

This glossary contains terms excerpted from documents produced by several sources deemed reliable.

medicine is considered complementary and alternative medicine. The aim of Ayurvedic medicine is to integrate and balance the body, mind, and spirit. This is believed to help prevent illness and promote wellness.

biofeedback: A method of learning to voluntarily control certain body functions such as heartbeat, blood pressure, and muscle tension with the help of a special machine. This method can help control pain.2

biologically based therapy: This area of CAM includes, but is not limited to, botanicals, animal-derived extracts, vitamins, minerals, fatty acids, amino acids, proteins, prebiotics and probiotics, whole diets, and functional foods.

botanical: A plant or plant part valued for its medicinal or therapeu- tic properties, flavor, and/or scent. Herbs are a subset of botanicals. Products made from botanicals that are used to maintain or improve health may be called herbal products, botanical products, or phyto- medicines.

chelation therapy: Chelation therapy is an investigational therapy using a man-made amino acid, called EDTA (ethylene-diamine-tetra-acetic acid). It is added to the blood through a vein. Disodium EDTA has been in widespread use since the 1970s for disease of the heart and arteries.

chiropractic: A whole medical system that focuses on the relation-ship between the body's structure—mainly the spine—and function. Practitioners perform adjustments (also called manipulation) with the goal of correcting structural alignment problems to assist the body in healing.

chiropractic care: This care involves the adjustment of the spine and joints to influence the body's nervous system and natural defense mechanisms to alleviate pain and improve general health. It is pri-marily used to treat back problems, headaches, nerve inflammation, muscle spasms, and other injuries and traumas.

cholesterol: Cholesterol is a fat-like substance that is made by your body and found naturally in animal foods such as dairy products, eggs, meat, poultry, and seafood. Foods high in cholesterol include dairy fats, egg yolks, and organ meats such as liver. Cholesterol is needed to carry out functions such as hormone and vitamin production. It is carried through the blood by [lipoproteins].

clinical trial: A type of research study that uses volunteers to test the safety and efficacy (the ability to produce a beneficial effect) of new methods of screening (checking for disease when there are no symp- toms), prevention, diagnosis, or treatment of a disease. Also called a clinical study.

complementary and alternative medicine: A group of diverse medical and health care systems, practices, and products that are not presently considered to be part of conventional medicine. Complementary medicine is used together with conventional medicine, and alternative medicine is used in place of conventional medicine.

conventional medicine: Medicine as practiced by holders of MD (medical doctor) or DO (doctor of osteopathy) degrees and by their allied health professionals such as physical therapists, psychologists, and registered nurses.

Daily Value (DV): A term used on a food or dietary supplement product label to describe the recommended levels of intake of a nutrient. The percent Daily Value (% DV) represents how much of a nutrient is provided in one serving of the food or dietary supplement. For example, the DV for calcium is 1,000 mg (milligrams); a food that has 200 mg of calcium per serving would state on the label that the % DV for calcium is 20%.

dietary supplement: A product that is intended to supplement the diet; contains one or more dietary ingredients (including vitamins, minerals, herbs or other botanicals, amino acids, and certain other substances) or their constituents; and is intended to be taken by mouth, in forms such as tablet, capsule, powder, softgel, gelcap, or liquid.

Energy healing therapy: Energy healing therapy involves the channeling of healing energy through the hands of a practitioner into the client's body to restore a normal energy balance and, therefore, health. Energy healing therapy has been used to treat a wide variety of ailments and health problems, and is often used in conjunction with other alternative and conventional medical treatments.

Feldenkrais: Feldenkrais is a movement therapy that uses a method of education in physical coordination and movement. Practitioners use verbal guidance and light touch to teach the method through one-on-one lessons and group classes. The intent is to help the person become more aware of how the body moves through space and to improve physical functioning.

guided imagery: A type of CAM that encourages imagining a pleasant scene to take your mind off your pain or anxiety.

herbal supplements: One type of dietary supplement. An herb is a plant or plant part (such as leaves, flowers, or seeds) that is used for its flavor, scent, and/or therapeutic properties. Botanical is often used as a synonym for herb. An herbal supplement may contain a single herb or mixtures of herbs.

homeopathy: A whole medical system that originated in Europe. Homeopathy seeks to stimulate the body's ability to heal itself by giv- ing very small doses of highly diluted substances that in larger doses would produce illness or symptoms (an approach called "like cures like").

hypnosis: A trance-like state in which a person becomes more aware and focused and is more open to suggestion.

magnet therapy: A magnet produces a measurable force called a magnetic field. Magnets are used for many different types of pain, including foot pain and back pain from conditions such as arthritis and fibromyalgia. Magnets in products such as magnetic patches and disks, shoe insoles, bracelets, and mattress pads are used for pain in the foot, wrist, back, and other parts of the body.

manipulation: The application of controlled force to a joint, moving it beyond the normal range of motion in an effort to aid in restoring health. Manipulation may be performed as a part of other therapies or whole medical systems, including chiropractic medicine, massage, and naturopathy.

manipulative and body-based practices: A group of CAM inter- ven- tions and therapies that include chiropractic and osteopathic manipulation, massage therapy, Tui Na, reflexology, Rolfing, Bowen technique, Trager bodywork, Alexander technique, Feldenkrais method, and a host of others.

massage: Pressing, rubbing, and moving muscles and other soft tis- sues of the body, primarily by using the hands and fingers. The aim is to increase the flow of blood and oxygen to the massaged area.

meditation: Refers to a variety of techniques or practices intended to focus or control attention. Most of them are rooted in Eastern religious or spiritual traditions. These techniques have been used by many dif- ferent cultures throughout the world for thousands of years.

mind-body medicine: Medicine that focuses on the interactions among the brain, mind, body, and behavior, and the powerful ways in which emotional, mental, social, spiritual, and behavioral factors can directly affect health. It regards as fundamental an approach that respects and enhances each person's capacity for self-knowledge and self-care, and it emphasizes techniques that are grounded in this ap- proach.

mineral: In nutrition, an inorganic substance found in the earth that is required to maintain health.

Native American Healer or Medicine Man: A Native American Healer or Medicine Man is a traditional healer who uses information from the "spirit world" in order to benefit the community. People see Native American healers for a variety of reasons, especially to find relief or a cure from illness or to find spiritual guidance.

naturopathy: A whole medical system that originated in Europe. Naturopathy aims to support the body's ability to heal itself through the use of dietary and lifestyle changes together with CAM therapies such as herbs, massage, and joint manipulation.

omega-3 fatty acids: Polyunsaturated fatty acids that come from foods such as fish, fish oil, vegetable oil (primarily canola and soybean), walnuts, and wheat germ. Omega-3s are important in a number of bodily functions, including the movement of calcium and other sub- stances in and out of cells, the relaxation and contraction of muscles, blood clotting, digestion, fertility, cell division, and growth. In addition, omega-3s are thought to protect against heart disease, reduce inflam- mation, and lower triglyceride levels.

osteopathic manipulation: Osteopathic manipulation is a full-body system of hands-on techniques to alleviate pain, restore function, and promote health and well-being.

pilates: Pilates is a movement therapy that uses a method of phys- ical exercise to strengthen and build control of muscles, especially those used for posture. Awareness of breathing and precise control of movements are integral components of Pilates. Special equipment, if available, is often used.

polyunsaturated fat: This type of fat is liquid at room temperature. There are two types of polyunsaturated fatty acids (PUFAs): omega-6 and omega-3. Omega-6 fatty acids are found in liquid vegetable oils, such as corn oil, safflower oil, and soybean oil. Omega-3 fatty acids come from plant sources—including canola oil, flaxseed, soybean oil, and walnuts—and from fish and shellfish.

probiotics: Live microorganisms (in most cases, bacteria) that are similar to beneficial microorganisms found in the human gut. They are also called friendly bacteria or good bacteria. Probiotics are available to consumers mainly in the form of dietary supplements and foods.

progressive relaxation: Progressive relaxation is used to relieve tension and stress by systematically tensing and relaxing successive muscle groups.

qi: In traditional Chinese medicine, the vital energy or life force proposed to regulate a person's spiritual, emotional, mental, and physical health and to be influenced by the opposing forces of yin and yang.

Qi gong: Qi gong is an ancient Chinese discipline combining the use of gentle physical movements, mental focus, and deep breathing directed toward specific parts of the body. Performed in repetitions, the exercises are normally performed two or more times a week for 30 minutes at a time.

reflexology: A type of massage, which applies pressure to the feet (or sometimes the hands or ears), to promote relaxation or healing in other parts of the body.

Reiki: A healing practice that originated in Japan. Reiki practitioners place their hands lightly on or just above the person receiving treatment, with the goal of facilitating the person's own healing response.

saturated fat: Fat that consists of triglycerides containing only saturated fatty acid radicals (i.e., they have no double bonds between the carbon atoms of the fatty acid chain and are fully saturated with hydrogen atoms). Dairy products, animal fats, coconut oil, cottonseed oil, palm kernel oil, and chocolate can contain high amounts of saturated fats.

spirituality: Spirituality may be defined as an individual's sense of peace, purpose, and connection to others, and beliefs about the meaning of life. Spirituality may be found and expressed through an organized religion or in other ways.

tai chi: Tai chi, which originated in China as a martial art, is a mind-body practice in complementary and alternative medicine. Tai chi is sometimes referred to as moving meditation—practitioners move their bodies slowly, gently, and with awareness, while breathing deeply.

traditional Chinese medicine: A whole medical system that originated in China. It is based on the concept that disease results from disruption in the flow of qi and imbalance in the forces of yin and yang. Practices such as herbs, meditation, massage, and acupuncture seek to aid healing by restoring the yin-yang balance and the flow of qi.

vegan: A person who does not eat any foods that come from animals, including meat, eggs, and dairy products.

vegetarian: A person who eats a diet free of meat. Lacto-vegetarians consume milk and milk products along with plant-based foods. They do not eat eggs. Lacto-ovo vegetarians eat eggs and milk and milk products, in addition to plant-based foods.

vitamin: A nutrient that the body needs in small amounts to function and maintain health. Examples are vitamins A, C, and E.

whole medical system: A complete system of theory and practice that has evolved over time in different cultures and apart from conventional medicine. Examples of whole medical systems include traditional Chinese medicine, Ayurvedic medicine, homeopathy, and naturopathy.

yin and yang: The concept of two opposing yet complementary forces described in traditional Chinese medicine. Yin represents cold, slow, or passive aspects of the person, while yang represents hot, excited, or active aspects. A major theory is that health is achieved through balancing yin and yang and disease is caused by an imbalance leading to a blockage in the flow of qi.

yoga: A mind-body practice in complementary and alternative medicine with origins in ancient Indian philosophy. The various styles of yoga that people use for health purposes typically combine physical postures, breathing techniques, and meditation or relaxation.

Chapter 58

Directory of Organizations That Provide Information about Complementary and Alternative Medicine

Government Agencies That Provide Information about Complementary and Alternative Medicine

Agency for Healthcare Research and Quality
Office of Communications and Knowledge Transfer
540 Gaither Rd., Second Fl.
Rockville, MD 20850
Phone: 301-427-1364
Fax: 301-427-1873
Website: www.ahrq.gov

Centers for Disease Control and Prevention
1600 Clifton Rd.
Atlanta, GA 30333
Toll-Free: 800-CDC-INFO (232-4636)
Phone: 404-639-3311
Website: www.cdc.gov
E-mail: cdcinfo@cdc.gov

Resources in this chapter were compiled from several sources deemed reliable; all contact information was verified and updated in August 2015.

Healthfinder®
National Health Information Center
P.O. Box 1133
Washington, DC 20013-1133
Toll-Free: 800-336-4797
Phone: 301-565-4167
Fax: 301-984-4256
Website: www.healthfinder.gov
E-mail: healthfinder@nhic.org

National Cancer Institute
6116 Executive Blvd.
Rm. 3036A
Bethesda, MD 20892-8322
Toll-Free: 800-4-CANCER
(422-6237)
Website: www.cancer.gov
E-mail: cancergovstaff@mail.nih
.gov

*National Institute
of Arthritis and
Musculoskeletal and Skin
Diseases*
National Institutes of Health
1 AMS Cir.
Bethesda, MD 20892-3675
Toll Free: 877-22-NIAMS
(226-4267)
Phone: 301-495-4484
Fax: 301-718-6366
Website: www.niams.nih.gov
E-mail: NIAMSinfo@mail.nih.
gov

*National Institute of
Diabetes, Digestive and
Kidney Diseases*
Bldg. 31, Rm. 9A06 31 Center Dr.
MSC 2560
Bethesda, MD 20892-2560
Phone: 301-496-3583
Website: www.niddk.nih.gov

*National Institute of
Neurological Disorders and
Stroke*
NIH Neurological Institute
P.O. Box 5801
Bethesda, MD 20824
Toll-Free: 800-352-9424
Phone: 301-496-5751
Website: www.ninds.nih.gov
E-mail: braininfo@ninds.nih.gov

National Institute on Aging
Bldg. 31, Rm. 5C27 31 Center
Dr., MSC 2292
Bethesda, MD 20892
Phone: 301-496-1752
Fax: 301-496-1072
Website: www.nia.nih.gov

National Institutes of Health
9000 Rockville Pike
Bethesda, MD 20892
Phone: 301-496-4000
Website: www.nih.gov
E-mail: NIHinfo@od.nih.gov

Substance Abuse and Mental Health Services Administration
SAMHSA's Health Information Network
P.O. Box 2345
Rockville, MD 20847-2345
Phone: 877-SAMHSA-7 (726-4727)
Fax: 240-221-4292
Website: www.samhsa.gov
E-mail: SHIN@samhsa.hhs.gov

U.S. Department of Health and Human Services
200 Independent Ave., S.W.
Washington, DC 20201
Toll-Free: 877-696-6775
Website: www.hhs.gov

U.S. Food and Drug Administration
10903 New Hampshire Ave.
Silver Spring, MD 20903
Toll-Free: 888-463-6332
Website: www.fda.gov

U.S. National Library of Medicine
8600 Rockville Pike
Bethesda, MD 20894
Toll-Free: 888-FIND-NLM (346-3656)
Phone: 301-594-5983
Fax: 301-402-1384
Website: www.nlm.nih.gov
E-mail: custserv@nlm.nih.gov

Private Agencies That Provide Information about Complementary and Alternative Medicine

Acupressure Institute
Website: www.acupressure.com
E-mail: info@acupressure.com

Alexander Technique International
1692 Massachusetts Ave., 3rd Fl.
Cambridge, MA 02138
Toll-Free: 888-668-8996
Phone: 617-497-5151
Fax: 617-497-2615
Website: www.ati-net.com

Alliance of International Aromatherapists
9956 W. Remington Pl., Unit A10 Ste. 323
Littleton, CO 80128
Toll Free: 877-531-6377
Phone: 303-531-6377
Fax: 303-979-7135
Website: www.alliance-aromatherapists.org
E-mail: info@alliance-aromatherapists.org

Alternative Medicine Foundation, Inc.
P.O. Box 60016
Potomac, MD 20859
Website: www.amfoundation.org

American Academy of Anti-Aging Medicine
301 Yamato Rd.
Ste. 2199
Boca Raton, FL 33431
Toll-Free: 888-997-0112
Fax: 561-997-0287
Website: www.worldhealth.net
E-mail: info@a4m.com

American Academy of Family Physicians
11400 Tomahawk Creek Pkwy
Leawood, KS 66211-2680
Toll-Free: 800-274-2237
Fax: 913-906-6075
Website: www.aafp.org

American Academy of Medical Acupuncture
1970 E. Grand Ave.
Ste. 330
El Segundo, CA 90245
Phone: 310-364-0193
Website: www.
medicalacupuncture.org
E-mail: administrator@
medicalacupuncture.org

American Apitherapy Society
500 Arthur St.
Centerport, NY 11721
Phone: 631-470-9446
Website: www.apitherapy.org

American Association of Acupuncture and Oriental Medicine
P.O. Box 162340
Sacramento, CA 95816
Toll-Free: 866-455-7999
Phone: 916-443-4770
Fax: 916-443-4766
Website: www.aaaomonline.org

American Association of Colleges of Osteopathic Medicine
5550 Friendship Blvd.
Ste. 310
Chevy Chase, MD 20815-7231
Phone: 301-968-4100
Fax: 301-968-4101
Website: www.aacom.org

American Association of Integrative Medicine
2750 E. Sunshine
Springfield, MO 65804
Toll-Free: 877-718-3053
Phone: 417-881-9995
Fax: 417-823-9959
Website: www.aaimedicine.com

American Association of Naturopathic Physicians
4435 Wisconsin Ave. N.W.
Ste. 403
Washington, DC 20016
Toll-Free: 866-538-2267
Phone: 202-237-8150
Fax: 202-237-8152
Website: www.naturopathic.org
E-mail: member.services@
naturopathic.org

American Botanical Council
6200 Manor Rd.
Austin, TX 78723
Phone: 512-926-4900
Fax: 512-926-2345
Website: abc.herbalgram.org
E-mail: abc@herbalgram.org

American Chiropractic Association
1701 Clarendon Blvd.
Arlington, VA 22209
Phone: 703-276-8800
Fax: 703-243-2593
Website: www.acatoday.org

American Dance Therapy Association
10632 Little Patuxent Pkwy
Ste. 108
Columbia, MD 21044-3263
Phone: 410-997-4040
Fax: 410-997-4048
Website: www.adta.org
E-mail: info@adta.org

American Feng Shui Institute
111 N. Atlantic Blvd.
Ste. 352
Monterey Park, CA 91754
Website: www.amfengshui.com
E-mail: fsinfo@amfengshui.com

American Herbalists Guild
141 Nob Hill Rd.
Cheshire, CT 06410
Phone: 203-272-6731
Fax: 203-272-8550
Website: www.
americanherbalistsguild.com
E-mail: ahgoffice@earthlink.net

American Holistic Health Association
P.O. Box 17400
Anaheim, CA 92817-7400
Phone: 714-779-6152
Website: www.ahha.org
E-mail: mail@ahha.org

American Massage Therapy Association
500 Davis St.
Ste. 900
Evanston, IL 60201
Toll-Free: 877-905-2700
Phone: 847-864-0123
Fax: 847-864-5196
Website: www.amtamassage.org
E-mail: info@amtamassage.org

American Music Therapy Association
8455 Colesville Rd.
Ste 1000
Silver Spring, MD 20910
Phone: 301-589-3300
Fax: 301-589-5175
Website: www.musictherapy.org
E-mail: info@musictherapy.org

American Naturopathic Medical Association
P.O. Box 96273
Las Vegas, NV 89193
Phone: 702-897-7053
Fax: 702-897-7140
Website: www.anma.org

American Oriental Bodywork Therapy Association
1010 Haddonfield-Berlin Rd.
Ste. 408
Voorhees, NJ 08043-3514
Phone: 856-782-1616
Fax: 856-782-1653
Website: www.aobta.org
E-mail: office@aobta.org

American Osteopathic Association
1090 Vermont Ave. N.W.
Ste. 510
Washington, DC 20005
Toll-Free: 800-962-9008
Phone: 202-414-0140
Fax: 202-544-3525
Website: www.osteopathic.org

American Polarity Therapy Association
122 N. Elm St.
Ste. 512
Greensboro, NC 27401
Phone: 336-574-1121
Fax: 336-574-1151
Website: www.polaritytherapy.
org
E-mail: APTAoffices@
polaritytherapy.org

American Psychological Association
750 First St. N.E.
Washington, DC 20002-4242
Toll-Free: 800-374-2721
Phone: 202-336-5500
Website: www.apa.org

American Reflexology Certification Board
P.O. Box 5147
Gulfport, FL 33737
Phone: 303-933-6921
Fax: 303-904-0460
Website: www.arcb.net
E-mail: info@arcb.net

American Society of Clinical Hypnosis
140 N. Bloomingdale Rd.
Bloomingdale, IL 60108
Phone: 630-980-4740
Fax: 630-351-8490
Website: www.asch.net
E-mail: info@asch.net

American Tai Chi and Qigong Association
2465 J-17 Centreville Rd.
Ste. 150
Herndon, VA 20171
Website: www.americantaichi.
org

American Yoga Association
P.O. Box 19986
Sarasota, FL 34276
Website: www.
americanyogaassociation.org
E-mail: info@
americanyogaassociation.org

Arizona Center for Integrative Medicine
P.O. Box 245153
Tucson, AZ 85724-5153
Phone: 520-626-6417
Fax: 520-626-3518
Website: integrativemedicine.
arizona.edu

Associated Bodywork and Massage Professionals
25188 Genesee Trail Rd.
Golden, CO 80401
Toll-Free: 800-458-2267
Fax: 800-667-8260
Website: www.abmp.com
E-mail: expectmore@abmp.com

Association for Applied Psychophysiology and Biofeedback
10200 West 44th Ave.
Ste. 304
Wheat Ridge, CO 80033
Toll-Free: 800-477-8892
Website: www.aapb.org
E-mail: aapb@resourcenter.com

Association of Reflexologists
5 Fore St. Taunton
Somerset TA1 1HX
Phone: 011-44-1823-351010
Website: www.aor.org.uk
E-mail: info@aor.org.uk

Atlantic Institute of Aromatherapy
16018 Saddlestring Dr.
Tampa, FL 33612
Phone: 813-265-2222
Website: www.atlanticinstitute.com

Ayurvedic Institute
P.O. Box 23445
Albuquerque, NM 87192-1445
Phone: 505-291-9698
Fax: 505-294-7572
Website: www.ayurveda.com

The Bach Centre
Mount Vernon, Baker's Lane
Brightwell-cum-Sotwell
Oxon OX10 0PZ
Phone: 011-44-1491-834678
Website: www.bachcentre.com

Bastyr Center for Natural Health
3670 Stone Way N.
Seattle, WA 98103
Phone: 206-834-4100
Website: www.bastyrcenter.org

Benson-Henry Institute for Mind Body Medicine
151 Merrimac St.
Fourth Fl.
Boston, MA 02114
Phone: 617-643-6090
Fax: 617-643-6077
Website: www.massgeneral.org/bhi
E-mail: mindbody@partners.org

Biodynamic Craniosacral Therapy Association of North America
150 Cross Creek Ct.
Chapel Hill, NC 27517
Phone: 734-904-0546
Website: www.craniosacraltherapy.org
E-mail: info@craniosacraltherapy.org

Biofeedback Certification Institute of America
10200 W. 44th Ave.
Ste. 310
Wheat Ridge, CO 80033-2840
Toll-Free: 866-908-8713
Phone: 303-420-2902
Fax: 303-422-8894
Website: www.bcia.org
E-mail: info@bcia.org

Center for Integrative Medicine
University of Maryland School of Medicine Kernan Hospital Mansion
2200 Kernan Dr.
Baltimore, MD 21207-6697
Phone: 410-448-6871
Fax: 410-448-6875
Website: www.compmed.umm.edu
E-mail: info@compmed.umm.edu

Center for Mindfulness in Medicine, Health Care, and Society
University of Massachusetts Medical School
55 Lake Ave. N.
Worcester, MA 01655
Phone: 508-856-2656
Fax: 508-856-1977
Website: www.umassmed.edu
E-mail: mindfulness@umassmed.edu

Chi Energy
Website: chienergy.co.uk

Complementary Healthcare Information Service
Website: www.chisuk.org.uk
E-mail: info@chisuk.org.uk

DrWeil.com
Website: www.drweil.com

Feldenkrais Educational Foundation of North America
5436 N. Albina Ave.
Portland, OR 97217
Toll-Free: 800-775-2118
Phone: 503-221-6612
Fax: 503-221-6616
Website: www.feldenkrais.com

Feldenkrais Resources
3680 6th Ave.
San Diego, CA 92103
Toll-Free: 800-765-1907
Phone: 619-220-8776
Fax: 619-330-4993
Website: www.feldenkraisresources.com
E-mail: office@feldenkraisresources.com

Flower Essence Society
P.O. Box 459
Nevada City, CA 95959
Toll-Free: 800-736-9222
Phone: 530-265-9163
Fax: 530-265-0584
Website: www.flowersociety.org
E-mail: info@flowersociety.org

Hellerwork International
P.O. Box 17373
Anaheim, CA 92817
Phone: 714-873-6131
Website: www.hellerwork.com
E-mail: info@hellerwork.com

Holistic Network
Website: www.holisticnetwork.
org

Homeopathic Educational Services
2124B Kittredge St.
Berkeley, CA 94704
Phone: 510-649-0294
Fax: 510-649-1955
Website: www.homeopathic.com

Institute of Traditional Medicine
2017 S.E. Hawthorne Blvd.
Portland, OR 97214
Phone: 503-233-4907
Website: www.itmonline.org

International Association of Reiki Professionals
Website: www.iarpreiki.org
E-mail: info@iarp.org

International Association of Yoga Therapists
P.O. Box 12890
Prescott, AZ 86304
Phone: 928-541-0004
Website: www.iayt.org

International Center for Reiki Training
21421 Hilltop St.
Unit #28
Southfield, MI 48033
Toll-Free: 800-332-8112
Phone: 248-948-8112
Fax: 248-948-9534
Website: www.reiki.org
E-mail: center@reiki.org

International Chiropractors Association
6400 Arlington Blvd.
Ste. 800
Falls Church, VA 22042
Toll-Free: 800-423-4690
Phone: 703-528-5000
Fax: 703-528-5023
Website: www.chiropractic.org

International College of Applied Kinesiology
Website: www.icak.com

International Feng Shui Guild
705 B S.E. Melody Ln.
Ste. 166
Lees Summit, MO 64063
Toll-Free: 888-881-IFSG
(881-4374)
Website: www.ifsguild.org
E-mail: office@ifsguild.org

International Institute of Reflexology
5650 First Ave. N.
St. Petersburg, FL 33733-2642
Phone: 727-343-4811
Fax: 727-381-2807
Website: www.reflexology-usa.net
E-mail: iir@reflexology-usa.net

International Medical and Dental Hypnotherapy Association
P.O. Box 2468
Laceyville, PA 18623
Toll-Free: 800-553-6886
Phone: 570-869-1021
Fax: 570-869-1249
Website: www.imdha.com
E-mail: info@imdha.com

Mayo Clinic
Website: www.mayoclinic.org

Moores Cancer Center
University of California–San Diego Medical Center
3855 Health Sciences Dr.
La Jolla, CA 92093
Phone: 858-822-6146
Website: cancer.ucsd.edu

National Association for Drama Therapy
44365 Premier Plaza
Ste. 220
Ashburn, VA 20147
Phone: 571-333-2991
Fax: 571-223-6440
Website: www.nadt.org
E-mail: nadt.office@nadt.org

National Association for Holistic Aromatherapy
P.O. Box 1868
Banner Elk, NC 28604
Phone: 828-898-6161
Fax: 828-898-1965
Website: www.naha.org
E-mail: info@naha.org

National Association of Cognitive-Behavioral Therapists
P.O. Box 2195
Weirton, WV 26062
Toll-Free: 800-853-1135
Website: www.nacbt.org
E-mail: nacbt@nacbt.org

National Association of Nutrition Professionals
P.O. 2752
Berkeley, CA 94702
Toll-Free: 800-342-8037
Fax: 510-580-9429
Website: www.nanp.org

National Ayurvedic Medical Association
8605 Santa Monica Blvd.
46789

National Center for Homeopathy
7918 Jones Branch Dr.
Ste. 300
McLean, VA 22102
Phone: 703-548-7790
Fax: 703-548-7792
Website: www.homeopathic.org

National Center on Physical Activity and Disability
1640 W. Roosevelt Rd.
Chicago, IL 60608-6904
Toll-Free: 800-900-8086
Website: www.ncpad.org
E-mail: ncpad@uic.edu

National Certification Commission for Acupuncture and Oriental Medicine
76 South Laura St.
Ste. 1290
Jacksonville, FL 32202
Phone: 904-598-1005
Fax: 904-598-5001
Website: www.nccaom.org

National College of Naturopathic Medicine
049 SW Porter St.
Portland, OR 97201
Phone: 503-552-1555
Website: www.ncnm.edu
E-mail: reception@ncnm.edu

National Headache Foundation
820 N. Orleans, Ste. 217
Chicago, IL 60610
Toll-Free: 888-NHF-5552 (643-5552)
Phone: 312-274-2650
Website: www.headaches.org
E-mail: info@headaches.org

National Qigong Association
P.O. Box 270065
St. Paul, MN 55127
Toll-Free: 888-815-1893
Fax: 888-359-9526
Website: www.nqa.org

Nemours Foundation Center for Children's Health Media
1600 Rockland Rd.
Wilmington, DE 19803
Phone: 302-651-4000
Website: www.kidshealth.org
E-mail: info@kidshealth.org

Physicians Association of Anthroposophic Medicine
1923 Geddes Ave.
Ann Arbor, MI 48104
Website: www.paam.net
E-mail: paam@anthroposophy.org

Reflexology Association of America
P.O. Box 1235
Evart, MI 49631
Phone: 980-234-0159
Fax: 401-568-6449
Website: www.reflexology-usa.org
E-mail: InfoRAA@reflexology-usa.org

Rolf Institute of Structural Integration
5055 Chaparral Ct.
Ste. 103
Boulder, CO 80301
Toll-Free: 800-530-8875
Phone: 303-449-5903
Fax: 303-449-5978
Website: www.rolf.org

Scripps Center for Integrative Medicine
10820 N. Torrey Pines Rd.
La Jolla, CA 92037
Phone: 858-554-3300
Fax: 858-554-2965
Website: www.scripps.org/
services/integrative-medicine

Thai Yoga Center / SomaVeda Institute
4715 Bruton Rd.
Plant City, FL 33565
Phone: 706-358-8646
Website: www.thaiyogacenter.
com

Therapeutic Touch International Association, Inc.
P.O. Box 419
Craryville, NY 12521
Phone: 518-325-1185
Fax: 509-693-3537
Website: www.therapeutic-
touch.org

Trager International
Website: www.trager.com
E-mail: admin@trager.com

University of Minnesota Center for Spirituality and Healing
420 Delaware St. SE Mayo
Memorial Bldg.
5th fl., MMC #505, C592
Minneapolis, MN 55455
Phone: 612-624-9459
Fax: 612-626-5280
Website: www.csh.umn.edu
E-mail: mclau033@umn.edu

University of Texas M.D. Anderson Cancer Center
1515 Holcombe Blvd.
Houston, TX 77030
Phone: 877-MDA-6789
(632-6789)
Website: www.mdanderson.org

Vegetarian Resource Group
P.O. Box 1463
Baltimore, MD 21203
Phone: 410-366-8343
Website: www.vrg.org
E-mail: vrg@vrg.org

WholeHealthMD
46040 Center Oak Plaza
Ste. 130
Sterling, VA 20166
Website: www.wholehealthmd.
com

Zero Balancing Health Association
Kings Contrivance Village
Center
8640 Guilford Rd.
Ste. 240
Columbia, MD 21046
Phone: 410-381-8956
Fax: 410-381-9634
Website: www.zerobalancing.
com
E-mail: zbha@zerobalancing.com

Index

Index